THE CHURCH IN A WORLD OF RELIGIONS

THE CHURCH IN A WORLD OF RELIGIONS

Working Papers in Theology

Tom Greggs
edited with J. Thomas Hewitt

LONDON · NEW YORK · OXFORD · NEW DELHI · SYDNEY

T&T CLARK
Bloomsbury Publishing Plc
50 Bedford Square, London, WC1B 3DP, UK
1385 Broadway, New York, NY 10018, USA
29 Earlsfort Terrace, Dublin 2, Ireland

BLOOMSBURY, T&T CLARK and the T&T Clark logo are trademarks of
Bloomsbury Publishing Plc

First published in Great Britain 2022
Paperback edition published 2023

Copyright © Tom Greggs, 2022

Tom Greggs has asserted his right under the Copyright, Designs and Patents Act, 1988, to be identified as Author of this work.

For legal purposes the Acknowledgements on pp. ix–x constitute an extension of this copyright page.

All rights reserved. No part of this publication may be reproduced or transmitted in any form or by any means, electronic or mechanical, including photocopying, recording, or any information storage or retrieval system, without prior permission in writing from the publishers.

Bloomsbury Publishing Plc does not have any control over, or responsibility for, any third-party websites referred to or in this book. All internet addresses given in this book were correct at the time of going to press. The author and publisher regret any inconvenience caused if addresses have changed or sites have ceased to exist, but can accept no responsibility for any such changes.

A catalogue record for this book is available from the British Library.

Library of Congress Cataloging-in-Publication Data
Names: Greggs, Tom, author.
Title: The church in a world of religions : working papers in theology / Tom Greggs.
Description: New York : T&T Clark, 2021. |
Includes bibliographical references and index. |
Identifiers: LCCN 2021019001 (print) | LCCN 2021019002 (ebook) |
ISBN 9780567701480 (hb) | ISBN 9780567701473 (paperback) |
ISBN 9780567701510 (epub) | ISBN 9780567701497 (epdf)
Subjects: LCSH: Church. | Christianity and other religions. |
LCGFT: Essays. Classification: LCC BV600.3 .G73295 2021 (print) |
LCC BV600.3 (ebook) | DDC 261.2–dc23
LC record available at https://lccn.loc.gov/2021019001
LC ebook record available at https://lccn.loc.gov/2021019002

ISBN: HB: 978-0-5677-0148-0
PB: 978-0-5677-0147-3
ePDF: 978-0-5677-0149-7
ePUB: 978-0-5677-0151-0

Typeset by Newgen Knowledgeworks Pvt. Ltd., Chennai, India

To find out more about our authors and books visit www.bloomsbury.com and sign up for our newsletters.

This book is for my teachers at the Liverpool Blue Coat School, many of whom saw something in me before I could ever see it myself: non sibi sed omnibus.

It is dedicated especially to Mr Phil Watson (who instilled in me deep respect for the thinkers of the long past, and – more importantly and profoundly – the importance of a deep humanity and integrity in life) and to Mr Tim Moore (who made me never forget decency and goodness are more important than academic success and – more importantly and profoundly – ensured my faith was deeply rooted and helped me never to be ashamed of the gospel). Both, for different reasons, will almost certainly disagree with much of what is written herein, but it is offered to them in gratitude and admiration. Qui docet in doctrina.

CONTENTS

Acknowledgements ix

INTRODUCTION 1

Part One
ESSAYS ON THE CHURCH

Chapter 1
PROPORTION AND TOPOGRAPHY IN ECCLESIOLOGY 9

Chapter 2
COMMUNIO ECCLESIOLOGY 27

Chapter 3
THE GLORY OF GOD IN THE PEOPLE OF GOD 43

Chapter 4
A STRANGELY WARMED HEART IN A STRANGE AND COMPLEX WORLD 59

Chapter 5
CHURCH AND SACRAMENTS 73

Chapter 6
A PROTESTANT ACCOUNT OF THE AUTHORITY OF THE CREEDS 87

Chapter 7
THE CATHOLIC SPIRIT OF PROTESTANTISM 105

Chapter 8
A CHURCH AGAINST RELIGION 125

Part Two
ESSAYS ON THE CHURCH IN A WORLD OF RELIGIONS

Chapter 9
BEYOND THE BINARY 151

Chapter 10
APOKATASTASIS   167

Chapter 11
THE MANY NAMES OF CHRIST IN WISDOM   183

Chapter 12
READING SCRIPTURE IN A PLURALIST WORLD   193

Chapter 13
PEOPLES OF THE COVENANTS   207

Chapter 14
LEGITIMIZING AND NECESSITATING INTER-FAITH DIALOGUE ON
EXCLUSIVIST GROUNDS   221

Chapter 15
PREACHING INTER-FAITH   237

CONCLUSION   247

Bibliography   251
Index   265

ACKNOWLEDGEMENTS

The author would like to thank Dr J. Thomas Hewitt for his detailed editorial assistance with the collation of this volume. The care and work he has undertaken is exemplary, and without his support the production of the volume would not have been possible, especially during an exceptionally busy time as head of divinity at Aberdeen. I am also grateful for the editors at T&T Clark, and to Dr Declan Kelly who assisted with the final proofs and indexing. Any errors which remain are, of course, the fault of the author.

The essays in this volume appeared in earlier forms as indicated below; some have been more fundamentally rewritten than others. We are grateful to these publishers for permission to use this material.

Chapter 1: 'Proportion and Topography in Ecclesiology: A Working Paper on the Dogmatic Location of the Doctrine of the Church', in *Theological Theology: Essays in Honour of John Webster*, ed. R. David Nelson, Darren Sarisky and Justin Stratis (London: T&T Clark, 2015), 89–106.

Chapter 2: '*Communio* Ecclesiology: The Spirit's Work of Salvation in the Life of the Church', in *Third Article Theology: A Pneumatological Dogmatics*, ed. Myk Habets (Minneapolis, MN: Fortress, 2016), 347–66.

Chapter 3: In Romanian as 'Glorificând în slava lui Dumnezeu: O prezentare contemporană despre slăvirea divină din perspectiva unui teolog metodist', *Revista Teologică* 99 (2017): 29–46; and in English as 'Glorifying in God's Glory: A Contemporary Account of Divine Glorification from a Methodist Theologian', *Revista Teologică* 99 (2017): 47–63.

Chapter 4: 'A Strangely Warmed Heart in a Strange and Complex World: On Assurance and Generous Hope', in *Generous Ecclesiology: Church, World and the Kingdom of God*, ed. Julie Gittoes, Brutus Green and James Heard (London: SCM, 2013), 120–39.

Chapter 5: 'The Church and Sacraments', in *Sanctified by Grace. A Theology of the Christian Life*, ed. Kent Eilers and Kyle Strobel (London: T&T Clark, 2014), 157–70.

Chapter 7: 'The Catholic Spirit of Protestantism: A Very Methodist Take on the Third Article, Visible Unity and Ecumenism', *Pro Ecclesia* 26 (2017): 353–72.

Chapter 8: 'Post-Christendom Ecclesiology', in Tom Greggs, *Theology against Religion: Constructive Dialogues with Bonhoeffer and Barth* (London: T&T Clark, 2011), 124–46.

Chapter 9: 'Beyond the Binary: Forming Evangelical Eschatology', in *New Perspectives for Evangelical Theology*, ed. Tom Greggs (Abingdon: Routledge, 2010), 153–67.

Chapter 10: '*Apokatastasis*: Particularist Universalism in Origen (*c*.185–*c*.254)', in *'All Shall Be Well': Explorations in Universal Salvation and Christian Theology from Origen to Moltmann*, ed. Gregory MacDonald (Eugene, OR: Cascade, 2010), 29–46.

Chapter 11: 'The Many Names of Christ in Wisdom: Reading Scripture with Origen for a Diverse World' in 'Spreading Rumours of Wisdom: Essays in Honour of David Ford', *Journal of Scriptural Reasoning* 7 (January 2008), http://jsr.shanti.virginia.edu/back-issues/vol-7-no-1-january-2008-spreading-rumours-of-wisdom/the-many-names-of-christ-in-wisdom/.

Chapter 12: 'Reading Scripture in a Pluralist Society: A Path to Discovering the Hermeneutics of *Agapē*', in *Horizons in Hermeneutics: A Festschrift in Honor of Anthony C. Thiselton*, ed. Stanley E. Porter and Matthew Malcolm (Grand Rapids, MI: Eerdmans, 2013), 201–16.

Chapter 13: 'Peoples of the Covenants: Evangelical Theology and the Plurality of the Covenants in Scripture', *Journal of Scriptural Reasoning* 11 (August 2012), http://jsr.shanti.virginia.edu/back-issues/volume-11-no-1-august-2012/peoples-of-the-covenants-evangelical-theology-and-the-plurality-of-the-covenants-in-scripture/.

Chapter 14: 'Legitimizing and Necessitating Inter-faith Dialogue: The Dynamics of Inter-faith for Individual Faith Communities', *International Journal of Public Theology* 4 (2010): 194–211.

Chapter 15: 'Preaching Inter-faith: Finding Hints about the Religious Other from the Good Samaritan', *Epworth Review* 36 (December 2009): 60–70.

INTRODUCTION

How does the church understand itself within and speak to a world of unbelief and religious pluralism? What wise ways are there to consider the life of the church which serves its witness and mission in the world? The essays in this volume seek to consider these questions in their discussions of ecclesiology and religious pluralism in a post-Christendom context. There is some sense in which these themes are deeply interrelated and intertwined. The great challenge of ecclesiology in the contemporary world is that the church must learn to express its purposes in a context of secularism and pluralism. From the age of Constantine the Great to the early twentieth century, the church (at least in the West) occupied a privileged role in a dominantly and homogeneously Christian context. Even in the nineteenth century, the perceived 'dangers' of pluralism were associated not with members of other faiths and none but with rival or alternative forms of Christianity within states. The Augsburg compromise of *cuius regio, eius religio* dominated the ecclesial and political landscape in which there was a unity of altar and throne. Ecclesiology was formulated and expressed within a generally harmonized Christian context: what issues were at stake pertained to the role of a given church within a Christian country, or a given form of polity in relation to any other given policy. Given the polemical nature of the relationships even within Christianity, between Nonconformity, Anglicanism and Roman Catholicism from the Reformation onwards, ecclesiological discourse has not been well-resourced in terms of the church's self-description in an age of not only Christian but also secular and religious pluralism. From the fourth century to the first part of the twentieth century, theological speech about the church has been conducted within and proceeded from the condition of understanding the church's role in a majority Christian context. The church's consideration of how it relates to a context of pluralism is, therefore, simultaneously a reflection on the church's own purpose and identity in society. Equally, the church's theological self-description necessarily has to take account of its role in a complexly secular and pluralist society: what the church is there *for* is important to what the church is.

For all, however, that there is a degree of cultural determinism about these essays, there is a determined desire not to allow this cultural context to overshadow theological speech. These essays mark in many ways my movement over the last fifteen years to being a dogmatician – and, indeed, being comfortable with such a self-description. The essays are not arranged chronologically, but there will be a certain sense of progression in the confidence of theological voice within them. While it is the case that the majority of the essays on religion preceded temporally the majority of those on ecclesiology, the decision has been made to reverse this order in the structure of the book itself. Materially, the chapters on religion help to describe in some concretion what it means to speak of the church being *for the world*. The nature of that world is significant in the manner in which the church exists *for* it. While in many ways the cultural condition of the society within which the church exists was in no small part the motivation for my focus over the last decade on ecclesiology, for Christian theology, there is a need to consider dogmatically the action and activity of God in the church *for the world* before unpacking something more about the ways in which the church might be operatively orientated upon being a light to the world in all its complexity. In other words, the questions of what the church is and how God is at work in it dogmatically precede questions of what the church's more particular purposes are and how God is at work *extra muros ecclesiam*. The purpose of the order in this book, therefore, is to indicate that this is not a cultural or culturally determined theology but rather a theology which seeks to be fundamentally 'theological' while at the same time recognizing that theology does not speak into a vacuum but always into a given, quotidian context. There is a terminus to revelation and it is the theatre of God's economy known within the church which exists in the world. The church itself is not an ahistoric or a-contextual body but one which is always an expression of God's economy in space-time – indeed, in a particular, given, space-time. The church's speech about God's activity (including the church's theological speech about itself) is always *into* a context in its particular givenness. And theology, as a critical reflection upon that speech, also speaks into the givenness of the situation however dogmatically and doctrinally theology seeks to speak. The essays in this volume seek collectively to show the interconnection between speech about the church and speech about the church's understanding of those secular and religious others outwith the church's own bounds. The given, current, quotidian space-time within which the church exists demands reflection on these interrelations: indeed, it is the dogmatic commitment to the contingent, spatio-temporal reality of the church as a body which only exists in a particular moment of space-time which is the key insight that drives the engagement in thinking theologically about the context in which the church lives and speaks. Discussions with doctoral students and with reviewers of the first volume of my *Dogmatic Ecclesiology* have indicated the degree to which there is continuity between my earlier work on salvation and religion, and how much my work on ecclesiology rests upon reflections of the cosmic nature of salvation in Christ and the self-critical humility which the church must have in relation to its sense of self and speech about itself and its place within the economy of God.[1] It is hoped that the essays in this volume show the interrelatedness of these themes in a single collected volume. Of course, the essays are occasional pieces, and were construed and written as such in the first

---

1. See Tom Greggs, *Dogmatic Ecclesiology Vol. 1: The Priestly Catholicity of the Church* (Grand Rapids, MI: Baker Academic, 2019).

place. They are not systematic in the overdetermined sense of some attempt at a false completeness or of a single, analytical and deductive mode of a priori argumentation. But they circle around shared themes and approaches in ways which hopefully demonstrate continuity and interdependence of thought in relation to these two areas of theological reflection.

While there is a sense throughout the essays of the complexly secular and pluralistic context in which the church lives, speaks and reflects upon its own life, as with all my theological work, the essays in this volume are consciously written in a deeply particularist way. They arise from an unwavering commitment to the absolute, sovereign uniqueness of Jesus Christ as the perfect revelation of God and the sole saviour of the world. By instinct, they are all evangelical – not only in the sense of pertaining to the good news of the gospel but also in the narrower sense of being formed by theological commitments and a life of faith associated with evangelicalism as a movement; I am a Wesleyan after all! However, in this commitment to an orthodoxly Protestant Christocentrism and to a sense of the supremacy of the gospel, there is an accompanying sense of the cosmic scope of this singular, particular act of God in Jesus Christ. While there is a uniqueness to the person and work of Christ, there is in this uniqueness a wideness in God's mercy, a majestic breadth in God's grace.

This commitment means, moreover, that the essays in this volume proceed in a determinedly *theological* way. Approaches to both questions of religious plurality and questions of ecclesiology have so often been followed from the perspective of social sciences. Since the significance of religious pluralism within society (especially in the West since the second half of the last century) is an observable phenomenon, and since churches are empirically observable communities, all too often theology has given way to social studies or in theology's own formulation and articulation has been formed by disciplines outwith theology. Questions very often on these topics have become practical, pragmatic and driven by non-theological agendas: What form should interreligious dialogue take? How should the church organize itself in an age of decline? What are the ethnographic forms of community which can be observed and what can we discover in these about how the church might improve? What practices does the church engage in in relation to reconciliation? In response to such questions, so often the answers are derived more from political, social or even managerial concerns than from any dogmatic commitments. The questions themselves derive from and give rise to approaches which are more shaped by practice, culture and observation than by reflection upon the works and life of God and all things in relation to those works and the living God.

How to understand the church within the salvific economy of God and the *Heilsgeschichte* is the way in which the essays on the church proceed. The first essay on this topic seeks to understand the theological proportion and topography necessary for ecclesiological speech: how and under which prior proximate and ultimate dogmatic *res* should the church be described theologically and what is it that we are doing in describing the church which articulates its life as an article of faith. The second of the essays on ecclesiology performs constructively, biblically and dogmatically the position argued for in the first chapter: locating the theological origins of the church within the salvific work of the Holy Spirit. The next chapter offers an account not of the origins of the church but of its life and its ends in terms of divine glory. Having spoken in confident dogmatic terms about the life of the church, the following chapter considers what an appropriate and an inappropriate form of assurance might look like for both the church and the individual – shifting discussion about the assured nature of the presence of the church from an inwards-looking, bounded and self-assured account to an account which is focused on the saving grace and activity of God which frees the church to live for the world. The next chapter brings these themes together in relation to the sanctified life, and in consideration of the church and sacraments from the proximate dogmatic trope of the Spirit's sanctifying grace – locating the church's constancy and being in history and space in the constancy of the Spirit's life. The final three chapters of the section on the church consider three issues which derive from the preceding dogmatic outlines: how the church reads scripture collectively and what this means in terms of understanding the traditions (especially the creedal traditions) of the church; how the churches might understand themselves ecumenically in relation to the church and its visible unity; and how the church might be understood in the context of a secular and religious pluralism.

This latter chapter forms a bridge to the section on religion. Once again, however, in the section on religion, the structure is one which seeks to lay the theological foundations relating to salvation and revelation from which the church can then examine issues pertaining to the complexity of the pluralistic societies within which it lives. The opening chapter of this section focuses on issues of eschatology in relation to the church to help the church in its speech both to be humble and to move beyond simply binaries and overly self-confident accounts of the church in relation to the eschatological *telos* of its life and members. This lays the foundation for, in the next chapter, a reflection – drawing from Origen – on what is termed 'particularist universalism'. As with the next chapter, the work of Origen (as a theologian who lived in the highly pluralist context of Alexandria) is used in order to resource (in the manner of *ressourcement*) a theology which might help the church to articulate its life and its sense of salvation in the pluralist context in which it now finds itself. The theology of the first three centuries is used to provide tradition and resources to speak of the church in relation to those of other (and no) faith outwith the conditions of Christendom. Discussion of Origen's nuanced, hopeful (and undogmatic) account of universalism is followed by an examination of his economic Christology in relation to the *epinoiai* of Christ. These essays are followed by a consideration of how to consider hermeneutics (or, as I would now prefer to consider it, illumination) for the church in the context in which it lives today – borrowing from tradition an understanding of the hermeneutics of love in order to retain a generous way of reading the particular and unique revelation of God known to us in the Bible. An example of the kind of approach which is advocated hermeneutically follows in a chapter devoted to a discussion of the multiple covenants that exist in scripture and what this might mean for the ways in which we understand the economy of God. This chapter itself forms a precursor for a discussion of the basis on which Christians might engage in inter-faith work: what is it which is particular to the revelation and economy of the God known by the Spirit in Jesus Christ through scripture that makes engagements with those of other faiths not only possible but even (perhaps) necessary as an expression of salvation? The final substantive chapter offers a more detailed example of the preceding two chapters in terms of the way in which these theological positions might 'preach' in relation to one particular narrative of Luke's Gospel—the Good Samaritan.

The essays collected in this volume seek to be biblically based and engage not infrequently in direct exegesis of particular texts. As well as the gospel narratives, there is a particular focus on the story of Pentecost and the fall narratives. This focus attempts to ground the economic dynamics of the Son and the Spirit in the narrative of salvation in scripture. The approach to scripture is one which prioritizes the illuminating grace of God through the work of the Spirit in the reception of the word of God in the life and context of the church. The living voice of scripture read through the tradition of the church is the foundation on which all theology is built. These essays, therefore, seek to offer a biblically formed and determined theology. In this task, there are certain, primary interlocutors with whom the essays engage: Origen is a significant figure on which the theology depends in its reflection on those who are not Christian; Wesley features significantly along the way to speak of the church; Barth and Bonhoeffer are ever present throughout;[2] Luther and Calvin inform much of the ecclesiological reflection contained herein (both implicitly and explicitly). But for as much as these essays seek to listen to scripture and to the voices of the past, they also seek to speak – to speak of the limitless grace of God in the world, a grace known and participated in actively by the church through the Spirit's multiply intensive activity in the extensity of the world.

---

2. It should be noted that the majority of work on Barth and Bonhoeffer is located in another book of essays: Tom Greggs, *Barth and Bonhoeffer as Contributors to a Post Liberal Ecclesiology: Essays of Hope for a Fallen and Complex World* (London: T&T Clark, forthcoming 2022).

Part One

ESSAYS ON THE CHURCH

Chapter 1

PROPORTION AND TOPOGRAPHY IN ECCLESIOLOGY: A WORKING PAPER ON THE DOGMATIC LOCATION OF THE DOCTRINE OF THE CHURCH

I

One of the most significant contributions that Professor John Webster has made to the field of ecclesiology within contemporary theology is to remind systematicians of the primacy of dogmatic content in accounts of the church over ecclesiological descriptions focused on social scientific description, ecclesial human reality, church polity, function, governance and/or modelling.[1] Against prevailing trends in attending to the empirical in ecclesiological discussion, Webster's voice has been something crying in the wilderness for a dogmatic account of the church. This is evident in his chapter in Pete Ward's recent edited collection *Perspectives on Ecclesiology and Ethnography*,[2] in which Webster's chapter stands as a challenge to the rest of the content of this volume – a prophetic warning against the conviction that the real is socio-historical in theological discussion.[3] Not unaware of the danger of falling into dogmatic idealism, Webster's essay fiercely rejects the position in ecclesiological discussion that 'the church is the people of God because certain events occur within a group of human beings – a causal order at which even the most frankly intrinsicist theology of grace might be dismayed'.[4] More

---

1. In mind here are the sorts of approaches that one sees in everything from the likes of Avery Dulles, SJ, *Models of the Church: A Critical Assessment of the Church in All Its Aspects* (Dublin: Gill & Macmillan, 1976); to John Drane, *The McDonaldization of the Church: Spirituality, Creativity, and the Future of the Church* (London: Darton, Longman & Todd, 2000); to Nicholas M. Healy, *Church, World, and the Christian Life: Practical-Prophetic Ecclesiology* (Cambridge: Cambridge University Press, 2000); to the Eerdmans' series 'Studies in Ecclesiology and Ethnography'.

2. John Webster, '"In the Society of God": Some Principles of Ecclesiology', in *Perspectives on Ecclesiology and Ethnography*, ed. Pete Ward (Grand Rapids, MI: Eerdmans, 2012), 200–22.

3. Webster, '"In the Society of God"', 202. For a response to this from the perspective of practical theology, see Christopher Brittain, 'Why Ecclesiology Cannot Live by Doctrine Alone: A Reply to John Webster's "In the Society of God"', *Ecclesial Practices* 1 (2014): 5–30.

4. Webster, '"In the Society of God"', 202.

acutely, however, Webster locates this propensity not only external to the dogmatic enterprise which has led away from dogmatic theology and towards the empirical and historical but also within certain decisions in dogmatic organization through appeals to elements of the Christian faith such as the incarnation or grace in a way which is 'often rather randomly chosen, abstractly conceived, and without much sense of their systematic linkages'.[5] In this, he sees the underlying problem resting in assumptions concerning the *res* of Christian theology, which leads to the following mistaken principle: 'since the object of Christian theology is the economy of God's works as creator and reconciler of humankind, then theology should naturally direct its attention to the temporal and social as the sphere of God's presence and activity'.[6] Helpfully, against this, Webster reminds the ecclesiologist:

> The temporal economy, including the social reality of the church in time, has its being not *in se* but by virtue of God who alone is *in se*. Time and society are derivative realities, and that derivation is not simply a matter of their origination; it is a permanent mark of their historical condition.[7]

This determines that ecclesiology must understand the church as a creaturely reality which stands under the metaphysics of grace. Thus, for Webster, to speak of a doctrine of the church means that one must first speak of the doctrine of God, on which for him ecclesiology hangs:[8] to speak of the sort of social history that the church is is to speak of its origin in God's goodness.

Thus, Webster sees the doctrine of the church as deriving from Trinitarian deduction. Seeing *credo in ecclesiam* as succeeding *credo in Deum Patrem omnipotentem ... et in Jesum Christum ... credo in Spiritum Sanctum*, he argues that ecclesiology has its place in the 'flow of Christian doctrine from teaching about God to teaching about everything else in God'.[9] In what follows, there is a masterful account, therefore, of the inner life of God who is 'alive with self-moved life'[10] before moving on to the (indeed any) discussion of divine operations in relation to the church per se. Here, Webster differentiates his position from that of social Trinitarians, about whom Webster is rightly nervous in that they use 'relation' to pass too quickly and easily between God and the church without adequately accounting for the gracious act of God in creating the church or the differentiation of the life of the church from God's own life.[11] Only once this ground

---

5. Webster, '"In the Society of God"', 202.
6. Webster, '"In the Society of God"', 202–3.
7. Webster, '"In the Society of God"', 203.
8. Webster, '"In the Society of God"', 204.
9. Webster, '"In the Society of God"', 205.
10. Webster, '"In the Society of God"', 206.
11. Webster, '"In the Society of God"', 206. Here he cites Gunton's concept of the church echoing the relations of the Trinity; see Colin Gunton, 'The Church on Earth: The Roots of Community', in *On Being the Church: Essays on the Christian Community*, ed. Colin Gunton and Daniel Hardy (Edinburgh: T&T Clark, 1989), 48–80.

has been cleared does Webster go on to describe the 'Trinitarian deduction of the church' in any detail, tracing how particular works of God might be appropriated to particular Trinitarian persons. There are (inevitably) three moves: (1) *'The church has being because of the eternal will of the God and Father of our Lord Jesus Christ,* who "destined us in love to be his children through Jesus Christ, according to the purpose of his will" (Eph. 1.5).'[12] (2) *'The church has its being because of the person and work of the eternal Son.'*[13] (3) *'The church is and acts by virtue of the Holy Spirit, the Lord and giver of life.'*[14] Each of these discussions emphasizes the inner divine life of a particular person of the Trinity before accounting for their role in the economy, and before moving to consider ecclesiology specifically.

Having established this, Webster subsequently addresses the socio-historical phenomena that characterize the church as the society which exists in God's society. The first emphasis here is on the creatureliness of the church and its current condition as those in whom 'the motion of God and the motion of creatures are not inversely but directly proportional'.[15] In this, Webster seeks to draw attention in ecclesiology away from simple empirical study and towards the nature and economy of God; away from notions of human self-realization of the church towards understanding the church as signs of the triune being and working; and from concerns with the phenomenological to a recognition that the temporal forms of the church are 'not unconditionally transparent'.[16] Only now will Webster hazard statements about the church's fundamental form ('the primary structures of its creaturely, social-historical existence').[17] In this, Webster lists the three examples (from what would be a larger set) of: assembly (a 'human act of assembly [which] follows, signifies, and mediates a divine act of gathering');[18] hearing the proclamation of the Word of God;[19] and order (as a 'ruled society, [of] common life under "law"').[20]

Webster sees all of this as essential for those who wish to engage in study of the church in whatever manner: without remembering this account of divine agency in the church, 'an ethnography [one could add any other social science here] of the church does not attain its object, misperceiving the motion to which its attention is to be directed, and so inhibited in understanding the creaturely movements of the communion of saints.'[21] Thus, there exists a hierarchy between modes of ecclesiological investigation: the first (and higher) mode is dogmatic, in offering

---

12. Webster, '"In the Society of God"', 207.
13. Webster, '"In the Society of God"', 208.
14. Webster, '"In the Society of God"', 213. This is the shortest of all of the sections.
15. Webster, '"In the Society of God"', 214.
16. Webster, '"In the Society of God"', 215.
17. Webster, '"In the Society of God"', 216.
18. Webster, '"In the Society of God"', 216.
19. Webster, '"In the Society of God"', 218–19.
20. Webster, '"In the Society of God"', 219.
21. Webster, '"In the Society of God"', 221.

a Trinitarian account of the church; the second relates to the phenomena of the church. This hierarchy has to be respected so as to resist treating the church as any other society – creating a 'naturalized ecclesiology' in which the true object of theology is in the background or covered over.[22] Dogmatic ecclesiology's purpose is in part, therefore, to 'resist this by keeping alive the distinction between and due order of uncreated and created being; by indicating that the phenomena of the church are not irreducible but significative; and by introducing into each ecclesiological description and passage of ecclesiological argument direct language about God, Christ, and the Spirit'.[23]

II

In a sense, the points in this chapter are made in order to attend with due proportion to ecclesiology and with a sense of the locus of this particular doctrine in relation to more foundational doctrines. The argument is made so that ecclesiological discussion does not become independent as a locus from the doctrine of God, and so that ecclesiology does not in its potential independence become disproportionate to the need for speech about God's superabundant grace and agency in creating and sustaining the church in its continuing spatio-historical existence. These are background concerns which Webster raises elsewhere in his discussions of ecclesiology. In an essay on episcopacy and church formation, he writes, for example: 'An evangelical ecclesiology will … have a particular concern to emphasize the asymmetry of divine and human action.'[24] Elsewhere, he cites approvingly Barth's railing 'against the over-inflation of ecclesiology and ethics into quasi-independent themes'.[25] In these independent accounts of the church's life,[26] there is too great an emphasis on the practices of the church and too little on the sheer free gracious act of God. Again, here, Webster has a concern for the proper order, speaking of the church in the light of reconciliation and advocating that *ek tou theou* in 2 Cor. 5.18 requires us 'to invest a great deal of theological energy in the depiction of the person and work of the reconciling God. Most of all, what will be required will be a rich description of divine aseity as it is manifest in the work of redemption.'[27] Quoting Schillebeeckx, what is needed is 'a bit of *negative theology*, church theology in a minor key';[28] and this for Webster is best

---

22. Webster, ' "In the Society of God" ', 221.
23. Webster, ' "In the Society of God" ', 221.
24. John Webster, *Word and Church: Essays in Christian Dogmatics* (Edinburgh: T&T Clark, 2001), 196.
25. Webster, *Word and Church*, 213.
26. Webster lists many examples; see *Word and Church*, 212, n. 2.
27. Webster, *Word and Church*, 215.
28. E. Schillebeeckx, *Church: The Human Story of God* (New York: Crossroads, 1990), xix. See also Webster, *Word and Church*, 214.

found in the passivity of the church as a community whose core activity is hearing the Word of reconciliation.[29]

But is divine aseity (traced through the doctrine of reconciliation) that which is required 'most of all' from an account of the church? In emphasizing God's life in itself and apart from creatures, is there potentially a danger of dogmatic disproportion? Even divine aseity is something that we cannot know apart from the economy of God. While attention should be directed to the order of being, it is precisely that – an *order*. And beyond recognizing that *creatio ex nihilo* means that all of God's ways with the world are gracious and without necessity, should we not (as scripture seems to) attend ourselves to God's presence with His creatures in spatio-history – the conditions by which He has determined that we should know Him? Aside from establishing the graciousness of God's operations in the world (a point that should never be forgotten or retreated from the foreground), there are few moments in scripture where there is direct attendance to the inner life of God. Instead, the accounts of the being of God that we have are those of God's ways with the world, rather than God's life *in se*. Even those which seem most directly to give an account of theology proper are *simultaneously* accounts of God's relation to the world. If we consider theophanies in the Old Testament, this is clear. The God who reveals Himself to Moses as 'I am who I am' is also the God who makes Himself known as the 'the God of your ancestors, the God of Abraham, the God of Isaac, and the God of Jacob' (Exod. 3.15). He is the God who promises to be with people and has seen their plight and will deliver them. Similarly, when Moses comes as close to seeing God as any human has, when the Lord passes before Him, what is proclaimed by God is thus:

> The LORD, the LORD,
> a God merciful and gracious,
> slow to anger,
> and abounding in steadfast love and faithfulness,
> keeping steadfast love for the thousandth generation,
> forgiving iniquity and transgression and sin,
> yet by no means clearing the guilty,
> but visiting the iniquity of the parents
> upon the children
> and the children's children,
> to the third and the fourth generation. (Exod. 34.6-7, NRSV)

Similarly, when Isaiah sees the Lord in Isa. 6, it is in the context of the calling of a prophet to speak to the people. Even 'The Lord is our God, the Lord alone' is the context of the *Shema*: '*Hear, O Israel:* The Lord is *our* God, the Lord alone. *You* shall love the Lord *your* God with all *your* heart, and with all *your* soul, and with

---

29. Webster, *Word and Church*, 228. Thus, Webster prefers ecclesiologies which centre on the Word.

all *your* might' (Deut. 6.4-5, emphasis added).[30] Or else, descriptions of God in the Psalms are in the context of prayer, praise and worship of the people. Description of God (even in recalling the differentiation of order of being and order of knowing) always involves simultaneously recognizing God's freedom *from* the creature in His own life *and* God's relationship *to* the creature through the community of the God's people: the basis for the latter (in the order of being) is the gracious nature that the former indicates; the purpose of the former (in the knowing) is the recognition of the gracious nature of God's acts in creation in the latter.

Yes; it is true that ecclesiology is different from the study of any other human society or organization because it is founded on God's promise 'I shall be your God', but the immediate accompanying statement with that is, 'And you shall be my people' (2 Cor. 6.16b). These two moments belong together, and both require appropriate attention. As St Augustine puts it, 'anyone who thinks that he has understood the divine scriptures or any part of them, but cannot by understanding build up this *double love* of God and neighbour has not succeeded in understanding them'.[31] Attendance to this 'double love', in which true love and enjoyment of neighbour is love and enjoyment of God,[32] is at the heart of ecclesiological investigation. To trace every dogmatic locus back to God's inner life in pretemporal eternity not only runs the risk of spending time discussing God outside of His revelation and economy, seeking to move behind it, but it also opens the possibility of a dominance of speech about God resting behind God's economy of salvation. Speaking of God's inner life (*most of all* of divine aseity) does not do justice to God's gracious *choosing* and *willing* to be God in this particular way with His people: aseity's purpose in theological speech is to indicate the gracious action of God who remains the same God even if there were no salvation. Without this dual manoeuvre, it will lead to the doctrine of the immanent life of God (important in the order of knowing primarily to establish the graciousness of God's acts in the world) being somewhat disproportionately present in discussions of other loci. The purpose of the doctrine of God's immanent life in the order of knowing is to emphasize the very graciousness of God's actions in the world: divine aseity fulfils the role of offering the relief against which all discussions of God's ways with the world can be built and shaped. In one sense, its role is as a warning: a necessary warning, but a warning nonetheless. Once it has been established that the church is an act of God's immeasurable and free grace rather than a community formed by human agency, the question is then what is it that can be said about the community formed by divine agency. In discussing divine aseity in ecclesiology, one establishes the foundational principle of the non-necessity of creation in order to be reminded of the divine gracious creation of the church external to the human society. Having

---

30. Furthermore, Jesus introduces to this immediately the idea of loving one's neighbour as oneself.

31. Augustine, *On Christian Teaching*, trans. R. P. H. Green (Oxford: Oxford University Press, 1997), 27 (I.86) (emphasis added).

32. Augustine, *On Christian Teaching*, 25 (I.79).

sounded the warning and protected ecclesiology from an overemphasis on human agency, it is then necessary to describe the form of community God creates in the body of His church. Just as Barth stated later in his life about his early theology that there was a need to learn to say 'yes' in the same way in which he had once said 'no',[33] ecclesiology (having received its warning – its 'no') must learn to say an appropriate 'yes' following from this admonitory 'no'.

III

The need to sound this warning is not an insignificant one. Not only should theology always be reminded that it stands before the immeasurable vastness of God's plenitude but ecclesiology also (and especially) must be aware in speaking of human community of the dangers of reducing speech about God and God's ways with the world with speech about humanity and society without recourse to divine action. Even in some of the greatest theologians, the capacity to 'forget God' when speaking about the church can be seen. Often concerned with the cultural conditions in which the church lives, numerous theologians have been insufficient in their account of the church in relation to the act and activity of God. Let us take, for example, John Owen. While Owen does address in passing the church as 'catholic and mystical', the unfolding of his ecclesiology certainly focuses on the secondary consideration of the church 'visible' and organized in 'a particular church or congregation'.[34] In the context of his time, the concern that Owen expresses in his ecclesiology is that of individual freedom, autonomy and the voluntary expression of the will to be a member of the church. For him in the context of seventeenth-century dissent, the focus is on the 'formal cause' of the church which rests in voluntary acts of obedience to the church; that the 'supreme efficient cause' of all human wills is Jesus Christ is discussed in passing. The church exists 'by *mutual confederation* or solemn agreement' to fulfil in obedience the duties Christ has prescribed.[35] In a highly individualized account of the nature of the church, Owen asserts:

> But if a church be such a society as is intrusted in itself with sundry powers and privileges depending on sundry duties prescribed unto it; if it constitute new relations between persons that neither naturally nor morally were before so related, as doth marriage between husband and wife; if it require new mutual duties and give new mutual rights among themselves, not required of either as unto their matter or as unto their manner before, – it is vain to imagine that

---

33. Cf. Karl Barth, *God, Grace and Gospel*, Scottish Journal of Theology Occasional Papers 8 (Edinburgh: Oliver and Boyd, 1959), 32–7.
34. John Owen, *The Works of John Owen*, vol. 16 (London: Banner of Truth Trust, 1968), 3.
35. Owen, *The Works of John Owen*, vol. 16, 25.

this state can arise from or have any other formal cause but *the joint consent and virtual confederation of those concerned* unto these ends: for there is none of them can have any other foundation; they are all of them resolved into the wills of men, brining themselves under an obligation unto them by their *voluntary consent*.[36]

It is thus evident that a functionalist focus on the form of the human society of the church is not a recent development. Its roots are not simply non-theological accounts of the church but rest in theological accounts of the freedom of the Christian in formation of particular assemblies by means of 'voluntary consent'. Indeed, such an emphasis on individualism brought together by human will may well arise from the Reformation itself. Often in polemic with Roman Catholic accounts of the nature and function of the church, its worship and its offices, Protestant accounts too frequently focused either on the freedom of the individual[37] or on the particular form of the church's polity, governance and sacraments.[38]

Part of the problem here is that ecclesiology was not until the fifteenth century a distinctive and separate locus in systematic presentation of Christian doctrine.[39] When ecclesiology does become a significant doctrinal locus, it is immediately preceding and then in the context of the Reformation: the Reformers introduce it often in polemical description of their position in contrast to that of Rome, and Roman Catholic theology responds by establishing a mode of ecclesiology which exists in contrast to that of the Protestant churches and in response to them. There is not, therefore, a dogmatic inheritance of the topography of ecclesiology such that order and proportion might govern dogmatic discussions of the church. What can result is a treatment of the church independent of other dogmatic loci, leading to functionalist descriptions of the life and order of the church, rather than dogmatic accounts of the church within the economy of God. It is possible to see, therefore, that treating ecclesiology as an independent locus runs the danger of disproportion in a dogmatic account of the church; the 'no' sounded by Webster is a wise one. But the question then arises as to how to say the 'yes'. Where there have

---

36. Owen, *The Works of John Owen*, vol. 16, 26 (emphasis added).

37. We see this, for example, in Luther's 'The Freedom of the Christian', in *Luther's Works*, vol. 31 (Philadelphia, PA: Fortress, 1957), 327–78, with its emphasis on inwardness, justification by faith and the priesthood of all believers. Similarly, in Calvin's *Institutes* discussion of the individual's appropriation of salvation precedes that of the church: Book 3 on the reception of the grace of Christ precedes Book 4's material on the church.

38. Compare for example, in Calvin's *Institutes*, Book 4, the amount of description of the ontology of the church (ch. 1) with that of form, function, polity and sacraments (chs 2–20, often in polemical mode).

39. Leo Dullaart, *Kirche und Ekklesiologie* (Munich: Chr. Kaiser, 1975), 190–7, albeit clearly theologians before this time had much to say individually about the church, but there is no distinctive or scholastic 'Doctrine of the Church'. See also Wolfhart Pannenberg, *Systematic Theology*, vol. 3 (Grand Rapids, MI: Eerdmans, 1997), 21–2.

been attempts at not treating the doctrine independently, however, dangers remain in being disproportionate in the other direction – a negative disproportionality. Here, we might identify two trends which both sublate direct ecclesiological speech, and which by virtue of that almost free ecclesiology once more from its dogmatic connections.

The first trend in attempting to ensure that ecclesiology is appropriately proportionate, but ultimately determining that it becomes disproportionate, is the dogmatic manoeuvre of making the doctrine of the church a subset or a consequence of the doctrine of God's work of salvation in Christ. This is the approach which discusses grace and justification in Christ, the benefits of Christ in the appropriation of His grace by faith and then the consequent discussion of the church. This order gives the doctrine of individual salvation priority over the doctrine of the life of the church. We see this in Calvin's *Institutes of the Christian Religion*, and this approach is largely normative for Reformed Dogmatics that follow from him.[40] As Pannenberg puts it, 'Right up to 19th and 20th century the account of individual appropriation of salvation usually preceded discussion of the concept of the church.'[41] Schleiermacher might be seen as indicative of this in differentiating Protestant and Roman Catholic ecclesiology on this principle: 'The antithesis between Protestantism and Catholicism may be provisionally conceived thus: the former makes the individual's relation to the Church dependent on his relation to Christ, while the latter contrariwise makes the individual's relation to Christ dependent on his relation to the Church.'[42] However, in this account, ecclesiology is given little concrete content. The church exists to hear the Word and receive the sacraments in order to foster faith. Thus, Calvin, 'in order that the preaching of the gospel might flourish, he [God] deposited this treasure in the church. … [H]e instituted sacraments, which we who have experienced them feel to be highly useful aids to foster and strengthen faith.'[43] But in this instance, is there not disproportion? What *actually* is said about *the church*? Why does God choose this *particular form* to be the locus of the preaching of His Word and the ministrations of His grace? Why create a *spatio-historical community*? And what is that community's nature? Is the church simply the gathered individuals in one location for the sake of efficiency of communication with no direct responsibility or relationship to one another, other than being placed in one geographical location at one point in history? Furthermore, it is not clear on the basis of the creed or the scriptures that functional Christology should be the doctrine under which (or as a consequence of) ecclesiology should exist. Christ did not found the church. Locating ecclesiology within functional Christology may well collapse the particular

---

40. Pannenberg, *Systematic Theology*, vol. 3, 23. Wollebius and Amesius do not follow this order, but discuss the theme of the church before that of the individual's appropriation of salvation.

41. Pannenberg, *Systematic Theology*, vol. 3, 24.

42. Friedrich Schleiermacher, *The Christian Faith* (Edinburgh: T&T Clark, 1928), 103 (see also paragraph 24).

43. Calvin, *Institutes*, 4.1.1 (pp. 1011–12).

acts and moments of the *Heilsgeschichte* singularly into the narrative of God's saving activity in Jesus Christ. The church's creation follows from the gift of the Spirit and is located following the description of the sovereignty of the Spirit in the creed.

This final point about the order of the narrative of God's saving work in the persons of the incarnate Son and the life-giving Spirit might also lie as the problematic point for the second trend in ecclesiology, which leads to its negatively disproportionate presentation in dogmatics. This trend is the mode of accounting for the doctrine of the church following an account of the divine life as Trinity. In this account, while the doctrine of the church is related to that of the doctrine of the divine life, the church becomes almost a separate article that follows from the divine life. There are three resultant possibilities here: (1) there is a (crude) modelling of the church after the life of God as can be seen in certain social Trinitarian accounts of the church;[44] or, (2) in the opposite direction, there is an account of divine agency in reference to the invisible church which can become overly separated from the church's concrete empirical form; or (3) the doctrine of the church is quashed by the doctrine of the divine life, such that the vast oceanic magnitude of the latter swallows up accounts of the miniscule droplet of the created *ekklesia*. In short, there is either too close an association of the divine life with the life of the church or too great a disconnect from the divine life in its immanent aseity from the life of the church and the work of God in this historical form in its spatio-historical existence and its particular polity. Furthermore, such a reading may well rest on a misreading of the creed that makes the church a separate fourth article preceded by the belief *in* Father, Son and Holy Spirit.[45] However, the church should not be understood to be a separate fourth article, but to exist under the third. There is no *in* preceding *ecclesiam*, as there is preceding the divine persons. This is clear in the Latin rendering of the Nicene-Constantinopolitan creed:

Et in Spiritum Sanctum, Dominum et vivificantem, qui ex Patre Filioque procedit.	And in the Holy Spirit, the Lord and giver of Life, Who proceeds from the Father and the Son.
Qui cum Patre et Filio simul adoratur et conglorificatur: qui locutus est per prophetas.	Who, with the Father and the Son, is adored and glorified: Who has spoken through the Prophets.
Et unam, sanctam, catholicam et apostolicam Ecclesiam.	And one holy, catholic and apostolic Church.
Confiteor unum baptisma in remissionem peccatorum. Et expecto resurrectionem mortuorum, et vitam venturi saeculi. Amen.	I confess one baptism for the remission of sins. And I look for the resurrection of the dead, and the life of the age to come. Amen.

44. We see this in Gunton's 'echo'; see above.

45. This seems to be how Webster reads the creed. He speaks of 'the creedal sequence in which *credo in ecclesiam* succeeds *credo in Deum Patrem omnipotententem ... et in Jesum Christum ... credo in Spiritum Sanctum*'. The concern I am expressing here rests with the '*in*' preceding *ecclesiam* which seems to indicate that it is a separate (and fourth) article of the creed.

Here, there is a clear differentiation between belief *in* the Holy Spirit, and the church which exists underneath the third article and not independent of it.[46] Similar to the way in which the account of salvation and judgement follow from the second article, so follows the church and its activity from the third article. The point is also clear even in the truncated Apostles creed:

> *Credo in Spiritum Sanctum,*
> *sanctam Ecclesiam catholicam, sanctorum communionem,*
> *remissionem peccatorum,*
> *carnis resurrectionem, vitam aeternam.*
> *Amen*

This is a point that Calvin makes very strongly at the start of his discussion of the church. Although he points to variance in the early church over the preposition, he nevertheless asserts: 'There is no good reason why many insert the preposition "in." Instead, it is important to be reminded that we simply believe the church (and not in the church).' For him, the reason for this distinction is clear: 'We testify that we believe *in* God because our mind reposes in him as truthful, and our trust rests in him.'[47] There are not four articles of the creed, therefore, but three. As Congar puts it,

> In the West ... the preposition *eis* or *in* has usually been omitted before *ecclesiam* and this fact has often been accorded a religious or theological significance ... When the great Scholastic theologians, then, came to consider the formula 'Credo in Spiritum Sanctum ... et in unam ... Ecclesiam' in the Niceno-Constantinopolitan Creed, they provided the following commentary: I believe in the Holy Spirit, not only in himself, but as the one who makes the Church one, holy, catholic and apostolic.[48]

The church is in the creed a mission of the Holy Spirit who is in Himself God and who acts in the economy of salvation to create the church.

Ecclesiology is certainly not an independent locus: we are only God's people because God has willed to be our God; this order is primary. But the deduction of the church on the basis of the creed and of scripture seems most appropriate on the basis not of strictly Trinitarian logic most immediately but of pneumatological logic most immediately.[49] Clearly, the life of the Spirit follows from God's life as Trinity,

---

46. This is a distinction between Eastern and Western versions of the creed. Western versions, including Western Greek texts, follow Augustine in stating that only the Triune God is the object of religious faith in the highest sense.

47. Calvin, *Institutes*, 4.1.2 (p. 1013) (emphasis original).

48. Yves Congar, *I Believe in the Holy Spirit*, vol. 2 (New York: Crossroad, 2013), 5.

49. While I recognize the principle of *opera ad extra sunt indivisa*, in speaking this way I am utilizing the doctrine of appropriations.

but moving from God's life in itself to the economy of salvation, pneumatology should be the mediating doctrine (the efficient cause) of ecclesiology. The doctrine of the church is not independent of other dogmatic loci, nor can it immediately be deduced from the divine life as Trinity *in se*, but must be articulated appropriately through the divine life of the Spirit as the divine person who is most immediately operative in creation and with creation in the time between the ascension of Christ and His return. The *res* of ecclesiology should be in 'The Holy Spirit, the Lord, the Giver of Life'; and the *res* of pneumatology in God's triune life. Proportionate space must be given for this move. And as a result of it, through the Spirit's life and work in the church and the believer, an account of the direct proportionality of created motion and divine motion might be accounted for. In other words, space might be afforded for both a description of divine agency and its connection to the human empirical spatio-historical nature and form of the church.

IV

Having a sense in dogmatics of a hierarchy of *res* (a tracing of efficient causality) through which one might have to trace more immediate economically orientated doctrines (such as the doctrine of the church) through the doctrine of appropriations to doctrines of functional personhood (economic pneumatology) to ontological personhood (pneumatology per se) to God's inner life (immanent Trinity) might determine that the topographical location of individual dogmas affords them both a degree of integrity and a sense of their interconnection to the whole nexus of God's being and God's ways with the world. Certainly, ecclesiology requires this mediated hierarchy, but it also requires discussion which is appropriate to its own subject in its own right – the life and being of the church. Tracing the doctrine of the church through the life and activity of the Spirit of God might allow in this mode of dogmatic ordering, furthermore, for a more appropriate sense of proportion in theological speech and prevent binarized choices between attending to the spatio-historical human community or the being of God as gracious source of that community in his acts.

Speech about the Holy Spirit of God in ecclesiology may be a way to emphasize the asymmetry of divine and human action, but to realize their interconnection in the life of the church which the Spirit creates, guides and will perfect. As Webster states, 'It is clearly important that this emphasis on the priority of divine action over the church as an act of human association should not be allowed to eclipse the "visibility" of the church.'[50] Or in Christoph Schwöbel's words: 'the way in which the Church is constituted by divine action determines the character and scope of human action in the Church'.[51] It is impossible to disconnect the two, and integral

---

50. Webster, *Word and Church*, 196.

51. Christoph Schwöbel, 'The Creature of the Word: Recovering the Ecclesiology of the Reformers', in *On Being the Church*, 122.

for the dogmatic ecclesiologist to describe the relationship between divine action and the community constituted by it, and to offer critical reflection to the church in its current form under this rubric. While asymmetry determines that there will always be a need to 'maximize' speech about God's action, this should relativize but not underplay speech about the human forms of community created by God's act.[52] Furthermore, attention to the relationship between these two realities (the efficient cause of the act of the Spirit in creating the derivative creaturely reality of the church) should be a priority. Thus, the foundational approach of Webster in his ecclesiology should be trumpeted:

> There emerge two fundamental principles for an evangelical ecclesiology. First, there can be no doctrine of God without a doctrine of the church, for according to the Christian confession God *is* the one who manifests who he is in the economy of his saving work in which he assembles a people for himself. Second, there can be no doctrine of the church which is not wholly referred to the doctrine of God, in whose being and action alone the church has its being and action.[53]

But how are these two principles, these two moments, dogmatically best to be related? What is the content of *kai* in 2 Cor. 6.16: *enoikēsō en autois kai emperipatēsō kai esomai autōn theos kai autoi esontai mou laos*? Certainly, there should be attention first to the action and agency of God in creating the church before any account of the church's form, activity or habits;[54] but how is it that we are to connect those two moments? What of God's action can we say should shape the particular spatio-historical (critical) description of the community of the church?

Emphasis on Trinitarian approaches, Christological accounts or a mix of economic Christology and pneumatology (as has traditionally been the case) tends to lead to disproportion in the doctrine of appropriations if one is to follow the reading of the creed offered above.[55] The Spirit's work can be somewhat short-changed.[56] Furthermore, these approaches can tend to offer accounts of the church in which there is a sense of exclusion of the empirical, spatio-historical church in place of the dogmatic account of God, or else can introduce competitive

---

52. Webster, *Word and Church*, 198.
53. Webster, *Word and Church*, 195.
54. Webster, *Word and Church*, 228.
55. We should bear in mind here Webster's early warning: 'To tie the Spirit too closely to the person and work of Christ is to underestimate that differentiation within the one divine life and thus to encourage the slow drift into modalism which is so common in western Trinitarian theology.' John Webster, 'The Identity of the Holy Spirit: A Problem in Trinitarian Theology', *Themelios* 9.1 (1983): 6.
56. We potentially see this in Webster's own account in *Word and Church* which focuses on Son and Spirit (with more said about the former), and in his '"In the Society of God"' in which the Spirit receives perhaps only one page of direct discussion.

sensitivities to the two. The Spirit is the person of God, however, who works within the creaturely to bring it to its creaturely perfection. As Origen's student, Didymus the Blind, puts it, all human progress in truth comes from 'that divine and magnificent Spirit, the author, leader and promoter of the Church'.[57] There is in the work of the Spirit an account that can be offered of what Webster describes as direct proportionality between the motion of God and the motion of the creature: 'the more God moves the creature, the more the creature moves itself'.[58] The Spirit works within the creature to perfect the creature's creatureliness: in this way the Spirit works from outwith the believer within the believer.

Here, it is worth pausing for a moment. As the one who *works in* the creature and *perfects* the creature (outwith itself) an account of the activity of the Spirit in the life of the church will always require recognition of the difference between God as creator and redeemer and the church as creation being redeemed; but as the one who works *in the creature* and perfects *the creature*, there is also a need to speak of the creaturely form which is created and is being redeemed as creature by God the Holy Spirit. Speech of God's person and work as Holy Spirit involves recognition first of all of the Spirit's divinity: the Holy Spirit is 'the Lord and giver of Life, Who proceeds from the Father and the Son. Who, with the Father and the Son, is adored and glorified'; the creed makes this clear. Here, we need to be careful always to remember that the Spirit is not the Spirit of the community and should not be confused with a given culture or form of community.[59] The Spirit is, after all, the *Holy* Spirit. He is the Spirit of God, and He should not be confused with the community but is Lord of, Creator of and Judge over the church. But, second, the Spirit is at work upon and within the church, creating it. As Luther succinctly puts it, '*Proprium opus spiritus sancti est, quod ecclesiam facit.*'[60] The Spirit that rested on Christ has come now (in a different way) to rest on the church in order that the church might make present the completed work of the ascended Christ in the world today. As the one who blows wherever He wills (as the *ruah* of God),[61] the presence of the Spirit is not seen in and of itself (as the Son in His earthly life is)[62] but in those who are moved by the Spirit's movement. The concrete form of the life of the Spirit in His works *ad extra* is the life of the church He creates. We perceive this as the work of the Spirit when it accords to the description of the Spirit's life and work – when its form is one moved by the Spirit in a manner which scripture suggests. It is necessary, therefore, in speaking of the activity of the Spirit to do justice at once to both the Spirit's sovereign freedom and the Spirit's presence in the community of the church.

---

57. Didymus, *Enarrat. Ep. Cath. 2 S. Petri*, 3, 5 (PG 39, 1774).
58. Webster, '"In the Society of God"', 214.
59. See Hans Küng, *The Church* (London: Burns and Oates, 1968), 173–86.
60. Luther, Katechismuspredigten (1523) (WA 11), 53.
61. See Jn 4.
62. Even if only in incarnate form (i.e. in relation to the economy).

Before moving to sketch what fundamental forms such a movement of the Spirit might have been revealed in scripture to take in the life of the church, it is necessary to address in a little further detail the fact there is imagery in scripture relating the church to Christ. Why should the dominant perspective of ecclesiology be from that of pneumatology and not that of Christology? The point here is that beyond the objective work of God in Christ, there is a further work of God in relating this completed act, which took place once and for all at a particular moment in history, to the present spatio-temporal conditions of the world. God does not only in His grace make Himself responsible for our salvation but offers us the gift of enabling us to receive the salvation He offers through the work of the Holy Spirit.[63] As Barth advocates, the Holy Spirit is the special element in the revelation of God's saving acts who provides for the creature the subjective aspect of the event of revelation. In this way, the Holy Spirit is the presence of God Himself to the creature in a way which does not reduce God's divinity. The Spirit effects a relation with the creature in order to grant the creature new life, and is the freedom of God to be present to the creature, enabling the possibility of humanity being open to revelation such that the presence of God comes not only from above but also from within the human.[64] It is by an event of the Spirit that this work of salvation which comes from Christ (the word and salvation of God) is enabled to penetrate spatio-historical contemporaneity in the institution of the church in advance of the parousia.[65] Webster puts the relationship between Son and Spirit in the work of salvation thus:

> In consequence of the Son's perfect work of reconciliation, the Spirit animates and preserves a human social world in which the old order of sin and death has been set aside and the life of the children of God is unleashed. Through the Spirit it comes about that there exists a temporal, cultural, bodily reality in fulfillment of the divine appointment: 'You shall be my people.'[66]

Proportion in ecclesiology determines that due account is given to the Spirit's life, being and work, as the one under whose sovereignty it is most appropriate to discuss the life, being and work of the church. This is not to the exclusion of functional Christology but with due attention to appropriate dogmatic topography and proportion.

The reason for this location is to enable a suitable description of the forms that we might deduce from scripture that the Spirit would create in animating and

---

63. For more on the economic dynamics of Spirit and Son, see Tom Greggs, *Barth, Origen, and Universal Salvation: Restoring Particularity* (Oxford: Oxford University Press, 2009) esp. chs. 4 and 7.

64. Barth, Karl. *Church Dogmatics*. Edited by Geoffrey W. Bromiley and Thomas F. Torrance. 2nd edn. London: T&T Clark, 2004 (hereafter *CD*). *CD* I/1, 449–51.

65. Congar, *I Believe in the Holy Spirit*, vol. 1, 80.

66. Webster, '"In the Society of God"', 213.

preserving the human community of the church. First of all, the community of the church, if it attends to the dogmatic observation that the church exists by the gracious act of God the Holy Spirit, will be a community of *epiclesis*. The being and the form of the church will be found in the constant prayer: 'Come Holy Spirit.' This prayer is a reminder of the created nature of the church as an act of God's free generosity. In *epiclesis*, there is a recognition that this community in space and time is not simply a coming together of human wills but a fulfilment of God's purpose and an act of God's salvation in bringing together in this particular time and this particular place and this particular form the people of God. This is not to overemphasize the charismatic at the expense of the institutional but to realize the miracle of God's grace that people are freed to be communities that are witness to His salvation. In this, a balance is to be struck between an overemphasis on form which confuses the church with God's objective work of salvation or His Kingdom, and an underemphasis on form which relies only on God's external operation. The prayer of *epiclesis* is that the Spirit comes to and within the community. This community is always contingent in its contemporary spatio-historical form, but this does not reduce its significance or importance: it is precisely in the contingency of its contemporary spatio-historical form that God the Holy Spirit works, because in this the eternal work of God is made present in the conditions God has created that humans may receive His salvation. Human history and human patterns are not unimportant because they are the way God chooses to work in the delay of Christ's parousia: it is the locus in which the Word of God is *heard* and then *proclaimed*. In this way, they are gifts of the patience of God. This is a form which is not yet perfected (and should not, therefore, confuse the Kingdom with itself by overemphasizing the institution) but which is being perfected by the activity of the *Holy* Spirit from without inside the community itself (and should, therefore, attend with all reverence to its form as the place where the Holy Spirit of God is asked to dwell). As a community of *epiclesis*, the community should seek to bear the marks of the Spirit who is known and seen as wind in the movement He effects in creation. These marks are the fruit the community bears by which it will be judged: love, joy, peace, forbearance, kindness, goodness, faithfulness, gentleness and self-control (Gal. 5.22-23). In these marks are the polity of the people of God, and can the Spirit's presence be seen. These are yet to be fulfilled, but as the one who is given as the guarantee of our salvation, the Holy Spirit is at work in the lives of communities and humans in perfecting them in creation.

Second, as the one who is perfecting creation, the Spirit is one through whom there is an internal twofold order in the community that the Spirit alone can establish. The Spirit works within the creature in time, bringing the creature to redemption. In this activity of redemption, the sinfulness of individualism and egoism is overcome as the Spirit opens the believer to God and other humans. In this moving beyond the ego (the opening of the heart turned in on itself), the community of the church is not only an incidental extra but also essential for redemption. As the locus of the gathered worship, the church is the place where the dynamic of being opened up for God (in worship) and for others (in the body of believers with whom we worship) is simultaneously present. The coming of the

Spirit (*epiclesis*) is to open the believer to God's activity of redemption in opening the believer to God and to God's creation. In that sense, we should say with Cyprian, '*extra ecclesiam nulla salus*'. This opening towards God and towards others is a gracious gift, and not one that fallen humanity can perform alone but only as it is enabled to be the creature it was always intended to be by God's redeeming grace. We see the Spirit at work in creation, therefore, in those communities which are most actively simultaneously ordered towards God and each other in complete openness and in a sense of the complete inextractable nature of those two directed orientations. This situation demands the contingent contemporaneity of a given community in a specific place at a particular time: it demands a gathering (an *ekklesia*) in which the deposit of salvation might be given for its completion when we know even as we are known (1 Cor. 13.12).

A third dynamic extends this visible presence of the Spirit in orientating the human beyond their ego despite the inevitability of this in their sin. In reordering the individual to the community in which there is worship of God and fraternity with fellow members, the Spirit does not displace individual egoism with collective ecclesial egoism. A mark of the Spirit's presence in the community of the church is that the *whole* church is orientated simultaneously on God and the world outside of its walls. There is an external ordering of the church which replicates ecclesially what the church fulfils internally for the individual. The gathered community does not gather simply for itself but for the sake of the world to whom and for whom it is a sign. In the account of Pentecost recorded in Acts, Luke directs us to the reality that the coming of the Spirit led the community out: the Spirit radically reordered the community from its inward facing direction to facing the world around it in proclamation of the gospel in the many tongues of those present. In this way, the presence of the Spirit in the church creates a community which is focused on mission and witness. In Pannenberg's words: 'The church … is nothing apart from its function as an eschatological community and therefore as an anticipatory sign of God's coming rule and its salvation for all humanity.'[67] The church is orientated beyond its own communal bounds to its future with God and to the world in which it dwells. This is a work of the Spirit who gathers to send, and the more orientated simultaneously on God in worship and on the community that surround the church in service any given church is, the more present the Spirit can be known to be within the community.

A pneumatological locus for the doctrine of the church should help to prevent falling into the traps of either describing only human society or only the life of God. In the church, both are present as in the church the Spirit is at work in the here and now, the time between the times, redeeming and perfecting as the reality of God's completed work of salvation is fulfilled in the contingent contemporaneity of human existence. This is *God's* work, but it is God's work *on and within His creatures*. In this, we cannot speak of the one who is our God without speaking of the people whom He has chosen; both must be spoken of together with due

---

67. Pannenberg, *Systematic Theology*, vol. 3, 32.

proportion and with the correct sensitivity to dogmatic topography. Congar's words seem particularly apt in thinking about the work of God in animating and preserving the church: 'The Spirit, who is both one and transcendent, is able to penetrate all things without violating or doing violence to them.'[68] Both this transcendence and the integrity of that which the Spirit penetrates must be held together in discussing the church, and any successful ecclesiology will seek proportion in that – a proportion which will be helped by locating the doctrine of the church under the doctrine of the Holy Spirit of God.

68. Congar, *I Believe in the Holy Spirit*, vol. 2, 17.

Chapter 2

COMMUNIO ECCLESIOLOGY: THE SPIRIT'S WORK OF SALVATION IN THE LIFE OF THE CHURCH

Human fallenness has a horizontal as well as a vertical dimension: the fall not only ruptures relations with God but also (and as a consequence of this) ruptures relations between humans and between humans and the rest of creation. Reconciliation and redemption, therefore, are needed not only for humans in relation to the vertical order (vis-à-vis God) but also in relation to the horizontal dimensions of sinfulness (in relation to the rest of creation). It is in this context that we might think most appropriately of the work of the Spirit in salvation,[1] and in this way that we might begin to understand St Cyprian's maxim *salus extra ecclesiam non est*.[2] The Spirit is the one who opens humans up to one another, incorporating them into the body of Christ, giving them a true and fundamental identity in baptism and through the life of the church (which the Spirit creates), and opening them up through the church to the world. In this communion, we see redemption being worked out by God through the person of his Spirit in space and time on the horizontal plane: this is the ongoing work of salvation (salvation to life in all its fullness) in the time between the resurrection of Jesus and the consummation of all things. In the life, death and resurrection of Jesus Christ, the God-human, reconciliation between God and humans is completed once and for all. In the time of the church (the time of God's patience),[3] this restored relationship between God and humanity begins to be worked out not only (vertically) in the praise, prayer and confession of God's people in the life of the church, by which the Spirit orders the human towards God, but also through the work of the Spirit in creating communion *with one another* (horizontally) in the church.

This chapter will outline the essence of sin as the *cor incurvatus in se*, and identify not only the vertical implications of this but also the horizontal impacts of the fall in terms of human individualism and self-centredness in relation to the rest of the created world. From here, the chapter will argue that it is necessary to

---

1. This said, it is important to attend here to the doctrine of appropriations. See Thomas Aquinas, *Summa theologica* I, q. 39.

2. More commonly rendered, *extra ecclesiam nulla salus est*, 'Outside the church there is no salvation.'

3. See *CD* II/1, 406–39.

examine the operation of God in salvation from the perspective of the effects of the fall on the horizontal plane as well as the vertical plane. The chapter will advance that through incorporation into the body of Christ the believer participates by the Spirit in the true humanity of Jesus (a humanity which is opened fully to God and fully to others), and the believer does this by receiving and sharing in the same Spirit as rested fully and intensely upon Christ in his full, perfect and complete humanity. The Spirit incorporates the individual into the body of Christ and creates in her the realization that humanity is co-humanity and that co-humanity is the re-orientated reality that arises in space and time from God's work of salvation. The concrete form of this new life that the believer has takes shape through the continuing work of the Spirit in establishing the life of the church. The establishing of the church itself is a salvific act of God which allows the outworking of the vertical reconciliation which God has effected in Jesus Christ to reverse the effects of the fall in time and space in both restoring the relationship of humanity to God *and, in the life of the church, restoring the relations between humans and between humans and creation.* This aspect of salvation is the operation of God the Holy Spirit in turning the heart in upon itself out towards that which is not itself in creation.

Horizontal fallenness

The origins of sin arise from the human breaking a relationship with God through disobedience: Adam and Eve disobey the one command God gives to them in the context of his superabundant grace in creation – they eat the forbidden fruit. But the immediate consequence and effect of this act, even before the description of the rupture in relationship with God which follows, is that the man and woman understood themselves to be naked in front of each other, and covered themselves (Gen. 3.7).[4] Furthermore, having hidden himself because of his nakedness from God when God walks in the garden, Adam immediately seeks to divert blame away from himself and towards Eve, and indeed through this to God: it is 'the woman you [God] gave to be with me' whom Adam blames for eating the fruit which, he is clear, was given by Eve (Gen. 3.12). The woman then also offers blame away from herself towards the serpent (Gen. 3.13).[5] We see disjointed and conflictual

---

4. Luther reflects on both the vertical and horizontal components of this verse. See Martin Luther, *Lectures on Genesis Chapters 1–5*, Luther's Works, ed. Jaroslav Pelikan (St Louis: Concordia, 1958), 163–9 (esp. 167–9 on the rupture between human beings).

5. Clearly, there are significant issues here to which feminist theology rightly draws our attention, such as the potentially problematic male–female power relations of the text, specifically with regard to man's fall through woman. For an initial survey of the literature on this theme, see, for example, Carol L. Meyers, 'Gender Roles and Genesis 3:16 Revisited', in *The Word of the Lord Shall Go Forth*, ed. Carol L. Myers and Patrick O'Connor (Philadelphia, PA: Eisenbrauns, 1983), 337–54; Ilana Pardes, *Countertraditions in the Bible: A Feminist Approach* (Cambridge, MA: Harvard University Press, 1992); Phyllis

individual reality arising immediately from the fall, with the sense of separate and individualized identity, not only in relation to God but also in relation to other humans and the rest of creation.

Human nature is thereby corrupted by sin, for this alters the relationship that exists not only between the human and God but also between human beings themselves. Because the human no longer seeks to be orientated on God and to share in the good gifts of his grace, the human shifts the focus of her orientation onto herself. There is an awareness of individual identity in a relationship of (potentially conflictual or hostile) alterity towards both God and other human beings. Indeed, to be aware of other options beyond immediate obedience is itself to be aware of one's self over and against God: no longer shared co-willing but a distinctive will aside from that which God has. It is an act of the grace of God, indeed a participating in his grace towards that which is other than himself in creation, for the human to be able to be orientated towards another – both God and other human beings. As soon as humanity is tempted to step outside of that relationship of grace, the consequence is that the human being ceases to participate in the grace which allows her to be orientated towards another and not herself: outside of grace, the human finds herself outside of the ability to receive and share in God's absolute free-loving kindness, which affects her orientation towards those around her. That the myth of Genesis records that it is one individual who is tempted to behave thus, and then the other also partakes of the forbidden fruit, further underlines the degree to which the individual's self-awareness and self-orientation is key: Eve and Adam do not make the decision together initially, but apart from each other; they blame each other; the man even blames God for giving him the woman. This is a long way from the origins of man and woman recorded in the second creation myth:

> This at last is bone of my bones
> and flesh of my flesh;
> this one shall be called Woman,
> for out of Man this one was taken. (Gen. 2.23)

The unity and sense of identity and unity between man and woman in the second myth (emphasized by the story of the rib taken from Adam) indicates that co-humanity was originally a (perhaps the) central feature of the creation of humanity. This is also evident in the first creation myth in which the unity of man and woman is linked with being made in the image of God:

Trible, *God and the Rhetoric of Sexuality* (Philadelphia, PA: Fortress, 1986); Mary Daly, *Beyond God the Father: Toward a Philosophy of Women's Liberation* (Boston, MA: Beacon, 1973). The points made in this essay do not seek to displace such critiques. However, this essay seeks to focus these critiques further in relation to the issue of individualistic alterity. Feminist critique of the text presupposes the very problem that the text intends to clarify, namely, the very individual power relations that arise from a distorted alterity.

> So God created humankind in his image,
> in the image of God he created them;
> male and female he created them. (Gen. 1.27)

Male and female are created together, and their joint creation is in the image of the gracious Creator: there is no individualism here, and human unity ('them') is related to the image of God who in creation determines himself to be for another.[6] In the story of the fall, it is the person's *individual* identity in relation to another (both God and another human being) that begins to take centre stage.

Accounts, therefore, of the restoration of creation from the fall require an account of the operation of God in restoring the relations of humans to other humans as well as humanity's relation to the rest of creation,[7] since these, too, are consequences of fallenness, along with broken relations between the divine life and the human. In general accounts of salvation have focused upon the economy of God in the incarnation of the second person of the Trinity, God the Son. Salvation comes through the God-human, Jesus Christ, who mediates God to humanity and humanity to God.[8] The key concern here is that the fall is overcome, and humanity is offered salvation by restoring the relationship between God and humanity. Clearly, this is the primary concern of salvation: humans are saved by the grace of God in Jesus, who while we were still sinners died for us (Rom. 5.8); for us and for our salvation, God became human as the Nicene creed attests. It is only as a gift of God's grace that humans are saved, and God's merciful free-loving kindness is such that God chooses not to be without the fallen human creature. Furthermore, for God, there cannot be differentiated horizontal or vertical (an ethical or ritual) sin: all sin is a falling short of God's glory; and it is only (as we have established) by participating in the good grace of God that the human can share in being orientated away from the self and towards the other in creation. However, God does not only in his salvific grace set right human relations with Godself (vertically); in God's economy of salvation, God also in God's grace sets right human relations to each other and to creation. This horizontal reorientation of humanity is no less a work of God's salvation than the vertical restoration.

This is no new discovery. But what might be of note is that where there is a concern to express the horizontal dimension of salvation, this again has tended to be in relation to the work of God in Jesus Christ – through a moral example,[9]

---

6. See *CD* III/1, §41; cf. *CD* II/2.

7. On this theme, see David L. Clough, *On Animals*, vol. 1 of *Systematic Theology* (London: T&T Clark, 2012), esp. ch. 7.

8. We might think of the *locus classicus* of this view as Anselm's Cur *Deus Homo*. See 'Cur Deus Homo', in Anselm, *Anselm: Basic Writings*, trans. Thomas Williams (Indianapolis, IN: Hackett, 2007), 237–326.

9. Perhaps the greatest example of such so-called 'subjective' theories of atonement – as Gustav Aulén dubbed them in his now classic *Christus Victor: An Historical Study of the Three Main Types of the Idea of the Atonement* (New York: Macmillan, 1969) – is that of Friedrich Schleiermacher, whose doctrine taught that the effects of the cross were of no

through Christ's command[10] or through an enhypostatic participation in Christ's humanity.[11] The operation of the Spirit in salvation is often somewhat overlooked or played only in a minor key.[12] The role of the Spirit in establishing the life of the church, and the church's salvific significance, can fall into the background – an added extra not theologically explored or related to other aspects of the economy of God's salvation. Such a perspective which underplays the Spirit's work may well, however, sublate God's economy of salvation, either reducing the church to a mere human structure negatively (as simply a gathering of humans with no recognition of the salvific miracle of the church's existence)[13] or heightening human authority in the institutions of the church (without a critical approach to an over-identification of God's work with human structures).[14] There is a need for accounts of salvation to have a deeper degree of reflection on the third person of the Trinity. While attending to the doctrine of appropriations (and remembering *opera trinitatis ad extra indivisa sunt*), no doubt we would wish to affirm with the most ancient traditions that the Father creates, the Son saves and the Spirit sanctifies the people

---

real effect outside of the new community of the church. See Friedrich Schleiermacher, *The Christian Faith*, 2nd edn, trans. H. R. Mackintosh and J. S. Stewart (Edinburgh: T&T Clark, 1928), 425–38. This idea was carried forward by Adolf von Harnack in his 'The Essence of Christianity' lectures, and later by Albrecht Ritschl in *The Christian Doctrine of Justification and Reconciliation* (New York: Scribner, 1902).

10. See Dietrich Bonhoeffer, *Discipleship*, ed. Geffrey B. Kelly and John D. Godsey, trans. Martin Kuske and Ilse Tödt, Dietrich Bonhoeffer Works 4 (Minneapolis, MN: Fortress, 2003), 77; and *CD* II/2, §37.

11. See my *Barth, Origen, and Universal Salvation: Restoring Particularity* (Oxford: Oxford University Press, 2009), 32. Cf. *CD* II/2, 7; George Hunsinger, *How to Read Karl Barth: The Shape of His Theology* (New York: Oxford University Press, 1991), 114; Bruce L. McCormack, 'Grace and Being: The Role of God's Gracious Election in Karl Barth's Theological Ontology', in *The Cambridge Companion to Karl Barth*, ed. John Webster (Cambridge: Cambridge University Press, 2000), 92–100.

12. This is potentially a more Protestant propensity, as there is nervousness about affording too much salvific 'power' to the church: only Christ saves. However, the point of this essay is to argue that in the life of the church there is a further salvific work not of the church as an institution but of God in the person of the Holy Spirit.

13. See John Webster, '"In the Society of God": Some Principles of Ecclesiology', in *Perspectives on Ecclesiology and Ethnography*, ed. Pete Ward (Cambridge: Eerdmans, 2012), 200–22.

14. We might think of these approaches as being crudely parallel to Ebionism or Docetism, respectively, and may correspond to low-church and high-church self-understandings accordingly. On such characterizations of ecclesiology, see Colin Gunton 'The Church on Earth: The Roots of Community', in *On Being the Church: Essays on the Christian Community*, ed. Colin E. Gunton and Daniel W. Hardy (Edinburgh: T&T Clark, 1997), 65.

of God;[15] we must also note that the act of sanctifying is a salvific act which reverses the effects of the fall by returning humans to communion, not only with God in Christ but also with each other in the work of the Holy Spirit in the life of the church. To speak of the work of the Holy Spirit is to speak of the acts and events of God in the time between the ascension and return of Jesus Christ; it is to speak to the acts of God in establishing the life and work of the church by an event of the Holy Spirit. Such a work of God is a continuing work of salvation before the consummation, for in time and space God establishes returned inter-human relations, which redefine the identity of the human not as those whose hearts are turned in upon themselves in self-preserving egoism but as those whose hearts are turned outwards towards God, and – as they are turned outwards towards God – turned outwards towards the church (i.e. as the corporate body of Christ in which the individual finds her primary and most basic identity).

Horizontal salvation through the Spirit in the communion of the church

Through the life, death and resurrection of Jesus Christ, humanity is reconciled to God. The restoration of this vertical relationship to that which it was in a prelapsarian condition also involves the restoration to the prelapsarian condition and a reversal of the effects of the broken relationship with God and his good grace: thereby, broken human-to-human relationships are also restored, as humans are able to participate in the grace of God, and are thus orientated away from themselves and towards others (the movement which is the foundational nature of God's grace as God wills to be for another other than Godself in creation – even in its fallen state). This reorientation of humanity and restoration of human-to-human relationality is an act of the Spirit of God, who makes us participants in the body of Christ, sons and daughters of God. As Paul recounts in 1 Corinthians: 'For in the one Spirit we were all baptized into one body – Jews or Greeks, slaves or free – and we were all made to drink of one Spirit' (1 Cor. 12.13).[16] Here, difference and individual identity is relativized and reduced in relation to the one Spirit and one body into which all individuals are baptized. This body is defined later in the chapter by Paul as the body of Christ: 'Now you are the body of Christ and individually members of it' (1 Cor. 12.27). It is the Spirit (with whom Christ baptizes) in whom members of the church are baptized, and through whom they

---

15. Classically, in the Niceno-Constantinopolitan Creed, the church confesses belief in 'God the Father, Maker of heaven and earth … in Jesus Christ … [who] for us and for our salvation came down from heaven … [and] in the Holy Spirit … [who] has spoken through the prophets' and whose presence enables 'one, holy, catholic, and apostolic church … the forgiveness of sins … and the resurrection of the body'.

16. On this verse, see: J. Ross Wagner, '"Baptism into Christ Jesus" and the Question of Universalism in Paul', *Horizons in Biblical Theology* 33 (2011): 45–61.

come to be members of the body of Christ.[17] To be a member of the body of Christ not only alters our relationship to God, from its broken post-lapsarian state, but also alters the anthropological status of individuals who are no longer essentially understood in their individual identity, but through the Spirit's baptism in their relationship to Christ: there is no longer Jew or Greek, slave or free, male or female, since the church is one in Jesus Christ (cf. Gal. 3.28). In Christ, we not only share in his mediating work between God and humans but also recover, by the Spirit with whom he baptizes, what it means to be fully human as God eternally determined – participating in God's grace through restored vertical relations, and so enabled to be turned away from ourselves and out towards other human beings. By being a member of the body of Christ, our humanity is transformed into the humanity it was created by God to be. This is a co-humanity, rather than an individualistic humanity – a humanity whereby we do not exist by ourselves or even in groups or organizations of individuals who gather together as individuals jointly, but in which we share in one another. As Paul puts it in Romans, 'so we, who are many, are one body in Christ, and individually we are members one of another' (Rom. 12.5). To be a member of the body of Christ is not only to aggregate together in the church, but it is to be 'members of one another' – to recognize that salvation makes our identity radically different. Or, put otherwise, the church is not simply a collection of individuals who come together and are dispersed; the church reveals our true and eternal identity as members of the body of Christ. We are not to think of ourselves first as individuals and second as those individuals who gather but rather as a communion of those who share in each other as we share in the body of Christ.

But what specifically has this to do with the Spirit? Is this not more second article than third article theology? Let us parse the above argument, and begin in relation to baptism, which itself exists under the third article of the creed.[18] In baptism, we are baptized into Christ, and in this we share with Christ in receiving the Holy Spirit (cf. Mt. 3.16 and parallels). This gift of God to humanity is not, however, a means by which we are transformed into something other than human, nor in baptism is something added to us beyond God's initial prelapsarian desire for creation. In receiving the Spirit in baptism, humanity is enabled to share and participate (both *de iure* and *de facto*) in the humanity of Christ. Christ's reception of the Holy Spirit in the baptismal narrative is not a pointer to his divine identity; this comes in the Father's announcement that Jesus is his beloved Son. Rather, it might be best to think of Christ's reception of the Holy Spirit (like his baptism itself) as a fitting sign and even fulfilment of Christ's full humanity. The reason for this can be found in the second Genesis account of creation: 'Then the Lord God

---

17. On the distinction between water baptism and baptism by the Spirit, see *CD* IV/4, 30–1.

18. The creed should not be read as four articles as if the discussion of the church were a separate, fourth moment: the creed's third article on the Holy Spirit is the one under which we read about the identity of the church.

formed man from the dust of the ground, and breathed into his nostrils the breath of life [ruah]; and the man became a living being' (Gen. 2.7). The use of ruah here is significant. The Spirit (who is, as the Constantinopolitan creed notes, the Giver of Life) is breathed into humanity: it is by the Spirit that humans become living beings. Job gives us a clear image of this, linking the presence of the Spirit, breath and human life:

> If he [God] should take back his spirit to himself,
> and gather to himself his breath,
> all flesh would perish together,
> and all mortals return to dust. (Job 34.14-16)

To be a true and real living human being involves receiving the breath (or Spirit) of God. If we are to think of the baptismal narrative as having some echoes of the creation,[19] we might wish to suggest that the Spirit's resting on Jesus in his baptism is a perfection of his full humanity:[20] the Spirit who is extensively present throughout the world is fully and intensively present in the human Jesus. The

---

19. A number of commentaries point to the reminiscence of Gen. 1.2 (the Spirit hovering over the waters of the deep) here; see, for example, C. E. B. Cranfield, *The Gospel According to St Mark* (Cambridge: Cambridge University Press, 1963), 53–4; Adela Yarbro Collins, *Mark: A Commentary*, Hermeneia (Minneapolis, MN: Fortress, 2007), 148; and Morna D. Hooker, *The Gospel According to St Mark* (London: A&C Black, 1991), 47. However, the connection to the presence of the Spirit in the creation of the first human in Gen. 2 does not seem to be considered, despite parallels that suggest themselves, especially in light of the Pauline idea of the first Adam becoming a living being, but the last Adam a life-giving Spirit (cf. 1 Cor. 15.45). There is space to explore further the connection between baptism and the creation of humanity. Paul relates baptism to inclusion in Abraham's family (Gal. 3), and passage with the messiah through death to new life (Rom. 6), and he frames the generation of Abraham's worldwide family as the act of a God who creates out of nothing and who resurrects (Rom. 4).

20. This is distinctive to Spirit Christology. This form of Christology, sometimes explained in distinction from (but not necessarily contradiction to) so-called Incarnation or Logos Christology, understands the work of the Spirit as integral to both Christ's identity as the second person of the Trinity (the Son) and Christ's salvific work as risen Lord. Specifically, Christ's baptism and mission in the Spirit, his giving of the Spirit to the church and his objective love with the Father, which is the Spirit, are each understood as integral to his divine person. See, for a range of examples, Walter Kasper, *Jesus the Christ*, 2nd edn (London: T&T Clark, 2011); Paul Tillich, *Systematic Theology*, vol. 2, *Existence and the Christ* (Chicago: University of Chicago Press, 1975); David Coffey, *Deus Trinitas: The Doctrine of the Triune God* (Oxford: Oxford University Press, 1999); and Ralph Del Colle, *Christ and the Spirit: Spirit-Christology in Trinitarian Perspective* (Oxford: Oxford University Press, 1997). The approach offered in this chapter seeks to associate the presence of the Spirit far more closely with what it means to speak of Christ as true human.

receiving of the Holy Spirit by Jesus is an active recognition or even consummation of his true humanity – the humanity which other humans as yet do not possess in fullness but which they will receive in the eschaton.[21] The reception is a fulfilment of creation, an eschatological anticipation of the true humanity to which humans were eternally predestined, seen in the prelapsarian creation narratives: the resting of the Spirit on Jesus is a confirmation of his complete and true humanity which is caused by and drenched or immersed with the Holy Spirit.

In short, to be wholly and truly human is to be wholly and truly open to the Spirit of God: to become more human and to increase our humanity is to be completely open to the Holy Spirit; the more the Spirit dwells with us, the more human we may become. The descent of the Spirit onto Jesus is the realization in time and completion of his true humanity; this is in part why the baptismal narrative follows the nativity and infancy narratives so closely. Since time and space are essential to created humanity, in time and space Jesus' humanity flourishes to be complete humanity, which all of humanity was determined to share in; the resting of the Spirit on Jesus is an indication of this. Yet, Jesus is not only the one who is baptized and receives the Holy Spirit; he is also the one who baptizes with the Holy Spirit. In the giving of the Holy Spirit in baptism, Jesus offers the gift of God's own self in the person of the Spirit in the economy of salvation, so as to restore humanity to the true humanity it was created to be: baptism by the Spirit is a way in which humanity is not only reconciled to God but made anew as true human beings. Paul picks up this link between Adam's creation, Jesus' baptism and the giving of the Spirit when he writes: 'Thus it is written, "The first man, Adam, became a living being"; the last Adam became a life-giving spirit' (1 Cor. 15.45).[22] In baptism, by receiving the Spirit of God, we become human (or open ourselves to the potential of becoming human), and in this are enabled to participate both passively (by the objective reality of God's grace in salvation) and actively (through acts and behaviour that correspond to that objective reality) in Christ's full humanity.[23] This true humanity is a humanity which shares in Christ, and which has an identity which is more foundational than any individual identity each human may possess. Clearly, Jesus' is a life which shares fully (in fact, uniquely) in God's life – the God who has become in the second person of his Trinity this particular human, Jesus. But by an act of the Spirit we share in Jesus' humanity, for the same Holy Spirit who breathed life into Adam and rested fully on Christ is present to his people and works within us. We share in Christ's humanity such that we become adopted children of God (Eph. 1.5).

However, reception of the Holy Spirit through baptism, in making us adopted children of God, not only makes us fully human on an individual level but

---

21. See Eberhard Jüngel, *Theological Essays II* (London: Bloomsbury, 2014), 216–40.

22. Cf. Luke Timothy Johnson, *Contested Issues in Christian Origins and the New Testament*, NovTSup 146 (Leiden: Brill, 2013), 227–93.

23. Cf. 2 Cor. 5.17: 'In Christ the old has passed away and the new has come.' This is a work from God, and in this God enables humanity to become righteous.

reorientates us towards our corporate and communal identity in Christ. The first sense of this is that our primary and ontological identity is in relation to being part of the body of Christ. The Spirit who is at work in creation redeems humanity from its individualism and enables us to share in our true identity, which is in its prelapsarian state 'naked and unashamed' (to quote Dietrich Bonhoeffer).[24] Through the presence of the Spirit in her life, the believer recovers the humanity that she was always to have: she becomes a new creation to herself, but this is the creation God eternally determined her to be. This humanity is not one where there is enmity between individuals but where all are one in Jesus Christ. As Eph. 4 reminds us:

> I therefore … beg you to lead a life worthy of the calling to which you have been called, with all humility and gentleness, with patience, bearing with one another in love, making every effort to maintain the unity of the Spirit in the bond of peace. There is one body and one Spirit, just as you were called to the one hope of your calling, one Lord, one faith, one baptism, one God and Father of all, who is above all and through all and in all. (Eph. 4.1-6)

The unity of the Spirit is the unity to which the believer is called. Humans are enabled to escape the effects of the fall through the work of the Holy Spirit, whose baptism enables us to share in the humanity of Christ. By this, horizontal relations are reordered, and co-humanity becomes the primary identity of the human being. Individual alterity in relation to God and fellow humans is reversed by a salvific act of God who makes us anew by his Spirit in baptism.

In time and space, the effects of this reorientation of horizontal relationality take form in the life of the church which the Spirit creates. The event of Pentecost, with the giving of the Holy Spirit, is the birth of the church. In the gift of the Spirit comes the capacity to be ordered not to oneself but to others. The life of the church in all of its variety provides the concrete form for the outworking in time and space of salvation on the horizontal plane. In the other within the life of the concrete community of the church, to whom one is united not by virtue of any other element except for unity in Christ through the baptism of the Spirit, one finds the form in which the life of the redeemed in time has. In the life of the church, the other human exists as a divine gift to whom, by a work of the Spirit, the individual not only becomes ordered but through whom and with whom the individual finds her true identity as not existing in and of herself, but as one who is in Christ and as such ordered to co-humanity. In the concrete life of the community of the church, there exist others who are enabled to be the objects of the turning out of our hearts through the work of the Spirit. These others are not those to whom we necessarily

---

24. Dietrich Bonhoeffer, *Creation and Fall: A Theological Exposition of Genesis 1–3*, ed. John W. de Gruchy, trans. Douglas Stephen Bax, Dietrich Bonhoeffer Works 3 (Minneapolis, MN: Fortress, 2004), 82: 'The human being is naked and not ashamed, speaks with, and has to do with, God as though they belong to each another.'

are attracted by virtue of some benefit to our selves or by virtue of a repetition of our own identities which we see mirrored in theirs. Instead, the others within the church are genuine others who are given by the Spirit as a gift of God within the church. As Bonhoeffer puts it, it is essential that we avoid the 'greatest danger':

> The danger of confusing Christian community with some wishful image of pious community, the danger of blending the devout heart's natural desire for community with the spiritual reality of Christian community. It is essential for Christian community that two things become clear right from the beginning. *First, Christian community is not an ideal, but a divine reality; second, Christian community is a spiritual [pneumatische] and not a psychic [psychische] reality.*[25]

For Bonhoeffer, there are no idealized images, no demands, no bonds of union other than the act of God in bringing the community together; and for that act and the gift of the other, the believer should be thankful.[26] The otherness of these others is a divine reality given to the believer in the life of the church. In them, we discover our truest identity (not in race, class, gender, status and so forth), but in the true co-humanity that we share in Jesus Christ through baptism as the Spirit, which rested fully in his humanity, dwells within us and makes us human. This means that variety in the life of the church is crucial: the community needs to be a community in which there is variance between individual members such that the believer is enabled genuinely to be turned out to other humans. The church is not a community like any other in which there might be some bond of attraction between members (whether shared or aggregated interests) but is a community formed by the Spirit of God where members are joined together through the redeeming activity of God's Holy Spirit, who frees individuals from sin in relation to the horizontal order of humanity: humans are freed to be for others and to share in the co-humanity of these others in Christ, and this is based on nothing other than the economy of God's salvation through the work of the Spirit, who enables humans to be saved from the *cor incurvatus in se* and to be genuinely focused on the full co-humanity of all others in Christ. In the gathering of the church, the Spirit becomes intensively present,[27] bringing together these others and saving them from their focus upon themselves in their sinful hearts turned in towards themselves. This bringing together and focus on co-humanity is a work of salvation which humans cannot achieve by themselves: in fallen sinfulness, human desire is ordered towards the self and the ego, but through the Spirit this fallenness is overcome.

---

25. Dietrich Bonhoeffer, *Life Together and Prayerbook of the Bible*, ed. Geffrey B. Kelly, trans. Daniel W. Bloesch and James H. Burtness, Dietrich Bonhoeffer Works 5 (Minneapolis, MN: Fortress, 2004), 35.

26. Bonhoeffer, *Life Together and Prayerbook of the Bible*, 36.

27. The language of intensity and extensity is borrowed from Daniel W. Hardy, *Finding the Church: The Dynamic Truth of Anglicanism* (London: SCM Press, 2001).

The church is not, therefore, a society of like-minded people or of friends but a community of salvation (a proleptic anticipation of redemption),[28] in which we are freed from our focus on ourselves and opened to the genuine otherness of the other in the church – the other as one who also shares in the fundamental identity in which we do in participating in the true humanity of Christ. We are able to see this in the earliest communities of the church, and in the description offered in Acts 2 of its character. Here, there are two things to note. The first is the political salvation that the giving of the Spirit brings in the gift of tongues. The passage makes the variety of nations from which various people at Pentecost were present plainly clear: 'every nation under heaven' (Acts 2.5) with a very long associated list (Acts 2.9-11). However, the differences that exist between them are overcome by an event of the Spirit who does not suppress the otherness of those present, but (affirming this otherness) transcends it and prevents it from preventing genuine communication between peoples:

> All of them were filled with the Holy Spirit and began to speak in other languages, as the Spirit gave them ability. Now there were devout Jews from every nation under heaven living in Jerusalem. And at this sound the crowd gathered and was bewildered, because each one heard them speaking in the native language of each. Amazed and astonished, they asked, 'Are not all these who are speaking Galileans? And how is it that we hear, each of us, in our own native language?' (Acts 2.4-8)

Cultural and linguistic difference and otherness are not removed, but they become the means for the work of God's Spirit: it is in each native language rather than some spiritual Esperanto that those on Pentecost hear the disciples speak. The church's form is such that it includes difference, but the Spirit brings us together in communion in that difference: otherness is essential for the conditions for the possibility of freeing our hearts from their propensity to be turned in upon themselves. This is profoundly political: one identity is not suppressed or removed for the sake of another, but identities are not an obstacle for communication, coming together and sociality.[29] The second point to note is the sociopolitical and economic consequences of the salvific work of the Spirit. Rather than individuals preserving the things God has given them for the sake of their own individual self-preservation, all things were held in common: the church becomes the primary identity of the believer who is so orientated towards those others within

---

28. For a detailed and systematic account of proleptic anticipation, see Wolfhart Pannenberg, *Jesus – God and Man*, 2nd edn, trans. Lewis L. Wilkins and Duane A. Priebe (Louisville, KY: Westminster John Knox, 1982); and Wolfhart Pannenberg, *Systematic Theology*, vol. 3, trans. Geoffrey W. Bromiley (Grand Rapids, MI: Eerdmans, 2009).

29. See Daniel W. Hardy, 'Created and Redeemed Sociality', in *On Being the Church: Essays on the Christian Community*, ed. Colin E. Gunton and Daniel W. Hardy (Edinburgh: T&T Clark, 1989), 21–47.

the church that she is prepared to share her individual possessions. This is clearly something that Luke finds remarkable in his recounting of the life of the first Christians: 'All who believed were together and had all things in common; they would sell their possessions and goods and distribute the proceeds to all, as any had need' (Acts 2.44-45). This is as much a miraculous work of the Spirit as the more 'supernatural' accompanying signs to Pentecost: the effects of the freeing of humans from hearts turned in on themselves are profound in and for the life of the church; and, if the story of Ananias and Sapphira is anything to go by, central to the identity of the redeemed spiritual community. Unity in the life of the church and a life ordered towards others is a sharing in the humanity of Christ, which is a gift of salvation of the Holy Spirit of God. In this, the horizontal effects of sin are overcome, and humans are freed to share humanity rather than seek to preserve their individual egos.[30] This is why there is no salvation outside the walls of the church.

Nonexclusive communio

Since the work of the Spirit in salvation brings the human being into the humanity of Christ, which is the humanity that humans were eternally destined towards (rather than the fallen humanity in which post-lapsarian humans currently participate), and by this redeems the human from the horizontal effects of the *cor incurvatus in se*, the form of the redeemed humanity which the Spirit brings corresponds to the humanity of Christ in which it participates. This is a body which is turned outwards towards others. There is, therefore, in the Spirit's work in salvation a double turning of the heart outwards: first, out towards concrete others in the life of the church in which the believer participates; second, as the body of the church out towards the world and the concrete others who are as yet not part of the church. This orientation out towards the world reflects the movement in narrative of Christ's life: when the Spirit is given and rests on Jesus in the baptism, Jesus begins his public ministry. The resting of the Spirit on Jesus leads him to be outwards focused.

The Spirit's salvific work of orientating us towards others establishes the church not only as a community in which there is unity focused on one another within the church but also a unity in being focused on others in the world. Having been gathered together corporately, in the event of Pentecost, the church receives its true identity by being ordered outwards towards the world. This is an activity of the Holy Spirit in forming humanity into the body of Christ. Just as Christ is the

---

30. This is something which overly individualized accounts of salvation need to recognize: salvation is not simply about an individual's relationship with God but also following from this the individual's relationship to the rest of humanity. There the greatest command involves not only loving God but also loving neighbour.

human for others,[31] so too his body of the church is enabled to be ordered to other human beings through the Spirit's work.

This outwards orientation through the Spirit has a double effect. First, individuals find their true identities in the body of Christ: true identity is not the individual ego, but the life of the Spirit in which we become human by being incorporated into the true humanity of the body of Christ. Second, that true humanity is such that there is no corporate egoism to replace individual egoism, but in which as the corporate body of the church, individuals are orientated not only on one another but also on the world. The individual *cor incurvatus in se* is not replaced by a corporate or ecclesial *cor incurvatus in se*. Since through the Spirit's work human fallenness and its horizontal propensity for individualism (whether singularly or collectively) is reversed by incorporation into the body of Christ, Christ's own body, by a gift of the Spirit of Christ, is reflected in the corporate body of the church; just as Christ is himself offered for and focused on others, so also the corporate body of Christ in its very communion and unity is not turned in on itself but is opened up to the world. It is the body of Christ given *for the world*. The Spirit's work in salvation in establishing the life of the church in which the believer is freed from focusing in on herself to focusing out to the concrete other in the community of the church is propelled beyond the confines of the community in and of itself. The reversal of human sinfulness in the heart turned towards itself terminates on the horizontal plane in the church's existence for the sake of the world. Individual hearts are turned out towards others by the Spirit within the church, and the corporate heart of the church community is turned out towards the world. Barth makes this point emphatically:

> The work of the Holy Spirit in the gathering and upbuilding of the community (C.D., IV, 1 § 62 and IV, 2 § 67) cannot merely lead to the blind alley of a new qualification, enhancement, deepening and enrichment of this being of the community as such. Wonderful and glorious as this is, it is not an end in itself even in what it includes for its individual members. The enlightening power of the Holy Spirit draws and impels and presses beyond its being as such, beyond all the reception and experience of its members, beyond all that is promised to them personally. And only as it follows this drawing and impelling is it the real community of Jesus Christ.[32]

As the community of witness to Jesus Christ, which is brought about by the Holy Spirit, the church cannot simply be an end in itself even in the individual salvific end of being freed from individualism and pointed towards the other in the life of the community. As a community, the task of the church, instead, is to be sent out

---

31. See Dietrich Bonhoeffer, *Letters and Papers from Prison*, ed. John W. de Gruchy, trans. Isabel Best et al., Dietrich Bonhoeffer Works 8 (Minneapolis, MN: Fortress, 2010), 228, 501.
32. *CD* IV/3, 764 (cf. *CD* IV/1 §62 and IV/2 §67).

to the world for which it exists. The church's orientation is not to be focused on itself even in its communion and corporeality, but out towards the rest of the world for which the church exists.

There is an important order here. The world does not exist for the sake of the church – to provide members, for self-preservation or to bring those others who are outwith its bounds within it. Corporately, the church exists for the world to witness through the power of the Spirit to the life, death and resurrection of Jesus Christ and to the reconciliation and redemption of humanity. The Spirit not only saves humanity from anthropological egoism through the community of the church but also saves humanity and the church from sacral communal egoism through the work of the Spirit in the church's existence for the world. Crucially, there must be a recognition of the provisionality of the church: the church is not an end in itself but a witness to the end prepared for all creation, when God will be all in all (1 Cor. 15.28). The church's existence is not to stand aside from the world but to stand for the world. It is not the world which is instrumental for the church, since there will be a new creation and a new heaven and new earth in the *Eschaton* (Rev. 21.1); it is instead the church which is instrumental for the world to make clear to the world that which it already is – the world reconciled by Jesus Christ. The Spirit frees the church to exist not for itself but for the world to which the church pays this testimony. This is a communal reversal of human fallenness: on the horizontal plane the community is freed from the sin of existing for self-preservation. Instead, participating in Christ's humanity, the church corporately mediates the message of salvation to the world: it is the presence of Christ in the context of the world in the time between his ascension and return. Again, this is a work of salvation, since only by the grace of God's Spirit is the church able to participate in the divine grace which is seen in God's being for another than himself in creation. As the community of humans who are freed by the Spirit from the effects of sin in individual self-preservation, the church is a community which also corresponds to that order of existence which is orientated on another.[33] Life in the Spirit is life ordered towards God *and others in the world*, and by this work the

---

33. Bonhoeffer takes this so far that he even claims that the church exists in order to take the sins of the world onto itself. This is a fulfilment of the church's existence for the sake of the world. Bonhoeffer arrestingly writes:

> The church is today the community of people who, grasped by the power of Christ's grace, acknowledge, confess, and take upon themselves not only their personal sins, but also the Western world's falling away from Jesus Christ as toward Jesus Christ … With this confession the whole guilt of the world falls on the church, on Christians, and because here it is confessed and not denied, the possibility of forgiveness is opened … for there are people here who take all – really all – guilt upon themselves, not in some heroic self-sacrificing decision, but simply overwhelmed by their very own guilt towards Christ. In that moment they can no longer think about retributive justice for the 'chief sinners' but only about the forgiveness of their own great guilt. (Dietrich

Spirit frees believers from replacing individual self-preservation with collective individual self-preservation. The concrete life of faith is one turned outwards away from the self (whether on a single or collective front) and out towards the others.

Conclusion

Salvation does not exist outside of the church since the church is a work of the Spirit in which salvation is worked out in space and time in the world in the time between the ascension and return of Christ. This work of the Spirit is a further work of the economy of God which undoes the horizontal effects of the fall by freeing humans from their individual or corporate egoism of the *cor incurvatus in se*. This reverses the effects of the fall and restores humanity to the humanity it was eternally determined to be by God. Through sharing in the same Spirit who rests on Christ and fulfils his true humanity, human beings are freed to become genuinely human and to increase the humanity that they currently have, since human existence is a work of God breathing his Spirit into Adam. The concrete form of this pneumatological inspired anthropology is that it is ordered not on the self (which is the effect of the fall) but on God and on others. On an individual level, the community of the church provides the divine gift of others in their otherness who are essential to the truest and deepest identity of any individual – an identity which comes only in sharing in the humanity of Jesus Christ. On a corporate level, just as the Spirit compelled Jesus to his public ministry following his baptism and the resting of the Spirit on him, so too the Spirit compels the church to exist for the world beyond its bounds for which it exists.

Bonhoeffer, *Ethics*, ed. Clifford J. Green, trans. Reinhard Krauss, Charles C. West and Douglas W. Stott, Dietrich Bonhoeffer Works 6 (Minneapolis, MN: Fortress, 2005), 135–6)

Chapter 3

THE GLORY OF GOD IN THE PEOPLE OF GOD: PARTICIPATING IN THE INTENSITY OF THE SPIRIT'S LIFE

The Westminster Catechism begins by posing the question: 'What is the chief end of humanity?' To this question, the catechism gives the following answer: 'Humanity's chief end is to glorify God, and to enjoy him forever.'[1] But what does it mean for humanity, or indeed more narrowly the people of God, to glorify God? Does God need our glory? If God does, what does that say of God? If God does not, what does it say of humanity's and (more narrowly) the church's giving glory to God? It is to these issues that this chapter turns in seeking to understand the people of God giving glory to God as a *responsive participation in God's infinite glory which is known in the radiance of its perfect effulgence*.[2] To unpack this account, the chapter begins by outlining the implications of the claim that God is perfectly glorious in Godself: that glory belongs properly to God. It then, in a second section, seeks to

---

1. Westminster Catechism, Question 1; language has been altered to make it gender inclusive.

2. This was the first academic chapter I wrote following the unexpected loss of my teacher, friend and colleague, Professor John Webster, at an all too early stage of his life. John had taught me at Oxford, and latterly we were colleagues and shared a doctoral seminar in Aberdeen. I cannot begin to account for the debts I owe to John. It was fitting that the occasion for this chapter being delivered was in St John's College, where John began his academic career as chaplain and tutor in systematic theology. I didn't always agree with John theologically; but the seriousness with which he took the task of theology was something I could never cease but be impressed by, and – having prayed with him most days while we were colleagues – the breadth and intensity of the vision of God John had, as a God supremely, unendingly, totally and incomprehensibly complete in Godself, always moved me – pietistically as well as intellectually. I have tried in this chapter to learn more from John than perhaps I have before. He did not, in fact, say so much about God's glory in his work, preferring other ways of expressing the majesty of the divine life – plenitude, sovereignty, perfection. But he never tired from challenging theologians to speak about God. I offer this chapter in memory of John Webster.

unpack what it means to see the glory of God as a perfection of divine *movement*,[3] in which the radiance of the effulgence of God's glory is made present in the theatre of creation: in the divine perfection of glory the creature is confronted with the reality that the perfection of the divine life is One which is never now without the creature; the radiance of glory, we might say, has a locus in which it is known and received by creation. Section three of the chapter turns to the Christian's glorification of God. This glorification is understood, in virtue of the preceding sections, as a responsive participation in the overflowing and superabundantly gracious, glorious life of God. This responsive participation by the Christian is the response of active (de facto) sanctification in which the creature is conformed by the Spirit to the image of Christ so as to participate in the perfection of God's eternal glory. This very response of the Christian is itself one of overflow and grace as she participates in and witnesses to the logics of the Lord's glory, the radiance of the effulgence of which touches the world that Lord is redeeming.

Sufficient glory – God is glorious and source of all glory

The divine life is complete in itself.[4] To account for God's glory is not to offer in the first instance an account of the recognition by the creature of the divine Creator's qualities and perfections, such that God's glory would not exist, be diminished or would exist in a changed manner, were God not Creator. Instead, to account for God's glory is in the first instance to claim that God *is* glorious – that God is perfectly and fully glorious in God's eternal life in and of itself. We might say that it is *proper* to God to be glorious. God's glory is a glory which has existed in the eternal triune life as the Father eternally glorifies the Son so that the Son may glorify the Father (Jn 17.1) in the unity of the Holy Spirit. This is a glory which the presence of God had 'before the world existed' (Jn 17.5) and is, therefore, not

---

3. For an excellent and thoroughgoing account of divine movement (though one distinct from the account offered in this chapter) in the history of Christian thought and in relation to philosophy and science, see Simon Oliver, *Philosophy, God and Motion* (London: Routledge, 2005); particularly relevant by way of contrast is ch. 4.

4. For an excellent contemporary account of divine aseity, see John Webster, *God without Measure: Working Papers in Christian Theology: Volume 1: God and the Works of God* (London: T&T Clark, 2016). Chapter 2 directly tackles this question, and the volume as a whole tackles the relationship between the divine life and God's outer works. The present author has some reservations about the dogmatic proportionality and topography of some of the material in this volume, but it remains the most helpful account of the divine life's freedom from and for creation in recent years. For the classical account of divine perfection and simplicity (from which much of Webster's own insights are drawn), see Thomas Aquinas, *Summa theologica*, prima pars, qq. 3 and 4. For all that the current author might disagree on *how* to express the relationship of the divine life in and of itself to the economy of God, that God's life is perfect in and of itself remains a point of full agreement.

a glory which is dependent on the theatre of creation as the condition for the radiance of glory's effulgence. The divine life is fully sufficient in its glory in the divine eternity of perichoretic relations. When creatures give glory to God, we do not add anything to the divine life which God lacked before our glorifying of God, but we simply acknowledge the perfection of glory in the eternal glorification of the Father, Son and Holy Spirit. The *Gloria* reminds us of this: 'Glory to the Father and to the Son and to the Holy Spirit, *As it was in the beginning, is now, and shall be forever.*' God's glory does not enhance itself through the glorification offered by the creature: God's is a glory already perfect in itself in the eternal Trinitarian relations of the divine life in which glory is given and received. God has no need of the creature for God's glorification: the plenitude of God's glorious life is infinite, and it is only in that infinite plenitude of glory that speech about the creature's glorification of God finds its appropriate place.

In understanding what it means to speak of the glory of God in the people of God, it is necessary, first, then, to establish that glory in relation to God does not reside in the creation's perception of or response to the divine life; instead, to speak of God's glory is to speak of who God is in and of God's perfect Self. God is wonderfully, superabundantly, perfectly glorious in God's own self in the eternity of God's life. God, we might say, *is* the God of glory. It is proper to God's own nature to be glorious. To speak of the glory of God in the people of God is to speak first of *God's* glory and only then of how it is perceived and responded to by God's people. God's is a glory which is not a greater or even maximal outworking of a scale of glory we imagine in our creaturely realm; God's is the glory of the One who is the King of glory. It is not like any other. To speak of the glory of God in God's people is to join in the first instance with the Psalmist in saying: 'Lift up your heads, O gates, And be lifted up, O ancient doors, That the King of glory may come in! Who is the King of glory? The LORD' (Ps. 24.7-8). It is not that we may know what is glorious and see God as the fulfilment of that; it is that by God's glory we may learn to see creation as the theatre of the radiance of the effulgence of God's glory. God's glory is the illuminating light which gives light to every other thing, and by which we might see glory (or its radiance, rather) in the creaturely sphere.

Habakkuk puts it well when he states: '[God's] radiance is like the sunlight' (Hab. 3.4a). In the light of God's glory, we do not simply see a kind of glory comparable to anything in creation; but we see the glory of the Creator which illuminates the creation with its radiance. Order and topography in systematic theology are important here. It is not that by the glory of God's people we see the glory (or the giving glory) of God; it is that by the radiance of the glory of God we see the glory (and giving glory) of God's people. And it is this principle of the perfect and plenitudinous sufficiency of God's divine glory which is best spoken of first in any systematic, doctrinal or dogmatic account of God's glory. A God who is not glorious in and of Godself is not a God worthy of glorification: that would be an idol who receives glory like anything else in creation, rather than the God who is the source and perfection of all that is glorious in the glories of God's eternal life.

But perfection itself in the divine life is an *infinite* perfection. It is not a perfection which is staid and static in its condition: God's perfect glory is a perfection which is supremely unconditioned. The divine eternity of glory is an eternal *life* in which God's glorious and infinite aliveness must not be forgotten. God is not only glorious in the glories of God's pretemporal life;[5] God is also simultaneously glorious *now* in the context of the theatre of the radiance of God's glory and in the context of creation's glorification of the eternal glory of God; just, indeed, as God will be perfectly glorious after creation forever more. By this is meant that God's perfect glory does not exist *competitively* in relation to the creature's act of glorification of the divine life, but exists as the infinity of the divine plenitude which now *includes* the creaturely act of the glorification of the eternally and sufficiently glorious God. God's existence before all time, in the perfection of God's eternity, already contained within it the glorification by the creature of God now: God's eternity is, as Boethius reminds, *interminabilis vitae tota simul et perfecta possessio*.[6] The simultaneity *and perfection* of God's presence to and possession of time is significant in terms of what it means for God to be glorious: God's glory is not dependent upon the creature's glorifying of God or upon creation as a theatre of the radiance of God's glory, but equally God's glory does not remove the integrity and significance of the creature's glorifying of God or the creation as a theatre of God's glory.

But how do we know of this perfectly sufficient glory of God? We know it because the God who is complete in God's own glory is glorious with an end point in that which is not God – in the theatre the radiance of glory's effulgence. God's glory for the creature has the logic of grace.[7] Glory is the perfection of the divine life in which the outwards movement of the immutable and constant perfection of the eternal triune life is known. Complete in itself, divine glory is known because it is glorious – because it shines forth in its infinite excess beyond itself, and thereby glory's radiance is known in creation.[8] Glory at once implies the free sovereign glory of the divine life, and the loving and gracious movement of the divine life to

---

5. By this is meant that we should not think of God's freedom from creation in God's free electing grace simply as being pre- or a-temporal in relation to God's glory: God's glory *is* glorious in the spatio-temporal theatre of creation also.

6. See Boethius, *de Cons. Philos.*, prose VI. For some survey material on the philosophical backgrounds and theological history of accounts of divine eternity, the reader is directed to the following works as examples: For a discussion of this see Wolfhart Pannenberg, *Metaphysics and the Idea of God* (Grand Rapids, MI: Eerdmans, 1990), 75–82; and Michael Chase, 'Time and Eternity from Plotinus and Boethius to Einstein', in ΣΧΟΛΗ 8, no. 1 (2014): 68–110. I have attempted to unpack some of the details of this material myself in my 'The Order and Movement of Eternity: Karl Barth on the Eternity of God and Creaturely Time', in *Eternal God, Eternal Life: Theological Investigations into the Concept of Immortality*, ed. Philip G. Ziegler (London: T&T Clark, 2016), ch. 1.

7. See Eph. 1.6 where grace and glory are connected.

8. The relation of glory to light in scripture can be found in Exod. 34 (in the Septuagint's rendering *doxa*); Jer. 13.16 in the contrast of light to darkness; Lk. 2.9 (in the shining of glory); and 2 Cor. 4.6; as well as the relation of glory and fire in the Old Testament.

that which is not Godself – the rays of the glory of God known in the terminus of the theatre in creation as the radiance of divine glory's effulgence.[9] It is to this topic which this chapter now turns.

The perfection of glory's movement

Although it is imperative to understand the glory of God as a perfection of the divine life in and of itself in the perfect, immutable eternity of the divine living, in the perfection of God's glory the creature is confronted with the reality that the perfection of the divine life is one which is *never now without the creature*. Here, the eternality of God's glory needs further unpacking. To say that God is glorious in God's own eternity is not to set up the divine life's eternality as an atemporal existence aside from creation in opposition to the creaturely sphere. It is not only that God's glory exists only as it was in the beginning; God's glory also exists as it is now and it will exist as it ever more shall be. There is no eternity aside from the eternity in which creation (in its temporality) also exists; there is no eternal glory of God aside also from the glorifying of God by creation. Eternity is not perfectly static in glory; eternity is perfectly alive in glory. There is a need for care here. It is not that God requires creation for the completion of God's glory; nor that creation adds anything to God's glory in conceiving God's glory as never now being without creation. These options presume false dichotomies (dualisms even) which imagine we can think of God without creation or of the creation without God. It is, rather, simply the case that God has in God's eternal, sovereign and wise freedom determined Godself to be God who is the Creator, Reconciler and Redeemer of creation. This determination is not the determination of a will dependent on the exercise of an intellect that chooses and then enacts a purpose. This determination is a determination of the One who is eternally (in the simultaneous and perfect possession of unending time) the LORD, the one who is *actus purus*. In her wonderful first volume of her systematic theology, Kate Sonderegger very helpfully reminds us of this in her account of the burning bush (in relation to Schleiermacher's interpretation):

> We intend ... to speak in the earthly words given us of the I AM who is cradled in the things of this world, the Person who Radiates Truth. As unearthly Fire, God explodes into the earth. His own Reality is itself impulsive, alive. But it is alive as Subject, not natural Emanation alone. It is Nature, Spiritual Substance. God can fittingly be described as Energy or Fire, *Dunamis*, and it scorches the earth. But in a mode unimaginable to us – the greater unlikeness of the likeness – God's

---

9. Speaking of the radiance of the effulgence of glory is an attempt at preserving the perfection of glory as that which belongs perfectly to God apart from the economy. It is a way of attempting to preserve something of the distance of the glory of God from the creaturely sphere, as is seen in Ezek. 1 (especially v. 28).

Nature is entirely, throughout, and inexhaustibly creative and subjective. God does not *elect* an action that He then executes in the power of His own willing. He does not *deliberate*, then *enact*. We do not mean personal, in that sense – precisely not that! God teaches in a divine sense: that is, He descends down through the individuals and kinds He has made with His own Life, His own Vitality and Truth, so that they catch Fire, they combust with the Life that is Divine – yet they remain their own kind, the bush not consumed.[10]

The God who is glorious, perfectly in and of Godself, has determined Godself in this way to be the God who creates, who binds Godself (covenants) with the creature as creature for all eternity. There is not a moment in pre-temporal eternity in which God decides to be the Creator; such a description ironically makes God all too temporally contingent. No; for all eternity God was eternally the One who would create, creates and has created.[11] The existence of creation does not add anything to God's glory, but is as the creation of God a place, a theatre, in which God in God's radiant glory is alive.

To speculate about a God who is glorious without God's creation is to create an abstractly atemporal being who is other than the God and Father of the Lord Jesus Christ who together with the Spirit is to be worshipped and glorified. The otherness of God's glory is not an otherness from creation but an otherness *for* creation, an otherness which is known only by God's self-disclosure in creation. To quote St Paul: 'For God, who said, "Light shall shine out of darkness," is the One who has shone in our hearts to give the Light of the knowledge of the glory of God in the face of Christ' (2 Cor. 4.6). Glory is that perfection of God which speaks of God's self-determining love to be the God who is eternally for the other as much as it bespeaks the God who is perfectly complete in Godself; to be for that which is not God, for the creation which becomes the theatre of the radiance of God's glory. That is why the Light of the knowledge of the glory of God is seen in the face of Jesus Christ: we know who God is because God's glory *comes, shines forth*, and in this coming, this shining forth, God has made Godself known; and God's glory is known in the locus in which the foundation for the eternal covenant of God with creation is to be seen – in the person of Jesus Christ.

The Creator–creature distinction, which is often employed in systematic theology at these points in the discussion, is a distinction which is helpful here; but we must remember that the distinction is not an expression of abstract metaphysics but of a *relation*. There is as much intimacy as there is ultimacy in speaking of God as Creator.[12] To speak of this distinction is not to speak simply of a demarcation

10. Katherine Sonderegger, *Systematic Theology: Volume 1: The Doctrine of God* (Minneapolis, MN: Fortress, 2015), 266.

11. The idea here is not so distant from the account of the relationship of Jesus to eternity and time given in Wolfhart Pannenberg, *Jesus – God and Man* (London: SCM, 1968), 367–9; cf. 320.

12. See Janet Soskice, *The Kindness of God: Metaphor, Gender, and Religious Language* (Oxford: Oxford University Press, 2007), 61.

of God and world but to speak instead of the creature's Creator and the Creator's creature – a distinction only meaningful in asymmetrical interrelationality.[13] Or, again, to quote Sonderegger:

> God's Reality is personal rather, in *this* sense: He is the One, the Utterly Unique One, who in His concrete Person makes possible the concrete, specific relation with creation, the unique relation that brings into being the creature. The *Relatio* between such a Creator and such a creature is itself *God* – that is another way to put this point. He alone can bridge the two; He alone can bring into existence another.[14]

That creation is a theatre in which the radiance of the effulgence of the glory of God may be known is an expression of precisely this relational Creator God, who is not perfected by the creature but is the perfect Creator of the creature, and the radiance of whose glory is manifest to the creature the Creator has created.

In this way, we may wish to speak of glory as the supreme perfection of divine loving since glory bespeaks the divine reality of the radiance of God in the theatre of that which is not God. While glory speaks of God's unique and unchangeable infinite majesty, we may also say that glory has a terminus in the radiance of the effulgence of God's glory as received and recognized by that which is not God – that is, by creation. Glory speaks at once of God's otherness from creation as God (God *is* glorious) and God's presence in creation as God (God's glory is *radiant*): *glory is God's otherness for creation*, we might say. To continue with the verse from Habakkuk already quoted: 'His radiance is like the sunlight; He has rays flashing from His hand, And there is the hiding of His power' (Hab. 3.4). In the sunlight, the rays which flash to creation are not only the presence of God's glory to creation but also the hiding of God's power (the veiling in God's unveiling to use one of Barth's dialectics):[15] God's glory at once speaks of the *knowledge* of God which radiates from God's infinitely perfect glory, *and* the knowledge of *God* towards whose infinite glory the creature can only bow her knee and squint her eyes as she seeks to behold the glory of the King. This glory of God is the glory of the God known in the face of Jesus Christ: such glory is what it means to behold God's hidden power in the context of the human Jesus hanging on the cross.[16]

---

13. This is the structure I observe in Augustine's *Confessions*: Augustine speaks of God's nature in relation to his own creation and climaxes the book with a commentary on Genesis' account of creation.

14. Sonderegger *Systematic Theology: Volume 1*, 267.

15. Cf. *CD* I/1, 178–9, 315–26.

16. For the best account of the relationship between the cross and theology proper, see Eberhard Jüngel, *God as the Mystery of the World: On the Foundation of the Theology of the Crucified One in the Dispute between Theism and Atheism* (London: Bloomsbury, 2014). In this book, Jüngel explores the effect on the doctrine of God of what it means for God to define Godself through identification with the crucified.

As Karl Barth reminds us, glory is the supreme perfection of God which can be understood only in terms of seeing the divine freedom as the divine freedom to love. Glory is the way God makes Godself conspicuous and apparent everywhere God is. In a captivating phrase, Barth writes: 'God's glory is His competence to make use of His omnipotence as the One who is omnipresent, and to exercise lordship in virtue of His ever-present knowledge and will.'[17] God's glory is both God's right in and of Godself, and God's power in the context of God's creation. Or again, to quote Barth: 'God's glory is God Himself in the truth and capacity and act in which He makes Himself known as God.'[18] That we know of the radiance of the effulgence of God's glory is in and of itself an expression of the divine determination to be for another that is not God: that we know of God's glory is an expression of the infinitely excessive gracious nature of the overflow of divine love. In the reality that God is glorious is the reality that God loves. Glory at once speaks not only of the fullness and sufficiency of God's divine perfection but also 'the emerging, self-expressing and self-manifesting reality of all that God is'.[19] Glory speaks of God's perfect being as that which always reaches beyond itself through the radiance of God's effulgence to that which is not God: glory speaks of the God who *declares* Godself, and of the other as one for whom in gracious love God determines Godself to be. *God's glory is identical with the plenitude of God's self-sufficiency in God's inner life, but God's glory is simultaneously the declaration of the plenitude of God's self-sufficiency to the creature who God never now is without.* The reason why we see the 'Light of the knowledge of the glory of God in the face of Christ' is because God's glory is God's loving: in the love expressed in the face of Jesus Christ is found the infinite glory of the God whose infinitely sufficient nature is one which is sufficient in the plenitudes of its grace which overflows towards that which is not God; in the face of Jesus Christ is the God who is Creator, Reconciler and Redeemer, and who in this never ceases to be fully, sufficiently and completely God. Glory is an account of God's divine Self-manifestation, which does not cease to be divine in its self-manifesting. John Webster writes as follows: 'God's glory is God himself in the perfect majesty and beauty of his being. This glory is resplendent. Because God himself is light, he pours forth light. God is glorious and therefore radiant. ... [There is an] unbroken continuity of being between God's glory and effulgence; light and its splendour are one.'[20] In attesting to the relationship between the divine light and the radiance of its effulgence which manifests that light, theology cannot help to be drawn back to the eternal relationship of the Father to the Son. As the One who is Light from Light, the Son is the effulgence of God's glory: glory and its effulgence are an eternal dynamic expression of the movement of the Father's paternity and the Son's filiation. This filiation itself is part of the double reality (or movement) of

---

17. *CD* II/1, 641.
18. *CD* II/1, 641.
19. *CD* II/1, 643.
20. Webster, *God without Measure: Volume 1*, 73.

the Son's relation to the Father and the Son's radiating of the presence of God's majesty. The presence of the radiance of the effulgence of the glory of God on earth is a manifestation of the eternal movement of glory and glorification in the divine life: the Son Himself as the *Verbum incarnandum* is already eternally the One determined as the effulgence of God's glory to bring light to the world in the radiance of His being.[21] Christ's divinity overflows in His glory in true God becoming true human in Him.[22] As the writer of the Epistle to the Hebrews puts it, 'In these last days [God] has spoken to us by a Son, whom he appointed heir of all things, through whom he also created all things. He is the reflection of God's glory and the exact imprint of God's very being, and he sustains all things by his powerful word.'[23] The glory of God is known to us in the manifestation of the Son, who manifests to creation the reality of the eternal triune Creator's glorifying and loving dynamic movement in the theatre of creation. Christ is the one who has glory in the presence of God before the world existed (Jn 17.5) but who also glorifies God on earth (Jn 17.4). This Son is the one who glorifies the Father, who is the reflection of God's glory, the effulgence of God's Light.[24] This Son is the One eternally destined to be for creation's salvation and redemption, as an expression of the Father's love for creation even as the love of the Father for the Son (Jn 17.23). Glory speaks of God's double movement: God's internal immanent life of paternity and filiation; and God's manifestation in the realm of God's creation with God's own presence in the effulgence of God's glory in the person of the Son – the very One who is eternally self-determined to be for the creation which was created through Him and reconciled by Him.

Put succinctly, the point of the preceding is to say that God's glory is the means of speaking of the very deity of God – in the eternal infinitely self-sufficient relation (movement) of the Father and the Son; and simultaneously of the manifestation of the deity in the movement of God towards that which is other than God – towards creation – in the effulgence of the glory of God known in the person of Jesus Christ. God's glory is both an account of God's immutable divinity aside from creation and of God's unbreakable covenant with creation. God is immutably the glorious Creator, Reconciler and Redeemer of the world. God's glory is distinct from the glory of every other being because it is *God's* being, and God is pre-eminent to every other being and therefore excels them perfectly, infinitely and absolutely. But a being can live in such contrast to others that is so marked off from them as to have no significance for those others – to have no meaning, no terminus. If this were true of God, however, this could not be the God to whom

---

21. Cf. Webster, *God without Measure: Volume 1*, 73–4; albeit the form of this in terms of the *Verbum Incarnandum* is expressed in a more Barthian register.

22. *CD* I/2, 662.

23. Heb. 1.2-3a.

24. Cf. Origen regarding the Son's filiation: 'This is an eternal and everlasting beginning, as brightness is begotten from light' (Origen, *On First Principles*, trans. G. W. Butterworth [New York: Harper & Row, 1966], 1.2.4).

belongs the glorifying of the creature who would be unreached by God's glorious otherness. Instead, God is not at one point (in God's immanent life) and we at another (in the economy of creation): what reaches creatures is the radiance of the effulgence of God's own glory – God Himself in Jesus Christ in whose face is found the light of the knowledge of the glory of God. God's glory is revealed when it is not just immanent but when recognized and acknowledged by humans, known in the illumination it brings – even in the darkness.[25] Glory speaks of God infinity and God's infinite capacity in God's infinity to love and move towards that which is not God, and speaks of God's very nature as being such. Put more dogmatically, we might say that in God's omnisufficiency, God's glory is God's love: divine glory is not just God's plenitude but God's superabundant plenitude of grace (of absolute free-loving kindness). The God of glory is the glory of this God: the God who is not glorious from creation but whose glory is radiant in creation; the God whose aseity is not static but eternally and infinitely on the move to that which is not God – an aseity which is *spoken in the economy of God's people*.

Responsive participation in glorification

What, then, is the creature's role in glorifying the perfectly glorious God who reaches the creature in God's effulgence? How are we to speak of the glory of God in the people of God, given the account of glory offered so far? First, it is necessary to affirm that the human creature's glorification and glorifying of God is a *response* to the overflowing and superabundantly glorious nature of divine grace. It may be possible further to say, second, that the people of God's giving glory to God is not a conditioning or an adding of anything to God; the people's glorifying is a responsive *participation* in God's own gloriously gracious life. The logics of grace (of the free and supreme divine self-giving) are logics of non-necessity. God has no need or necessity of the creature for God's own glory, but in God's grace the creature in glorifying God may join in God's own perfect glory. It is necessary to unpack this.

In faith in Jesus Christ, the believer not only confesses her faith in the glory of God but also that she is a sinner reconciled by God and in God. This faith in God's reconciling work is what enables the Christian to praise God as she is awakened by God to God's own glorious light – a light which in prevenient grace reaches her first.[26] In being reached by this illuminating light, the creature shares in God's glory as it reaches to her. The response to the illuminating light of God's glory is to give glory to God, and in giving glory to God we participate (as the creatures for whom God eternally determined Godself in God's infinitely glorious life) in the divine glorification: God makes this glorification of ours (this creaturely

---

25. The points made here are a reworking of *CD* II/1, 646–7, seeking to draw out more of the relation between filiation and manifestation in terms of divine glory.
26. Cf. *CD* II/1, 668.

glorification) God's own. Since God's glory is infinite, we cannot add anything to it in our giving glory. We can only participate in that perfect and infinite glory which already exists in God's own life. Glorification by the creature is a creaturely (and this side of the eschaton), therefore, imperfect giving of glory which is nevertheless being drawn up into the glorification of God by the Son: 'Changed from glory into glory', to quote Charles Wesley.[27] Because of Jesus Christ, what is done by God's people in gratitude to God's gracious glory is to share in glorifying God. Because this glorifying takes place in Jesus Christ in His body the Church, even though it is creaturely, it is still within the glory of God. Jesus is recorded as saying to the Father in John's Gospel: 'The glory you have given me, I have given them' (Jn 17.22a). The creature in Christ is taken up into the act of the Father and the Son's relationship of glorification. Pannenberg summarizes this well:

> The Son has glorified the Father (17.4) by proclaiming his lordship. He now asks the Father to glorify him by reaccepting him into his original fellowship with the Father (v. 4). In this way, and by the participation of the believers in the common glory of the Son and the Father (v. 22), the glorifying of the Father by the Son will come to fulfilment.[28]

The response of the creature receiving the revelation of the radiance of God's glory, being illuminated by God's glory and being caught up in God's glory, is for the creature itself to share in giving glory to God. This is not an addition of something to God which was lacking before, but a participating by the believer as a creature in Christ in the eternal glorification of the Father by the Son and the Son by the Father. Hardy and Ford describe this relationship to perfection helpfully as follows with regard to praise, but the same point could be made of glorifying: 'perfection would not be perfect if it had to require praise for its completion. Yet the odd fact is that in this way perfection itself can be perfected, and the more perfect it is the more wonderfully it evokes new forms of perfection. The logic is that of overflow, of freedom, of generosity.'[29] In responding to God's glory, the creature is drawn up and participates in the already perfect glorifying by the Son of the Father and the Father of the Son by virtue of the gracious and free excess and overflow of the radiance of the effulgence of God's glory.

This participative response in and to the glory of God is something even more than salvation from sin and reconciliation to God. Giving glory to God is something greater, something more abundant. As Barth puts it, the creature in knowing reconciliation should have joy and jubilation not only in the creature's reconciled nature but also in the act of glorifying God which accompanies it. He

---

27. Charles Wesley, *Love Divine* (hymn).
28. Wolfhart Pannenberg, *Systematic Theology: Volume 3* (Grand Rapids, MI: Eerdmans, 1997), 625.
29. David F. Ford and Daniel W. Hardy, *Living in Praise: Worshipping and Knowing God*, 2nd rev. edn (Grand Rapid, MI: Baker Academic, 2005), 9.

writes: 'This is the destiny which man received and lost, only to receive it again, inconceivably and infinitely increased by the personal participation of God in man's being accomplished in Jesus Christ.'[30] This capacity the people of God come to possess of being able to share in the glorifying of God is a further work and permission of God that comes following the reconciliatory work of Jesus Christ. The power to glorify God does not come from the creature (or else it would be an addition to God) but comes from the infinitely perfect glorious God. The glory of God speaks of divine superabundance, and the glorification of God may well equally take place as an overflowing in the people of God itself.[31]

At this point, the conspicuously absent member of the Trinity thus far in this essay must be discussed. Although the Spirit is absent in Jn 17, the Spirit is very present in ch. 16; and Jesus' prayer in ch. 17 is for the disciples for that time after He has gone, the time of another Counsellor. It is the Spirit of truth about whom John writes when he has Jesus state: 'He will glorify me, because he will take what is mine and declare it to you' (Jn 16.14). It is the Spirit who is the one who glorifies the Son in believers by bringing to them the memory of Jesus and His work of glorifying the Father. Pannenberg is worth quoting at length on this point:

> The glorifying of believers, however, their transforming by the light of divine glory, draws them into the eternal fellowship of the Father and the Son by the Spirit. It is the same Spirit who is already conferred on believers by their baptism and who enables them, as they participate in the filial relationship of Jesus Christ to the Father, to call on God as their Father, and in so doing to have a foretaste of their own eschatological consummation as participation in the eternal life of the trinitarian God in the fellowship of the Son and the Father by the Spirit.[32]

The work of enabling the creature to glorify God in response to God's own glory is an expression of the overflowing of the self-glorification of God to establish fellowship between God and our created being. This is not by virtue of any mediatorial *tertium quid* or common element (spirit, with a lower case 's', so-called) between humanity and God. The One who is Spirit, too, is God, and is – as the creed of Constantinople reminds us – with the Father and Son worshipped and glorified. The glorification of God in God's people through the Spirit consists in nothing short of God's coexistence with us and our coexistence with God.[33] Therefore, to engage in glorifying God is to have a foretaste of the eternal life with (our perfect coexistence with) God in which creatures will share. 2 Cor. 3.18 puts it thus: 'But we all, with unveiled face, beholding as in a mirror the glory of the Lord, are being transformed into the same image from glory to glory, just as from the Lord, the Spirit.' Glorifying God is a proleptic anticipation (for all of its fallen

30. *CD* II/1, 648.
31. Cf. *CD* II/1, 671.
32. Pannenberg, *Systematic Theology: Volume 3*, 626.
33. Cf. *CD* II/1, 673.

creaturely form) of the life with God to which creation is determined; it is through the Spirit in the life of the believer that this proleptic anticipation is offered and is possible.

The reality of this anticipation of an eschatological presence with God in participating in glorifying God should not result, however, in some cheap, one-dimensional and prosperous ecclesial headiness. The same light of God which is glorious is also the fire which consumes. Sin itself is, after all, a falling short of the glory of God (Rom. 3.23),[34] and as the people of God participate in the eternal act of glorifying God so too we participate in the divine judgement on that which is not glorious in our lives.[35] To glorify God is not simply to be caught up in the raptures of praise and song; to glorify is also to call to mind and confess our sins on bended knee as the King of glory comes.

To participate in God's glory is to become the image of God that the human was eternally destined to be:[36] remembering that the new creature is in Jesus Christ freed from sin, and lives in the freedom of the Spirit, as the creature conforms more and more to the image of Christ, so she shares more and more in the eternal glorifying of the Father and the Son in the Spirit. Just as God breathed life into the first human, so being filled (or baptized) with the Spirit of God breathes new life into the new creature: Jesus is the One most filled with the Spirit in all creation and shows the people of God what a life filled with the intensity of the Spirit looks like. Indeed, it might be best to think of Christ's receiving the Holy Spirit in His baptism as a fitting sign or perhaps the greatest expression of Christ's full humanity – the humanity we as yet do not possess but which was determined for us for all eternity – a perfect humanity perfectly drenched in the Spirit. The Spirit who is the Giver of Life gives life (breath) to humanity: it is by God's own Spirit that humans become living beings, as the book of Job attests.[37] To be a true and real living human being involves receiving the breath (or Spirit) of God. Since we have scope to receive the Spirit of God more fully, we are not yet, we might say, fully human. If we are to be images of the image of God in Jesus Christ, it is the presence of the Spirit within the creature which is required in overflowing abundance for us to be conformed to the form of Christ. Only in the form of correspondence to Jesus Christ through the work of the Holy Spirit can there be the glory of God in the glorification of God, whose glory is perfect, by the creature.[38] The glorification of God by the creature in response to God's eternal and infinite glory is the Spirit's work of de facto sanctification in the life of the believer as the believer participates

---

34. On 'falling short of glory' in Rom. 3.23 as referring specifically to alienation from God's (cultic) presence (cf. Rom. 9.4), see: W. Daniel Jackson, 'The Logic of Divine Presence in Romans 3:23', *CBQ* 80 (2018): 293–305.

35. Cf. Karl Rahner, 'Purgatory', in *Theological Investigations: Volume 19: Faith and Ministry* (London: Darton, Longman & Todd, 1984), 181–93.

36. Cf. *CD* II/1, 673.

37. See, for example, Job 34.14-16.

38. *CD* II/1, 674.

in God in Christ. 1 Thess. 2.12 has it thus: 'So that you would walk in a manner worthy of the God who calls you into His own kingdom and glory.' Glorifying God is for the people of God about living lives worthy of the glory of God, lives conformed to Christ as we (like Christ) are filled with overflowing abundance with the Spirit. Barth understands this well when he writes in his long discussion of the glory of God that glorifying can only ever mean imitating. For him, if the people of God wish to offer glory to God, they simply need to live a life of obedience in which as creatures they seek to know God, and in knowing God (through God's gracious and illuminating radiance) have no option but to offer glory to God. In this imitation of Christ, which the Spirit enables, we share in what it means to give glory to God and to share in God's glory.

Since for the people of God to engage in responsive participation in the glory of God involves being filled with the Spirit so as to imitate Christ, the glory of God in the people of God has a horizontal as well as a vertical axis.[39] Glorifying God is not simply something the believer participates in when she engages in acts of worship and adoration of the divine life and is orientated upwards, vertically to God in praise and thanksgiving. Glorifying God involves responding to the radiance of the effulgence of God's glory and participating in that. To participate in that glory means that the creature participates in the form of that glory – a form which has been described in terms of its movement, overflow, excess and freedom to be for that which is not God. A creaturely participation in divine glory is, therefore, a participation in the excessive overflow of glory, in the glory which produces an effulgence, in the effulgence which is radiant. The believer's participation in glorifying God is, therefore, not simply one which is ordered ever more to the depths and intensities of God's being, but also one in which the creature is (like the glory in which she participates) pushed outwards towards the creation, the world in and for which the light shines. The intensity which the Spirit brings in the believer who participates in the glory of God is an intensity which propels the believer to the outward reaches of the radiance of the effulgence of God's glory in the world. If the believer is not pressed outwards in this way by the glory of God, it is not the Lord's own glory which moves towards creation in the radiance of its effulgence in which she participates, but some other glory which does not have the logics of the infinitely sufficient plenitude of the Lord's own glory. To quote Barth, God 'is God who is glorious in His community, and for that reason and in that way in all the world'.[40]

What does the horizontal component of glory look like? The space allotted does not allow a thoroughgoing entry into this topic. But we might point initially to two dimensions of this glory the people of God have by virtue of their participation in

---

39. Gregory of Nyssa points to this well in his *Life of Moses* when he discusses how receiving the revelation of the glory of God (the vertical axis, in the terms of his paper) is immediately followed by Moses descending with the law (the horizontal axis, in the terms of this paper). See Gregory of Nyssa, *Life of Moses*, trans. Abraham J. Malherbe and Everett Ferguson (Mahwah: Paulist Press, 1978).

40. *CD* II/1, 677.

God's own glory, a glory which in its infinite sufficiency is infinitely radiant in its effulgence, a glory which extensively illuminates that which is not God. The first dimension is that of witness. The people of God join in Christ's work of witnessing to the glory of God, of bringing light in the darkness, of pointing to the light, of (as we participate in it) shining with the radiance of the effulgence of the glory of God. This is a witness across space and time in the world in the time between the ascension of Jesus and the *eschaton*. The second dimension is that of existence towards one another. Since we have said that the otherness of God's glory is not an otherness from creation but an otherness for creation, for the creature in her creaturely integrity to participate in the otherness of God's glory in response to being reached by God's glory determines that in her participation there will always be an otherness *for* creation. Worship so deeply and individualistically orientated on God's glory is no glorification of God: such worship does not participate in *God's* glory. We know God's glory as by it we are moved to be orientated beyond ourselves towards others, in the corporate life of the church, and perhaps most pertinently towards those others in situations where there is darkness. A triumphalist glorifying of God will not be a genuine response to, participation in or engagement with the God, the knowledge of whose glory is known in the face of Christ – the crucified, the man for others, the one who is the great intercessor, the one who laid down His life not just for His friends but also His enemies. There is not, despite the protestations no doubt of some Lutheran friends, in the end a choice between a theology of glory and a theology of the cross: the glory of God known in the face of Christ is a glory which is cruciform (as a shorthand for the whole Self-giving of God in the life, death and resurrection of Christ), and to participate in the reality of that glory is (in both witness and living – or even dying – for the other) to be given the power by the Spirit of God in the hope of the resurrection to take up our crosses and follow Christ.[41] In Calvin's Commentary on the book of Ephesians, he writes: 'We will receive God's glory in its highest when we are no longer anything other than the vessels of his mercy.'[42] To be a vessel of God's mercy (to move with God's movement) is, I think, what it means for the people of God to join with the writer of the Ephesians in praying: 'to Him [God] be the glory in the church and in Christ Jesus to all generations forever and ever. Amen' (Eph. 3.21).[43]

---

41. Cf. Rom. 8.17: 'Those who suffer with Christ will be glorified with Him.' For an unpacking of the call to cruciform living, see John Howard Yoder, *The Politics of Jesus* (Grand Rapids, MI: Eerdmans, 1996).

42. Calvin, On Eph. 1.11 (identify translation, etc.); CO 51.152.

43. Another parallel approach to these themes can be found in Grant Macaskill, 'Apocalypse and the Gospel of Mark', in *The Jewish Apocalyptic Tradition and the Shaping of New Testament Thought*, ed. Benjamin E. Reynolds and Loren T. Stuckenbruck (Minneapolis, MN: Fortress, 2017), 53–77, esp. 67–71. Macaskill argues that the glory of Jesus in the transfiguration should not be understood as angelic glory or even the glory of human transformation sometimes associated with heavenly ascent but rather with the glory of God himself. He argues this on the basis of literary cues in Mark and imagistic correspondences with theophanies in Jewish apocalyptic literature.

Chapter 4

A STRANGELY WARMED HEART IN A STRANGE AND COMPLEX WORLD: ON ASSURANCE AND GENEROUS WORLDLINESS

There is a strange and perhaps unexpected by-product of living in an age of what appears to be the rapid de-Christianization of Western Europe, with projections about the disappearance of denominations and the terminal decline of the church.[1] The unexpected by-product is: locating the church with assurance has become an increasingly easy task. We are no longer as concerned about those who attend out of societal and cultural expectation, and congregations largely consist of those who wish to identify with the active community of faith. The increasingly counter-cultural nature of the decision to attend church both demarcates the church and its members, and makes the church community a visible, identifiable and distinguishable community in contradistinction to the world. In the context of secularization and pluralism, the very continued existence of the church has meant that the church has come (over and against prevailing cultures which 'believe' but do not 'belong' to an institutional form of Christianity)[2] in almost all forms to understand itself with some sense of the ecclesiology of the radical reformation:[3] there is a clear distinction to the rest of society. For those from more evangelical traditions, this identifiable confidence has expressed itself in terms of individualized personal salvation: in contrast to the rest of society, 'I' am saved. For those from more catholic traditions, this identifiable self-confidence has expressed itself communally in the locatedness of the visible church: the church's sacred

---

1. For example, the Right Reverend Paul Richardson in his article, 'Britain is no longer a Christian nation', *Sunday Telegraph*, 27 June 2009, suggests the Church of England could disappear within a generation, given that the falling numbers in Sunday morning congregations is accelerating at around 1 per cent per annum, and on this basis it is difficult to see the church surviving for more than thirty years. For more on church attendance figures and the situation in Europe, see Gracie Davie, *Europe: The Exceptional Case: Parameters of Faith and the Modern World* (London: Darton, Longman & Todd, 2002), 6–7; and her *Religion in Britain since 1945: Believing without Belonging* (London: Blackwell, 1994), 46–9.

2. See Davie, *Religion in Britain since 1945*, ch. 6.

3. Cf. David Fergusson, *State, Church and Civil Society* (Cambridge: Cambridge University Press, 2004), 44.

space is clearly distinguishable (in its traditions, forms and practices) from secular space. In both cases, unhelpful (ungenerous) forms of ecclesial self-understanding and practice arise.

In this chapter, I wish – from a Methodist perspective – to reflect on the theological understanding of assurance that underlies such self-certainty, either in terms of a collection of individually assured believers or of the church's form and practice. I will then reflect on the doctrine of assurance in relation to the expression of it by John Wesley during the evangelical revival of the eighteenth century, using this as a mode of repair to unhelpful contemporary understandings of assurance that underlie the current ecclesial setting. I will then apply this repaired understanding of assurance to ecclesiology to demonstrate how a properly understood doctrine of assurance has the potential to provide a basis for a more generous understanding in which there nevertheless remains a clear distinction between the church and the rest of society.

Unhelpful binaries and confident self-assurance

The contemporary situation of declining church attendance has rightly drawn attention from all kinds of ecclesial traditions. At times, decline has brought about (in the words of Michael Jinkins) 'the hyperactivity of panic. This manifests itself in clutching for any and every programmatic solution and structural reorganization in the desperate hope that survival is just another project or organizational chart away.'[4] Usually, survival concerns getting those 'outside' into the 'inside'; those who do not attend church to attend church; those who are not 'saved' to be saved; those who do not receive sacraments to receive sacraments; and so on. In other words, in response to the contemporary setting, the church has presumed that it operates with clear identifiable binaries, and that the activity of the church is to move people from one side of a binary, across a relatively clearly defined boundary, to the other side of the binary. In forms of piety that are associated with evangelical Protestantism, this binary is usually expressed as some form of the saved–damned distinction (believer or non-believer; Christian or non-Christian).[5] But even if expressed differently, such a distinction is found in other forms of piety and ecclesial settings: secular–sacred, church–world and so on. What underlies such binaries is an assurance about who counts as 'us' and who counts as 'them', whether expressed in terms of personal salvation or ecclesial identity. Although there might be considerations around where the boundary lies, there is nevertheless clarity that such a boundary exists and is relatively easy to

---

4. Michael Jinkins, *The Church Faces Death: Ecclesiology in a Post-Modern Context* (Oxford: Oxford University Press, 1999), 9.

5. For more on binaries in relation to salvation, see Tom Greggs, *Barth, Origen, and Universal Salvation: Restoring Particularity* (Oxford: Oxford University Press, 2009), especially preface and ch. 7. On binaries more generally, see Peter Ochs, *Pierce, Pragmatism and the Logic of Scripture* (Cambridge: Cambridge University Press, 1998), ch. 8.

spot: a little like an elephant, it may be difficult to describe, but you know where it is. Furthermore, and perhaps unexpectedly, even in modes of church expression that are oriented on being 'culturally relevant', such a binary underscores missional practice and ecclesial identity. So, for example, *Mission-Shaped Church* speaks of the transformed approach to mission in the following ways:

> Church plants and fresh expressions of church represent the emergence of a diametrically different approach that is both theologically appropriate and strategically significant. Instead of 'come to *us*', this new approach is 'go to *them*'. We need to find expressions of church that communicate with *post-Christian people*, and which enable them to become committed followers of Jesus Christ. Then *they*, in turn, can continue to engage in mission with and beyond *their own culture*.[6]

This issue at stake is more profound for a generous ecclesiology than simply whether the church is (or is best) expressed as a parish or gathered community or some other mode of community: the point is not geographical.[7] The issue at stake concerns more what the church is, and how that nature determines the way the church understands its relation to the *rest of* the world as part of the world itself.[8] Or, put otherwise: what is the church assured of, and how does this determine its self-understanding and actions?

Current discussions of ecclesiology that focus so much on form, and that do so to be clear about (or to justify) where we might have assurance that the church is, are in large part preoccupied with the self: either the self of an individual believer or of the communal ego of the particular form of the church (parish versus network and so on). This issue of ecclesial/believers' self-understanding in relation to a society that identifies itself in large part as non-Christian (or at least non-practising) is obviously in certain ways a particularly modern problem: when societies were religiously homogeneous, such issues were not as pronounced; previously the issue might have been *degree* of fervour, or *regularity* of participation, but not whether or not one belonged to the church. Given that there are those in society who do not identify as believers or communicant church members, it is hardly surprising that the church thinks of itself in distinction to those others. But care must be taken that those thought processes about the relation of the church to *the rest of society* (of which the church is also a part) use appropriate theological categories. Care must be taken that the assurance that underlies the discussions of church identity is an assurance that comes from the activity of God, and not an ill-found self-confidence. John Wesley's pronouncement (in characteristic

---

6. Graham Cray, ed., *Mission-Shaped Church: Church Planting and Fresh Expressions of Church in Changing Contexts* (London: Church House, 2004), 12, emphasis added.

7. Cf. the concerns in *Mission-Shaped Church*, 7, over networks or parishes.

8. Note here that I do not speak in terms of church-world, but in terms of church (as part of the world)-rest of the world.

eighteenth-century tones) sounds a warning that the contemporary church would do well to heed: 'How many have mistaken the voice of their own imagination for this "witness of the Spirit" of God, and thence idly presumed they were the children of God while they were doing the work of the devil!'[9] Even if we might not wish to use the same language to express the point, the issue of self-deception and the importance of self-critical examination have much to say to a contemporary church that argues over its form but is confident of its nature.

One way to overcome this problem would be (and perhaps has been) to lose all confidence in the church altogether: to see the broken and created church with all its propensity to sin and self-deception as entirely unredeemable; to see the feeling and assurance of salvation for the children of God as located in the human psyche; to see God as so objective and distant that the experience of salvation could have no appropriately theological grounds. Thus, perhaps, lies the road to the sort of deism that most people in Western Europe effectively practice.[10] But a community without any confidence could not be described in terms of a generous ecclesiology: it would have nothing to be generous with. Experience of God and assurance has always been part of faith: we need only to pray the Psalms to discover that; scripture is full of descriptions of what it means to be the children of God.[11] The problem is not *whether* God allows Godself to be experienced in the life of the believer and the life of the church. The problem is *how* we think about that experience and assurance. Wesley makes the point that a madman's imagining himself to be the king does not mean that there are no kings.[12] Unhelpful ways of thinking about the assurance of being God's children do not mean that assurance is not offered to believers and the church. The issue is what sort of assurance God offers to God's people, and how are we to understand that assurance. It is to this issue that this chapter now turns in examining John Wesley's account of assurance.

Re-examining assurance

In the theology of John Wesley we find an account of assurance that helpfully cuts through many of the problematic features identified thus far with particular forms of assurance associated with contemporary expressions of pietism and evangelicalism in relation to the individual, and – perhaps indeed – contemporary forms of ecclesial assurance in more catholic traditions in relation to the whole church. In Wesley's three sermons on assurance (Sermons 10–12), he recognizes problematic features of Christian assurance and offers an account of assurance that

---

9. John Wesley, *The Works of John Wesley: Volume 1: Sermons 1 (1–33)*, ed. Albert C. Outler (Nashville, TN: Abingdon, 1984) (henceforth in this essay *Sermons I*), 267.
10. Cf. Davie, *Religion in Britain since 1945*, ch. 5, where Davie discusses people's belief in the 'ordinary god'.
11. *Sermons I*, 271.
12. *Sermons I*, 293.

is potentially fruitful for a generous ecclesiology. Three of Wesley's central points will be examined to identify a pneumatological, humble, world-oriented account of assurance that could have positive effects on ecclesial self-understanding in relation to the world.

Assurance is not self-assurance: The activity of the Spirit and the message of scripture

For Wesley, it is very clear that the source of assurance is located in the activity of God the Holy Spirit and that this is known through the testimony of holy scripture.[13] Unlike accounts which locate assurance in humanity and in feelings,[14] Wesley sees (in terms of the order of being) assurance to be located in the Spirit of God, who is at work in believers. The account of human assurance is an account of the economy of God who works from outwith the believer within the believer: 'Since therefore the testimony of his [God's] Spirit must precede the love of God and all holiness, of consequence it must precede our consciousness thereof.'[15] This consciousness must be 'distinguished from the presumption of a natural mind'.[16] The joy of the assured Christian is not based upon any anthropological condition or cause: 'This is not a *natural* joy.'[17] Furthermore, in terms of the order of knowing in relation to this assurance, Wesley is clear that the reality that a believer can feel the assurance of the Spirit is derived from the teaching of scripture: the activity of the life of the Spirit in the believer is paid testimony to in scripture, and thus the believer might be assured because she is taught in scripture that the Spirit assures the believer. For Wesley, the experience of assurance is a reality not primarily because of the experience (which could be one of self-deception) but because the Bible teaches that the Spirit works within hearts of the children of God.[18] The text for Sermons 10 and 11 is Rom. 8.16: 'The Spirit itself beareth witness with our spirit that we are the children of God' (KJV). Since scripture teaches this, Wesley asserts that it must be a reality for the believer today; and it is only in applying to oneself the marks of the children of God as described in the Bible that one might know if one is a child of God. Thus, writes Wesley, in scripture: 'He that now loves God – that delights and rejoices in him with a humble joy, an holy delight, and an obedient love – is called a child of God; But I thus love, delight, and rejoice in God; Therefore I am a child of God; then a Christian can in no wise doubt of his being a child of God.'[19]

---

13. In identifying the economy of the Spirit as the locus for assurance, Wesley makes use of the doctrine of appropriations.

14. Cf. Friedrich Schleiermacher, *The Christian Faith* (Edinburgh: T&T Clark, 1968), 12. Schleiermacher is concerned here with the feeling of 'absolute dependence', which he identifies as a feeling of being in relation to God.

15. *Sermons I*, 290.
16. *Sermons I*, 277.
17. *Sermons I*, 310.
18. *Sermons I*, 271.
19. *Sermons I*, 276.

Both in terms of the order of being and in terms of the order of knowing, individual feeling and interiority comprise the *final* stage of assurance, and not the foundation of assurance: the activity of God and knowledge of God's economy in scripture are foundational.[20] Indeed, Wesley identifies a stage *before* the inward assurance of being a child of God that is discernible in his above deduction – the active life of a child of God. For Wesley, exteriority is the first product of the life in which the Spirit acts, and which the Bible teaches is the life of a child of God: 'We must be holy of heart and holy in life *before* we can be conscious that we are so, before we can have "the testimony of our spirit" that we are inwardly and outwardly holy.'[21] The faithful are assured of being children of God only after they are holy of heart and in life. In Wesley, therefore, consciousness of being a child of God (assurance) follows from the activity of the Spirit in human lives; from the knowledge that God does this work, as it is taught in scripture; and from the reality of lives that are being transformed into holiness. It is only after the latter that one might become assured.

At this point, the question arises as to what it is that Christians can be assured of, and how is it that they know that their assurance is the activity of the Spirit and not anthropological self-assurance, which is a deception. Here, Wesley offers an account based on repentance and on the outwards orientation of the believer and the fruits of the Spirit. It is to these that this chapter now turns.

The assurance of radical de-assurance: Assured of the need to repent

For Wesley, the first identifying feature of assurance is in one sense the radical de-assurance that is found in the need for repentance. Assurance is not about a self-confident approach to God and the gifts of God, nor is it a single momentary confirmation of one's salvation to carry one through life. Instead, the first mark of assurance is the conviction of sin in the believer.[22] In comparison to the 'presumptuous self-deceiver', the assured believer is described by Wesley in the following terms:

---

20. This is a point on which Wesley does not move (*Sermons I*, 287), despite the fact that he does shift from initially believing that assurance was necessary for salvation to believing, in his more mature thought, that it was not (cf. Colin W. Williams, *John Wesley's Theology Today* [London: Epworth Press, 1962], 112).

21. *Sermons I*, 274, emphasis added. This seems to differ from the order offered by Schleiermacher: feeling, for him, is distinguished from (and more primary than) doing. See Schleiermacher, *The Christian Faith*, 5–12.

22. This is a point that is paralleled in the work of the nineteenth-century German pietist Blumhardt. See Simeon Zahl, 'The Spirit and the Cross: Engaging a Key Critique of Charismatic Pneumatology', in *The Holy Spirit and the World Today*, ed. Jane Williams (London: Alpha, 2011), 111–29.

The Scriptures describe that joy in the Lord which accompanies the witness of his Spirit as an humble joy, a joy that abases to the dust; that makes a pardoned sinner cry out, 'I am vile! ...' And wherever lowliness is, there is patience, gentleness, long-suffering. There is a soft, yielding spirit, a mildness and sweetness, a tenderness of soul which words cannot express. But do these fruits attend that *supposed* testimony of the Spirit in a presumptuous man? Just the reverse.[23]

The one who does not – in being conscious of God's presence in her spirit – repent, but becomes confident of her assurance, grows haughty in her behaviour. To her, Wesley proclaims: 'Discover thyself, thou poor self-deceiver! Thou who art confident of being a child of God ... O cry unto him, that the scales may fall from thine eyes.'[24] For Wesley, assurance comes not after the act of repentance, but in the very act of repentance: only in hearing the sentence of death do Christians hear the voice of the one who says 'Your sins are forgiven'.[25] Furthermore, for Wesley, this is far from a single moment or event: it is rather a continuous state of being. As Karl Barth points out, when we have to do with the Spirit, we have to do with the eschatological presence of God in the present: in St Paul's language, the Spirit is a 'guarantee' or 'deposit' (*arrabōn*) of a future reality.[26] This reminds us that, in Barth's words, in the present, we 'believe in an eternal life even in the midst of the valley of death. In this way, in this futurity, we have it. The assurance with which we know this having is the assurance of faith, and the assurance of faith means concretely the assurance of hope.'[27] According to Wesley, therefore, we are wise

---

23. *Sermons I*, 280. Cf. Luther:

> God receives none but those who are forsaken, restores health to none but those who are sick, gives sight to none but the blind, and life to one but the dead. He does not give saintliness to any but sinners, nor wisdom to any but fools. In short: He has mercy on none but the wretched and gives grace to none but those who are in disgrace. Therefore no arrogant saint, or just or wise man can be material for God, neither can he do the work of God, but he remains confined within his own work and makes of himself a fictitious, ostensible, false, and deceitful saint, that is, a hypocrite.(Jaroslav Pelikan and Daniel E. Poellot, eds, *Luther's Works*, vol. 14 (St. Louis: Concordia Publishing House, 1958), 163)

24. *Sermons I*, 281.
25. Williams, *John Wesley's Theology Today*, 106.
26. For the classic treatment of Pauline pneumatology, discussing 2 Cor. 5.5 and eschatology, see Gordon Fee, *God's Empowering Presence: The Holy Spirit in the Letters of Paul* (Peabody, MA: Hendrickson, 1994), 324–7.

For a more recent account, discussing the Old Testament background of 'deposit', see John R. Levison, *Filled with the Spirit* (Cambridge: Eerdmans, 2009), 253–63.

27. *CD* I/1, 463.

to continually cry to God.[28] Assurance is a state of continual crying out to God in repentance, as opposed to a state of confidence in one's status based on some singular event.

Outwards orientation: Assurance from loving the world and fruits of the Spirit

In contrast to understandings of assurance focused upon the interiority of a believer, who is able to concentrate on her own personal salvation rather than be concerned with the communities and lives of those around her, Wesley's account of assurance is focused radically away from the self and towards others. For Wesley, beyond repentance, one's assurance comes from being 'saved from the pain of proud wrath'. In concrete terms, this is an orientation away from self and towards neighbour.[29] Indeed, this echoes Luther's assertion that those who lack assurance are in fact self-centred;[30] and Wesley states overtly that 'you must be directly assured if you love your neighbour as yourself; if you are kindly affectioned to all mankind, and full of gentleness and long-suffering'.[31] The activity of loving one's neighbour and *all* humankind is a basis by which one might know that one is assured: it is not an outworking of assurance but a basis for assurance. Wesley presses this point. To know assurance we must be 'embracing every child of man with earnest, tender affection, so as to be ready to lay down our life for our brother, as Christ laid down his life for us'.[32] It is this activity (along with the activity of loving God) which gives believers 'a consciousness that we are inwardly conformed by the Spirit of God to the image of his Son'.[33] This pattern of thought structurally seems to follow 1 Jn 4: because God has loved us we are able to love him; and because of God's love towards us, we ought to love one another. Wesley, however, recognizing the distinction between the order of knowing and the order of being, reverses the order in relation to assurance, beginning with the concrete existence of the believer: she may know that she is assured if she loves her neighbour because only God's love is capable of allowing her to do so; if she loves her neighbour, she can know that she is loved of God since God loved humanity before humanity loved God or neighbour.

Wesley makes a similarly structured argument in relation to the fruits of the Spirit. Again, the way in which the believer is able to know the assurance of salvation is through fruits of the Spirit displayed in her life. Only the Spirit can

---

28. Cf. *Sermons I*, 298. Wesley makes the point here in relation to prevenient grace, but the point regarding continuation remains: indeed, the context of these remarks is within times of strong temptation when the fruits of the Spirit are 'clouded' (*Sermons I*, 297).

29. *Sermons I*, 273.

30. Cf. Cf. Gerhard Ebling, *Luther: An Introduction to His Thought* (London: Collins, 1970), 37–8.

31. *Sermons I*, 273.

32. *Sermons I*, 274.

33. *Sermons I*, 274.

produce such fruit, and so – if a believer produces fruit – that fruit is testimony to the activity of the Spirit in the life of the believer. Thus Wesley writes: 'By the fruits which he hath wrought in your spirit you shall know the "testimony of the Spirit of God". Hereby you shall know that you are in no delusion; that you have not deceived your own soul.'[34] This too is outwards oriented, rather than concerned with the interior life of the believer. Were it not enough that the gifts are displayed and known in relation to others, Wesley makes the point emphatically that he is talking not only about transformed pneumatological personality traits but 'outward fruits' – 'the doing good to all men, the doing no evil to any'.[35] This is far from a self-occupied concern with personal salvation: personal salvation is known through a reorientation of one's life away from self-occupied concerns about one's salvation and towards the other.

In one sense, we might think that this concern with fruits ostensibly stands in tension with the teaching about repentance as a sign of assurance, but is that so? There is a sense in which continued calling upon God in confession is precisely a downplaying of the ego that this type of reorientation also describes. In confession, one reorientates oneself towards God's self and away from one's own self; in orientation towards the other and in fruits of the Spirit, one moves from preoccupation with one's sake to preoccupation with the other's sake.

Ecclesial implications

It may seem strange to deal with what seems on first glance to be a doctrinal locus that operates primarily in relation to the life of the individual believer (in her assurance of salvation) within a discussion of ecclesiology. However, not only is it the case that (as I have argued) unhelpful forms of assurance underlay forms of ecclesial operation, but it is also the case that an important feature of assurance for Wesley is the ecclesial context in which assurance is located. For him, assurance is not simply an issue for individual believers. He writes:

> And here properly comes in, to confirm this scriptural doctrine [assurance of salvation], the experience of the children of God – the experience not of two or three, not of a few, but of a great multitude which no man can number. It has been confirmed, both in this and in all ages, by 'a cloud of' living and dying 'witnesses'.[36]

34. *Sermons I*, 283.
35. *Sermons I*, 283. We should note that, since these are activities of the Spirit in the life of the believer, there is nothing of a works-based righteousness here: the activity of the Spirit in the life of the believer in the order of being precedes the fruits; but in the order of knowing, the fruits are the means by which one might know that one is a child of God. Cf. *Sermons I*, 296, and Ralph Del Colle, 'John Wesley's Doctrine of Grace in Light of the Christian Tradition', *International Journal of Systematic Theology* 4 (2002): 176.
36. *Sermons I*, 290.

The experience of assurance, on which the doctrinal considerations reflect, is one that concerns the whole body of believers – the larger category of the *communio sanctorum*. It is a common and genuinely ecclesial experience that confirms the experience of the individual. But given that the experience of assurance is an internal concern for members of the church, what has it to do with the 'generosity' with which the current chapter is concerned? Here, three points can be identified (corresponding to each of the three features of assurance identified in the section above) regarding assurance in relation to ecclesiological concerns. The sort of understanding of assurance proposed in the above section may offer ways to think creatively and generously about the nature of the church and its engagement with the world.

Pneumatological priority

The recognition of pneumatological priority over personal assurance is deeply significant. There are important implications to locating both the life of faith and the church under the third article of the creed and the activity of the Holy Spirit. Centrally, such a prioritization of the doctrine of the Spirit over that of the life of faith determines that it is necessary to reflect on the true condition of the life of faith and of the church. This true condition is primarily the presence of the Holy Spirit, and not any external set of conditions. The presence of the Spirit is the only true assurance of the present reality of the church, and not the particular form that the church takes: there can be no ecclesio-Pelagianism.

This prioritization of the Spirit over the church is borne out by the testimony of scripture. In Acts 1.12 we get what seems to be the beginnings of the church. In the Methodist Church, every year the superintendent minister in each circuit reads out the list of preachers; there is something similar with the list of the disciples in v. 13. We then get a description of worship (v. 14). We have a count of membership in v. 15 (a pastoral roll almost). After that, there is even a parish or church council meeting, with an election of officers (vv. 23-6) and Matthias being elected to a new position. The description of what is going on in Acts 1 looks as though it is a description of the church. But it is not: what is described is something that only has the semblance of a church. The church begins in Acts 2, with the coming of the Spirit. The essence of the church is not in the first instance connected to form. The essence of the church is ultimately the act of the presence of the Holy Spirit who is present within the variety and plurality of the community in time in all its contingency and diversity.

That the Spirit is the essence of, condition for and basis of the church should help us to avoid confusing self-assurance with God's assurance; and the reality that the Spirit blows wherever he wills should open us up to be surprised about the forms that the community of the people of God will take. Recognizing the priority of the Spirit may also break down the binary views of salvation and the church that many hold. The Spirit cuts through such binaries – establishing the church *within* the world and time and history; working in unexpected and surprising places; forming a visible witness of faith through his invisible presence. Furthermore, the reality that the ultimate condition of the church is the presence of the Spirit should lead us all to a self-reflective and self-critical engagement with our own senses of self-assurance, and a greater generosity towards other forms of ecclesial practice. After all, Wesley is clear (as we all must be if we live with open eyes in the world) that the fruits of the Spirit are not confined to those who identify themselves, as the church in various forms does, as *the* 'assured'.[37]

This point about the critical implications that the importance of pneumatological priority brings does not simply apply to those who affirm traditional patterns of church only: the issue is, rather, that form is only secondary to nature in relation to the church, and therefore all prioritizations of form over reflections on nature should be self-critical. Indeed, there is as much (if not more) assurance about who the 'we' are in less traditional forms of church as there is in traditional forms. And the recent movement towards speaking of the church in terms of 'incarnational' language concretizes the idea of the church in unhealthy ways:[38] such language is not only theologically unhelpful (the incarnation is a single and particular event of God at a particular historical moment in Jesus Christ) but also pushes us towards speaking about the substantialization of the church in people rather than the actualization of the church by the presence of the Spirit. Through the doctrine of appropriations, it is proper to speak of the activity of God in relation to the church as being most appropriately spoken about in relation to the third member of the Trinity. The effect of this is that we should be aware of the dynamic and fluid nature of the church, whose substance exists only because it is founded as an act of the *eternal* Holy Spirit: that is, the Spirit's eternity and holiness assures the temporal continuity of the church over time, not the particular created human forms of the church. God does not 'incarnate' himself in the church; God has already incarnated himself once and for all in the person of Jesus Christ. Instead, God's Spirit founds the church as a community of his presence, enabling the church in time to participate in the body of Jesus Christ, to encounter the living and speaking Word, and to be transformed into a community of holiness. This is an activity of God, and not of human form and practice: the Spirit is the sine qua non of the church; the church is not the sine qua non of the Spirit. The children of God need to realize that their assurance both individually and corporately rests on the activity of God, and they should not aggregate to themselves any sense that their own created forms condition the presence of God into resting upon them. This should give the church a greater generosity in relation to the rest of the world, and it should also make us realize that it is not so easy to identify in a binary way where the church is: even if we use the idea of logical inference back to the presence of the Spirit that Wesley suggests (see above), as we look around to the rest of the world we will find our categories disrupted as we make inferences about the presence of the Spirit of God in unexpected places.

---

37. Cf. *Sermons I*, 298 and 310.
38. Cf. *Mission-Shaped Church*, vii and 8.

Humility alongside the world

This breaking down of binarized understandings of the church in relation to the world through realizing that the church exists only as an activity of the Spirit of God is also underscored when we consider the first outwards identifier of the children of God – repentance. The church's assurance is not one that exists to raise it over and above the rest of the world; to give it a sense of superiority in relation to the rest of the world; or to enable it to be against the rest of the world. The assurance of the children of God is an assurance that conjoins the church to the rest of the world: it is an assurance that is expressed in confession of sin, in repentance and in recognition of its continued worldliness. Assurance, resting in the activity of the Spirit and leading to a life of repentance, should create an ethic of humility in the church, as it realizes that it stands alongside the world, as it confesses its own sinfulness. In this way, the church is conjoined to the rest of the world, and believers are conjoined to unbelievers: all creation stands in need of salvation, and the church are those who recognize this as chief among the sinners – those who have the Word of God, and still fail to keep it.

Furthermore, the centrality of repentance to the identity of the assured avoids the tendency to identify a binary demarcated space between the church and the world, as the promises offered to the church are promises about the *future*: assurance is something which is felt as *promise*, and thereby is not an assurance of something fully realized in the present. Assurance is in anticipation: it is the assurance of 'things hoped for'. In that way, assurance is only a present experience of the proleptic anticipation of the ultimate.[39] This status does not deny the church any importance: the penultimate is not only important in terms of its waiting for the ultimate but is also important in and of itself. Bonhoeffer writes: 'the penultimate also has its seriousness, which consists, to be sure, precisely in never confusing the penultimate with the ultimate and never making light of the penultimate over and against the ultimate'.[40] Because of the ultimacy of Christ, attending to the penultimate is central. Assurance is important as it points ultimately to the work of Christ in reconciling and redeeming the whole of creation; but assurance itself should not be confused with this ultimate work of Christ. In that way, assurance should lead to a humble identification with the rest of the world, as part of all those in need of salvation. Indeed, for all the importance Wesley attached to assurance, later in his life he became convinced that assurance was not necessary for salvation.[41] For the church, such an understanding of assurance should lead us to an identification with the rest of the world, and the communities around us, rather than a separation from them: even for the church, assurance is eschatological; it is

---

39. Cf. Dietrich Bonhoeffer, *Ethics*, ed. Clifford Green, trans. Reinhard Krauss, Douglas W. Stott and Charles C. West, Dietrich Bonhoeffer Works 6 (Minneapolis, MN: Fortress Press, 2005), 168.
40. Bonhoeffer, *Ethics*, 168.
41. *Sermons I*, 200–1; cf. Williams, *John Wesley's Theology Today*, 112.

for things *hoped for*. The church should dare to hope for all creation, recognizing in humility its own failings.[42]

Outwards orientation: Greatest intensity at fringes

If the gift of assurance is not to separate the church from the world as those who are saved in contradistinction to those who are damned, what purpose does assurance fulfil for the church? The purpose of assurance is to free the children of God from preoccupation with personal salvation and the question of one's own standing before God, and to orientate the church on those other children of God in the world who do not yet know the status they enjoy before the king of all creation. Assurance is not for the sake of the church: it is for the sake of the rest of the world, as the church is freed to be church *for* the world. Here, we are able to see the true direction of God's instrumentalization of creation. It is not that the rest of the world is an instrument by which the church might know that it is saved; rather it is that the church is an instrument by which the rest of the world might know its standing and status as the creation of God. The church exists for the rest of the world; the rest of the world does not exist for the church.

The implications of this ordering of instrumentalization determine that the greatest intensity of assurance that the church has is found not at the visibly clear centre of the church (in its services, institutions, offices, etc.) but at the fringe and circumference of the church, as it meets the rest of the world. Because the church only exists for the rest of the world, it is in those places where the church is most actively engaged with the rest of the world that the church is most intensively the church, that the church is most assured that it is the people of God. Wesley's insistence that assurance enables the Christian to love *all* creation and *every* person suggests that it is in loving the very breadth of the *every* and *all* that the true assurance of the church can be found.[43]

Contrary to models of the church that rest on forms of assurance that are binary, interior and supposedly clear-cut, a church that seeks to understand its assurance as the children of God in line with Wesley's teaching should be one that is concerned with the sorts of false assurance that the goats in the gospel narrative have:[44] those so ordered on themselves that they do not recognize Christ as present in the rest of the world; those whose binary divides place them in a precarious position before the judgement of God.[45] In the end, the assured are those who are so consumed with loving the rest of the world that they are able to be unconcerned

---

42. Cf. Tom Greggs 'Pessimistic Universalism: Rethinking the Wider Hope with Bonhoeffer and Barth', *Modern Theology* 26 (2010): 495–510.

43. Cf. *Sermons I*, 274.

44. Cf. *Sermons I*, 281–2.

45. For more on this, see Tom Greggs, 'Beyond the Binary: Forming Evangelical Eschatology', in *New Perspectives for Evangelical Theology: Engaging with God, Scripture and the World*, ed. Tom Greggs (Abingdon: Routledge, 2010), 153–67.

for their own salvation, and are instead oriented on serving the world and seeing it as the world created, sustained and being brought to redemption by God. The church needs to become the community of the sheep in Mt. 25, who think that they are goats because they have so loved the world around them that they have not realized it was God they were serving all along, and yet who, in loving creation so much, have treated those others as they would have done had Christ been in their midst. Such a church can be assured of the salvation offered to the children of God; such a church rests on a form of assurance founded by the Spirit's work, who opens the church up to the present activity of God in the world.

Chapter 5

CHURCH AND SACRAMENTS

The church is a sanctified community that bears witness to the salvation of God. This means that it is not only a society made up of individuals who are sanctified by the activity of God in their lives (as is articulated in John Wesley's theology),[1] but the church is also *in itself a community* which God creates and sanctifies in the person of the Holy Spirit. In this chapter, we seek to give an account of that community.

In some ways there are no theological themes which exist outside of speech about the church. We should note, for example, that Karl Barth's *magnum opus* was a *Church Dogmatics* which sought to engage in the scientific self-examination of the *church's* proclamation.[2] But there is also a profound sense that any speech about God is meaningful only within the context of the worship of God by the community of faith: the meaning we attach to the word 'God' is determined by the way it is used by the community. Bonhoeffer in his earliest work is wise to remind us, therefore, that *'the concepts of person, community, and God* are inseparably and essentially interrelated'.[3] Thus, it is important that we understand the nature of the community (or church) appropriately not simply for the sake of this single doctrinal *locus* but also for theology more broadly. It is important to understand the condition that God creates in which proclamation of the Christian Gospel takes place (i.e. the church) so as to understand the very conditions in which we undertake the theological task, as a task orientated on reflection on the proclamation of the church. Put simply: there is no Christian theology which does not begin with the church in terms of the order of knowing.

In seeking to describe the church, two principal options are open to us: the theological and the social-scientific. This could be stated otherwise as the view from above and the view from below, respectively. Should an account of the church begin by seeking to understand the operation of God in forming a community

---

1. See, for example, John Wesley, *The Works of John Wesley: Volume 3: Sermons III (71–114)*, ed. Albert C. Outler (Nashville, TN: Abingdon Press, 1986), 46–57.

2. *CD* I/1, 3.

3. Dietrich Bonhoeffer, *Sanctorum Communio: A Theological Study of the Sociology of the Church*, ed. Clifford J. Green, trans. Reinhard Krauss, Nancy Lukens and Dietrich Bonhoeffer Works 1 (Minneapolis, MN: Fortress 1998), 34 (italics original).

in time to bear witness to the world? Or should an account of the church begin by describing the phenomenon of the church through empirical study and description? In this chapter, we shall seek to take the first option so as to answer the former question. We will thus ask: what theological account can we give of the church in relation to the sanctified life? However, in so doing, we seek to give a theological account of the very existence of the empirical church in phenomenal space and time: what is the operation of God that creates this community in the world in history?

There have been many different attempts at answering these questions, and different typologies and catalogues of typologies exist in relation to the responses: models of the church which are ontological (as is often the case in Roman Catholic theologies); mystical (in the Orthodox tradition); actualist (in the Reformed tradition); historical (in Anglican accounts); and so on.[4] The account given in this chapter, in relation to the overarching theme of the sanctified life, might be considered to be 'actualist pneumatological' in its attempt to consider the nature of the church and its sacraments in relation to the sanctifying activity of the Holy Spirit. The church has in its creeds traditionally taught that the church which says 'We believe' does so only as it exists by the activity of the Spirit. It is under its third article (on the Holy Spirit) that the following is listed in the Nicene-Constantinopolitan creed: '[we believe] in one holy catholic and apostolic church; in one baptism for the forgiveness of sins.' As with its other articles, in its third article the creed offers a dense coda on the teaching of scripture. Scripture is clear that the Spirit is given to the community for its upbuilding and growth (1 Cor. 12) and for the production of fruitful and holy lives (Gal. 5.22-23). Scripture is also clear that it is only by the Spirit that we can say 'Jesus is Lord' (1 Cor. 12.3), and that the Spirit of God bears witness to our spirit that we are children of God (Rom. 8.16). The activity of the Spirit, therefore, is the basis by which the church is created, built up, able to teach and worship and able to know the assurance of salvation.

In reflecting further on what an actualist pneumatological account of the church and sacraments might be in relation to the sanctified life, this chapter will consider the event of the Spirit as the condition for the existence of the church; outline the significance of the church as a community in history; describe the features of the visible church in the proclamation of the Gospel and the administration of the sacraments; consider the relation of the church to the sanctified life; and discuss the identity of the church as a community which exists for the world.

---

4. Daniel W. Hardy, *Finding the Church: The Dynamic Truth of Anglicanism* (London: SCM, 2001), 30-2. Cf. Nicholas M. Healy, *Church, Word and the Christian Life: Practical-Prophetic Ecclesiology* (Cambridge: Cambridge University Press, 2000), 27-51; and Avery Dulles, SJ, *Models of the Church: A Critical Assessment of the Church in All Aspects* (Towbridge: Gill & Macmillan, 1981), 27-51.

The condition of the church: The activity of the Holy Spirit

God's Holy Spirit alone gives life to the concrete historical church in time. Properly speaking the church is primarily invisible or hidden, since God alone sees it and since it is created only by God through the event of the coming of His Spirit. The church is in the first instance an object of faith and not of sight.[5] A properly ordered account of the nature of the church should, therefore, give priority to the person and activity of the Spirit, whose active presence alone is the condition of the church's existence. We see the importance of this proper ordering in the opening two chapters of the book of Acts.

In the first chapter of Acts there is what seems to be an account of the church. It is a phenomenological account of the form of the church which describes its officers, liturgy and polity. Acts 1.12 seems to present the beginnings of the church, as the disciples return to Jerusalem and gather together. There is the identification of the church's leadership and officers with the reading of the list of the disciples in v. 13. We then get a description of worship (v. 14). We have count of membership in v. 15 (a pastoral roll, almost), then a sermon and readings led by Peter. After that, there is even an equivalent to a parish or church council meeting, with an election of officers (vv. 23-26), and Matthias taking the new position.

The description of Acts 1 looks as though what we are dealing with is ecclesiology. But it is not. In Acts 1 all that we are dealing with is something with the semblance of a church – an empirical description of the form of a human society, but something that is not yet the church. The church begins in Acts 2:

> When the day of Pentecost had come, they were all together in one place. And suddenly from heaven there came a sound like the rush of a violent wind, and it filled the entire house where they were sitting. Divided tongues, as of fire, appeared among them, and a tongue rested on each of them. All of them were filled with the Holy Spirit and began to speak in other languages, as the Spirit gave them ability. (Acts 2.1-4, NRSV)

The church begins at Pentecost with the coming of the Holy Spirit. The primary condition of the church is not ecclesial form, patterns of worship or structures of ministry. The primary condition of the church is the event of the coming of the Holy Spirit, who is present within the variety and plurality of the community in all its diversity, and acts upon the community to make it the church. The church is made holy (is sanctified) from without by an event of the *Holy* Spirit.

We will consider below what this means in terms of the visible community which is created. However, we should pause to consider this issue in greater depth, since it has profound effects on the way in which ecclesiology, as a discipline which studies the life of the church, is pursued. There is wisdom in the words of Robert

---

5. For a discussion of the dominical ordinances of baptism and holy communion, see below.

Jenson: 'If the church understands herself as founded in events prior to Pentecost and not also in the event of Pentecost *as* a divine initiative commensurate to the Resurrection, she will be tempted to seek her self-identity through time in a sanctified but still worldly institutionalism.'[6]

The vast majority of engagements in contemporary ecclesiology fall prey to precisely the problem of locating the identity of the church in the institutional organization of the church to which Jenson points. This has become all the more acute a problem in a situation of de-Christianization, in which many people have posed the question of Bonhoeffer to his own (somewhat different context): 'What does a church, a congregation, a sermon, a liturgy, a Christian life, mean in a religionless world?'[7] In seeking to offer a response to this, many accounts of the church have sought to focus on form and to concern themselves with the question of whether the church ought to be countercultural or culturally relevant. We see this in the ecclesiology behind the emergent or emerging church, or in fresh expressions of church, as much as we see it in so-called classical accounts of the nature of the church in movements such as Anglo-Catholicism: Being a 'true' church comes to be associated with being organized into a particular form, be that culturally responsive, episcopal, liturgical and so on. In seeking to answer the question of what the church means in the current age, much ecclesiological investigation has descended, in the words of Michael Jinkins, into 'the hyperactivity of panic'. This manifests itself in clutching for any and every programmatic solution and structural reorganization in the desperate hope that survival is just another project or organizational chart away.[8]

As a result, there has been a propensity in many ecclesial settings to think about the church in resolutely non-theological categories; and this runs deep. Much discussion of the church has focused on aping the church of Acts 1, and not attending to the condition of the existence of the church in Acts 2 – the event of the outpouring of the Holy Spirit of God. Much ecclesiological discussion has become obsessed with questions of *how* to be church, sometimes at the expense of thinking about the question of what the church actually is.

However, in accounting for the nature of the church, we should observe that in the first instance the church is a dynamic community of the Holy Spirit of God. In terms of theological ordering, we need to attend to the pneumatological priority over ecclesiology if we are to have any hope of being a church which is meaningful to the world, because it is the Holy Spirit who makes God present in the contingent situations in which we find ourselves in the here and now. Calvin writes that there is no reason to 'pretend … that God is so bound to persons and places, and

---

6. Robert W. Jenson, *Systematic Theology: Volume 2: The Triune God* (Oxford: Oxford University Press, 1999), 180.

7. Dietrich Bonhoeffer, *Letters and Papers from Prison*, ed. John W. de Gruchy, trans. Isabel Best et al., Dietrich Bonhoeffer Works 8 (Minneapolis, MN: Fortress, 2010), 364.

8. Michael Jinkins, *The Church Faces Death: Ecclesiology in a Post-Modern Context* (Oxford: Oxford University Press, 1999), 9.

attached to external observances, that he has to remain among those who have only the title and appearance of a church [Rom. 9.6]'.[9] If, as I suggest, that is true of the players in Acts 1, then it is no less true today – whatever those external observances might be (whether contemporary or traditional, low or high church). It is the Holy Spirit of God alone who gives life to the church. While the church is formed into the body of Christ, it is the Holy Spirit who does this. The order is important. We pray 'Come Holy Spirit' in order that we may learn what it means to say 'Jesus is Lord'; we pray 'Come Holy Spirit' because the Spirit is the one who makes present the reality of Christ in the multiplicity, diversity and plurality of the communities which form the universal church, as the body of which He is the Head. This plurality and diversity is important, lest we should confuse our own preferred style of worship or community with *the best* style or even *the* worship or community.

How we are a true church (rather than something with the semblance of a church) is related to the presence of the Spirit, who is the Spirit of Christ and who makes the Word known to us in present historical contexts in all their contingency. Seeking not only to have the semblance of a church is not under any circumstances about focusing on one form of church practice or liturgy or worship which trumps all others. It is not about that claim that one's own form of worship is true worship because it is low church and modern, and other forms of worship are only the worship of a community which has the semblance of a church because they are high, formal and traditional; or vice versa. Identifying the event of the Spirit as the basis for the existence of the church should prevent us from confusing ecclesial form or cultures of any kind, which can all have the semblance of a church, with the reality of the event of God the Holy Spirit which is the primary condition for the presence of the church as the Spirit makes Christ known to communities of peoples in all their variety in the present. This ordering can only enrich and deepen (rather than homogenize) the church today, and challenge both the old and new semblances of the church to focus on what it really means to be church. The priority of pneumatology over ecclesiology should remind the church that its holiness does not come from within its own form, organization and structures; the holiness of the church comes from without the church, as God who alone is holy creates a community by God's Holy Spirit for God's own purposes.

Furthermore, this should open up the community of the church, rather than close it down, to the belief that God's Spirit may be active outside the walls of the institutional church. Since the church is a subset of the activity of the Holy Spirit, the appropriate order here teaches us that the Holy Spirit is not only confined to the church: while the Holy Spirit is the sine qua non of the church, the church is

---

9. John Calvin, *Institutes of the Christian Religion*, ed. John T. McNeill (Louisville, KY: John Knox Press, 1960), 4.2.3 (p. 1044). These discussions concern Roman Catholicism polemically. However, outside of that polemic, the dogmatic content remains helpful and can usefully be redirected back to the Protestant church as itself an *ecclesia semper reformanda*.

not the sine qua non of the Holy Spirit.[10] The condition for the existence of the church is the presence of the Spirit; the condition for the presence of the Spirit (who blows wherever He wills) is not the church, nor located only within the church.

The historical church: The time and continuity of the Spirit

Although the church is an event of the Holy Spirit of God, it is nevertheless an event of the Holy Spirit of God *in time and history*. More precisely, it is an event of the Holy Spirit of God in the time between the resurrection and the return of Jesus. The coming of the Spirit at Pentecost marks the beginning of the time of the church, and the activity of God in history before the close of the age and the coming of the *parousia*. The time of the church is, therefore, a time of the patience of God with the world in history, before the coming of the Kingdom. There are a number of implications to this reality.

First, the church is a contemporary, time-bound and contingent reality, and not a romantic, timeless ideal. The church is a community which exists in the 'not yet' and in its 'becoming'. It is important to note that the church is not the Kingdom of God, nor will the Kingdom of God be the church: the imagery of the Kingdom involves political and not ecclesial imagery – a city where there is no temple as God Himself is the temple (Rev. 21.22). However, the church remains the event of God by God's Spirit in this 'not yet'; the church's penultimacy does not reduce its significance. In its penultimacy and historical contingency, the church is nevertheless an anticipation and a sign of the coming kingdom, a sign which signifies God's salvation of the world. As Pannenberg puts it, 'The church must distinguish itself from the future fellowship of men and women in the kingdom of God in order that it may be seen as a sign of the kingdom by which its saving future is already present for people in their own day.'[11] Its role as a sign is a real role in the history of God's patience with the world before the *eschaton*. But as a sign, the church is not the thing it signifies: the church is not the salvation or kingdom to which it points but is the sign that as an event of the Holy Spirit points to them proleptically in history.

As a sign of the kingdom and not the kingdom itself, the church must always remember, second, that it is still historical and human. Although it is an event of the Holy Spirit, the church which is made holy in time and space is still historical, contingent and creaturely. The church is created as a divine reality in time, but this is an operation of God with human beings and creation which does not nullify the creatureliness of the church. The existence of the church as an event of the

---

10. Cf. Tom Greggs, *Theology against Religion: Constructive Dialogues with Bonheoffer and Barth* (London: T&T Clark, 2011).

11. Wolfhart Pannenberg, *Systematic Theology: Volume 3* (Grand Rapids, MI: Eerdmans), 32.

Holy Spirit should make the church less, rather than more, confident of its own authority – questioning its own propensity to ignore or disobey God's action, and remembering that it is still only a sign (in all of its creatureliness) of the ultimate. Colin Gunton argues wisely:

> Sometimes it has appeared that because a *logical* link has been claimed between the Spirit and institution, the institution has made too confident claims to be possessed of divine authority. The outcome ... has been too 'realised' an eschatology of the institution, too near a claim for the coincidence of the Church's action with the action of God. Against such a tendency it must be emphasised that, as christology universalises, the direction of pneumatology is to particularise. The action of the Spirit is to anticipate, in the present and by means of the finite and contingent, the things of the age to come.[12]

As we were reminded by Calvin in the above section, we should not forget the danger of the human community having only the semblance of a church (as in Acts 1), rather than being a true event of the Holy Spirit. Indeed, Calvin also points to the fact that the church's holiness (which comes from God) is one in which the church advances but is not yet perfect:[13] the creed's affirmation of the communion of saints is followed immediately by its affirmation of the forgiveness of sins.

A third issue arises in relation to the historical form of the church in terms of its continuity and constancy. If the church is an event of the Holy Spirit, which cannot be guaranteed by any human activity *ex opere operato*, how can we account for the ongoing presence of the witness of the church on earth in time? Is the church so contingent on the event of the Spirit that one cannot have faith in its ongoing presence and existence? This is certainly a concern, but we should be careful that such concerns do not force us back to engaging in ecclesiology by describing the human phenomenon of the community rather than the action of God. Since the church is an event of the Holy Spirit in time, its constancy comes not in its own forms, which are historical, contingent and passing, but in the constancy and holiness of God the Holy Spirit: it is the holiness and constancy of the Spirit that provides the faithfulness of the church. This is why the church is a subset of the communion of saints of all times and places: the church of each age and place is preserved by God's faithfulness. Because of the promise of Jesus to send His Spirit, and because of the holiness, constancy and faithfulness of God the Holy Spirit, the church in time exists dependent upon God and sustained by God.

---

12. Colin E. Gunton, 'The Church on Earth: The Roots of Community', in *On Being the Church: Essays on the Christian Community*, ed. Colin E. Gunton and Daniel W. Hardy (Edinburgh: T&T Clark, 1989), 61.

13. Calvin, *Institutes*, 4.1.17 (p. 1031).

The visibility of the church: Word and sacraments

Having considered the activity of God's Spirit in establishing the church ever anew and sustaining the church in time, we may now ask what the visible church looks like as a sign of the kingdom and of salvation. The visible church exists in a community (of whatever size) where the Gospel is preached and the sacraments (baptism and holy communion) are celebrated. It is these two identifiers which mark both the possibility and the boundary of the existence of the church. As Calvin succinctly puts it, 'Wherever we see the Word of God purely preached and heard, and the sacraments administered according to Christ's institution, there, it is not to be doubted, a church of God exists.'[14] It is these two features which provide the base-level descriptor of the visible church formed by the activity of the Holy Spirit of God.

The visibility that exists in the church's preaching is the operation of the Holy Spirit, without whom no-one can say 'Jesus is Lord', in the life of the community. The first action of the disciples after the coming of the Spirit is to 'speak about God's deeds of power' (Acts 2.11) in the languages of all of those in Jerusalem. This is followed by a sermon delivered by Peter. The visible presence of the Holy Spirit is known, therefore, in the hearing and in the proclamation of the Lordship of Jesus Christ, in the receiving and preaching of the good news, in the public listening to and speaking of God's Word. A primary marker of the existence of a church is a community in which the scriptures are read publicly and preached. The church is, therefore, a community which proclaims (in its sermons and worship) the Gospel and a community which instructs in the faith. This involves both an outwards expression of the Gospel to those who do not know it; and an inward-facing teaching for the purpose of growth into maturity of faith. In this latter way, the church aids the believer as she seeks to live out the sanctified life, as in its preaching, the church enables the believer to encounter the words of the Living God and to grow in faith and maturity. Thus, the very existence of the church as an act of the Holy Spirit reminds the believer that her faith is not simply a single momentary conversion: her faith is a schooling in the ways of God, which she is taught in unity with her Christian sisters and brothers through the proclamation of God's word. The public component of this proclamation is important: it is an attestation of the unity of the faith of believers in the church. It is for this reason many churches recite one of the ecumenical creeds in worship. Furthermore, the public nature of Bible reading and teaching means that believers are to seek the wisdom of the community in the interpretation of scripture, so as to prevent misguided private interpretation. In this way, the church's apostolic function comes to be expressed through the passing on of the *regula fidei* through the church.

It is by baptism in the name of the Father, Son and Holy Spirit that an individual believer becomes a member of this visible community. In baptism, a believer dies to self and sin, and is raised to a new sanctified life, as she becomes incorporated into

---

14. Calvin, *Institutes*, 4.1.9 (p. 1023).

the body of Christ. Although it is a visible and public act, the belief in one baptism that the creeds express demonstrates that we are baptized into the universal and catholic church. Baptism is not into a particular denomination or into a particular expression of Christianity. It is, instead, in the first instance a visible expression of belonging to an invisible community of God. In scripture, baptism is the first act that follows repentance, and it is the way the first community in Acts 2 identified and included the earliest converts into the church (Acts 2.38), as the mark which denoted confession of Jesus Christ, forgiveness of sins and reception of the Holy Spirit. In being baptized, the Christian enters a communion with those earliest members of the church and with the saints of all ages. As Paul teaches, 'There is one body and one Spirit, just as you were called to one hope of your calling, one Lord, one faith, one baptism, one God and Father of all, who is above all and through all and in all' (Eph. 4.4-5).

In sharing in the act of holy communion, the church attests visibly its continued unity. Holy communion is an event in which the reciprocity of the community's relationship with God and between its members is attested. Coming together (in communion with one another), members of the church come into communion with God; coming in communion with God, the church comes together. In this act, the church is reminded, in the words of Dan Hardy, that 'human sociality arises in (is given with) relationship with God – as a necessary part of it, not as a *post facto* addition to it. Therefore human sociality is inseparable from community with God; human and human-divine community are mutually necessary.'[15] In this way, holy communion sustains the community of the church in its communion with God. In receiving bread and wine, and following the instruction of Christ, the church looks back in memorial to the saving activity of God in the life, death and resurrection of Jesus, and forwards to the future salvation awaiting creation. As such, communion is a visible promissory act in history which is a sign to the church of its temporal purpose as a sign to the world of God's communion with and in the community before the return of Christ. In holy communion, the believer receives in humility a sign of God's gracious forgiveness of sins and the new life promised through the death and resurrection of Jesus, remembering and sustaining her baptism in her ongoing life of faith and the ongoing life of the church.

The church and the sanctified life

Having described the features of the visible church, it is necessary to ask what the purpose is of this particular operation of God in creating the church through an act of the Holy Spirit beyond gathering people together to form community. It is here, particularly, where this chapter's focus on the sanctified life comes to the fore; for in the church (in all its humanity, temporality and contingency), we see in God's act a sign of the restoration of God's plan for creation. The church is an

---

15. Daniel W. Hardy, 'Created and Redeemed Sociality', in *On Being the Church*, 38.

anticipation of future salvation in its reversal of human fallenness. This has both a vertical dimension in relation to God and a horizontal dimension in relation to creation, since in the fall humans are led into a state of solitude in relation both to God and to each other. In the fall narrative, the immediate response of Adam and Even to their fallen situation is to hide from God; to cover themselves from each other in shame; and to blame each other and creation (Adam blames Eve; Eve blames the serpent).

In terms of its vertical relation, the church is a community in which God by God's grace through the Holy Spirit makes Godself immediately available to His people. As the Spirit enables people, they are able to proclaim the Lordship of Jesus and to direct themselves to the activity of glorifying God in worship and praise. In sermons and Bible readings, the church is able to hear God speaking. In confession, the church is able to ask forgiveness of God and to be assured in its thanksgiving of God's pardoning of sins. In prayer, the community is able to petition God and to intercede on behalf of the world. In holy communion, the church is able to receive the sign of the promise of God's salvation in the body and blood of Jesus Christ. In benediction, the church is able to bless the community and the world. It is this immediacy of relation to God that the classical Protestant traditions speak of when they articulate the doctrine of the priesthood of all believers: each person is able to go in praise, confession and prayer directly to God without the need of another mediator. That there is no need for a mediator determines that before anything is said of the polity and orders of ministry in the church, it is necessary to say something of the equality of believers in their immediate relation to God: as Paul teaches, 'There is no longer Jew or Greek, there is no longer slave or free, there is no longer male and female; for all of you are one in Christ Jesus' (Gal. 3.28).[16]

The equality of immediate relations with God in the church determines, second, therefore, that there is a reordering in the church of the horizontal relations that exist between individuals (and more generally in creation). Bonhoeffer puts this well: 'When God restores community between human beings and God's own self, community among us also is restored once again, in accordance with [the] proposition about the essential interrelation of our community with God and human community'.[17] These horizontal and vertical relations should not be thought of as two distinct moments but should be thought of as a simultaneous moment – a single event of God's grace in which God reverses human sinfulness by reordering human lives in relation to Godself and to creation. As a community of vast differences between individual believers, the church (in the broadest geographical and historical sense) is enabled to become a community in which

---

16. On this verse, see: Karin B. Neutel, *A Cosmopolitan Ideal: Paul's Declaration 'Neither Jew Nor Greek, Neither Slave Nor Free, Nor Male and Female' in the Context of First-Century Thought*. LNTS 513 (London: Bloomsbury, 2015). In particular, Neutel makes the point that even if Paul is appropriating a traditional liturgical saying that predates him (majority position), it is nevertheless integral to his thought (pp. 24–8 of the monograph).

17. Bonhoeffer, *Sanctorum Communio*, 145–6.

individual members are freed to be for one another only as the Spirit works within it to create the community: the church is not a gathering of aligned human wills but a gracious act of God that creates a community so that our neighbour can become a gift to be loved in order to fulfil the command of Christ (and it is here where accounts of the different ministries of members of the church might be appropriately discussed). The church is, thus, a community of people orientated simultaneously on God and on other humans – a community of people freed from hearts turned in upon themselves. In this much, the church is a saving and sanctifying activity of God for the individual believer.

An outward-facing witness: The reason for the visible church

This orientation away from the self and towards God and other human beings forms the internal structural sociality of the church. However, this internal structure within the church is also reflective of the structural relation of the church in its external relations beyond its own walls. The church is created as an event of the Holy Spirit not for its own ends in the time between the ascension and the return of Christ but as a sign for the sake of the world.

Lots of the imagery surrounding the foundation of the church by the Holy Spirit in scripture is imagery that we might think of as being *intense*. In Acts 2, we have a picture of this deep intensity: the language concerns the sound of rushing violent winds (*ēchos hōsper pheromenēs pnoēs biaias*, v. 2), tongues as if on fire (*glōssai hōsei pyros*, v. 3), every nation under heaven (*pantos ethnous tōn hypo ton ouranon*, v. 5), fulfilment of prophecy (vv. 16, 25, 30–31) and so forth.[18] The immediate relation to God which the church provides is a relation of intensity: worship is of the *holy* God, and – whether high church, charismatic or formal – reflects something of God's holy intensity. However, this intensity is not to be confused with interiority, or with a self-understanding of ecclesial purity which is such that the church understands itself as being sanctified over and against the world. The church's holiness, brought about by the intense presence of the Holy Spirit of God in the present in the communities He creates, is a holy intensity created *for* the world. The event of the proclamation of the Gospel which accompanies the coming of the Spirit in Acts and the foundation of the church is an event which reflects the outwards movement of the church to all the world – a point emphasized in the long list of nations who heard about God's acts in their own languages (Acts 2.5-11). The intensive presence of the Spirit in the church is an event of God for the sake of the extensity of the world;[19] the intensive presence

---

18. For discussion of this language and its background(s) in historical context, see Richard I. Pervo, *Acts*, Hermeneia (Minneapolis, MN: Fortress, 2009), 61–6. For a more theological account, discussing the symbolism of these descriptors with reference to the Old Testament, see I. H. Marshall, *Acts*, TNTC (Cambridge: Eerdmans, 1980), 67–9.

19. The language of 'intensity' and 'extensity' is borrowed from Daniel W. Hardy, *God's Ways with the World: Thinking and Practising Christian Faith* (Edinburgh: T&T Clark, 1996).

of God's Spirit in the community orientates the community beyond its own bounds and out towards the world to which the community is a sign of the salvation of God. The Spirit, who leads church into deep worship and love of God and each other, leads us outwards to the world.

Karl Barth wrote:

> The work of the Holy Spirit in the gathering and upbuilding of the community ... cannot merely lead to the blind alley of a new qualification, enhancement, deepening and enrichment of this being of the community as such. Wonderful and glorious as this is, *it is not an end in itself even in what it includes for its individual members*. The enlightening power of the Holy Spirit draws and impels and presses beyond its being as such, beyond all the reception and experience of its members, beyond all that is promised to them personally. And only as it follows this drawing and impelling is it the real community of Jesus Christ.[20]

The Spirit who creates the church as a sanctified community is the same Spirit who leads the church at once ever deeper into the world, for the world. These two operations cannot be pried apart since the church exists in this time as a sign of the coming salvation. A church with a singularly inwards concern for its community, even a good community of praise and of love of God with preaching and administration of sacraments, is not a church in the theological sense; it is only a church in a sociological sense – to end where we began, it is only the society of Acts 1 and not the church created by the Holy Spirit in Acts 2. As the church is created by the Spirit, it presses beyond its own existence for the world both through the narration of the salvific events of the life, death and resurrection of Jesus *and* in the life of a community formed by the teaching of Jesus. As Acts 2 makes clear, there are political, social and economic implications to this outwards orientation of the church. Politically, the church is a sign of a society in which cultural and national differences do not lead to a breakdown of communication (through the tongues which the disciples speak).[21] Socially, the church is a sign of a society in which age, gender and social status do not express themselves in hierarchical power relations (through the fulfilment of the prophecy of Joel 2). And economically, the church is a sign of graciousness and generosity (through the sharing of all things in common and the breaking of bread together). As an event of the Spirit, the church not only is able internally to live beyond its individualism in relation to God and to other humans but is also made able to live beyond its own internal concerns. As Bonhoeffer asserts,

> The space of the church does not, therefore, exist just for itself, but its existence is already always something that reaches far beyond it. ... [T]he space of the

---

20. *CD* IV/4, 764, emphasis added.
21. Cf. Stanley Hauerwas, *Christian Existence Today: Essays on Church, World, and Living In Between* (Grand Rapids, MI: Brazos, 2001), 53.

church is the place where witness is given to the foundation of all reality in Jesus Christ. ... The space of the church is not there in order to fight with the world for a piece of territory, but precisely to testify to the world that it is still the world, namely the world that is loved and reconciled by God.[22]

The church receives the Spirit of God in deep and intense ways to enable it to exist for the world in all its extensity, plurality and diversity. As the Spirit creates the church in this way, the church is able to become the body of Christ – a body which lives not for itself but for the sake of God and the rest of the world. In this way, the church is sanctified community – not by being cut off from the world but by being for the world.

---

22. Dietrich Bonhoeffer, *Ethics*, ed. Clifford J. Green, trans. Reinhard Krauss, Charles C. West and Douglas W. Stott, Dietrich Bonhoeffer Works 6 (Minneapolis, MN: Fortress, 2005), 63.

Chapter 6

A PROTESTANT ACCOUNT OF THE AUTHORITY OF THE CREEDS

A problem exists for contemporary evangelical theology, and this problem is twofold: first, the affirmation of the principle of *sola scriptura* has been marked by the prioritization of the individual in relation to the text of scripture that has followed the Enlightenment; second, such a prioritization has determined that it is difficult to read the biblical testimony without a sense of the tension that exists in interpreting the text honestly and critically (in relation to its *Eklärungen*) and in a way which affirms the church's traditional interpretation of the text of scripture as read through the early ecumenical creeds and symbols. When we read the texts of scripture by ourselves as individuals and as critical academics, it is difficult not to be clear that the Christology of each of the Gospel writers or of Paul is not that of Chalcedon; or that Pauline Trinitarian theology (if there is such a thing) is not the same as that of Nicea-Constantinople. For those Christian traditions which prioritize the teaching of the church and have an account of the priority of the development of tradition from and over scripture, the problem is not so acute: the church's authority has determined that this is the way the texts are to be interpreted and this is their meaning, and that meaning has developed; in some way, the teachings of the church rule over the *viva voce* of scripture, which (crudely speaking) is itself after all in this account a creation of the church in its canonical form. For those of us who emphasize the *sola* of *sola scriptura*, however, such an account of the historic (and we might also add ongoing) development of tradition cannot so straightforwardly be given: crudely, what if the tradition has read the scripture wrongly – an issue at the heart of the Reformation itself? Surely we should return *ad fontes*? Is not the very activity of engaging in strict and precise exegesis, identifying what an individual biblical text or writer says and thinks, an activity of *sola scritpura* in its purest form – an individual with the text of scripture reading out of it what it says, rather than reading tradition into it? Were Strauss, Spinoza and Wellhausen the Luther, Calvin and Zwingli of their generations?

Thus, attempts at biblical interpretation from within the magisterial Protestant traditions face a number of difficulties which arise from the traditions' affirmation of the scripture principle.[1] Although the tradition of *sola scriptura* claims that

---

1. Wolfhart Pannenberg identifies difficulties in relation to hermeneutics *and* biblical criticism. This essay will deal only with the former of these two concerns. See Wolfhart

scripture is sufficient and clear, we must surely have enough honesty to face up to the reality that two hundred years of biblical criticism points to the reality that scripture is not uni-vocal (if vocal at all) on many classical doctrinal loci (such as the hypostatic union or the doctrine of the Trinity); and biblical hermeneutics must inevitably remind contemporary Protestant readers of scripture that they read through the lens of confessional documents, and certainly through the lens of the four principal ecumenical councils (and most especially through the lens of the Nicene-Constantinopolitan creed and the Chalcedonian symbol). However, elements of the symbols and creeds do not clearly and straightforwardly say what scripture seems to, about, for example, the relation of the Father to the Son.[2]

On the one hand, this has led a number of evangelically minded Protestant systematic theologians to undertake a path well-trodden by more Radical Reformers in questioning the veracity of the creedal and symbolical reception in light of a more direct biblical engagement. Individual engagements with the biblical texts have been used to deny, for example, the eternal generation of the Son, effectively advocating some form of subordinationism.[3] One can understand how particular (perhaps modern) understandings of *sola scriptura* might easily lead one to this conclusion. After all, does not Jesus make clear that the Father

---

Pannenberg, *Basic Questions in Theology: Volume 1* (Minneapolis, MN: Fortress, 2008), 1–14. An interesting (if somewhat basic) discussion of tradition in relation to canon, development and church history can be found in Emil Brunner, *The Misunderstanding of the Church* (Philadelphia, PA: Westminster, 1951), ch. 4.

2. We see this, for example, in recent literature about Arius, in which he is presented as one who understands himself to be a biblicist. See, for example, Rowan D. Williams, *Arius: Heresy and Tradition* (London: SCM Press, 2001); and Robert C. Gregg and Dennis E. Groh, *Early Arianism: A View of Salvation* (London: SCM Press, 1981). This perspective certainly seems appropriate to what primary sources there are, and even Athanasius resisted use of the non-biblical term *homoousios* until *c.* 355 CE, preferring biblical terminology to point towards the same concept instead in his pre-355 CE works.

3. See, for example, Bruce Ware, *Father, Son, and Holy Spirit: Relations, Roles, and Relevance* (Wheaton: Crossway, 2006); Bruce Ware, 'How Shall We Think about the Trinity?' in *God under Fire: Modern Scholarship Reinvents God*, ed. Douglas S. Huffman and Eric L. Johnson (Grand Rapids, MI: Zondervan, 2002); Wayne Grudem, *Systematic Theology: An Introduction to Biblical Doctrine* (Downers Grove: IVP, 1994), 248–52; Wayne Grudem, *Evangelical Feminism and Biblical Truth* (Sisters: Multnomah, 2004); Stephen D. Kovach and Peter R. Schemm, Jr, 'A Defense of the Doctrine of the Eternal Subordination of the Son', *JETS* 42 (1999): 461–76. These claim that the creed is supportive of their position. However, also see the replies to this issue in defence of the classical doctrinal position, including: Kevin Giles, *The Eternal Generation of the Son: Maintaining Orthodoxy in Trinitarian Theology* (Downers Grove: IVP, 2012); Thomas H. McCall, *Which Trinity? Whose Monotheism?* (Grand Rapids, MI: Eerdmans, 2010), 175–88; Kevin Giles, *The Trinity and Subordinationism* (Downers Grove: IVP, 2002); Kevin Giles, *Jesus and the Father: Modern Evangelicals Reinvent the Doctrine of the Trinity* (Grand Rapids, MI: Zondervan, 2006).

is greater than He is (Jn 14.20)? Is not Wisdom the first of God's creations (Prov. 8.22)? Is not Jesus identified with pre-existent Wisdom as 'the first born of creation' (Col. 1.15)? As one evangelically minded biblical scholar (who will remain anonymous) recently put it to me, reading the symbols and creeds with any sense of the importance of responsible exegesis and then still expecting them to be able to be read as genuinely appropriate to biblical exegesis is like taking a fish out of the water, holding it in your hand until it is dead, putting it back to the bowl again and then still expecting it to swim. The scripture principle creates a very real problem if we wish to maintain the creeds.

On the other hand, a number of people have recognized some of the tensions that exist in terms of the relation of the traditions of classical Christianity to the texts of scripture, and have sought to explain this issue in a way which does not give hierarchical priority to scripture, in the way that *sola scriptura* classically has done. For example, in a recent book published by InterVarsity Press, Jim Belcher describes the approach of what he calls 'relational hermeneutics' as follows: 'Nothing is privileged, not even the Bible, over the community in discovering and living out truth. The Bible is just one of the conversation partners.'[4] This understanding of the issues relating to the relative authority of scripture and church is a long way from *sola scriptura* as classically articulated in the Protestant tradition.

In this chapter, I will advocate that the activity of reading scripture through the creeds and symbols of the first four councils is an exercise in reading scripture with ecclesial responsibility not only to the church of our own day but also to the communion of saints through all ages. When I speak of 'ecclesial responsibility' or 'ecclesial hermeneutics', I am using such terms to point towards the concrete reality that in the life of the church scripture is not only read privately and understood individually, but it is *first* heard and read publicly, and interpreted and understood corporately. The *church* (as individual believers united in the body of Christ) has always sought to understand scripture, and the individual has read and heard the texts of scripture in the context of and in relation to the church; and it has been scripture and its interpretation that has created and defined the church, as – in relation to one another and to the text – the church has sought to hear and understand the Word of God. This process of identification of the church around shared and ecclesially negotiated interpretation of scripture is something we see in the church's path towards creedal and symbolic statements in the first five centuries. Furthermore, in setting a dense coda on scripture, creeds and symbols offer minimal parameters within which scripture continues to be interpreted for those who identify themselves as existing in relation to the church in every age, through the communion of saints. Thus, for creedal Christians, the exercise of understanding holy scripture is always in the first sense corporate, and an exercise which displays ecclesial responsibility in interpretation, since the Christian does not exist except as part of the body of Christ.

---

4. Jim Belcher, *Deep Church: A Third Way beyond Emerging and Traditional* (Downers Grove: IVP, 2009), 145.

By identifying the creeds and symbols as the church's exercise in reading texts ecclesially, in order to offer minimal parameters for responsible reading in the formation of doctrine for the community that identifies as the church, I will seek to demonstrate that creedal interpretation of the Bible does not stand at odds with classical Protestant accounts of *sola scriptura*. I will do this, first, through identifying the hierarchical priority of Jesus Christ over scripture, and of scripture over the church; second, by seeking to understand councils and symbols as arising from ecclesial readings of the biblical canon, and as giving form to ecclesial patterns of responsible scriptural reading for subsequent generations; third, by reflecting on the communion of saints and what it means to read with members of the body of Christ from all ages, and to be connected to this mode of reading not only across space but also across time; and fourth, from this, by offering some tentative conclusions about the significance of ecclesially responsible readings of scripture for a contemporary doctrine of *sola scriptura*, identifying the necessity of reading scripture through the creeds and symbols in order that scripture can form the community of the church as a community under the authority of Jesus Christ.

The importance of the hierarchical priority of scripture over tradition

Over and against progressive, developmental understandings of church dogma, which exist under the authority of the church which also defines the canon and offers its (singular and sometimes new) true interpretation,[5] the Magisterial Protestant tradition advocates the principle of *sola scriptura*. Calvin, following Augustine,[6] rightly points out that it is more appropriate to render the 381 CE creed's clause on the church 'I believe the church' than it is to render it 'I believe in the church' in order to differentiate between the object of faith and the means of knowing faith – that is, between God in whom Christians place their faith and the church which hears revelation and makes this God known.[7] The church is not the locus of faith for the individual, but the temporal and spatial body which directs the believer in her faith in God.

Potentially, one implication that we may seek to draw from this for evangelical theology is, however, that it is also inappropriate to state that we believe *in* scripture: it is appropriate for the believer to believe scripture which makes the God of salvation known, but not *in* scripture as itself the saving object; scripture is rather witness and testimony to this saving God. It is because salvation and faith is

---

5. Cf. John Henry Newman, *An Essay on the Development of Christian Doctrine* (London: Penguin, 1974).

6. Augustine, *On Faith and the Creed*, 10.21, Nicene and Post-Nicene Fathers series 3, 331. This recognizes the difference between the use of *eis* in Eusebius's *Ecclesiastical History* and *The Acts of the Council of Chalcedon*.

7. John Calvin, *Institutes of the Christian Religion* (Louisville, KY: Westminster John Knox, 1960), 4.1.2 (p. 1013).

appropriately located in Christ alone (*solus Christus*) that the Reformers advocate that scripture governs and rules the church, since Christ is to be *discovered* in the testimony of the witnesses to the encounter with Him. There is an important hierarchy to be noted here. As Barth puts it,

> In the 16th century ... the Evangelical [*Evangelisch*] decision was taken that the Church has not to seek and find the Word and authority of Jesus Christ except where He Himself has established it, that it and its word and authority can derive only from the word and authority of the biblical witnesses, that its word and authority are always confronted by those of the biblical witnesses, and are measured and must be judged by them. This is what the Reformation was trying to say and did say in its affirmation that Holy Scripture alone has divine authority in the Church. It was not ascribing a godlike value to the book as a book and the letter as a letter – in some sinister antithesis to spirit, and power and life. But it wanted Jesus Christ to be known and acknowledged as the Lord of the Church, whose revelation would not have been revelation if it had not created apostles and prophets, and even in the present-day Church can only be revelation in this its primary sign.[8]

The hierarchy we see is this: Christ as sovereign over scripture; and scripture as sovereign over the church. But this hierarchy does not exist in such a way that the revelation of the Word of God does not confront the believer in the church. Instead, it points to the mediated revelation of God in the church through scripture:[9] scripture is, according to Barth, 'the sign of a sign', and only in reading this 'sign of a sign' can the church hear the apostles and prophets, in order to hear and meet Jesus Christ.[10] Since Jesus Christ is the sovereign Lord of the church, it is only under scripture (which testifies to Christ), and by being obedient to scripture, that the church has authority; and this authority is a humble and mediated authority through scripture, rather than an authority which might appeal to Christ and the Holy Spirit directly in support of its beliefs and actions without recourse to the Bible.[11] Thus, both because the authority of scripture derives from its testimony to Jesus Christ, and because the believer truly confronts Jesus Christ in the church and only in scripture do we learn about Jesus Christ, scripture rules over the church.

When we come, therefore, to creeds and symbols, we must note that their authority is an authority which exists *under* scripture rather than over scripture. This is an issue that the Reformers are at pains to emphasize. Calvin advocates that the very right of councils to gather and claim any authority rests in the

---

8. *CD* I/2, 581.
9. On ecclesial mediation in Barth, see John Yocum, *Ecclesial Mediation in Karl Barth* (Aldershot: Ashgate, 2004).
10. *CD* I/2, 583.
11. *CD* I/2, 586.

promise of scripture that where two or three are gathered, Christ will be present.[12] Furthermore, the judgements of councils are authoritative only because they are based solely on scripture,[13] and these judgements are therefore meaningful, by virtue of this, not only in the contexts in which they take place but also now and in the future, since the church still stands under the authority of scripture.[14] In this way, we might say that councils, symbols and creeds are, therefore, exercises in biblical interpretation, in hermeneutics.[15] Furthermore, from a Protestant perspective, they are ecclesially responsible exercises in hermeneutics, in which the church universally (catholically) engages, and whether councils are correct in their decisions rests on the appropriateness of their biblical interpretation.[16] But this interpretation is not one which arises from the thoughts of an individual but from the negotiated interpretation of the whole body of the church: to be a member of the catholic church (small 'c') is to read scripture with our brothers and sisters in this way, realizing that this is how the church has sought corporately to interpret scripture, how the church has heard the Word of God. It is not, crudely, therefore, for an individual sat in her office to decide that the creeds are incorrect on the basis of their interpretation of scripture; this is a modernist doctrine but not the doctrine of *sola scriptura* as described by the Magisterial Reformation. Instead, it is for the whole body of Christ collectively and ecclesially to discuss and interpret scripture together, and to work out corporately the way in which scripture should be understood. This corporate interpretation is that which sets the parameters for those who interpret and seek to hear the text while claiming to belong to the church. It is correct ecclesial interpretation and wisdom which takes priority over and (for those who wish to interpret the texts within the context of the church) sets the boundaries for individual interpretation and wisdom. Councils are ecclesial forms of hermeneutics: they are the church interpreting scripture together as one. It is to this that we now turn.

Councils are exercises in ecclesially responsible hermeneutics

Much recent patristic scholarship has pointed to the priority of scriptural interpretation for the theology of the fathers and in conciliar debates and statements. As Lewis Ayres makes clear in his work, the fourth century saw

12. Calvin, *Institutes*, 4.9.2 (pp. 1166–7).
13. Calvin, *Institutes*, 4.9.14 (p. 1178).
14. Calvin, *Institutes*, 4.9.9 (p. 1173).
15. In this way, I wish to draw a stronger demarcation than Pannenberg does between scripture and tradition; see Pannenberg, *Basic Questions in Theology: Volume 1*, 186. However, I agree with his argument later in the same piece that 'later tradition is viewed not as completing the content of scripture, but as having a purely hermeneutical function' (188).
16. Cf. Calvin, *Institutes*, 4.9.13–14 (pp. 1176–9). For the Reformers, it is key that the councils can be wrong.

debates about the explication of the (so-called) plain sense of scripture, with theological argument about the best way to explicate scripture and the best philosophical and terminological resources to do so.[17] For the fathers, there were not differing disciplines with differing data on which to reflect (be that systematic theology, history, philosophy or the Bible); there was only the task of reflecting on the narrative of scripture and the best way in which to express from that the grammar of the divine.[18] In this, to borrow terminology from Lindbeck, the governing vocabulary lexical core was scripture as the locus in which the narrative of salvation was to be found and the God of that salvation was to be known.[19]

The centrality of biblical interpretation to the decisions, creeds and symbols of the first four councils determines in the first instance that scripture is the yardstick (*kanon*) by which all decisions of councils are measured, and the basis on which they are made. Thus, even when councils seem to make statements that are not contained directly in scripture, they do so arising out of the activity of offering a condensed interpretation of or coda on scripture having sought to listen to the Word of God in it. For example, Calvin asks those who argue that the term 'consubstantial' is not found in scripture the following question: 'What else are the Nicene fathers doing when they declare them [the Father and the Son] of one essence but simply expounding the real meaning of scripture?'[20] For both Calvin and Luther, the role of councils is not to *create* doctrine but to *preserve* the teachings of scripture as understood by the church and in so doing to refute heresy:[21] councils, for them, simply state what the scriptures say. Again, to quote Calvin,

> We willingly embrace and reverence as holy the early councils ... which were concerned with refuting errors – in so far as they relate to the teachings of faith. For they [the councils] contain nothing but the pure and genuine exposition of Scripture, which the holy fathers applied with spiritual prudence to crush the enemies of religion who had arisen.[22]

---

17. Lewis Ayres, *Nicea and Its Legacy: An Approach to Fourth-Century Trinitarian Theology* (Oxford: Oxford University Press, 2004), esp. 38–40; cf. David Yeago, 'The New Testament and Nicene Dogma', *Pro Ecclesia* 3 (1994): 152–64.

18. See here, Ayres, *Nicea and Its Legacy*, 14–15; cf. George A. Lindbeck, *The Nature of Doctrine: Religion and Theology in a Postliberal Age* (London: SPCK, 1982), esp. 79–84.

19. Lindbeck, *The Nature of Doctrine*, 81.

20. Calvin, *Institutes*, 4.8.16 (p. 1165).

21. This is, indeed, how the fathers understood themselves. See, for example, Athanasius, *Contra Arianos*.

22. Calvin, *Institutes*, 4.9.8 (pp. 1171–2). Luther makes a parallel argument about the condensing of the biblical narrative into the term *homoousios*; see Martin Luther, *On the Councils and the Church*, in *Church and Ministry III*, ed. Eric W. Gitsch, Luther Works vol. 41 (Philadelphia, PA: Fortress, 1966), 83.

This is a point which is also made repeatedly by Luther in his treatise *On the Councils and the Church*. In this, Luther argues that councils do not do anything new but only confirm inherited truth from scripture against heresies and innovations. His argument thereby reduces the authority of councils since they do not innovate in terms of doctrine but only confirm what is already in scripture if appropriately heard. Since the four principal councils did not innovate, according to Luther's interpretation, in terms of church teaching, the church presently cannot do so.[23] The early councils are exercises in the church interpreting scripture as the church.

Even if contemporary historiography determines that we can no longer take such a view of the history of orthodoxy and heresy,[24] two important points should be made here. First, the Reformers correctly identify the centrality of biblical interpretation performed ecclesially to the decisions of councils, and – in this – the Reformers recognize the authority of scripture over councils. Second, the Reformers identify a key *ecclesial* aspect for this means of interpretation: the way in which one reads the biblical narrative becomes the determining feature of the identity of the church. Despite historiographical issues, the theological, ecclesial and hermeneutical points still stand: to be a part of the one, holy, catholic and apostolic church means reading scripture with that church in a particular way, and in a way which will determine the minimal parameters in which subsequent readings will take place within that community. Indeed, modern critical historiography may in fact add support to the case being made here: out of various interpretative options (and there are many of them), the holy, catholic and apostolic church identifies itself in relation to the particular interpretative framework it finds most compelling and scriptural; the issues at stake between what we might refer to anachronistically as orthodox and heterodox communities are hermeneutical in the formation of their identities. The church is, therefore, created by and sets its parameters in relation to the reading of scripture: the Bible is the foundation for the church, since the way in which one reads the Bible and hears the Word of God with others determines whether one is within or outwith the catholic church.

Let us consider these points in a little more detail. First, in understanding the councils as ecclesial exercises in biblical hermeneutics, we see the fathers as engaging in negotiated, ecclesial and catholic interpretations of scripture for the church. That these interpretations are enacted corporately is of central concern to the Magisterial Protestant traditions. Calvin points to the fact that councils and synods arise out of a crisis or in order to solve a major issue through *common* deliberation. It is the very collectivity of the decisions of the pastors about the interpretation of scripture that gives the decision weight, in comparison to the decisions and findings of a few individuals with regard to scriptural interpretation.[25]

---

23. See Luther, *On the Councils and the Church*, 9–178.

24. See on this, for example, Walter Bauer, *Orthodoxy and Heresy in Earliest Christianity* (Philadelphia, PA: Fortress, 1971); and Mark J. Edwards, *Catholicity and Heresy in the Early Church* (Aldershot: Ashgate, 2009).

25. Calvin, *Institutes*, 4.9.13 (pp. 1176–7).

For Luther, we know the truth of these conciliar decisions because the sheep (i.e. the whole body of the church) recognize the voice of Christ. Thus, the whole church engages together in judgement on the appropriate interpretation of texts by virtue of the church's affirmation of what is true in their acceptance of creeds and symbols: it is not that bishops and councils judge the church, but that all Christians judge the truthfulness of the claims of councils. Symbols and creeds are supreme exercises, therefore, in ecclesial modes of scriptural interpretation since they involve the *whole* church's (in the broadest and plainest sense) reading of scripture, taking the power of interpretation away from bishops and scholars, and placing the responsibility in the hands of the entire church. Thus, writes Luther: 'Bishops, popes, scholars, and everyone else have the power to teach, but it is the sheep who are to judge whether they teach the voice [i.e., the words] of Christ or the voice of strangers.'[26] In this sense, *sola scriptura* is a fundamentally ecclesial-hermeneutical account both of the authority of councils under scripture (through the church's common interpretation of scripture) and of the authority of creedal statements in relation to the church. There is a cycle here: scripture is the authority on which the symbol and creed rests as it is negotiated by those at the councils; this authority is recognized by the broader body of the church, whose collective assent is the true catholicity of the creedal or symbolic formula. Church interpretation has priority over individual interpretation.

This relates to the second issue – that the way in which one reads the biblical narrative becomes the determining feature of the identity of the church. Here, the issue is not primarily that creeds offer dense narratives of the *sensus plenior* of scripture in relation to the central character of God, Father, Son and Holy Spirit, though this is certainly part of the story. The issue is more that creeds offer means to help to prevent getting the references of scripture wrong, or more appropriately offer minimal frameworks in which the references of scripture might be understood and interpreted. Councils were – in one sense – about community formation and identity in relation to the parameters of the interpretation of scriptural texts.[27] In terms of their contemporary use in relation to biblical interpretation, creeds and symbols continue to set the ecclesially responsible means of interpreting scripture for the community that identifies itself as part of the one, holy, catholic and apostolic church. Thus, creeds and symbols are not only formed ecclesially, but they continue to form the ecclesiality that exists within the church in terms of the minimal parameters they set for biblical interpretation. This minimalism is crucially important: within these minimal parameters is a whole host of open

---

26. Martin Luther, *That a Christian Assembly or Congregation Has the Right and Power to Judge All Teaching and to Call, Appoint, and Dismiss Teachers, Established and Proven by Scripture*, in *Church and Ministry I*, ed. Eric W. Gritsch, Luther Works vol. 93 (Philadelphia, PA: Fortress, 1970), 307 (cf. 305–14); cf. Luther, *On the Councils and the Church*, 61, where Luther argues that we can identify past heresy because it died away, and the church universal did not recognize it.

27. See Frances Young, *The Making of the Creeds* (London: SCM, 2002), xiv, 14.

possibilities both in terms of theological loci (such as salvation or sacraments) and in terms of culturally and temporally meaningful interpretation of scripture. To quote Thiselton on tradition: 'It yields, in Wittgenstein's language, sufficient regularities of beliefs and practices to offer an identifiable continuity within the public world, but sufficient development, change, and particularity to allow for the growth of new socio-linguistic horizons as new socio-historical contexts emerge.'[28] Thus, the ecclesial effect of creedal and symbolic interpretation of biblical texts is the formation of a community identity shaped around a shared set of minimal parameters for the reading of scripture: corporate interpretation of the scripture shapes the ecclesial identity of the church, and the ecclesial identity of the church shapes the way the church continues to read the Holy Bible. Thus, the church is created by the Word: the church comes into being not only when the Word is proclaimed, but the church also sets its identity in relation to the collective reading and interpretation of scripture. The minimal particularities of this reading in the dense coda it offers to avoid getting the references of scripture wrong provide a corporately formed *sensus plenior* which is the framework within which the Word is read, heard and proclaimed. In one sense, one may say that scripture rules over the church because the church is created by scripture and its identity and boundaries are formed in relation to its collective hearing and reading of scripture.

Crucially, however, this second point cannot be held without the first point: the authority of symbols and creeds rests on their interpretation of scripture which is affirmed by the universal catholicity of the entire church (i.e. all of its members; it is worth noting well here the baptismal use of the Nicene-Constantinopolitan creed). With Barth, we must say first about any church confession that 'its authority is simply its content as scriptural exposition, which is necessarily confirmed or judged by scripture itself'.[29] But we need to say in the same breath the following: 'To make a confession, *confiteri*, is to proclaim its content, to publish it, to make it known, to make it known as widely and universally as possible. A confession demands publicity. This derives from its nature as the word of the whole Church to the whole Church.'[30] An ecclesial interpretation of scripture is affirmed by the *full* ecclesiality of the church, and forms the minimal parameters of the church in relation to its interpretation of biblical texts.[31] Ecclesial interpretation gathers the church around the reading and exegeting of the Word as a whole church, forming what it means to be church or a member of it in relation to the reading of scripture.

---

28. Anthony C. Thiselton, *New Horizons in Hermeneutics: The Theory and Practice of Transforming Biblical Reading* (Grand Rapids, MI: Zondervan, 1992), 9.

29. CD I/2, 638.

30. CD I/2, 639.

31. The issue of *church* interpretation is obviously important here. I am deliberately focusing this on the community of interpretation of the church. Outside of this community, these parameters hold no sway, and a much broader range of interpretations are possible. But *within the community that interprets scripture this way*, creeds and symbols set this parameter.

Reading with the communion of saints of all ages

In one sense this might all be well and good, but does this not mean that we can today collectively challenge these symbols and statements of the creed? What does this mean for us today in light of our reading of scripture, however? That is how the body of the church read scripture then, surely we now know better and should read it differently now? Is it not necessary for us to be responsible to modernity, not to be responsible academics with critical faculties in full play? Does not the body of the university with all its learning offer another mode of interpretation of the texts which is equally corporate? And what of the importance of academic freedom and the thoughts of the individual?

Reading ecclesially, however, is not just about reading corporately with the church of a given moment, but it is also about reading the Word of God with an acknowledgement that it has spoken and been heard across time: when we read scripture ecclesially, we read with the great cloud of witnesses who have gone before and who will come after us. To read scripture through the creeds is to realize that the Bible and its interpretation creates and sets minimal parameters for the church of all ages and times. It is to read scripture with Athanasius and Augustine and Luther and Calvin and Wesley and so on, recognizing that God's faithful constancy means he has addressed each generation with His self-same Word which is a sure foundation. Reading these texts in a non-ecclesial way is, after all, relatively new. We have eighteen hundred years of reading these texts in a way which did not prioritize individuals' interpretations over the church's, and as the church we do not read only with other late-moderns; we hear God's Word with and within the whole body of Christ across space and time. It is here that the doctrine of the communion of saints comes into prominence.[32]

The article of the creed '*sanctorum communionem*' finds its origins in late fourth-century Gaul. Although its original meaning was probably little more than a further description of the preceding article ('Holy Catholic Church'), and although its insertion into the creed perhaps came only in protest against the Donatist schism, it is clear that very soon the phrase was interpreted as meaning the fellowship of all believers with the holy of all ages (both living and in heaven). The idea of a participation of the contemporary church in the eternal communion of saints joins the church in the present to the church in every age. This is a recognition of the *ekklesia* not simply as the gathered community of a given place and time, but as a part of the one universal church, not only geographically but also historically. When the present expressions of the church seek to understand themselves in continuity with the past, they do so, therefore, as part of the one

---

32. For a more detailed account of the implications of this doctrine for contemporary theology, see Tom Greggs, 'Being a Wise Apprentice to the Communion of Modern Saints: On the Need for Conversation with a Plurality of Theological Interlocutors', in *The Vocation of Theology Today: A Festschrift for David Ford*, ed. Tom Greggs, Rachel Muers, and Simeon Zahl (Eugene, OR: Cascade, 2013), 21–4.

communion of saints. When the church seeks to offer an ecclesial interpretation of scripture, it does so in relation not only to the catholicity of worldwide creedal Christianity today but also in relation to those who have heard God's Word and confessed the creeds in all ages and across boundaries of historical difference.

This determines that in reading scripture ecclesially, not only must individuals within the church engage in interpretation in recognition of their responsibility to the rest of the church of their given day, which is created as it is gathered and defined in relation to the hearing and reading of God's Word, but also the church today has responsibility to and shares in reading God's Word with the church of every age through the communion of saints. In the doctrine of the communion of saints we might hope to find the basis of the theological grounds for the engagement with reading scripture through the creeds. But what does that engagement look like? In what way does it allow the genuine practice of *sola scriptura* while recognizing this doctrine is primarily an account of the church's (and only subsequently) the individual's reading of scripture, as the church collectively and relationally seeks to hear and interpret the Word of God? How does such an engagement with the whole of the church across time through the communion of saints avoid either idolizing the past church and the creeds and symbols at the expense of the present reading of scripture, or making a god of the contemporary at the expense of the wise readings of scripture that have gone before?

First of all, in hearing, reading and interpreting scripture today, it is necessary for the church to be engaged in the serious acquisition of the thought of the past, staying alert to the dangers of the cult of the modern and the propensity to fad or vogue in the way in which scripture is interpreted. In theology, as in all academic discourse, whoever is married to the Spirit of the Age is a widow in the next.[33] In theology's case, however, this is not because of some notion of progress in knowledge or the like on the one hand (though that certainly may have its place), nor because of an attempt at an identification with anachronistic antiquarian eccentricities on the other. Instead, the critical rejection of the readings of past generations on the basis of any given external norm,[34] which clashes with the traditional claims of the church in the first four ecumenical councils, is primarily a denial and rejection of the creedal affirmation of the communion of saints. While those who do reject claims of the creeds on the basis of *sola scriptura* will no doubt rush to defend their connection to the church of all ages on the basis of various linguistic expressions of extra-linguistic categories, it is clear that for them, even so, the learning of the church in the present has become the master which judges the church of the past, and to which the way that scripture has been

---

33. This is surely why those theologies which aim to be most modern date more easily than those which do not: Tillich and Bultmann, for example, now feel very dated in comparison to Barth, not least because the philosophical assumptions to which they wedded themselves are no longer vogue or contemporary.

34. Cf. Hans Frei, *Types of Christian Theology* (New Haven, CT: Yale University Press, 1994), 28–30 (type 1).

read in past must always be subject. Modern thought, in its desire for universal rational categories (with a very limited definition of the *ratio*), judges that which is pre-modern as unscientific and insufficient, seeing true knowledge as always lying ahead in future human capacity, and nervous of tradition and any claim it makes to authority.[35] However, an affirmation of the communion of saints must surely remind us of the equidistance of the church of any age to the Kingdom of God, and to God's *eschaton*: what we have in the church of any given 'today' (whether in the twenty-first century or the fifth century) is always a (lesser) witness to that universal and eternal communion of all ages. The way in which the catholic church has read scripture ecumenically in the past must be treated with seriousness and the respect that it deserves, as part of God's revelatory work by the power of the Holy Spirit in communities of faith throughout all ages and times: God has spoken His Word and continues to speak in His faithful constancy to each age and generation through His Spirit. Faithful retrieval of the readings of the church in the past is integral to the church's hearing and reading of scripture today and integral to the principle of *sola scriptura*, since *sola scriptura* is in the first instance a doctrine about the church's reading of scripture, and through the communion of saints the church catholic is connected to the church of every age. This need to engage with the ecumenical readings of scripture of the past is not only to learn from what past theological thinkers might offer but also to ensure that theology speaks with an appropriate level of humility even when engaging in hearing and reading scripture and affirming the principle of *sola scriptura*. The hubris of much modern thought is reminded not only of its own passing nature, in light of past vogues, but is ultimately humbled in light of the object of theological science – the eternal and infinite God who has made Himself known through His Word in the church of every generation.

Second, engagement with the reading and interpretation of scripture in the church of the past cannot be a simple repetition of the past, for the sake of historical interest only. Such engagement needs to be creative and living since the church of today is also part of the communion of saints and part of the universal church which is created by and defined by its reading and interpretation of scripture.[36] The confession of a belief in the communion of saints not only affirms the importance of the creeds, councils and saints of the past but also affirms the connectedness of the church today to the church of all ages: the church today is as important as any other historical instantiation of God's community. This has two implications. First of all, study of the interpretation of scripture in the church of earlier generations and of creeds and councils cannot *theologically* simply be for its own sake. The authority of these councils, as already established, rests on their interpretation of scripture. To learn from these councils and earlier figures in their interpretation

---

35. We might see this as arising from Kant's desire for us to be liberated from our 'self-incurred tutelage', something which invites a challenge to tradition in Enlightenment thinking.

36. David F. Ford, *The Future of Christian Theology* (Oxford: Wiley-Blackwell, 2011), 101.

of scripture certainly involves careful exegesis of their work, linguistic tools and contextual appreciation. But those skills are there in order that an engagement in understanding these theologians *today* might take place: *Erklärung* is essential for the purpose of *Verstehen*. Reading and rereading these creeds, symbols and earlier interpretations of scripture is a mode of establishing for the contemporary theologian 'relationships of cohabitation'[37] with the communion of saints in order to hear the Word of God in the reading of scripture today. Reading scripture through and with the creeds is a means of communing and hearing scripture with the saints of old, rather than simply observing them in some laboratory setting, or hardening and crystallizing their readings. As Karl Barth puts it,

> It is always a misunderstanding of the communion of saints and a misunderstanding also of the fathers when their confession is later understood as chains, so that Christian doctrine today could only be a repetition of their confession. In the communion of the saints there should be *reverence* and *thankfulness* for the fathers of the church, those who have gone before us and in their time have reflected on the gospel. But there is also *freedom* in the communion of the saints. Real respect and real thanksgiving are free.[38]

Related to this, the second implication of this need for living and creative retrieval of creeds is that theology (and the church) today cannot pick some arbitrary point in history or any given single historical figure to be the yardstick by which the benefits and validity of all other theology or readings of scripture are understood and measured. This is a propensity in much contemporary theology.[39] The principle of *sola scriptura* will simply not allow this, however. As we have already established, this principle means that scripture rules sovereignly over the church. The church in every generation as part of the communion of saints has to read scripture and to seek to hear it appropriately, and allow scripture always to govern or rule over tradition. This ecclesial reading cannot prioritize the readings of the past (any given moment in the life of the church) any more than it can prioritize the readings of the present. To use one single point as the basis for all theological judgements runs entirely contrary to *sola scriptura* and fails to appreciate the plurality of saints with whom, and the full breadth of the catholic church of all generations with which, today's church and theologian is to be in dialogue.

---

37. Ford, *The Future of Christian Theology*, 99.

38. Karl Barth, *Learning Jesus Christ through the Heidelberg Catechism* (Grand Rapids, MI: Eerdmans, 1964), 21.

39. Nicholas Healy sees this as associated primarily with the church, rather than theology; see Nicholas M. Healy, 'What Is Systematic Theology?' *International Journal of Systematic Theology* 11 (2009): 25. Surely his point about *status quo ante* could be applied to Radical Orthodoxy, or any systematic theology which engages a single historical figure as the basis for all contemporary theological claims.

Reading scripture ecclesially as part of the communion of saints is a wise way to realize the contemporaneity of all interpretations of scripture, the contextual nature of all theological claims and the limits of all theology (and each theologian, even the greatest). This is not, however, to ignore the authority of past hearings and interpretations of the Word. To quote Barth once again,

> It is impossible to speak without having first heard. All speaking is a response to these fathers and brethren. Therefore these fathers and brethren have a definite authority, the authority of prior witnesses of the Word of God, who have to be respected as such. Just because the Evangelical confession is a confession of the vitality and the presence of God's Word actualised again and again, it is also a confession of the communion of saints and therefore of what is, in a sense, an authoritative tradition of the Word of God, that is, of a human form in which that Word comes to all those who are summoned by it to faith and witness in the sphere of the Church and by its mouth – of a human form which is proper to it in the witness of these fathers and brethren.[40]

Furthermore, we cannot elide the difficulties and problems that exist in seeking to read scripture with these saints of old. The process of hearing what they have to say and what scripture has to say through them will involve careful and detailed historical work, which will point out how different these figures and their thoughts are from our own and those of our contemporary society. But the recognition of that very strangeness is in and of itself important to the church's reading of scripture today. It is a reminder of the significance of *sola scriptura* and the dangers of taming scripture through comfortable assumptions about the text (or even eisegesis), when it should be heard and read in its very otherness as *God's* Word. In the theological epilogue of his book *Arius*, Rowan Williams puts the matter thus:

> The loyal and uncritical repetition of formulae is seen to be inadequate as a means of securing continuity at anything more than a formal level; Scripture and tradition require to be read in a way that brings out their strangeness, their non-obvious and non-contemporary qualities, in order that they may be read both freshly and truthfully from one generation to another. They need to be made more *difficult* before we can actually grasp their simplicities. Otherwise, we read with eyes not our own and think them through with minds not our own; the 'deposit of faith' does not really come into contact with *ourselves*.[41]

The very process of careful (and respectful) historical exegesis brings out the strangeness of scripture and the way in which scripture has been appropriated by past generations of the church which along with the church today are a part of the communion of saints. In affirming that *sola scriptura* is in the first instance a

---

40. *CD* I/2, 573.
41. Williams, *Arius*, 236.

doctrine about the church's relationship to scripture, and in remembering that in reading scripture ecclesially we hear it as part of the communion of saints of every generation, when the church reads scripture today (and when we as members of the church do so) we need to move between two poles – learning from the church's past readings of scripture, but not simply repeating those readings since scripture rules over all the church in every generation.

Provisional conclusions: Some implications for a contemporary doctrine of sola scriptura

Put in the starkest terms, what I am trying to argue is that within the community which identifies itself in relation to this particular ecclesial hermeneutic of creedal and symbolic statements, the doctrine of *sola scriptura* demands that scripture is read through creedal and symbolic statements in the way outlined thus far within this chapter. This is because *sola scriptura* is a doctrine concerning the *church's* relationship to the sovereignty of scripture over it *before* it is a doctrine of the *individual's* relationship to scripture: the latter only arises out of the former, as the former concerns the 'public' hearing and reading of scripture.[42] Luther famously puts the matter thus:

> Whenever you hear or see this word preached, believed, professed, and lived, do not doubt that the true *ecclesia sancta catholica*, 'a Christian holy people' must be there ... for God's word cannot be without God's people, and conversely, God's people cannot be without God's word. Otherwise, who would preach or hear it preached, if there were no people of God?[43]

The Word of God stands in a hierarchical relationship to the church, which is formed by it and derives its authority from scripture. But this Word is known only with a terminus of encounter – only within the ecclesiality of God's people, the church. Tillich is quite wrong, therefore, when he sates: 'It is a demonic and therefore destructive act for the community of faith to be interpreted as unconditional subjection to the doctrinal statements of faith as they have developed in the rather ambiguous history of the churches.'[44] It is the very identity of the church in relation to the interpretation of scripture that concerns the statements of creeds and symbols; it is out of the authority of scripture that these statements arise; and it is because of the ecclesiality of the church that such statements are made catholically. In one sense, ambiguity is the very point: creedal and symbolic statements arise to give identity to the community of the church in relation to its

---

42. Calvin points to the dangers of private reading of scripture without the church; see, for example, *Institutes*, 4.1.5 (p. 1018).
43. Luther, *On the Councils and the Church*, 150.
44. Paul Tillich, *Systematic Theology* (Digswell Place: James Nisbet, 1968), 3:186.

reading of scripture *within* the ambiguity of history, and they continue to provide an ecclesial hermeneutic in changing contexts of interpretation. These statements connect the church's interpretation of scripture not only to the geographical breadth of the catholic church but also to the historical communion of saints of all ages – past, present and future.[45] Through the communion of saints, there is an authoritative tradition of the Word of God as it has been read ecclesially by the catholic church of all generations. However, this is not an independent authority of tradition over scripture, but a subordination of the *entire* church in its ecclesiality to scripture. Barth also states:

> Ecclesiastical history can be heard and respected as ecclesiastical authority only when there is discussion on the basis of a common hearing and receiving of the Word of God, and in that discussion one of those agreements, and in the documenting of that agreement a common confession, in matters of faith – hence, only when answers are given to the question of a true faith by way of speech and counter-speech, agreement and a common declaration in the face of Holy Scripture.[46]

In recognizing that the church confronts Jesus Christ in scripture in every age, the believer must seek to orientate her reading of scripture ecclesially onto the ecclesial readings of scripture that have taken place throughout the history of the church in the statements of the first four councils.

Sola scriptura is ultimately, therefore, an ecclesial account of the way in which scripture is read. If the believer wishes to recognize the authority of scripture over the church, it is meaningless for her to read scripture to this end *extra muros ecclesiae*. For that reason, her reading must be ecclesially responsible to the catholicity of the communion of saints if it is to be orientated towards understanding scripture as authoritative over the life of the church. In the continuation of history, in all its contingency, to proclaim a belief in *sola scriptura* is not to proclaim a belief in individual autonomy in relation to the biblical text but to proclaim a belief in the sovereignty of Christ, who is known only through scripture, over *the body of the church*. This is what the true humility of the present-day Magisterial Protestant churches must be, as the church seeks to stand under scripture alone, a present-day catholic church made up of individuals related to one another in Christ, and seeking to hear in scripture the proclamation of Christ to the church of which He is the head in all places and times.[47] Although this stands contrary to more radical or liberal understandings of *sola scriptura* which might well emphasize the freedom of individual readings, the framework for reading in this ecclesial way still allows tremendous breadth and freedom in reading scripture. The creeds

---

45. Pannenberg explores this in relation to continuity into the future; see *Basic Questions in Theology Volume 1*, 205–9.
46. *CD* I/2, 594.
47. Cf. *CD* I/2, 693.

and symbols only offer a minimal framework for interpretation, and within that framework there is much scope for freedom: the catholic church (in the broadest sense) leaves open understandings of salvation, church order, sacraments and a whole host of other areas which dogma and doctrine take up.

However, in seeking to read scripture ecclesially within the communion of saints of all places and times through sharing in the interpretation of the first four councils, the church will begin to discover the true hierarchy of relations of authority. This is ultimately in terms of the sovereignty of the true God. While symbolic and creedal statements may seem to offer ever more technical, precise and fine-grained accounts of the nature of the Trinitarian God, their purpose is to provide this definition for the communion of believers in order to prevent idolatry,[48] or as Nicholas Lash puts it, 'of getting the reference wrong: of taking that to be God which is not God, of making some fact or thing or nation or person or dream or possession or ideal for our heart's desire and the mystery "that moves the sun and other stars".'[49] The process of symbolic and creedal formulation is one of seeking from scripture the proper reference for 'God' in the narrative of God's encounter with creation, and in this, that reference is made more (and not less) mysterious.[50] The ecclesial responsibility of individual believers in connection to scriptural hermeneutics is not about the aggregation of power to the church; it is rather – even in its most detailed and confident claims – about the humility of the church ultimately before the God of our salvation; before Jesus Christ; before the testimony of prophets and apostles who bear witness to Him; and before the body of Christ of which each individual is only ever one part. *Sola scriptura* as a doctrine seeks that proper ordering, and for that reason is meaningful in the church, and to individuals within the church only in their relation to one another and ultimately to God: in *sola scriptura*, therefore, one might hope to find a truly ecclesially responsible mode of hearing God's Word and of biblical hermeneutics.

---

48. Cf. Young, *The Making of the Creeds*, 103.

49. Nicholas Lash, *The Beginning and End of 'Religion'* (Cambridge: Cambridge University Press, 1996), 134.

50. Cf. Williams, *Arius*, 236.

Chapter 7

THE CATHOLIC SPIRIT OF PROTESTANTISM: A VERY METHODIST TAKE ON THE THIRD ARTICLE, VISIBLE UNITY AND ECUMENISM

Protestants have a reputation for being schismatic. Were it not enough that they broke with Rome in the sixteenth century, from the very start Protestants have been divided among themselves: Luther and Zwingli could not find agreement over the nature of holy communion at the Marburg Colloquy; more profoundly, Radical and Magisterial Reform divided; and ever since the Reformation, there has been division upon division of churches who have all protested against their parent church that it has not proclaimed scripture or performed church practice or celebrated the sacraments or ordered itself or articulated its doctrine correctly. Moving to Scotland in recent years, I have been particularly aware of this propensity to divide. Reading Scottish church history can feel a little similar to reading a script from an episode of *Dallas*: unending fall outs, divisions and divorces, followed by the odd make-up and ostentatiously glamourous wedding. Diagrams of Protestant church history can bear an unhealthy similarity to complex plumbing maps, with lines dividing off and coming back together in almost inscrutable ways. It is rumoured indeed that one particularly narrow and exclusive Protestant sect even has a hymn that goes:

> Heaven's not a big place;
> It won't be very crammed.
> We alone are the chosen few,
> And all the rest stand damned.

While this is obviously a satire on schismatic propensities within Protestantism, there can nevertheless often exist (particularly within ecumenical circles) the sense that it is the Reformation's fault that we no longer have visible ecclesial unity in the West. As such, some ecumenical discourses can give the appearance (if they really and honestly examine themselves) of route plans for the journey back to Rome en route to Constantinople.

This essay considers what catholicity and visible unity in an ecumenical context might mean for a Protestant family of churches;[1] and in relation to the

---

1. In referring here to the Protestant family of churches, the essay primarily refers to those Protestant churches which are non-episcopally structured, though the points herein

understanding of catholicity and visible unity offered, how to account for the plurality of churches and opinions that the Protestant emphasis on conscience seems to give rise to. The chapter seeks to locate the theological reasoning for a Protestant account of visible unity in proximity to the way in which Protestantism understands the relationship between the Holy Spirit and the institutional church. In articulating the relationship between ecclesiology and pneumatology thus, the chapter wishes to offer what might potentially be a corrective to the dogmatic topography of ecclesiology within the broader Protestant tradition in order to make it possible to understand the manner in which Protestantism can understand itself as a visibly catholic church.

The title of this chapter arises in part from one of John Wesley's sermons, 'A Catholic Spirit', and it is this sermon with which I will be in dialogue throughout the chapter. The sermon obviously refers to spirit with a lower case 's'. However, this chapter seeks to examine how the account of catholicity offered by Wesley relates to a particular understanding of the Holy Spirit and the Spirit's work in and in relation to the church; and to unpack the constructive benefits of this account for a Protestant understanding of visible unity in the context of ecumenical discourse. Section one of this chapter will exegete Wesley's sermon. This sermon is described to offer a hypothesis about the manner in which Protestantism understands visible unity and catholicity. The second section of this chapter seeks to explore what is meant in theological terms by visible unity from a Protestant perspective. The third section offers a theological reason for this re-description of visible unity, locating the church in relation to the work of the Spirit, and considering the significance of dogmatic topography in placing ecclesiology in the proximate dogmatic *res* of pneumatology. The conclusion points to the sanctifying work of God the Spirit in the lives of believers, and its effects, as the basis for catholicity in a context of the multiple illuminative work of the Spirit.

Wesley's sermon, 'A Catholic Spirit'

John Wesley's sermon, 'A Catholic Spirit', is based on a text from 2 Kgs 10 concerning Jehu:

may well be directly relevant to episcopal Protestant churches as well. The essay notes that particularly the Anglican churches would require a more detailed engagement with the office of the bishop and the role of episcopacy in maintaining unity. While the points in this chapter do not necessary debar such an account, for historically episcopal Protestant churches, a more detailed engagement with the office, role and function of the bishop would need to supplement the account offered herein. To that end, the reader is directed to the helpful and nuanced account of episcopacy in the context of ecumenism in Paul Avis, *Reshaping Ecumenical Theology: The Church Made Whole?* (London: T&T Clark, 2010), esp. ch. 7; and his *Becoming a Bishop: A Theological Handbook of Episcopal Ministry* (London: Bloomsbury, 2015), esp. chs 7 and 8.

And when he was departed thence, he lighted on Jehonadab the son of Rechab coming to meet him. And he saluted him, and said to him, Is thine heart right, as my heart is with thy heart? And Jehonadab answered, It is. If it be, give me thine hand.[2]

Wesley takes this text as his basis to explore relationships between Christians from different Christian traditions.[3] Wesley's argument is that this is a text that can be used as a way of accounting for Christian brotherly and sisterly love. The question Christians of different traditions need to ask each other is the question that Jehu asks of Jehonadab: 'Is thine heart right, as my heart is with thy heart?' Wesley uses his exegesis of this text to differentiate between thinking alike and walking alike in the faith, and bemoans that failing to think alike is often the grounds and justification for failures in Christian love, and failures of Christians to share visibly in fellowship and the work of the faith. Christians who do not agree with the form of the other's Christianity should, according to Wesley, focus on the question of love for the other and whether their *hearts* are one such that they can walk together, rather than agreement between them in relation to opinions about the church.[4] Wesley does not expect there to be a thoroughgoing and absolute need for what he terms 'external union' between people who have different opinions about the faith or practice different modes of worship. The question he poses is this: 'Though we cannot think alike, may we not love alike? May we not be of one heart, though we are not of one opinion?' And for Wesley the answer is clear: 'Without all doubt we may. Herein all the children of God may unite, notwithstanding these smaller differences.'[5] For Wesley, love of the one with whom he disagrees trumps the disagreement that exists.

Wesley's prioritization of love of the other even in contexts of disagreement does not mean that for him questions of the truth are or should be set aside; or that one should pretend to agree. Instead, there is to be a recognition of the liberty of the Spirit present here in the context of disagreement: 'Every wise man, therefore, will allow others the same liberty of thinking which he desires they should allow

---

2. 2 Kgs 10.15; as cited in John Wesley, 'Catholic Spirit' (Sermon 39), in *The Works of John Wesley Volume 2: Sermons II*, ed. Albert C. Outler (Nashville, TN: Abingdon, 1985), 79-95. Henceforth, 'Catholic Spirit' will be cited as CS with section and paragraph given. The quotations from Wesley are quoted exactly and have not been repaired in relation to gender inclusive language.

3. Although clearly written more than a century before the nascence of the ecumenical movement, Wesley's writing of this sermon coincided with the writing and publication of his open Letter to a Roman Catholic, which also stressed an emphasis on a right heart, and a greater openness and degree of tolerance than might be expected for a churchman of his generation. See Richard P. Heitzenrater, *Wesley and the People Called Methodist* (Nashville, TN: Abingdon, 1995), 173.

4. CS, I.3.

5. CS, I.4.

him; and will no more insist on their embracing his opinions, than he would have them to insist on his embracing theirs.'[6] The single criterion that is to be applied in relation to a member of the faith with whom one disagrees is the refrain question: Is thy heart right, as my heart is with thy heart? This point is something to which Wesley returns at the end of the sermon. Almost as a postscript, Wesley states that there are three issues that the listener or reader should not confuse his point over. First, for Wesley, there is no sense that doctrine does not matter. Wesley does not subscribe to latitudinarian thought. Wesley writes that 'a catholic spirit is not *speculative latitudinarianism*. It is not an indifference to all opinions. This is the spawn of hell, not the offspring of heaven.'[7] Second, a catholic spirit does not mean latitudinarianism in practice either. Wesley states that a catholic spirit is:

> not any kind of *practical latitudinarianism*. It is not indifference as to public worship or as to the outward manner of performing it. This likewise would not be a blessing but a curse. … But the man of a truly catholic spirit, having weighed all things in the balance of the sanctuary, has no doubt, no scruple at all concerning that particular mode of worship wherein he joins. He is clearly convinced that *this* manner of worshipping God is both scriptural and rational.[8]

Third, there can be no indifference according to Wesley in relation to which congregation it is that one chooses to worship within. One should belong to a particular congregation with particular patterns of order: someone with a truly catholic spirit 'is fixed in his congregation as well as his principles. He is united to one, not only in spirit, but by all the outward ties of Christian fellowship. There he partakes of all the ordinances of God.'[9] Catholicity for Wesley is not an account of universality within the church by virtue of relativism or a laissez-faire attitude to forms of church order or governance, or the truthfulness of doctrinal standards and statements. However, for him, disagreement over such matters should not prevent loving Christian fellowship in relation to those of the Christian faith persuaded differently in relation to denominational commitments. Put otherwise, catholicity for Wesley is not brought about by a negative denial of the significance of doctrines and practices but is brought about by a positive loving enactment of fellowship in the context of disagreement: catholicity is the context in which we learn to disagree better, to improve the quality of our differences and disagreements within the Christian faith.[10]

6. CS, I.6.
7. CS, III.1 (italics original).
8. CS, III.2 (italics original).
9. CS, III.3.
10. Scriptural Reasoning follows this logic in relation to members of other faiths, and it is from colleagues in Scriptural Reasoning that I owe this insight; see Ben Quash, 'Deep Calls to Deep: The Practice of Scriptural Reasoning'. Available online: http://www.interfaith.cam.ac.uk/resources/scripturalreasoningresources/deepcallstodeep (accessed 3 June 2016). However, the same logic can be applied ecumenically as much as between religions.

Wesley recognizes that there has always been difference in the church in relation to beliefs about God and the form of practice that worship of God should take,[11] and that it is down to the individual and the individual's conscience to choose which form of the faith he or she should follow.[12] Here, Wesley points to the difference between the creator and the creature in terms of knowledge of the Deity: God has not given 'any *creature* power to constrain another to walk by his own rule.'[13] Wesley goes on to state: 'God has given no right to any of the children of men thus to lord it over the conscience of his brethren. But every man must judge for himself, as every man must give an account of himself to God.'[14] Modern individualism is plain for all to see here, but the theological basis of this for Wesley is grounded in the creator–creature distinction and the very otherness of God (as much as the rights of the individual and her conscience). Since no creature has the mind of God, no creature can impose his or her view on another: the implications of this distinction do not make the truth unimportant, but the point at stake is one which recognizes that none of us possess a monopoly on the truth of God.[15] Geographical location also cannot be the reason for a person being a member of a particular denomination: the idea that if one is born in England one should be Anglican and so forth; the ecclesiastical settlement of the Augsburg Compromise (*cuius regio, eius religio*). Wesley confesses that he was once a zealous believer in this idea, but has come to reject it since, if the place of one's birth had been the basis for denominational affiliation, there could not have been a Reformation: instead, there should only be the right of private judgement on which, he states, the whole of the Reformation stands.[16]

Having cleared this ground, Wesley moves on to speak materially about what it is positively that he believes a catholic spirit should consist of in a believer. Stating that he believes his own practice and doctrine to be 'truly primitive and apostolical'

---

11. CS, I.8. For an outworking of the kind of logic on display in this sermon, see Wesley's sermon which takes up the question of the imputation and impartation of Christ's righteousness (a point of debate between himself and the Calvinists): 'The Lord our Righteousness' (Sermon 20), in *The Works of John Wesley Volume 1: Sermons I*, ed. Albert C. Outler (Nashville, TN: Abingdon, 1984), 444–65. Cf. Heitzenrater, *Wesley*, 221–3. For a discussion of Wesley's understanding of the variety of approaches to the pattern and order of the church even in apostolic times, see Colin W. Williams, *John Wesley's Theology Today* (London: Epworth, 1960), 145–9. Also of relevance as a contrastive case is Wesley' sermon, 'On Schism' (Sermon 75), in *The Works of John Wesley Volume 3: Sermons III*, ed. Albert C. Outler (Nashville, TN: Abingdon, 1986), 58–69.

12. CS, I.9.

13. CS, I.9, emphasis added.

14. CS, I.9.

15. CS, I.10. This point about not having the monopoly on truth about God is something I have devoted considerable discussion to in Tom Greggs, *Theology against Religion: Constructive Dialogues with Bonhoeffer and Barth* (London: Continuum, 2011).

16. CS, I.10.

but does not intend to enforce his belief onto another, Wesley advocates his belief that the basis on which he should unite with another in love should be a question not of denominational affiliation, order, liturgy or sacramental beliefs but of whether the other's heart is right with one's own heart, as one's own heart is right with the other's.[17] The differences in opinion should stand, and can be talked of in a convenient season and in the context of a mutual recognition of the rightness of each other's hearts, but the principal concern should be an outward posture of love towards the other.

Wesley works out the content of what the basis for this posture means in seven steps. First, Wesley asks questions of belief in God. Wesley does so in a manner which mirrors creedal formulations themselves, but – significantly – he relates the articles of faith to the *life* of faith. The first question, he states, implied by the question 'Is thine heart right, as my heart is with thy heart?' is the question of whether one's heart is right with God: 'Is they heart right with God?' asks Wesley.[18] For him, seemingly, to have a heart which is right with God is to believe in the classical attributes of the Divine Life, and in God's justice, mercy, truth and providential governance.

Second, Wesley wishes to establish the same with Jesus Christ. Wesley is not only concerned that one believes in Christ, but he asks further:

> Is he 'revealed in' thy *soul*? Dost thou 'know Jesus Christ and him crucified'? Does he '*dwell* in thee, and thou in him'? Is he 'formed in thy *heart* by faith'? Having absolutely disclaimed all thy own works, thy own righteousness, hast thou 'submitted thyself unto the righteousness of God', 'which is by faith in Christ Jesus'?[19]

Wesley finds one whose heart is right as his is with theirs in one who has received the *benefits* of Christ's work of salvation, expressed by him in terms of justification by grace through faith. This clearly establishes some level of generous doctrinal commitment in his catholicity around receiving the works and benefits of Christ, but these works and benefits are in themselves pietistically described in their effects: it is necessary to know Christ and his works *in one's soul*. The pietistic posture seems more important than the Christological dogmatic formulae.

From this point, the third criterion is established in relation to the response and posture of the believer to God and God's work of salvation. Wesley sees someone who has a catholic spirit as someone whose faith is *energoumene di agapes* – 'filled with the energy of love'. Put otherwise, a catholic spirit will exist in one who is on a path of de facto sanctification – one who lives a life of grateful thanks to God.[20]

---

17. CS, I.11.
18. CS, I.12.
19. CS, I.13, emphasis added.
20. CS, I.14.

This spiritual posture, fourth, should impel the one in whom one can identify a catholic spirit to good works. Wesley sees the one with a catholic spirit as employed in doing the will of the Father, and in aiming in work, business and conversation at glorifying God in all that one does.[21] The seriousness with which one should do this is, fifth, as a result of the urgency of the gospel: the reality of the possibility of hell should provoke the believer to hate all evil ways and to avoid sin.[22] The way that this sense of urgency is to be recognized and the law fulfilled rests, sixth, for Wesley, in the one with a catholic spirit loving their neighbour and enemies, feeling moved by them and praying for them.[23] This love has to be shown, seventh, in acts and works – in doing good to all people, giving to them and 'assisting them both in body and soul'.[24]

For Wesley, if a Christian is able to fulfil these conditions, or desires to fulfil them, then he or she can be adjudged to have a heart which is right as one's own heart is right towards that other.[25] This identifies a Christian with whom one can walk. These seven conditions are the conditions for Wesley of a catholic Christian faith and are, as such, the basis on which one can have Christian unity with another from a different denomination or of a different doctrinal persuasion. That love of God and the other is the condition for Christian unity reduces the significance of the capacity of doctrine, liturgy, order or polity to be the basis on which the catholicity of a Christian is judged. There is no need, according to Wesley, for Christians to be of the same opinion; or to dispute points constantly; and fail to engage with each other as a result of these differences. Instead, the Christian with a catholic spirit is, like Jehu and Jehonadab, to walk together with others of the same spirit. At this point in the sermon, Wesley shifts the refrain from 'Is thine heart right, as my heart is with thy heart?' to the end of the verse: 'give me thine hand'.[26] Wesley identifies examples of difference over polity (between episcopal and Presbyterian order) and in sacramentology, and yet states that he does not want the Christians who hold different opinions on such matters to change their minds in relation to their commitments, only to be prepared – having satisfied the conditions of a catholic spirit – to walk in the faith with other Christians.[27] The Christian's concern should not be the relatively minor (to Wesley's mind) differences that exist between different denominations, but whether the self and the other love God and love humankind. Having described the seven conditions of a catholic spirit, Wesley *requires* four things of the one with a catholic spirit to walk with him in faith – four demonstrations, we might say, of *active catholicity*. First, he requires love from Christians of different traditions. This love, however,

21. CS, I.15.
22. CS, I.16.
23. CS, I.17.
24. CS, I.18.
25. CS, I.18.
26. CS, II.1.
27. CS, II.2.

is a particular form of love – a love which is greater than love for neighbour or for enemy. Wesley requests of the other who can assent to his seven conditions:

> 'If thine heart be right, as mine with thy heart', then love me with a very tender affection, as a friend that is closer than a brother; as a brother in Christ, a fellow-citizen of the New Jerusalem, a fellow-soldier engaged in the same warfare, under the same Captain of our salvation. Love me as a companion in the kingdom and patience of Jesus, and a joint heir of his glory.[28]

This kind of love, for Wesley, is a higher degree of love than that for the rest of humankind. Christians' love for each other should – as the saying goes – cover a multitude of sins such that whatever the other considers amiss in him should be pardoned in the hope that the grace of God will correct it, and whatever is considered wanting in him should be supplied through the riches of the mercy of Jesus Christ.[29] In addition to this love, second, the one with a catholic spirit should pray for the other. Rather than argue with the other, Wesley commands the one with a catholic spirit to wrestle with God on the other's behalf that *God* (and not the believer) would correct what is amiss and supply that which is wanting. The one with a catholic spirit is to pray earnestly for the other, for the other's growth in faith in and love of God.[30] Third, these prayers should be accompanied by good works directed towards the other which have the intent of provoking the other also to love and good works (a competitive outstripping one another in love effectively) – that is to a more faithful and active form of discipleship.[31] And fourth, the one with the catholic spirit can walk with the other in working together and joining together (even while retaining their own opinions and modes of worship) in the work of God, and in supporting the other in the other's work for the Kingdom (including speaking well of the other, sympathizing with them and assisting them in any difficulty or distress).[32] The catholic spirit which arises from a sanctified life must display this life in relation to the other (of different denominational affiliation and doctrinal commitments) in enacting these marks of sanctification in the joint journey of discipleship all Christians are to undertake. Differences of opinion do not require Christians to cut themselves off from one another. Instead, these differences require the Christian to orientate their love towards other Christians and – to a degree – to recognize that which is primary in the faith (a sanctified life in response to God's grace) and that which is secondary (distinctions in polity and theological commitment).

---

28. CS, II.3.
29. CS, II.4. There is a parallel here with Augustine's interpretation of Cyprian during the Donatist controversy; see Augustine, *On Baptism: Against the Donatists*, Book 2.
30. CS, II.5.
31. CS, II.6.
32. CS, II.7.

What are we to make of these claims of Wesley in the contemporary ecumenical context? It is to this that we now turn in addressing visible unity in Protestantism.

Visible unity in Protestantism

In order to understand the significance of this move by Wesley, it is necessary to trace (albeit briefly) the idea of catholicity as it develops in the early centuries of the Christian church.[33] Classical patristic accounts of catholicity rest in figures such as Ignatius, Cyprian and Augustine. As early as Ignatius in the late first/early second century, the idea of unity for the church was connected innately to that of the church's polity and order. While clearly the need for Ignatius to make this case suggests that reality was otherwise in the church, and while as well the material content of the nature of the orders is not set out in a way that corresponds to present understandings, it is Ignatius who seems to connect the idea of unity under a bishop, and to the clergy who serve under him, to the idea of catholicity: the symbiotic relationship we might say between catholicity, apostolicity and the institutional forms of the church. (Ignatius is, in fact, the first to coin the term 'catholic'.) The church is to be united, for Ignatius, as the clergy are to the bishop, so as to praise Jesus in 'unison' and 'harmony'.[34] The point, therefore, is not only that the church is subject to the bishop, but that the bishop in his apostolic authority teaches them how to be united to one another in Christ and fulfils the condition of ecclesial unity (or – we might say – catholicity). For Ignatius, the need for this unity is so that members of the church can be united so as not to fail at the last to offer the ultimate sacrifice to God in martyrdom, being confident in their unity in receiving the eucharist that they are 'with undivided minds … to share in the one common breaking of bread – the medicine of immortality, and the sovereign remedy by which we escape death and live in Jesus Christ for evermore'.[35] Unity under the bishop is the condition for the efficacy of the eucharist and this is in itself the way in which a martyr can be confident of immortality.

The *locus classicus* of the mature version of this account of Christian unity related to orders is found in St Cyprian. In Cyprian's thought there is a clear relation of causation between the presence of appropriately ordained clergy and efficacy of the sacrifice of the eucharist.[36] It is this which guarantees the unity and universality of the church. It is only in being connected to the priest who stands

---

33. On this topic, see Mark J. Edwards, *Catholicity and Heresy in the Early Church* (Aldershot: Ashgate, 2009); and the classic, Walter Bauer, *Orthodoxy and Heresy in Earliest Christianity* (Mifflintown: Sigler, 1996).

34. Ignatius, *Eph.*, 4.

35. Ignatius, *Eph.*, 20.

36. Cyprian, *De Lapsis: The Unity of the Catholic Church*, trans. Maurice Bévenot (Oxford: Clarendon, 1971), 18.

under the apostolic authority of the bishop that the Christian can understand herself as a member of the church catholic. Cyprian states:

> Does a man think he is with Christ when he acts in opposition to the bishops of Christ, when he cuts himself off from the society of His clergy and people? He is ... waging war upon God's institutions. An enemy of the altar, a rebel against the sacrifice of Christ; giving up faith for perfidy, religion for sacrilege; an unruly servant, an undutiful son and hostile brother, despising the bishops and deserting the priests of God, he presumes to set up a new altar, to raise unauthorized voices in a rival liturgy, to profile the reality of the divine Victim by pseudo-sacrifices.[37]

Only by being in full communion with a priest who is in full communion with his bishop (who is in communion with the bishop of Rome as Peter's successor and heir to the keys of the kingdom) is the Christian a true Christian: unity in the church exists only in this way – a visible expression which has a causal effect in guaranteeing salvation and preserving the Christian in the faith and in salvation through the sacrifice of the eucharist. For Cyprian, visible unity as thus expressed is the manner by which the church is able to preserve the unity of the body of Christ:[38] visible unity grounded in the institutions and polity of the church is the way in which catholicity is expressed. We see this emphatically in the discussions which follow his talk about the clergy:

> God is one and Christ is one, and His Church is one; one is the faith, and one the people cemented together by harmony into the strong unity of a body. This unity cannot be split; that one body cannot be divided by any cleavage of its structure, nor cut up in fragments with its vitals torn apart. Nothing that is separated from the parent stock can ever live or breath apart; all hope of its salvation is lost.[39]

What is key, however, for Cyprian is that this unity and catholicity are found in a set aside priesthood: it is a single group exclusively within the church that (in its relation to bishops and the bishop of Rome) grounds the church's unity and sets the limits of universality. The guarantee of catholicity is expressed by the polity of the church and its unity is guaranteed episcopally and ultimately in relation to the episcopate's communion with the pope. The episcopally ordained clergy, we might say, provide the catholic limits of the church, and this limit is indexed to their institutional expression of dependence on apostolic authority which is traced ultimately back to Peter's successor.

---

37. Cyprian, *De Lapsis*, 17.
38. We should note that claims for the clergy are variously grounded in the idea of apostolicity in Cyprian; see, for example, Cyprian, *De Lapsis*, 2–5.
39. Cyprian, *De Lapsis*, 23.

Unity and catholicity as found under the clergy who are united under a bishop who are united under the bishop of Rome is a long way from the account of unity and catholicity that Wesley expresses.[40] Does this mean that Wesley and the Protestant theologians who like him are not in communion with Rome (and furthermore participate in or have even given rise to non-episcopal forms of the church) are schismatics whose Christianity falls outwith the bounds of catholicity?[41] Is the very act of reform a breaking from the universality of the church, a rejection of the idea of the church catholic? For Wesley and others from a Protestant persuasion in relation to the visible church, the answer must surely be no. Indeed, it may be that the reasoning for this answer in the negative rests in the Protestant critique of the institutional church's propensity to over-identification with the work and activity of the Spirit. Calvin perhaps summarizes this best when he writes that the church should not be tempted 'to pretend … that God is so bound to persons and places, and attached to external observances, that he has to remain among those who have only the title and appearance of a church [Rom. 9.6]'.[42] Unity is not,

---

40. Cf. *Lumen Gentium*, in Vatican Council II:

> Fully incorporated into the society of the church are those who, possessing the Spirit of Christ, accept its entire structure and all the means of salvation established within it and who in its visible structure are united with Christ, who rules it through the Supreme Pontiff and the bishops, by the bonds of profession of faith, the sacraments, ecclesiastical government, and communion. (14)

For the most comprehensive account of catholicity from a Roman Catholic perspective, see Avery Dulles, *The Catholicity of the Church* (Oxford: Oxford University Press, 1985); see also Karl Rahner, *Bishops: Their Status and Function* (London: Burns and Oates, 1964), especially ch. 6. For further discussion of obedience to the pope, see Joseph Cardinal Lefèbvre, 'Obedience to the Pope' in *Obedience and the Church* (London: Geoffrey Chapman, 1968). The account offered in this chapter is equally a long way from the account of unity offered by the Orthodox Church. See Pantelis Kalaitzidis, 'Theological, Historical, and Cultural Reasons for Anti-Ecumenical Movements in Eastern Orthodoxy', in *Orthodox Handbook on Ecumenism: Resources for Theological Education; 'That They All May Be One' (John 17:21)*, ed. Pantelis Kalaitzidis (Oxford: Regnum Books International, 2014), 135–6; Alexander Schmemann, 'Ecclesiological Notes', *St Vladimir's Seminary Quarterly* 11 (1967): 38 (point 6); John A. Jillions, 'Three Orthodox Models of Christian Unity: Traditionalist, Mainstream, Prophetic', *International Journal for the Study of the Christian Church* 9 (2009): 295–311; and for an excellent recent and constructive overview of the idea of unity in relation to ecumenical discourse, see Petre Maican, 'The Form of Christ: Sketching an Ecumenical Ecclesiology for Eastern Orthodoxy' (PhD diss., University of Aberdeen, Aberdeen, 2016), especially the introduction.

41. Wesley had a complex relationship to questions of church order and polity. For a helpful overview of this topic, see David Rainey, 'The Established Church and Evangelical Theology', *International Journal of Systematic Theology* 12 (2010): 420–34.

42. Calvin, *Institutes*, 4.2.3 (p. 1044). These discussions concern Roman Catholicism polemically. However, outside of that polemic, the dogmatic content remains helpful

indeed, for the Reformers, to be found in any visible unity of the institutions of the church catholic, since – after all – the church itself is in the first instance hidden and known ultimately only to God.[43] For the Protestant churches, there cannot be an un-self-reflective over-identification of the salvific works of God with the institutions and polity of the church.[44] Unity to the polity of the church might well be unity to that which has only the semblance of a church; and this can be no true catholicity. Catholicity has to be described otherwise, and to be located elsewhere than in the concrete institutions of the empirical church.

In Wesley's 'A Catholic Spirit', it is possible to see, therefore, an account of visible unity whereby the visibility of the unity is differentiated from that which had traditionally been considered to be the markers of unity and catholicity. Wesley does not differ from the Catholic (upper case) concern for catholicity and unity; nor indeed does he differ in wanting this unity to be visible. Where Wesley differs is in terms of *how* he expresses, understands and identifies this unity and catholicity. Rather than understanding visible unity to reside in the Eucharistic and/or clerical (episcopal or pontifical) polity of the church with bounds created by the apostolic limits on catholicity, Wesley understands visible unity to rest in the capacity to identify visibly the fruits of the life of faith in different Christians from across the universal church. Wesley is neither a latitudinarian nor a schismatic. Instead, Wesley is one who identifies the visibility of a Christian, and the unity with that Christian to which we are called, as resting in sanctification not primarily in its *de iure* condition but in its *de facto* reality in the life of the Christian, as this is effected by the work of the Holy Spirit. This, it seems, is a distinctive Protestant (or more narrowly, Pietistic) contribution to understandings of visible unity; and such an account does not rest on a particular account of scripture or of doctrine or of the polity of the church. Instead, such an account rests on the visible fruits

---

and can usefully be redirected back to the Protestant church as itself an *ecclesia semper reformanda*.

43. Schwöbel summarizes nicely the approach of the reformation churches to catholicity: 'The catholicity of the Church does not guarantee the universality of the truth of revelation. The universality of the truth of revelation is the foundation for the catholicity of the church' (Christoph Schwöbel, 'The Creature of the Word: Recovering the Ecclesiology of the Reformers', in *On Being the Church: Essays on the Christian Community*, ed. Colin E. Gunton and Daniel W. Hardy (Edinburgh: T&T Clark, 1989), 128). This point is also made by one from an episcopal tradition in the work of Michael Ramsay: 'Catholicism, created by the gospel, finds its power in terms of the gospel alone. Neither the massive polity of the Church, nor its tradition in order and worship, can in themselves seem to define Catholicism; for all these things have their meaning in the gospel, wherein the true doctrine of Catholicism can be found' (Michael Ramsay, *The Gospel and the Catholic Church* [London: Longman's, 1936], 179–80).

44. The concern here is the repeated reformation concern to ensure that there is appropriate and strict demarcation between divine and human action, even in their relationality. For an overview, see Schwöbel, 'The Creature of the Word'.

of the sanctified life of the Christian. It is the life of faith visibly enacted which is the grounds for visible unity between members of different denominations. For Wesley, it is not so much the case that he is uninterested in visible unity, but it is rather the case that visible unity is described differently and located elsewhere than in more classical Roman Catholic (or for that matter Orthodox) accounts. In this way, it might be easier to see greater unity between the different forms of Protestant churches than the histories of divisions might suggest: those divisions do not undermine unity and catholicity but express the individual integrity and freedom of conscience of the Christian (in the context of the recognition of the creator–creature distinction and a critique of the over-identification of the empirical church with the exclusive actions and activities of God's saving grace), an integrity and freedom of conscience that should recognize the same commitments in others, and still see oneself – despite all differences – united to them through the sanctifying presence of the Spirit within the lives of the believers in the church catholic.[45] It is then for these Christians to live lives sanctified by grace that orientate them towards those other Christians who similarly recognize a heart which is right with their own hearts, such that there is an attractiveness to one another or a resonance between the lives of faith and commitment each believer lives.

The church, the Spirit and the third article

I have taken a long time to get to a central aspect of the title of this chapter – pneumatology and the third article. But I hope in the foundations that I have laid the direction of travel might be clear. The point that this chapter is moving towards is that in Protestant theology there is a distinctive account of the relationship of the work of the Spirit and the church to that which is articulated in more Roman Catholic or Orthodox theology. There exists within Protestantism an account of the church which recognizes its continual dependence on the ongoing *act* and *events* of the Spirit for its existence. The church comes into being in time in a Protestant account by the activity of the Spirit in space and time. It is not in the church's institutions or forms that the church's genuine being rests, but in the act of the Spirit who brings the church into being in a given place at a given point in history. Put formally, we might say that the ontology of the church is actualistic, and its being rests in the reality that the Spirit who acts is the eternal and holy Spirit of God; the church's being rests in the eternality of the acts of the Spirit who brings it into being time and time again in history – not in the continuance of its

---

45. Cf. the words of the dissenter Thomas Binney in nineteenth-century Britain: 'I am a dissenter because I am a catholic; I am a separatist because I cannot be schismatical; I stand apart from some because I love all; I oppose establishments because I am not sectarian; I care not about subordinate differences with my brother, for *Christ* has received him, and so will I' (Thomas Binney, *Dissent Not Schism* [London: Robinson, 1885], 65).

temporal forms. However, for Protestantism, while the Spirit is the sine qua non of the true church, the church and its institutions (of whatever form) are not the sine qua non of the Spirit. The visibility of the church, and the unity of the church, on a Protestant account, is not, therefore, grounded on the structure or polity of the church, but upon the epicletic call of the church for the descent of the Spirit and upon the sanctifying activity of the Spirit in the life of the believer.[46] As Colin Gunton puts it,

> Sometimes it has appeared that because a *logical* link has been claimed between the Spirit and institution, the institution has made too confident claims to be possessed of divine authority. The outcome ... has been too 'realised' an eschatology of the institution, too near a claim for the coincidence of the Church's action with the action of God. Against such a tendency it must be emphasised that, as christology universalises, the direction of pneumatology is to particularise. The action of the Spirit is to anticipate, in the present and by means of the finite and contingent, the things of the age to come.[47]

The church (as a contingent anticipation in space-time of the eschatological Redemption of God) does not have the capacity to determine its own conditions of unity on the basis of its external polity and form. Instead, for Protestants, the church exists *under* the third article of the creed – under the sovereignty of the Spirit, the Lord, the Giver of Life. It is the presence of the Spirit which gives life to the church, not the church which dictates or demarcates or limits the universality of the presence of the Spirit. There is a prevalence at times to think of the Spirit as 'an essentially immanent force: as something *within* an already given person or institution qualifying its existence'.[48] In contrast to this, with Gunton, it seems best to understand the Spirit as the one who constitutes the church from 'time to time' in a Protestant account.[49] This determines that one should not recognize the catholicity and validity of the church in the church's own composition and form, but in the inworking power of the Holy Spirit who comes from without the church to create the conditions that Wesley lists in his 'A Catholic Spirit'. Unity can, therefore, be visible for Protestant churches, but the form of the visible unity rests on the *de facto* sanctifying presence of the Spirit in the life of the believer, not the

---

46. As Alan Sell puts it, 'Far from this being an exclusive claim, the Spirit's work is Church-creating no matter by which confessional body it is processed' (Alan Sell, 'The Holy Spirit and the Church: Some Historical Soundings and Ecumenical Implications' [paper presented at the Society for the Study of Theology Conference, 2012], 8).

47. Colin E. Gunton, 'The Church on Earth: The Roots of Community', in *On Being the Church*, ed. Colin E. Gunton and Daniel W. Hardy (Edinburgh: T&T Clark, 1989), 61.

48. Colin Gunton, *Theology through the Theologians: Selected Essays 1972–1995* (London: T&T Clark, 1996), 191.

49. Gunton, 'The Church on Earth', 137.

de iure structures of the churches to which the believers belong.[50] This sanctifying presence of the Spirit need not be any less visible than the structure of the church (indeed, it may be more so), but an account which rests on sanctification does determine that unity does not rest in human forms and practices of doctrine, polity and liturgy, but in the free and active presence of the Sovereign Spirit of God who – as part of God's saving and sanctifying work – gathers people together for the outworking of salvation in the horizontal conditions of time and space.

The church which comes into being in time is the church of Pentecost – the church brought about by the descent and presence of the Spirit who comes again and again to the church in time and creation. The visible structures of the church are in place in the first chapter of Acts (liturgy, polity, etc.), but it is only in the second chapter that the church comes into being. The words of Robert Jenson are wise:

> If the church understands herself as founded in events prior to Pentecost and not also in the event of Pentecost *as* a divine initiative commensurate to the Resurrection, she will be tempted to seek her self-identity through time in a sanctified but still worldly institutionalism.[51]

Visible unity as attached to a form of ecclesial polity is not the only way in which visible unity can be understood. In fact, as Jenson suggests, there may be good reasons for being nervous of such approaches. Indeed, it is worth noting that 'an inescapable characteristic of the Church is … that as part of creation it, too, is finite and contingent'.[52] The church is not the perfect expression of the presence of the Spirit (even if it might be the most intense presence of the Spirit in creation) but a contingent and created reality which is not yet (nor ever will it be the totality of) the Kingdom of God. As a result, Protestant churches with their different understandings of the relationship between the Spirit and the church need a distinctive account of visible unity rather than presuming that there is only one account of what visible unity might mean:[53] rather than an account of visible unity

---

50. This is a point which is made powerfully by Gordon Rupp who cites it as a mistake to confuse catholicity with a system of polity, dogma or order rather than 'the fellowship of a great experience … fellowship with the saints through common access to God' (E. Gordon Rupp, *Protestant Catholicity* (London: Epworth, 1960), 44–5 (cf. 34–5).

51. Robert W. Jenson, *Systematic Theology: Volume 2* (Oxford: Oxford University Press, 1999), 180.

52. Gunton, 'The Church on Earth', 67.

53. This point gestures towards the account that Daniel Hardy gives of the need for ecumenical discussion to take place with full attendance to and within the different dimensions and dynamics of different ecclesial self-understandings. Ecumenical discourse cannot presume partners that share the same bases for approach or presume a static mode of or basis for multi- or bilateral discourse. See Daniel W. Hardy, 'Receptive Ecumenism – Learning by Engagement', in *Receptive Ecumenism and the Call to Catholic Learning*, ed. Paul D. Murray (Oxford: Oxford University Press, 2008), 428–41.

on the basis of an institutional ecclesiastical unity, the Protestant account may well be of the sort that Wesley offers – an account based on the free presence of the sanctifying Spirit which resonates with those others in whom the Spirit is also working out their sanctification.

However, often Protestant theology has failed to address the way it understands its visible unity in a manner which has allowed it to seem schismatic. It is here, as a Pietist, I wish to offer a small potential corrective to Protestant theology in the mainstream – a corrective which arises from seeking to understand the logics of Wesley's account of the catholic spirit. This corrective involves the dogmatic topography of ecclesiology. Much Protestant theology locates the church in relation to the second article of the creed as its proximate dogmatic *res*, to Jesus Christ and to the Word of God. The test of the truthfulness of the church is found, for example, in Calvin in relation to the preaching of the Word and the correct celebration of the sacraments. In Calvin's words, 'Wherever we see the Word of God purely preached and heard, and the sacraments administered according to Christ's institution, there, it is not to be doubted, a church of God exists.'[54] For Luther, also, it is the mutual ministering of Christ to each other in sharing the Word of God and in prayer that is the mark of the church. To those worried about how to identify a church, Luther states: 'If you are troubled and anxious as to whether or not you are truly a church of God, I would say to you, that a church is not known by customs but by the Word.'[55] These accounts are correct in disinvesting ideas of unity from polities of the institutional church, but they may well replicate the same problems as those they critique, just in a slightly distinctive form. This propensity to locate the proximate dogmatic *res* of ecclesiology in the second article can render visible unity in the church needing to be expressed in relation to a particular form of the preached word or a particular theological commitment – replacing particular structural polity with particular understandings of the Word of God's interpretation and potentially a distinctive polity which arises from that. This can lead, in the words of Daniel Hardy, to a certain '"purism" of the Word,'[56] which can exclude others and produce a non-generous, schismatic so-called catholicity in which one understanding of the true church unity (based on church polity) is replaced with another based on particular interpretation of scripture and forms of its preaching (potentially the 'soundness' of its preachers and ministers). What can arise is a replication of the logic of the more classical accounts of catholicity, but in a form which imagines an idealized pure church separate from the human reality of difference. As Gunton highlights, 'An overweighting of the christological as against the pneumatological determinants of ecclesiology together with an overemphasis on the divine over against the human Christ has led to a "docetic" doctrine of the church.'[57] This docetism also presumes a particular form of the

---

54. Calvin, *Institutes*, 4.1.9 (p. 1023).
55. Martin Luther, *Luther Works*, vol. 40 (Minneapolis, MN: Fortress, 1958), 41.
56. Daniel W. Hardy, *Finding the Church* (London: SCM, 2001), 33.
57. Gunton, 'The Church on Earth', 65.

visible church to which all others should be ordered – a divine church with is not able to unite with the material reality of the created-empirical *ekklesia*.

The other option in terms of problematic approaches to ecclesiology within Protestantism is to see the church as entirely independent to the work of God, and to locate ecclesiology in relation to the proximate dogmatic *res* of anthropology and human will: this is the account of the church as a free and voluntarist organization.[58] As such unity does not matter at all, but only a sense of the purity of the given community to which one voluntarily belongs by virtue only of one's conscience. If the preceding problem is to locate the church under the second article (the effects of the work of Jesus Christ), the current problem is one which concerns the location of the church under an independent article of the creed – a fourth, one might say, potentially a proximate dogmatic *res*, independent of the divine life and works, or at best in relation to a theological account of anthropology. However, structurally, this is a wrong reading of the creed. The church should not be understood to be a separate fourth article of the Constantinopolitan creed, but to exist under the third, under the summary of the work of the Spirit. There is no *eis* preceding *ekklēsian* in the earliest editions of the creed, as there is preceding the divine persons – a point Calvin is at pains to remind us. There is a clear differentiation between belief *in* the Holy Spirit, and the church which exists underneath the third article and not independent of it.[59] Similar to the way in which the account of salvation and judgement follows from the second article, so follows the church and its activity from the third article. The point is also clear even in the truncated Apostle's creed: '*Credo in Spiritum Sanctum, sanctam Ecclesiam catholicam*' and so on. The proximate dogmatic *res* of ecclesiology is properly, creedally, pneumatology: ecclesiology is not its own independent dogmatic *res*. The reason for this is that the church rests on the work of the Spirit who sanctifies the people of God; the church is not independent of the Spirit, nor is the church the condition of the presence of the Spirit.

Protestantism would be wise in its account of visible unity to emphasize this particular articulation of the relationship between the work of the Spirit and the institutional church.[60] It is the sanctifying work of the Spirit which is the basis for the church's existence and the content of the church's self-description. Sanctification is that work of God the Holy Spirit which takes effect within people (corporately and individually). It is the sanctifying presence of the Spirit which is

---

58. One can see this type of account of the church in the likes of John Owen. See, for example, *The Works of John Owen*, vols 15 and 16 (Edinburgh: Banner of Truth, 1965).

59. The point is also clear in the Greek: one can compare *Kai eis to Pneuma to Hagion, to kyrion* and *Eis mian, hagian, katholikēn kai apostolikēn ekklēsian*.

60. In a very helpful article that engages Roman Catholic and Methodist reflections on catholicity, David Carter argues in a similar vein to this chapter that catholicity rests in a given church tradition's ability to observe the Spirit's work both within its own life and the lives of other ecclesial traditions. See David Carter, 'Catholicity and Unity', *One in Christ* 40 (2005): 67–84.

material content of the church's sense of its universality and catholicity: where the Spirit is present sanctifying the lives of believers, there the church is visibly present and believers being sanctified should recognize this in the hearts of others (by way of resonance with them and the work of the Spirit's sanctifying grace within them). Wesley's account of the catholic spirit is an account of the Spirit's activity within the believer, and the way in which the believer can recognize another as a member of the catholic church. Far from being schismatic, the Protestant church on this basis has the potential to offer a broader and more capacious understanding of catholicity and visible unity (in line with the argument offered by Wesley). The account offered here has the capacity to include a wider range of churches even in the description of the Protestant Reformation and its heritage: more narrowly theological discussion moves away, by virtue of this kind of description, from majority or minority Protestantism, Pietist or Scholastic Protestantism, Radical or Magisterial Protestantism, authority or dissent, experience or scripture; and moves instead to the question of whether we are able to recognize the sanctifying work of the Spirit in the other, and – if so – whether we are prepared to follow the charge to walk with one another in an active catholicity which arises from a visible unity which exists in the context of disagreement over theology and polity. Catholicity on this basis concerns recognizing the visible work of the same Spirit in the other universally within broad experiential bounds of the sort Wesley describes: the more the Spirit is at work in our lives, the more catholic we are able to be, and the more visible the church.[61]

Conclusion: Visibility, disagreement and illumination

In an age of ecumenism, it is important to understand the basis on which we are to speak of the ecumenical task: it is necessary to be clear what is meant by the visible unity for which the churches strive, as the terms 'visible unity' and 'catholicity' are themselves disputed in terms of their meanings; and different churches enter into the quest for visible unity with vastly different expectations of what that might mean. The Protestant spirit is one which recognizes the church as a work of the Spirit of God, and sees the church's dependence on God as one not related to visible institutional form and authority, but to the visible sanctifying presence of the Spirit in believers – a presence which traverses denominational bounds.[62] As

---

61. Although his focus is more on the relation of faith and merit, and although he has an eye to the postmodern context, Ralph Del Colle raises the ecumenical possibilities of Wesley's thought in his 'John Wesley's Doctrine of Grace in Light of the Christian Tradition', *International Journal of Systematic Theology* 4 (2002): 172–89, esp. 185–9.

62. This has profound effects upon the ecumenical task of establishing visible unity. If one were to consider, for example, the World Council of Churches, *Baptism, Eucharist and Ministry*, Faith and Order Paper No. 111 (Geneva: WCC, 1982), the paper describes itself as arising from 'obligation to work towards manifesting more visibly God's gift of Church unity' (v). However, it may well be that for some Protestants, this obligation is not

Wesley makes clear in his 'A Catholic Spirit' such an account does not neglect the differences that exist nor think that they are unimportant. But such an account does not make questions of catholicity dependent on particular institutional commitments either. It is perhaps here where we are to think of the work of the Spirit in illumination. The Word of God has an end point: its terminus is as it is heard and received in the lives of the believers. Believers vary; the times they live in vary; the geographical locations they have vary; their contexts, philosophical paradigms and their presumptions vary. It is the Spirit whose work of illuminating grace relates the unchanging Word of God to the changing contexts of peoples, times and places. Such an account is no disguised relativism but a recognition of the Spirit's work in reaching into the hearts of human beings who are not replications of a single idealized Platonic form but who exist in contingency, difference and vast variety across geographical and historical bounds. It is such an account of the work of the same Spirit in illuminating the hearts of human beings and sanctifying them by God's grace, which is the basis for the catholicity of the church, for its universality across space and time. As the Spirit works within the believer, so the effects of the Spirit's work are seen in the life of the believer, and so the believer can be enabled by the Spirit to recognize those effects in another, and to resonate with them. When we recognize this work of illumination in our lives as creatures, we are perhaps more likely, in a context of difference in which the Spirit works in meeting us in our human difference, to say: 'Is thine heart right, as my heart is with thy heart?', and to answer: 'It is.' 'Well, if it be, give me thine hand.'

expressed in discussing the baptism, eucharist and ministry of the church but the shared life of sanctification.

Chapter 8

A CHURCH AGAINST RELIGION

The decline of church attendance in Western Europe has been such that from a position in which the church once held power and influence in individual, local and national lives, it now finds itself almost on the brink of empirical disappearance.[1] The question Bonhoeffer poses to the situation of de-Christianization seems more pertinent today than it even did in the situation in which Bonhoeffer found himself: 'What does a church, a congregation, a sermon, a liturgy, a Christian life, mean in a religionless world?'[2]

Responses to this have, in the words of a scholar from the United States about his own ecclesial situation which is far less desperate than the European one, been marked by 'the hyperactivity of panic. This manifests itself in clutching for any and every programmatic solution and structural reorganization in the desperate hope that survival is just another project or organizational chart away.'[3] Furthermore, where there has been reflection by churches on this situation of de-Christianization in society, it has often led to the determinately countercultural ecclesiologies of the radical reformation.[4] Added to the fact that de-Christianization has taken place simultaneous to a growth of religious plurality, it is not simply the case that now less people are going to church: more people are now attending mosques, temples and gurdwaras in societies once divided only by which form of Christian denomination one chose to worship at on a Sunday. Indeed, perhaps Bonhoeffer's

---

1. The Right Reverend Paul Richardson, 'Britain is no longer a Christian nation', *Sunday Telegraph*, 27 June 2009, For more on church attendance figures and the situation in Europe, see Gracie Davie, *Europe: The Exceptional Case: Parameters of Faith and the Modern World* (London: Darton, Longman & Todd, 2002), 6–7; and her *Religion in Britain sSince 1945: Believing without Belonging* (London: Blackwell, 1994), 46–9.

2. Dietrich Bonhoeffer, *Letters and Papers from Prison*, ed. John W. de Gruchy, trans. Isabel Best et al., Dietrich Bonhoeffer Works 8 (Minneapolis, MN: Fortress, 2010), 364.

3. Michael Jinkins, *The Church Faces Death: Ecclesiology in a Post-Modern Context* (Oxford: Oxford University Press, 1999), 9.

4. David Fergusson, *State, Church and Civil Society* (Cambridge: Cambridge University Press, 2004), 44. Other approaches to this issue which have sought to be tied more firmly to culture have simultaneously been too liberal, imbibing *Kulturprotestantismus*, and have failed to be clear about what distinctiveness the church has.

question needs to be rephrased as 'What do a church, a community, a sermon, a liturgy, a Christian life mean in a simultaneously de-Christianized *and religiously pluralist* society?' In this situation, the concerns associated with individual egoism in terms of salvation[5] run the danger of reforming themselves tribally as communal egoisms: there can all too easily be a replacement of the individual person with the collective identity of the church, but the base concerns are the same. By this is meant that the danger of expressing a favoured soteriological future for a section of society, or a favoured providential position within the world for a singular group with whom God is singularly concerned in a way in which He is not with others lurks behind much discussion of ecclesiology. In the contemporary religious and secular setting, this danger is all too real, and there is a need to discuss issues surrounding ecclesiology with an awareness of the complex societal and global situation in which the church operates. Discussing ecclesiology after Christendom requires significant attention to the situation in which the church now finds itself: in what ways does the church live in, with and for the world of which it is a part, a world marked by pluralism and secularism with regard to religion?

Bonhoeffer unpacks some of the questions arising from his initial discussion of a religionless expression of the church thus:

> How do we go about being 'religionless-worldly' Christians, how can we be *ek-klesia*, those called out, without understanding ourselves as privileged, but instead seeing ourselves as belonging wholly to the world? Christ would then no longer be the object of religion, but something else entirely, truly Lord of the world. But what does that mean? In a religionless situation, what do rituals [Kultus] and prayer mean? Is this where the 'arcane discipline' [Arkandisziplin], or the difference (which you've heard about from me before) between the penultimate and the ultimate, have new significance?[6]

It is to these concerns that this chapter wishes to turn in seeking to articulate theologically the nature and purpose of the church in light of the contemporary religious sociological setting. Are we merely a holy remnant by which God announces His judgement against the rest of His creation? Or does the church have no or little role in an age which (while it might believe) very often does not express belief in God in an ecclesial way by belonging to the church?[7]

This chapter will discuss these themes in dialogue with Bonhoeffer and Barth by considering the nature of the church as dynamic and actualistic.[8] It will go on

---

5. See 'Saviour of All: Soteriology against Religion', in Tom Greggs, *Theology against Religion: Constructive Dialogues with Bonhoeffer and Barth* (London: T&T Clark, 2011), ch. 5.

6. Bonhoeffer, *Letters and Papers from Prison*, 364–5.

7. See Davie, *Religion in Britain since 1945*, ch. 6, in her discussion of believing without belonging as a description of contemporary societal religiosity.

8. Actualism is a feature that pervades Barth's theology and is a term which is variously used within 'Barthiana'. For an overview of actualism beyond the parameters of its use in

to articulate this in terms of the intense and active presence of God's Spirit, before attending to the church's role within and for the world.

Dynamic and actualistic ecclesiology of the Spirit

There are various models with which one might proceed in describing the church, and taxonomies of such models are various and variously complex.[9] In his work *Finding the Church*, the Anglican ecclesiologist Daniel W. Hardy sets out a helpful broad analysis of these models of the church, which he describes in a fourfold form: the ontological model (as is found in traditional Roman Catholic ecclesiologies); the mystical model (as is associated with the Eastern churches); the actualist model (as present in Reformed church ecclesiologies); and the historical model (associated with Anglicanism).[10] An Anglican himself, Hardy expounds the historical model in his own work, but his description of the actualist model may find more resonance with anti-religious theology. His description of Reformed ecclesiology is expounded in terms of the church being 'an assembly that is always being reconstituted by the graceful act (election) of God in the Word of God as received in faith'.[11]

This dynamic and actualistic ecclesiological framework is certainly an appropriate description of Calvin's work. Calvin writes that there is no reason 'to pretend … that God is so bound to persons and places, and attached to external observances, that he has to remain among those who have only the title and appearance of a church [Rom. 9.6]'.[12] It is, therefore, the Holy Spirit of God alone who gives life to the church. The church is properly speaking invisible, as God alone sees it; and empirical and visible expressions of the church exist only in groups constituted by gathering around the Word of God in scripture. This visible and empirical constitution is no guarantee of salvation, however: 'Although they put forward a Temple, priesthood, and the rest of the outward shows, this empty glitter which blinds the eyes of the simple ought not to move a whit to grant

---

this chapter in relation to ecclesiology, see Paul T. Nimmo, *Being in Action: The Theological Shape of Barth's Ethical Vision* (London: T&T Clark, 2007), 4–12.

9. See, for example, Avery Dulles, SJ, *Models of the Church* (New York: Doubleday, 1987); and Nicholas M. Healy, *Church, World and the Christian Life: Practical-Prophetic Ecclesiology* (Cambridge: Cambridge University Press, 2000), ch. 2.

10. Daniel W. Hardy, *Finding the Church: The Dynamic Truth of Anglicanism* (London: SCM, 2001), 30–4.

11. Hardy, *Finding the Church*, 32.

12. John Calvin, *Institutes of the Christian Religion*, ed. John T. McNeill (Louisville, KY: John Knox Press 1960), 4.2.3 (p. 1044). These discussions concern Roman Catholicism polemically. However, outside of that polemic, the dogmatic content remains helpful and can usefully be redirected back to the Protestant church as itself an *ecclesia semper reformanda*.

that the church exists where God's Word is not found.'[13] Indeed, Calvin quotes Augustine: 'Many sheep are without, and many wolves are within.'[14] No direct or exact correspondence can be made between the church empirical and the church spiritual and invisible.

Although this form of ecclesiology is sometimes associated with a certain '"purism" of the Word',[15] with the suggestion that only the appropriate expounding of scripture can bring about the constitution of the church, one crucial aspect of this actualistic ecclesiological model is its recognition of the appropriate ordering of doctrines. Ecclesiology is always a subset of pneumatology:[16] the Spirit creates the church at Pentecost, and the creed lists the church's existence under the third article. Put formally one might say that the presence of the Spirit is the sine qua non of the church, but the church is not the sine qua non of the presence of the Spirit, who in His freedom blows wherever He wills. Ordering the doctrines appropriately helps us to recognize this. It is thus only as an act of the Spirit that the church is brought into being in time, but the acts of the Spirit are not simply the bringing into being of the *ecclesia* in history.

The concern to deal appropriately with the invisibility of the church, and with God's act as the basis of the church is one which is found in the theologies of Barth and Bonhoeffer. For Barth, it is clear that the church exists only as an act of the Holy Spirit who enables the community of Jesus Christ to exist: 'The Holy Spirit is the power of God proper to the being of Jesus Christ in the exercise and operation of which He causes His community to become what it is.'[17] That the church's nature is dependent on an act of the Spirit determines, in Barth's words, that its nature is always 'mobile', 'dynamic' and 'historical':

> The being of Jesus Christ to that of His community is not static nor immobile, but mobile and dynamic, and therefore historical. As the act of the Holy Spirit which underlies the existence of the community takes place in the order of the being of Jesus Christ and His community, the latter existing as He exists, so this order of the being of Jesus Christ and His community is the order of grace, the order of the act of the Holy Spirit, the community existing as Jesus Christ causes it to exist by His Holy Spirit.[18]

---

13. Calvin, *Institutes*, 4.2.4 (p. 1046).

14. Calvin, *Institutes*, 4.1.8 (p. 1022). For Calvin, however, a church is constituted as a place where the Word is preached and the sacraments are celebrated (ibid., 4.1.9).

15. Hardy, *Finding the Church*, 33.

16. For a survey of different ways in which the relationship between the Spirit and the church might be mapped, the reader is referred to John McIntyre, *The Shape of Pneumatology: Studies in the Doctrine of the Holy Spirit* (Edinburgh: T&T Clark, 1997), ch. 8.

17. *CD* IV/3, 759.

18. *CD* IV/3, 759.

This dynamism need not bring with it a purism or Puritanicalism as is sometimes the case, but should bring with it a proper recognition of the dependence of the church on the work and operation of the Holy Spirit, and not on the basis of any religious ecclesial essentialism. This in turn means that one cannot be too firm about where the boundary of the church lies: 'For all the seriousness with which we must distinguish between Christian and non-Christian, we can never think in terms of a rigid separation.'[19] The inability to identify this boundary exists because the church properly speaking is invisible, a creation of the freedom of the Holy Spirit of God.[20] The church is not a function of the collectivism of religion: indeed, there is no direct evidence that religion is innately social (as its interior and mystical forms demonstrate).[21] And no particular form of religion (whether centred on purity of word or liturgy) can ever be the basis for the presence of the true church – only the basis for something with the semblance of a church. The Holy Spirit alone forms the church in history.

Indeed, scripture itself provides that one should be sceptical about seeing religious affiliation as the basis and determination of the community of God. Barth points in this direction clearly in his discussion of those other people of God (outside of the Jewish community) who are prominent in the text of the Bible. In differentiating between the visible and the invisible church, Barth is able to claim that 'We can expect this hidden neighbour, who stands outside the visible Church, just because there is a visible Church.'[22] Outside of the walls of the church are those who are nevertheless 'hidden neighbours' of the *visible* church, members of the true and *invisible* church of God. These neighbours have a function for the church:

> Individual figures whom we must not overlook … also have a present place in the redemptive history attested by the Bible. They are strangers, and yet as such adherents; strangers who as such have some very important and incisive things to say to the children of the household; strangers who from the most unexpected

---

19. *CD* IV/3, 494. This is a theme which will be returned to below and discussed in Greggs, *Theology against Religion*, ch. 8.

20. However, importantly for Barth, it is only from within the context of the visible church that this inability to identify the boundary is known. O'Grady helpfully observes: 'Visibility is so essential to the community that even what it is invisibly must not be sought apart from its being visible, but in it. … Ecclesiological docetism is just as impossible as Christological docetism.' (Colm O'Grady, *The Church in the Theology of Karl Barth* (Washington, DC: Corpus Books, 1969), 255.)

21. Dietrich Bonhoeffer, *Sanctorum Communio: A Theological Study of the Sociology of the Church*, ed. Clifford J. Green, trans. Reinhard Krauss, Nancy Lukens and Dietrich Bonhoeffer Works 1 (Minneapolis, MN: Fortress, 1998), 128. However, Bonhoeffer's assertion in this section of *Sanctorum Communio* that only the Christian religion is social needs to be rejected (130–1): it is plainly untrue as simply looking to Islam and *Ummah* or the Jewish community demonstrates.

22. *CD* I/2, 425.

distances come right into the apparently closed circle of the divine election and calling and carry out a kind of commission, fulfil an office for which there is no name, but the content of which is quite obviously a service which they have to render.[23]

Barth lists Balaam, Rahab, Ruth, Hiram, Cyrus, the Magi, the centurion of Capernaum, centurion Cornelius at Cæsarea, the Syro-Phoenician woman, the centurion at the cross with his messianic confession and the many who shall come from the East and from the West who shall sit down with Abraham and Isaac and Jacob. But for Barth the most significant of all of these figures is the priest of Salem, Melchizedek:

> According to Heb. 5:6f., 6:20, 7:1f., he is the type of Jesus Christ Himself and of His supreme and definitive high priesthood. It is therefore not merely legitimate but obligatory to regard the figure of Melchisedek as the hermeneutic key to this whole succession. It is not on the basis of a natural knowledge of God and a relationship with God that all these strangers play their striking role. What happens is rather that in them Jesus Christ proclaims Himself to be the great Samaritan: as it were, in a second and outer circle of His revelation, which by its very nature can only be hinted at. It must be noted that no independent significance can be ascribed to any of the revelations as we can call them in a wider sense. There is no Melchisedek apart from Abraham, just as there is no Abraham apart from Jesus Christ.[24]

The priestly role of Melchizedek here is significant and ecclesial. While Barth discusses the significance of this enigmatic priestly figure from the perspective of Christology, to consider the priest's position pneumatologically may be helpful in establishing the proper ordering of the relationship between the Spirit and the church. The Spirit rests on Melchizedek,[25] making him a priest despite his not

---

23. *CD* I/2, 425.
24. *CD* I/2, 426.
25. The reasons for this relation to the Spirit are threefold. First, traditionally, the priests and kings of ancient Israel were anointed (with oil and perhaps sometimes the Spirit). Second, Ps. 110 likens the anointed David to Melchizedek who is presented as an enigmatic priest-king, a historical oddity that occasioned the author of Hebrew to reflect on Christology, especially the legitimacy of the Judahite Jesus's priesthood, in light of Ps. 110. And third, the author of Hebrews claims that Jesus entered the order of Melchizedekian priests (one might say he was 'anointed' to that order) 'according to the power of indestructible life (*kata dynamin zōēs akatalytou*)', that his resurrected life (Heb. 7.15-16). The New Testament is elsewhere clear that Jesus' entry into the resurrected life, especially as reigning Son of God, is effected by the Holy Spirit (Rom. 1.4; 8.11). Given this, and given that the author of Hebrews explicitly states that Melchizedek 'resembles the Son of God' (Heb. 7.3), one can defensibly surmise that the scriptures present Melchizedek as a priest anointed with the Spirit, the same Spirit that bestows resurrection life on the ultimate Anointed One. For

being clearly within the visible community of God; it is not his religion or his priestliness (or any priestliness within or without the visible community of God) which determines that the Spirit rests upon him. The church can neither be so assured in its own religiosity to presuppose the Spirit's presence nor so assured of its singularity as to presuppose the Spirit's exclusivity to it.

For Bonhoeffer, similar concerns also permeate his thought. Bonhoeffer's 'Outline for a Book' includes in it the statement: 'We cannot ... simply identify ourselves with the church.'[26] This is a problem that he associates with Roman Catholicism and significantly also with the Confessing Church. Similar concerns (though more traditionally expressed) are present in Bonhoeffer's early writings. In these, he is clear that the Kingdom of God is always greater than the church. Even in his most ecclesial writings, Bonhoeffer realizes that the activity of God is always greater than the activity of God within the bounds of the *ecclesia*. He writes, for example:

> The purpose of God's rule is the Realm of God. This Realm includes all those who are predestined; the church, in contrast, includes only those who are elected in Christ as church-community (Eph. 1:4; 1 Peter 1:20). Thus the former exists from eternity to eternity, while the latter has its beginning in history.[27]

While Bonhoeffer is concerned that the empirical church receives due consideration in order that reflection on ecclesiology is conducted with due attention to the being of the lived church of believers, he is, even in his earliest work, emphatic that this should not simply be identified with a religious society:

> The empirical church is not at all identical with religious community. Rather, as a concrete historical community, in the relativity of its forms and in its imperfect and modest appearance, it is the body of Christ, Christ's presence on earth, for it has his word. An understanding of the empirical church is possible only in a movement from above to below, or from inner to outer, but not vice versa.[28]

Due ordering of the discussion of ecclesiology is present in this in terms of the categories of 'the movement above to below': we must begin with understanding the church as the act of God and then examining that act, not examining the church and seeking to understand how or why it is that God acts within it.[29] Only

---

the best recent work on these themes, see David M. Moffitt, A*tonement and the Logic of Resurrection in the Epistle to the Hebrews*, NovTSup 141 (Leiden: Brill, 2011), 200-8.

26. Bonhoeffer, *Letters and Papers from Prison*, 503.

27. Bonhoeffer, *Sanctorum Communio*, 217-18.

28. Bonhoeffer, *Sanctorum Communio*, 209. Bonhoeffer goes on to discuss the way in which the church can, following this statement, be understood to be a religious community which is really established by God.

29. This distinction is important with regard to many church growth strategies, or the likes, which seek to create the conditions in the church by which God might be present

in the context of recognizing the church as a community dependent upon God's gracious act is it then possible to reflect on the narrower category of the empirical church. In this narrower reflection, it is then possible to recognize openly and primarily that the latter is always imperfect, incomplete and modest.[30]

What, however, is the significance of this ecclesiological modelling for a theology against religion? This is in the first instance threefold. First, recognizing the proper ordering of theological reflection, and prioritizing pneumatology over ecclesiology, which exists only as a subset of the former, determines that God's Spirit is not institutionalized into a religious prison. The Spirit who is free to blow wherever He wills establishes the church by His gracious act; the church does not determine the presence of the Spirit. This allows for a greater openness to the idea that God is present outside the walls and confines of the church.[31] Second, realizing the dependence of the church on the presence of the Spirit, who enables the church to proclaim the Lordship of Jesus Christ, guards the church against any purism or idealization of its nature: since the church arises from the gracious act of the Spirit, there is the space for the reality of lived, human contingent life in failed and broken communities; the quality of the community does not determine the presence of the Spirit as the Spirit generates the community. Thus, the church is protected from purism or Puritanicalism, as the Spirit is God's operation with real human beings in real lived contexts and situations in all of their complexity and messiness.[32] The nature of the church as a people gathered and made the *ecclesia* by an act of the Spirit protects ecclesiology from a preoccupation with *form* and reminds the church universal of its primary identity. In this way, avenues for ecumenism are opened which do not rely on the oppressive monotony of sameness and uniformity, but are open to genuine and visible unity in brokenness. Third, prioritizing the work of the Spirit in the establishment of the church provides the church with the possibility of not replacing one religious essentialist ecclesiology with another. Many recent developments in ecclesiology have focused around *how* best to be church, often concerned with the mode of practice that a church group engages in. Dominant in British ecclesial cultures has been the rise of the

---

(or present more powerfully), in contrast to recognizing that the presence of God is the condition for the creation of the church ex nihilo.

30. Cf. *CD* IV/2, 621.

31. There is obviously a related issue here of discernment. One may well seek to understand this in terms of the fruits of the Spirit. This theme, and that of the discernment of the presence of the Spirit outside of the walls of the institutional church is discussed further in Greggs, *Theology against Religion*, ch. 8.

32. Cf. 'An overweighting of the christological as against the pneumatological determinants of ecclesiology together with an overemphasis on the divine over against the human Christ has led to a "docetic" doctrine of the church.' Colin E. Gunton, 'The Church on Earth: The Roots of Community', in *On Being the Church: Essays on the Christian Community*, ed. Colin E. Gunton (Edinburgh: T&T Clark, 1989), 65.

Emerging Church and/or Fresh Expressions of Church groups.[33] Working to relate social and cultural movements in society more broadly to modes of being church, these groups have nevertheless worked within a framework of asking *how* best to be church, rather than seeking primarily to identify the operative and dynamic work of the Holy Spirit. Their ecclesial framework is no different from other essentialist models of church; and their ecclesial framework is definitively from below to above, seeking to locate in physical and spatial communities the presence of God, and to get people on the 'inside' of a (modified but substantially defined notion of) church in which the visible takes prioritization over God's invisible and universal acts.[34]

Having discussed the nature of the church as an operation of the Holy Spirit, it is now possible to discuss the nature of the church in relation to believers before going on to discuss its nature in relation to the world.

Church as community of intensity and activism

In Bonhoeffer's *Ethics*, he proposes a problem:

> This belonging together of God and the world that is grounded in Christ does not allow static spatial boundaries, nor does it remove the difference between church-community and world. This leads to the question of how to think about this difference without falling back into spatial images.[35]

Indeed, Bonhoeffer sees this as a religious problem, in which by fighting for space, the church becomes a 'religious society' or a 'cult'.[36] An emphasis on the actualistic nature of God's operations with His church is one way to overcome this problem – a problem which to some degree is innate to all religious speech which seeks (unhelpfully) to differentiate secular and sacred spaces. As an act of the Holy Spirit, the church is established as a community of the intensive presence of God for active participation in His service and for His purposes. The

---

33. For more on these groups, see, for example, Eddie Gibbs and Ryan K. Bolger, *Emerging Churches: Creating Christian Community in Postmodern Cultures* (Grand Rapids, MI: Baker Academic, 2005); and Graham Cray, ed., *Mission-Shaped Church: Church Planting and Fresh Expressions of Church in a Changing Context* (London: Church House, 2004).

34. See, for example, John Drane, *The McDonaldization of the Church: Spirituality, Creativity, and the Future of the Church* (London: Darton, Longman & Todd, 2000); and John Drane, *After McDonaldization: Mission, Ministry and Christian Discipleship in an Age of Uncertainty* (London: Darton, Longman & Todd, 2008).

35. Dietrich Bonhoeffer, *Ethics*, ed. Clifford J. Green, trans. Reinhard Krauss, Charles C. West, and Douglas W. Stott, Dietrich Bonhoeffer Works 6 (Minneapolis, MN: Fortress, 2005), 68.

36. Bonhoeffer, *Ethics*, 63–4.

Spirit who is present extensively in the world dwells intensively with particular communities in time for the service and performance of God's will.[37] The church is not, therefore, a place in which one might think of a binary dividing line from the world. It is, instead, the people in which the presence of God, which in God's omnipresence cannot be spatially limited, dwells in intensity by the power of His Spirit in a community in time. This people is thus enabled to proclaim the Lordship of Jesus Christ, and to participate in God's salvific and redemptive work for all creation. Bonhoeffer states: 'The church-community is separated from the world only by this: it believes in the reality of being accepted by God – a reality that belongs to the whole world.'[38] There is a temporality to this operation of God. Not an essentialized and eternal institution, the church is a temporal people in which the actualization of God's eternal purposes takes place by the present by the Holy Spirit.[39] Thus, as Bonhoeffer advocates, 'in order for the church … to build itself up in time, the will of God must be actualized ever anew, now no longer in a fundamental way for all people, but in the personal appropriation of the individual.'[40] This is a calling for individuals to participate in the community which is not extensively and universally operative, but intensively and particularly determined as a vocation for some: 'the vocation of man is a particular and unique event in God's encounter with man which is as such a history, the occurrence and coming into being of a relationship which does not exist always, everywhere and from the very first. Not all men, therefore, are called as such.'[41]

The calling and active engagement of the church is, therefore, a particular calling upon some people to an active participation in the work of God in the present. It is in the context of the church community that this calling is exercised and fulfilled. As Bonhoeffer states, 'We experience our election only in the church-community, which is already established in Christ, by personally appropriating it through the Holy Spirit, by standing in the actualized church.'[42] While this experience is itself the result primarily of God's activity, it is hardly less real for that. The experience

---

37. Language of 'intensity' and 'extensity' is borrowed from Hardy, *Finding the Church*. For more on the dynamic operations of the Spirit and the Son in salvation in relation to God's universal and particular works, see Tom Greggs, *Barth, Origen, and Universal Salvation: Restoring Particularity* (Oxford: Oxford University Press, 2009), esp. chs 5 and 7.

38. Bonhoeffer, *Ethics*, 67–8.

39. Cf. Bonhoeffer, *Sanctorum Communio*, 139. As Gunton puts it, 'Sometimes it has appeared that because a *logical* link has been claimed between the Spirit and institution, the institution has made too confident claims to be possessed of divine authority. The outcome … has been too "realised" an eschatology of the institution, too near a claim for the coincidence of the Church's action with the action of God' (Gunton, 'The Church on Earth', 61).

40. Bonhoeffer, *Sanctorum Communio*, 143.

41. *CD* IV/3, 483. Albeit, it is necessary to keep in mind Barth's comments on IV/3, 491 also.

42. Bonhoeffer, *Sanctorum Communio*, 143.

of election is not a mere and passive assent to a body of knowledge but an active recognition and engagement in the movement of God towards humanity.[43] Barth is worth quoting at some length here:

> The invocation of God by Christians is the subjective, or, as one might simply say, the human factor and element in this history and these dealings. We remember that it is due only to the free grace of God that as there can be dealings with God at all, so there can be the special dealings between God and these men, the history of their encounter, the concrete intercourse and exchange between them, a living relation in which not only God acts but these specific people may and should be truly active as well. The grace of God is the liberation of these specific people for free, spontaneous, and responsible cooperation in this history. In his free grace God purges himself from the base suspicion that he is an unchangeable, untouchable, and immutable deity whose divine nature condemns him to be the only one at work. By God's free grace these people are not marionettes who move only at his will. They are given the status of subjects who are able and willing to act, able and willing to do what is appropriate to them in dealing with him, able and willing to call upon him as the Father of Jesus Christ and therefore as their Father and also as the Father of all men.[44]

The Spirit frees individual humans to participate actively in a community of God's gracious and intensive presence in and for the world.

The nature of this active engagement can be seen in terms of a differentiation between the work of sanctification that has already taken place *de iure* in Jesus Christ and that which takes places *de facto*. This purpose of this *de facto* participation is 'the revelation of the sanctification of all humanity and human life as it has already taken place *de iure* in Jesus Christ'.[45] The church has a purpose directed not towards its own end but one for the sake of the world (see below). As the 'all' of humanity moves towards this goal, so, writes Barth,

> Christianity, or Christendom, is the holy community of the intervening period; the congregation or people which knows this elevation and establishment, this

---

43. Cf. Stanley Hauerwas, *Hannah's Child: A Theologian's Memoir* (London: SCM, 2010), x:

> I do not put much stock in 'believing in God.' The grammar of 'belief' invites a far too rationalistic account of what it means to be a Christian. 'Belief' implies propositions about which you get to make up your mind before you know the work they are meant to do … I am far more interested in what a declaration of belief entails for how I live my life.

44. Karl Barth. *The Christian Life: Church Dogmatics IV/4 Lecture Fragments*, trans. Geoffrey W. Bromiley (Edinburgh: T&T Clark, 1981), 102.

45. *CD* IV/2, 620.

sanctification, not merely *de iure* but already *de facto*, and which is therefore a witness to all others, representing the sanctification which has already come upon them too in Jesus Christ.[46]

The distinctive role for the church, therefore, in God's ultimate salvific purposes for creation is the active engagement in God's ways with the world. There is, thus, a realization of the ontological (for the whole world) in the ontic (for the church).[47] As a member of the church, the Christian is made free by the Spirit and undertakes to engage actively in faith in Christ, obedience to Christ and confession of Christ.[48] This active engagement in God's work will always run the threat of falling into sin (and is already, indeed, an engagement in God's activity by sinners), but the purpose of the church is always to point beyond itself and its present broken and worldly provisionality.[49]

It is in this active engagement in the Christian life that one can find the necessary unity of the Spirit and the word in the church. As the Spirit dwells with intensity on the community of the church, so the church is freed beyond its own parameters. Those who hear God's word are now enabled to proclaim that message as well, repeating what God has already spoken to them. For Barth, the biblical witness testifies that those whom God calls, He commands to speak:

> As God speaks His Word to these men in and with what He does, and as He is heard by them, He gives them the freedom, but also claims and commissions them, to confess that they are hearers of His Word within the world and humanity which has not heard it but for which His work is dumb, and in this way to make the world and humanity hear. This is their *raison d'être*.[50]

The Spirit who enables the Word of God to be heard in communities of His intensive presence calls those communities to engage extensively in proclaiming God's salvation to the world which God has created, saved and will redeem. In Bonhoeffer's words, the church 'must tell people in every calling [Beruf] what a life with Christ is … It will have to speak of moderation, authenticity, trust, faithfulness, steadfastness, patience, discipline, humility, modesty, contentment.'[51] It is this activity to which the Spirit calls *some* in the world for the world. As

---

46. *CD* IV/2, 620.

47. This theme is discussed by Jeannine Michele Graham, *Representation and Substitution in the Atonement Theologies of Dorothee Sölle, John Macquarrie and Karl Barth* (New York: Peter Lang, 2005), 318–20; and in detail in Adam Neder, *Participation in Christ: An Entry into Karl Barth's Church Dogmatics* (Louisville, KY: Westminster John Knox, 2009).

48. *CD* IV/3, 544.

49. *CD* IV/3, 623.

50. *CD* IV/3, 576.

51. Bonhoeffer, *Letters and Papers from Prison*, 503; cf. Bonhoeffer, *Ethics*, 396–9.

Bonhoeffer's words demonstrate, however, this activity is not a preaching which is associated with the purism of the Word, but a preaching with our whole lives of the presence of the Spirit by the fruits He produces: it is more active than simple proclamation-reception; it involves wholeness.

However, when the church feels assured that it is created and formed by the Holy Spirit as a community of intensity and activism, the need once again to turn the critique of religion back upon itself (even in a church's self-perceived purist form) returns. The nature of the church as an event dependent upon the action of the Holy Spirit cannot itself be essentialized into some version of ecclesial purism: the church's very nature as dynamic and actualistic requires a constant alertness to the need to turn the critique of religion back onto itself and its own religiosity even in its quest to be a community formed by the dynamic and actualistic presence of the Spirit. A church against religion can never believe that it has arrived. The point is not that altars must be stripped, but that the very activity of stripping altars is as likely itself to arise from religious desires expressed in ecclesial essentialist forms as the activity of building the altar in the first place.[52] Turning the critique of religion back onto the church which seeks to follow this path away from religion is the critical point: when one thinks one has arrived at avoiding religion as a church, the likelihood is that one has precisely essentialized some form of ecclesial purism which prevents the church from recognizing its dependence on the free activity of the Holy Spirit. The church must avoid the arrogance of believing its form is anything other than that of the broken body in which the Spirit freely chooses

---

52. One of the best examples of the point that is trying to be made here comes from C. S. Lewis' *The Screwtape Letters* in which the senior devil addresses his nephew with the following point:

> I warned you before that if your patient can't be kept out of the Church, he ought at least to be violently attached to some party within it. I don't mean on really doctrinal issues; about those, the more lukewarm he is the better. And it isn't the doctrines on which we chiefly depend for producing malice. The real fun is working up hatred between those who say 'mass' and those who say 'holy communion' … And all the purely indifferent things – candles and clothes and what not – are an admirable ground for our activities. We have quite removed from men's minds what that pestilent fellow Paul used to teach about food and other unessentials – namely, that the human without scruples should always give in to the human with scruples. You would think they could not fail to see the application. You would expect to find the 'low' churchman genuflecting and crossing himself lest the weak conscience of his 'high' brother should be moved to irreverence, and the 'high' one refraining from these exercises lest he should betray his 'low' brother into idolatry. And so it would have been but for our ceaseless labour. (C. S. Lewis, *The Screwtape Letters: Letter from a Senior to a Junior Devil* (London: Collins, 1942), 84–5)

to act intensively.⁵³ There can be no absolute and sharp dividing line between the church and the world both because of God's freedom to work outside the bounds of the church and because of the church's own broken and failed form – even if that form is an attempted enactment of the avoidance of religion.⁵⁴

Church: A community within the world

It is important, moreover, in recognizing this intensive work of God's Spirit as being the basis of the church's existence that one does not confuse this intensity of God's presence with a spatial exclusivity of God's presence as if God were not present elsewhere in the world. The purpose of the church is not to become a reclusive sect separated from the world but to dwell deeply and fully within the world.⁵⁵ While the Holy Spirit sanctifies and makes holy (from without) the community and individuals, this is not done by separating humanity into camps of sanctified and sinners, and engaging only with those whom we perceive as the former. Not only does the gospel message tell of a Jesus who ate and drank with sinners and tax collectors, but it also tells of a Jesus who transformed those categories. Jesus condemned the religiously puritanical Pharisees and suggested that tax collectors and prostitutes would precede them in their entry into the Kingdom of God.⁵⁶ The church must be a place, therefore, which stands with and within the world, not against it.

Even in the very community identifiers of the church in its sacramental order, the unity of the church with the world is found. The symbols through which God initiates and sustains the members of His church are not ones which remove the church from the world but are ones which bind the church to the world. Water is itself the very basic necessity of life for all humanity (indeed, all creatures), and it is by this basic reality that a person is made a member of the people of God,

---

53. This is, I believe, the point at which the presentation of ecclesiology here differs from those of the Radical Reformation as much as from those of Roman Catholicism. Both prioritize the visibility of the church and do not turn the critique of religion back onto themselves. This is particularly the case in ecclesiologies of the Radical Reformation, which have too great a confidence in the visible church (even in its stripped back form). I have far less confidence in the capacity of the church to 'arrive', or the capacity to draw as sharp a dividing line between church and world. In this way, while I have personal sympathy with the ecclesiologies of the likes of Yoder, I am nervous of the quest for the 'pure' church and the ecclesial essentialism in contrast to the world which underlies such approaches.

54. This parallels (ecclesially) Greggs, *Theology against Religion*, ch. 5 on continued existence of sin in the believer and the broader hope of salvation.

55. There are dangers not only in sects which separate themselves from the world but also in radical ecclesiologies which appear at times to shun engagement with secular powers and society.

56. There is an interesting discussion of the Pharisees in Bonhoeffer, *Ethics*, 309–15.

Father, Son and Holy Spirit. The same degree of ordinariness is present in the sacred meal of the Christian church, the Lord's Supper. At the Lord's Table, we are not offered the 'special' elements of the Passover meal – the Passover lamb or the bitter herbs – but we are presented with the body of Christ in the most universal of food substances, bread, and his blood in the normality and 'everydayness' of wine. These elements of grace bind us to the world, as well as to the other members of the church. Furthermore, in the eschatological dimension of the Lord's Supper, the church is also bound to the Kingdom in which the many shall come from East and West to feast with Abraham, Isaac and Jacob. While these symbols of initiation and community membership present in themselves a unity of believers to one another,[57] as those baptized into the community of faith and sustained by the consumption of the bread and wine as the body and blood of Christ, these very sacramental elements not only bind Christians to one another but also, in the simplicity and ordinariness (one could say, in the secularity) of the signs God has chosen of bread and wine and water, to the very created order and to the ordinariness of everyday life in which God's Spirit is at work. Indeed, there is a degree to which the church is the place which demonstrates true sociality with the world, as opposed to any antisocial religious expression of individual or collective egoism. As Barth puts it,

> Solidarity with the world means that those who are genuinely pious approach the children of the world as such, that those who are genuinely righteous are not ashamed to sit down with the unrighteous as friends, that those who are genuinely wise do not hesitate to seem to be fools among fools, and that those who are genuinely holy are not too good or irreproachable to go down 'into hell' in a very secular fashion.[58]

Genuine piety and faith involve deep sociality with the world, not a collective egoistical separation from the world.[59]

---

57. The importance of unity for the sacraments was present in the church from earliest times. See, for example, 1 Cor. 11.19; *Did.* 9: 'As this broken bread, once dispersed over the hills, was brought together and became one loaf, so may thy Church be brought together'; and Ignatius, *Magn.* 7.2, *Trall.* 7.2 and *Phld.* 4 (translation taken from Maxwell Stamforth and Andrew Louth, eds, *Early Christian Writings: The Apostolic Fathers* (London: Penguin, 1987).

58. *CD* IV/3, 774.

59. Clifford Green discusses this in terms of Bonhoeffer's Christology in *Sanctorum Communio* thus:

> The new humanity of Christ, socially concrete in the church, is presented in the third act of the drama of all humanity from creation (primal community), through fall (broken community), to reconciliation. This Christology and ecclesiology, therefore, is concerned with the rehabilitation and renovation of genuine humanity for all people. Christ is the Kollektivperson of the new

As has already been discussed, it is significant to note that the direction of Barth's writing is always from the world to the community to the individual, and therefore our capacity to understand God's being *pro me* (even in the collective *pro me*) exists only within the context of God's being radically and firstly *pro nobis*.[60] This has profound effects on expressions of the community: 'The solidarity of the community with the world consists quite simply in the active recognition that it, too, since Jesus Christ is the Saviour of the world, can exist in worldly fashion, not unwillingly nor with a bad conscience, but willingly and with a good conscience.'[61] There is thus a need for the church to stand on the side of the world, and not simply against it. This involves community engagement with the world, a deep sociality with the non-Christian:

> As those who are called we are constrained to be absolutely open in respect of *all other men without exception*, exercising towards them the same openness as that in which alone, because the event of our calling can never be behind us in such a way that it is not also before us, we can see and understand ourselves as those who are called. If our assertion has the validity which it can have only as grounded in Jesus Christ and therefore in the work and Word of God, then we cannot view any man only in the light of those factors, e.g., the corruption of his mode of life, the perverted and evil nature of his actions, the untenability of the ideas and convictions expressed by him, which obviously seem to characterise, and in very many cases do actually characterise him, as one who is not called, as non-Christian, unchristian and even anti-Christian.[62]

The church is not, therefore, a community whose concern is its own religion and self-preservation apart from and separate to the world. It is, instead, by the Holy Spirit a community of Christ with and in the world.[63] As such, the church is 'the society in which it is given to men to be under obligation to the world. As they know it, and are united in solidarity with it, they are made jointly responsible for it, for its future, for what is to become of it.'[64] To be the church is not simply to be on the side of the world but to be in part responsible for the world.

The reason for this commitment to the world, and connection to it, arises from the provisional and representative nature of the church. The church's only real

humanity, superseding Adam as the Kollektivperson of the old humanity. Bonhoeffer's thinking is the very opposite of sectarian exclusivism; it moves, like Paul and Irenaeus, on the level of universal humanity. (Green, *Bonhoeffer: A Theology of Sociality*, rev. edn (Grand Rapids, MI: Eerdmans, 1999), 53)

60. *CD* IV/3, 496.
61. *CD* IV/3, 774.
62. *CD* IV/3, 493.
63. Cf. Bonhoeffer, *Ethics*, 96–7, in which Bonhoeffer differentiates a community that reveres Christ (religiously) and in whom Christ takes form.
64. *CD* IV/3, 776.

role is to be a provisional representation of all of humanity in the time before the eschaton – an expression of hope for all humanity which is justified in Christ. It is this which is the church's purpose and meaning in the world.[65] The church's direction is pointed towards the end in these end times, but this is not an end which will see the church's glorification. The end is one which will see the church's own end:

> The end-time is the time of the community. It does not have it and its existence in it merely for its own sake. As we have seen, it cannot be an end in itself. It has it for God, who is so very much for us men that He will not have it otherwise than that before He has finished speaking His last Word some, and even many, should already be for Him. And it has it for the world in order that as a provisional representation of the justification which has taken place in Jesus Christ it may be the sign which is set up in it, which is given to it, which summons it, in order that it may be to it a shining light-a feeble and defective but still a shining light-until the dawning of the great light which will be the end of all time and therefore of this end-time, the coming Jerusalem in which Rev. 21[22] tells us there will be no more temple because the Almighty God will Himself be its temple. The Christian community will then have rendered its service.[66]

Far from an everlasting religious community,[67] the apocalyptic community will need no temple as God will be the temple, and all of humanity will share in this eschatologically fulfilled community.

Given this eschatological direction to the nature of the church (an eschatological direction which will see its fulfilment in there being no need for the church), the church's nature is such that it is directed towards its end. The purpose of the church is thus not to seek to glorify itself but to seek to serve the world by speaking of and demonstrating the justification and sanctification awaiting all humanity. While the distinction already discussed between *de iure* and *de facto* participation exists, this is not eternally determinative. Instead, Barth continues in his discussion of this distinction by stating of the church's representative function in relation to the *de facto* the following:

> This representation is provisional. It is provisional because it has not yet achieved it, nor will it do so. It can only attest it 'in the puzzling form of a reflection' (1 Cor. 13[12]). And it is provisional because, although it comes from the resurrection of Jesus Christ, it is only on the way with others to His return, and therefore to the direct and universal and definitive revelation of His work as it has been accomplished for them and for all men.[68]

65. *CD* IV/1, 727.
66. *CD* IV/1, 739.
67. 'An inescapable characteristic of the Church is … that as part of creation it, too, is finite and contingent' (Gunton, 'The Church on Earth', 67).
68. *CD* IV/3, 620–1.

This provisionality does not mean that divine work is not done effectively and genuinely within the church,[69] but it does mean that the church is not the only community destined for eternal salvation as one religious sect in distinction from all other religious or non-religious sects. The church is, instead, representational of all humanity, and it is the task of representation with which the church is charged. The church is thus 'savingly necessary', but as a demonstration of God's present (and not simply past or future eschatological) saving work each day:[70] 'For the Jesus Christ who rules the world *ad dexteram Patris omnipotentis* is identical with the King of this people of His which on earth finds itself on this way and in this movement.'[71] However, this movement is a 'fitting of the Christian community for the provisional representation of the universal scope (concealed as yet) of the person and work of Jesus Christ.'[72] Indeed, the sin into which the church is constantly in danger of falling is precisely that of 'trying to represent itself rather than the sanctification which has taken place in Jesus Christ; of trying to forget that its existence is provisional, and that it can exist only as it points beyond itself'.[73]

Bonhoeffer engages in similar reflections to Barth on provisional representation in terms of his categories of the ultimate and the penultimate, categories indeed which Bonhoeffer thinks may have special reference to his reflections on religionless Christianity and the church.[74] While the context of Bonhoeffer's discussion of the ultimate and the penultimate is ethical, the implications of his thought may well bear fruit (as he thought it might) for ecclesiological reflections after Christendom. Bonhoeffer is deeply concerned with a Christianity or a theology or ethics which fails properly to attend to the simultaneity of the ultimate and the penultimate. Prioritizing one or other of these, advocates Bonhoeffer, leads to one of two extreme resolutions (extreme because they set the ultimate and the penultimate up as oppositions) – either the radical approach or the approach of compromise.[75] The radical solution attends only to the ultimate, seeking to break free from all that is penultimate;[76] the opposite solution of compromise attends only to the penultimate, breaking with the ultimate.[77] Bonhoeffer neatly summarizes these positions as follows:

Radicalism hates time. Compromise hates eternity.
Radicalism hates patience. Compromise hates decision.
Radicalism hates wisdom. Compromise hates simplicity.

69. *CD* IV/3, 621.
70. *CD* IV/3, 621.
71. *CD* IV/3, 622.
72. *CD* IV/3, 623.
73. *CD* IV/3, 622–3.
74. Bonhoeffer, *Letters and Papers from Prison*, 365.
75. Bonhoeffer, *Ethics*, 153.
76. Bonhoeffer, *Ethics*, 153.
77. Bonhoeffer, *Ethics*, 154.

Radicalism hates measure. Compromise hates the immeasurable.
Radicalism hates the real. Compromise hates the word.[78]

For Bonhoeffer, the only true relationship between these two positions can rest in the person of Jesus Christ, the incarnation of God in human flesh.[79] However, his perspective on the ultimate and the penultimate may well prove useful in thinking of the church as created ex nihilo as the Body of Christ in the present by an act of the Spirit. The danger of the church understanding itself as a radicalized community set against the world is precisely the danger of a religious church community which sees itself as God's presence on earth in opposition to all of the rest of the world (indeed, Bonhoeffer himself sees this as pharisaical);[80] this negative engagement fails to recognize the provisionality of the church in the present, as a community orientated towards its end when God shall be all in all. Indeed, Bonhoeffer hints at these concerns even in his earliest writings:

> A society and a community relate differently to time. If we describe the temporal intention of a community as reaching the boundary of time [*grenzzeitlich*], that of a society would be timebound [*zeitbegrenzt*]. Because of the eschatological character of community, which it shares with history, the deepest significance of community is 'from God to God'.[81]

However, the danger of compromise also lurks within an ecclesiology which fails properly to understand the church's representative function, or else its nature as an intensive community of the act of the Holy Spirit of God. The church is within and with the world, but it is not simply the same as the world, and as Barth puts it, *absolute* tolerance of the non-Christian would not take the non-Christian seriously. Again, Bonhoeffer's earliest writings display these kinds of concerns: 'Only in faith do human beings know the being of revelation, their own being in the church of Christ, to be independent of faith.'[82] The world and the church constitute a differentiated whole, not an undifferentiated one.[83] For the church to exist within and with the world involves the church existing for the world as well.

This existing within the world for the world is precisely a non-religious engagement in ecclesiology, and a fitting expression of ecclesiology in a post-Christendom era. There is something deeply significant in what Bonhoeffer calls the 'structural being-with-each-other [*Miteinander*] of church-community and

---

78. Bonhoeffer, *Ethics*, 156.
79. Bonhoeffer, *Ethics*, 155–9.
80. Bonhoeffer, *Ethics*, 156.
81. Bonhoeffer, *Sanctorum Communio*, 101.
82. Dietrich Bonhoeffer, *Act and Being*, ed. Wayne Whitson Floyd and Hans-Richard Reuter, trans. Martin H. Rumscheidt, Dietrich Bonhoeffer Works (Minneapolis, MN: Fortress, 1996), 118.
83. Cf. *CD* IV/3, 826.

its members, and the members acting-for-each-other [*Füreinander*] as vicarious representatives':[84] this deep sociality recognizes the interconnection of human beings, and (rather than being set against those one sees as other) is deeply engaged in being for others. In Bonhoeffer's early work (from which the preceding quotation is taken) this 'being for' is orientated towards others within the church. However, as his thought develops, so too does the extent to which this 'being for' is a determinative feature of the church for the world:

> The concept of vicarious representative action [*Stellvertretung*] defines this dual relationship most clearly. The Christian community stands in the place in which the whole world should stand. In this respect it serves the world as its vicarious representative; it is there for the world's sake.[85]

As with Barth, this 'being for' is an existence orientated on those outside the walls of the church,[86] in a manner which breaks the introverted and communally egotistical self-imaged idols of the church's creating. Being for the world involves the church prioritizing the serving of others over its own benefits, even to the point of cost to itself or self-sacrifice. In an age in which the church in the West is increasingly small (at least in the European context), the need to attend to the nature of the church within the world as for the world is pressing. Here, emphasizing the Reformation doctrine of the priesthood of all believers takes on new importance.[87] At a time when the church and the society of which the church is a part are no longer the same, and therefore when individual and clerical priests are not able to be vicarious for society at large, the whole community of the church is now more than ever needed to be the vicarious representatives of Christ in the world. How this is so is suggested in the next section of this chapter.

Church: A community for the world

Religion is not as innately communal as is often presumed: the mystic and ascetic often climb to religious heights through solitude and introversion; and even the most communal of religious groups often exercise intra-sociality for the preservation and survival of the communal ego. Bonhoeffer recognizes how these

---

84. Bonhoeffer, *Sanctorum Communio*, 191.
85. Bonhoeffer, *Ethics*, 404.
86. This point provides the foundation for the engagements. Greggs, *Theology against Religion*, chs 7–9.
87. Jinkins notes: 'The church as sign cannot merely point to or signify itself (self-representation) without losing its existence as sign. But the church's existence as sign conveys more than justification; the church signals God's continuing priestly event of sharing God's life with humanity' (Jinkins, *The Church Faces Death*, 83).

tendencies are related to a movement away from God and other human beings, and towards self-alienation and religion. The matters interrelate:

> Human beings have torn themselves loose from community with God and, therefore, also from that with other human beings, and now they stand alone, that is, in untruth. Because human beings are alone, the world is 'their' world, and other human beings have sunk into the world of things ... God has become a religious object, and human beings themselves have become their own creator and lord, belonging to themselves.[88]

In light of such a description, it is not surprising, therefore, that Jinkins argues, 'ironically the church is most attractive when it pursues its vocation unconcerned with its own survival'.[89] The concern for others beyond the collective ego of religion allows that the existence of others is not merely an existence of other human beings within one's own self-created world, in which one's self-created God also exists. The church's vocation is, therefore, communion with God found not by belonging to oneself (individually or collectively), but found instead in the sociality that the act of the Spirit brings about. This vocation of the church is its existence for the sake of the world, and not for the sake of itself. Being a community determined to be for the world itself presupposes a depth of sociality to enable a reaching beyond its own communitarian bounds. This, too, is an act of the Holy Spirit: the Spirit who dwells intensively in the church pushes the church beyond its own walls into the extensity of the world. Put otherwise, one might say that, while faith and hope are gifts to be desired, the gift of love is the greatest to be desired because of its orientation on the other. Barth asserts this emphatically:

> The work of the Holy Spirit in the gathering and upbuilding of the community (*C.D.*, IV, 1 § 62 and IV, 2 § 67) cannot merely lead to the blind alley of a new qualification, enhancement, deepening and enrichment of this being of the community as such. Wonderful and glorious as this is, it is not an end in itself even in what it includes for its individual members. The enlightening power of the Holy Spirit draws and impels and presses beyond its being as such, beyond all the reception and experience of its members, beyond all that is promised to them personally. And only as it follows this drawing and impelling is it the real community of Jesus Christ.[90]

As is demonstrated in the person of Jesus Christ, God is not simply for Himself, but for the world.[91] As the community of witness to Jesus Christ, which brought about by the Holy Spirit, the church cannot simply be an end in itself. The task

---

88. Bonhoeffer, *Act and Being*, 137.
89. Jinkins, *The Church Faces Death*, 32.
90. *CD* IV/3, 764.
91. *CD* IV/3, 763.

of the church, instead, is to be sent into the world within which and with which and for which it exists. The church's orientation is not to be focused on itself as a pure religious community, but on the world, which is no less really God's creation than the church is. Thus far in this chapter, it might seem that there has been little discussion of the church being for God. However, it is in this very being for others that the church is for God, that it executes the purpose for which God has created it and that it fulfils the task God has set it. In the church's reaching beyond itself to the other in love, the church is enabled by the Spirit to participate in mutual love of God the Holy Trinity. In being for others, the church is enabled genuinely to be for God.

Although one should use spatial language with a degree of caution, Bonhoeffer's discussion of these themes is helpful:

> The space of the church does not, therefore, exist just for itself, but its existence is already always something that reaches far beyond it. This is because it is not the space of a cult that would have to fight for its own existence in the world. Rather, the space of the church is the place where witness is given to the foundation of all reality in Jesus Christ. ... The space of the church is not there in order to fight with the world for a piece of territory, but precisely to testify to the world that it is still the world, namely the world that is loved and reconciled by God.[92]

According to Bonhoeffer, a church which fights for its own interests rather than those of the world can only ever be a religious society rather than the church of God. The church's role is instead to be for the world, a witness to the world of the reality it already knows.[93] This task of witness is one which Barth sees as being primary to the role and purpose of the church.[94] The vocation of humans is to be Christian, and by this to be witnesses to God's word.[95] This vocation leads the church out towards the world:

> The Christian is a witness, a witness of the living Jesus Christ as the Word of God and therefore a witness to the whole world and to all men of the divine act of grace which has taken place for all men. Thus, in what makes him a Christian the first concern is not with his own person. He is referred, not to himself, but to

---

92. Bonhoeffer, *Ethics*, 63.
93. Bonhoeffer, *Ethics*, 67.
94. In his excellent work on the post-liberal theologians (themselves heavily influenced by Barth), it is the category of witness that Paul DeHart sees as being the heartbeat of the theologies of both Frei and Lindbeck. See Paul J. DeHart, *The Trial of the Witnesses: The Rise and Decline of Postliberal Theology* (Oxford: Blackwell, 2006), esp. ch. 6.
95. One should note that Barth also discusses the lesser lights in *CD IV/3*, §69, and the reader is directed to Greggs, *Theology against Religion*, chs 4 and 8 for further reflection.

God who points him to his neighbour, and to his neighbour who points him to God. He does not look into himself, but in the most pregnant sense outwards.[96]

The concern of Christians is not for themselves, or their religious purism, but for the neighbours around them. This is because realizing the graciousness of God, the Christian is able to recognize that she exists in the 'most profound solidarity with the great and little sinners' with whom she lives, and to whom she witnesses as most likely 'the first and greatest sinner'.[97] Not only is this the case on an individual level. For Barth, this service of witness is a communal calling: 'The *community* dares to hope in Jesus Christ and therefore it dares to hope for the world.'[98] The church is a community in which there is intensive activity of the Holy Spirit in order that it may witness to the world within which and for which it exists.

For Bonhoeffer, the degree to which the church is for the world as a witness finds new depths in his provocative assertion that the role of the church is to bear the guilt of the world. In this discussion, one might see a creative and contextually appropriate version of the priesthood of all believers in a post-Christendom society. In Bonhoeffer's presentation, it is clear that the church is a minority, but one which should not seek to be a moralistic religious remnant. Bonhoeffer arrestingly writes:

> The church is today the community of people who, grasped by the power of Christ's grace, acknowledge, confess, and take upon themselves not only their personal sins, but also the Western world's falling away from Jesus Christ as toward Jesus Christ.[99]

Bonhoeffer develops this idea thus:

> With this confession the whole guilt of the world falls on the church, on Christians, and because here it is confessed and not denied, the possibility of forgiveness is opened … for there are people here who take all – really all – guilt upon themselves, not in some heroic self-sacrificing decision, but simply overwhelmed by their very own guilt towards Christ. In that moment they can no longer think about retributive justice for the 'chief sinners' but only about the forgiveness of their own great guilt.[100]

---

96. *CD* IV/3, 652. See also the discussion of the category of witness in relation to mission in Greggs, *Theology against Religion*, ch. 5.
97. *CD* IV/3, 653. This is a theme I have addressed in detail in the sub-section 'The co-sinfulness of all humanity', in Greggs, *Theology against Religion*, ch. 5.
98. *CD* IV/3, 720.
99. Bonhoeffer, *Ethics*, 135.
100. Bonhoeffer, *Ethics*, 136. When one considers the situation in which Bonhoeffer is writing about the 'chief sinners', the force of what he is saying is even greater.

In this description of the role of the church, we see a version of ecclesiology entirely at odds with religious approaches: rather than a community identity determined for eternal glorification, one sees a community of the Spirit which is truly enabled to be the body of Christ, bearing the world's guilt and sacrificing itself for the sake of the other. It is here that we see the real self-sacrifice involved for the church which seeks to be for the world. This is a true act in correspondence with the life of Jesus; it is genuinely being within the world for the world.

Conclusion

In the situation of post-Christendom, with visibly reduced power and status for the church, the need to think about ecclesiology is pressing. If salvation (from a Christian perspective) is not simply tied to religious affiliation,[101] the purpose of the church in the world requires rethinking: the normal categories of the church as the setting in which a person may come to have eternal life are no longer appropriate. Barth asks:

> Did the Son of God clothe Himself with humanity, and shed His blood, and go out as the Sower, simply in order that He might create for these people – in free grace, yet why specifically for them and only for them? – this indescribably magnificent private good fortune, permitting them to obtain and possess a gracious God, opening to them the gates of Paradise which are closed to others?[102]

The answer to this question of suspect *sacro egoism* is quite determinately 'Nein!'. The church is not a society that exists for its own purposes or benefit, declaring dividing spatial lines of where God is or is not present, confining God in its own temples and precincts, and establishing itself as a remnant and a moral minority. Its purpose is not religious, but concerns an orientation on the world within which and for which it exists. It is this message which needs to be heard so that liturgies can be transformed in order to praise not an idol but the God of all creation,[103] and so that sermons may begin to share the good news to a post-Christendom world. It is this message which needs to be heard in order that the lives of the saints can demonstrate a wise ordering on God and neighbour. How this good news might relate to the public sphere, and how the church is to be for the world in society is the topic to which this book now turns.

---

101. I argue this in Greggs, *Theology against Religion*, ch. 5.
102. *CD* IV/3, 567.
103. On these themes and worship, see Matthew Myer Boulton, *God against Religion: Rethinking Christian Theology through Worship* (Grand Rapids, MI: Eerdmans, 2008).

Part Two

ESSAYS ON THE CHURCH IN A WORLD OF RELIGIONS

Chapter 9

BEYOND THE BINARY: FORMING EVANGELICAL ESCHATOLOGY

Evangelical identity has its origins in strongly particularist senses of Christian self-identity and has tended to form its own social culture over and against that of the world around (as witnessed to in its puritan and pietist past). While evangelicalism has been happy to assimilate itself to certain cultural phenomena, especially around economic market forces, its desire to be 'in the world but not of the world' determines that many evangelical impulses arise from a form of separationism which relies on straightforward binary descriptors of insider–outsider, saved–damned, elect–reject. Strong particularism gives rise to strong separationism, and underpinning this separationism is often a degree of eschatological self-certainty which seeks such utter self-assurance as to push to the outside anyone who seems vaguely other or an outsider to the central issues perceived to be definitive for inclusion in the Kingdom of God. For this reason, we evangelicals often engage in seeking ever-narrower circles of acceptability – from the reformation to puritanism to pietism to card-carrying evangelicalism of various kinds.[1] Even within the latter, there are often issues which become 'fundamental' to being seen to be insiders, whether that be certain attitudes to the manner in which the Spirit inspires scripture, timetables of the *eschaton* or scholastic arguments about the minutiae of dogma which become defining issues for salvation. What is most pernicious is that often these issues that determine insider 'soundness' arise not from articulations of what we stand for but of what we stand against. Assurance of our place within the Kingdom comes to be governed by what it is we are able to stand against in order to stand on the Lord's side, and the other's otherness to us all too easily becomes the other's otherness to God: perceptions about the present become predictions about the future and judgements upon a person or a group.

Even when, as evangelicals, we seek to be more charitable, our conversation frequently revolves around where we place that binary dividing line. In our more charitable moments, evangelicals may ponder about the pious Muslim, or those who have never heard the gospel, or those who do not have the capacity to

---

1. For a brief history of this, see Stanley J. Grenz, *Revisioning Evangelical Theology: A Fresh Agenda for the 21st Century* (Downers Grove: IVP, 1993), 22–7.

proclaim faith in Christ, or those who die in infancy.[2] However, the question is still commonly who is on the inside and who is on the outside, and shows a worrying preparedness to make eschatological judgements about people today. While we may wish to shout that the judgement in the end is God's, the language of our own theology so often suggests that we are party to the knowledge of who will fall on each side of the divide: to say that God in the end will decide but simultaneously to ponder about the fate of different groups of those outside of the empirical church (and sometimes outside of the soundly empirical evangelical churches) is to make judgements that do not belong to now but properly to the *eschaton*, and do not belong to us but properly to God.[3] In that way, this form of strong separationism is simply the flip side of poor forms of dogmatic universalism – depreciating God's sovereignty and inevitably making judgements about individuals.[4]

No more can this form of binary line-drawing form the basis of our eschatological doctrinal reflection; our binary judgement-making as human beings must be moved beyond the sense that we are able to determine what is meant by *extra ecclesia nulla salus*. The desire to move beyond binaries may be difficult to justify given that the separationist tenor of scripture sounds so clear.[5] However, dogmatic separationist accounts of Christian eschatology often fail to attend to the alarming complexity of scripture and the scandalous particularism which undermines the binary categorization of people in what seems to be a most clear meta-narrative of salvation for the insider and destruction for the outsider. As Barclay puts it, 'a brighter hope can flicker around those dark expectations, often vaguely expressed or seemingly in contradiction to the prediction of utter destruction'.[6] There can be no doubt of the urgency of choosing to be on the Lord's side arising from the

---

2. One can see this sort of enterprise in Nigel M. de S. Cameron, 'Universalism and the Logic of Revelation', in *The Best in Theology*, vol. 3, ed. J. I. Packer (Carol Stream: Christianity Today, 1989), 153–68.

3. To suggest that these dividing lines are necessary in order to know who it is one should try to convert and who it is one should welcome into the church relies on far too substantialized a doctrine of the church. The church is present where the Holy Spirit calls it into being, and its existence is never simply for the sake of itself but for the sake of the other. The church exists, therefore, for those outside of the church: to that end, serving the other (in a manner which recognizes that pastoral work is missionary activity and vice versa) is what is of paramount importance – a point which relativizes the needs to draw such binary dividing lines for ecclesial purposes.

4. In dogmatic universalism, saying all are saved logically determines that each individual is saved and thereby also includes judgements over individuals.

5. David Fergusson, 'Eschatology', in *The Cambridge Companion to Christian Doctrine*, ed. C. E. Gunton (Cambridge: Cambridge University Press, 1997), 241.

6. John M. G. Barclay, 'Universalism and Particularism: Twin Components of Both Judaism and Early Christianity', in *A Vision for the Church: Studies in Early Christian Eschatology in Honour of J. P. M. Swete*, ed. Markus Bockmeuhl and Michael B. Thompson (Edinburgh: T&T Clark, 1997), 216.

call of scripture, but this should not in turn lead to antagonistic and pernicious self-definitions targeted at the dehumanizing condemnation of the other as if we were God, or as if the image of God in scripture is of a God who dehumanizes and condemns.

This essay seeks to address these issues by pointing to the reality that the categorizing of people into two binary opposed camps does not sit easily with either our tradition or the complexities of scripture. The need to move beyond simple binaries in our eschatological speech is considered by pointing to the centrality of grace in salvation (which places the seeming insider beside the seeming outsider). This is followed by a consideration of who the outsiders are in the New Testament and a discussion of the non-absolute nature of individual human beings (which determines the need to look to our own acts which are judged by God). It is hoped that in doing this, evangelical eschatologies will be enabled to be properly refocused on God and the present historical and worldly temporality in which God has placed us, with implications for social, political and economic structures and involvement.

Salvation by grace as the beginnings of evangelical eschatology

Although variously described, evangelicalism must have as its basis the grace of God as displayed in the life, death and resurrection of Jesus Christ.[7] One might say that it is the *sola gratia* which stands as the basis of each of the other great *solas*: only because of God's graciousness does God reveal Himself in scripture; only because of God's graciousness does God elect to be God in Jesus Christ; only because of God's graciousness does God grant us the gift of faith. It is only in living in response to the graciousness of God that evangelicals can understand their piety: the desire to follow Christ, to grow in faith, to engage in works of goodness is enabled uniquely as a response to God's underserved and absolute free-loving kindness. That God calls us to Himself, however God may do that, determines that the relationship with God for humanity is one which results from God's graciousness and not from human work or deserving. Faith is created within the believer ex nihilo from outside of the believer by the Holy Spirit. Undeserving of salvation and of God's fellowship, the believer is granted both of these things by God in God's gracious election of humanity. A belief in the absolute depravity of

---

7. This is implied in both the 'Bebbington quadrilateral' and the 'Larsen pentagon'. Larsen, furthermore, very helpfully differentiates between the (objective) reconciliation with God through Christ's atoning death and the (subjective) work of the Holy Spirit in bringing about conversion and the life of Christian faith. See Timothy Larsen, 'Defining and Locating Evangelicalism', in *The Cambridge Companion to Evangelical Theology*, ed. Timothy Larsen and Daniel J. Treier (Cambridge: Cambridge University Press, 2007), 1, 9–12; and David W. Bebbington, *Evangelicalism in Modern Britain: A History from the 1730s to the 1980s* (London: Unwin Hyman, 1989), 2–17.

humanity underscores this point firmly. No believer deserves God, 'since all have sinned and fall short of the glory of God'.[8]

The centrality of grace determines that conversion should never be understood as a work. Conversion is, instead, a response to God's graciousness which recognizes that grace as undeserved – that is, as gracious. The initiator of our conversion is not the self but the God who makes Himself known by the power of His Holy Spirit. A convert's response to God is only ever a response which is at best abductive,[9] moving towards or turning towards the God who in His movement to us attracts us to Himself. Conversion is not a work which conditions God into salvation, but a response to God to whom salvation properly belongs: 'Salvation belongs to our God who is seated on the throne, and to the Lamb!'[10] Frequently, there exists a confusion of the subjective realization of God's graciousness in conversion and the life of faith with the objective reality of God's saving work on the cross; this in turn can begin to undermine the centrality of grace as the determining feature of the evangelical, as one who pertains to the good news. This does not remove the urgency of response to God's grace, or the call to proclaim God's grace and seek people to follow His will. However, it does determine that we do not understand the act of conversion as a work which brings about salvation. In turn, this determines that we do not equate conversion with God's grace, as if our conversion lulls God into being gracious. Moreover, it determines that we do not place limits on the higher and broader category of God's grace by identifying it only with the response to that grace in salvation. Put otherwise, grace both precedes and brings about conversion, but grace is not simply conversion and should not be empirically equated with conversion.

Recognizing the priority of grace begins to unpick the dangerous binary tendencies of evangelical eschatologies that engage in identifying insiders and outsiders based on judgements about the empirical (evangelical) church. The undermining that focusing on God's grace brings to eschatological reflection can be seen at this juncture in two principal ways.

The first implication that the prioritizing of grace brings for evangelical eschatologies is the recognition of the fallenness and depravity of *all* humanity – even those who have converted. The continued presence of sin in the life of the believer as *simul iustus et peccator* must bring with it the realization that believers

---

8. Rom. 3.10.

9. On the formal nature of abductive logic, see Peter Ochs, *Pierce, Pragmatism and the Logic of Scripture* (Cambridge: Cambridge University Press, 2004), 28–30, 235–40. As applied to Christian theology, see Peter Ochs, *Another Reformation: Postliberal Christianity and the Jews* (Grand Rapids, MI: Brazos Press, 2009); Daniel W. Hardy, *Wording a Radiance: Parting Conversations on God and the Church* (London: SCM, 2010), 40–56; and Robert Leigh, 'The Energetics of Attraction: Daniel Hardy's Theological Imagination, Sociopoiesis, and the Measurement of Scriptural Reasoning', *JSR* 17.1 (2018), https://jsr.shanti.virginia.edu/files/2018/08/LEIGH-READY-FOR-PUB.pdf (accessed on 11 June 2021).

10. Rev. 7.10.

stand side by side with unbelievers as those who have brought and continue to bring sin into the world. Salvation *sola gratia* relies on the knowledge of the undeserved nature of salvation by God. The universality of human sinfulness is such that far from feeling aggrandized or special (and certainly far from feeling an insider), the believer is continually confronted with her wilful disobedience even in the face of her conversion and turning to God. Applied to the contemporary church, Paul's language about the universality of sin not only places the convert in the same boat as the unbeliever, but in a far more precarious position within that boat. Paul asks the question 'Are we any better off?', to which the reply is not simply 'No' but 'No, not at all':[11] given that we who have turned to God know what we should be doing and fail to do it, we surely have no grounds to point to any supposed superior position before God in comparison to those who fail to obey God's will without knowing it. For our purposes, we may put it thus: realizing the grace of God as the source of salvation means that we realize that we stand together with all of fallen humanity – not in one binary category as insiders over and against another as outsiders. With characteristic wisdom, Bonhoeffer states this:

> On the one hand, the concept of the church, as Christ's presence in the world which calls for a decision, necessarily demands the dual outcome. The recognition that the gift of God's boundless love has been received without any merit would, on the other hand, make it seem just as impossible to exclude others from this gift and this love. The strongest reason for accepting the idea of *apocatastasis* would seem to be that all Christians must be aware of having brought sin into the world, and thus aware of being bound together with the whole of humanity in sin, aware of having the sins of humanity on their conscience.[12]

Finding ourselves undeservedly seeming to be on the inside brings with it a realization of the undeserved nature of being on the inside and a co-identity with those who seem to be on the outside.[13] This is no denial of God's holiness (which is often pitted against those who hope for a wider hope) in favour of a monochromic dull version of love, but is instead a wider hope that arises out of realizing God's holiness and our undeserving sinfulness: the more holy we understand God to be, the more our own sin comes into sharp focus and our unity with those we may be tempted to see as outsiders is realized. To recognize this in turn means that the evangelical must question the sharp eschatological dividing line she may be

---

11. Rom. 3.9. Clearly in the context of Romans, this is directed at the Jewish believers, but can equally well be applied to the Christian church in our own position before God.

12. Dietrich Bonhoeffer, *Sanctorum Communio: A Theological Study of the Sociology of the Church*, ed. Clifford J. Green, trans. Reinhard Krauss and Nancy Lukens, Dietrich Bonhoeffer Works 1 (Minneapolis, MN: Fortress, 1998), 286–7.

13. One can see these kinds of thought processes in Barth's considerations of the atheist thought of Max Bense: Karl Barth, *Fragments Grave and Gay* (London: Collins Fortress, 1971), 45–6.

inclined to place between herself and other converts on one side and those many others on the other who are no less deserving of God's love than she is.[14]

It is this blurring of the lines which leads to the second implication that salvation by grace alone brings to bear on evangelical eschatology. This is that we have no right (especially in our precarious position before God) in positing a limitation on the grace of God or to the friendliness of Jesus Christ. Indeed, rather than introduce grace as a principle or almost a new version of the law which is assented to through conversion,[15] it is necessary to understand grace as an outworking of the love and friendliness of the person of Jesus. Knowledge of Christ's love towards humanity, even to fallen sinners as ourselves, should guard us from rushing to place boundaries around where Christ's love and grace can be felt. Much wisdom is to be gained from Karl Barth's own expressed fears concerning those who rejoice in just such a limiting of God's friendliness by jumping anxiously away from the possibilities of a wider salvific hope:

> It would be well, in view of the 'danger' with which the expression is ever and again seen to be encompassed, to ask for a moment, whether on the whole the 'danger' from those theologians who are forever sceptically critical, who are again and again suspiciously questioning, because they are always fundamentally legalistic, and who are therefore in essentials sullen and dismal, is not in the meantime always more threatening amongst us than that of an unsuitably cheerful indifferentism or even antinomianism, to which one could in fact yield oneself on one definite understanding of that conception. One thing is sure, that there is no theological justification for setting any limits on our side to the friendliness of God towards man which appeared in Jesus Christ.[16]

While we may not wish to move from a dogmatic form of separationism to a dogmatic form of universalism,[17] to have a wider hope grounded in the graciousness of God we may wish to point to the tension that exists in understanding our conversion as responses to God's undeserved free-loving kindness – a tension which sees the insider on the inside undeservedly and united to the outsider in shared sinfulness, and which thus makes us undogmatic about where the friendliness of God in Jesus Christ may be found because we are so dogmatic that the friendliness of God in Jesus Christ has found us.[18]

---

14. The doctrine of sanctification does not invalidate my point here: sanctification is not tantamount to salvation.

15. Here is not the place to consider the third use of the law.

16. Karl Barth, *God, Grace and Gospel* (Edinburgh: Oliver & Boyd, 1959), 49–50.

17. 'As propositions, they can only contradict each other. As pictures, they can both be held up, either alternatively or, occasionally, together, as pointers to the God whose grace and judgment both resist capture in a system, or in a single picture.' M. Eugene Boring, 'The Language of Universal Salvation in Paul', *JBL* 105 (1986): 292.

18. 'This very talk of *apocatastasis* may never be more than the sigh of theology wherever it has to speak of faith and unfaith, election and rejection.' Dietrich Bonhoeffer, *Act and*

This tension must lead us to an uneasiness with binary approaches to eschatology: not divided from the outsider but united to her, the evangelical must become cautious of making eschatological predictions regarding the other. Such an emphasis on grace as is appropriate to evangelical theology begins to break down this self-definition in terms of an eschatological otherness to one perceived to be an outsider. However, even if evangelical conversionism and crucicentrism lead to this, it is my contention that biblicism leads us to go further. Taking seriously all of scripture and scripture's ability to address the church today, the evangelical is directed to ask the question: 'Could it possibly be that we are the outsiders?' It is this to which it is necessary now to turn.

Beyond the insider and outsider: Where are we?

To speak of grace as the defining characteristic of evangelical theology, and to address some of the implications of that, does not go far enough. For grace is not an abstract principle that relates to God but is a second-order description of the nature of God as revealed in the person of Jesus Christ. God's personhood determines that theology should never seek to establish propositional principles as if they are able to bind God's person in a prison of our own dogmatic making. The narrative of scripture testifies to God's personhood and His activity with His people. Thus, rather than establishing principles that flow from the abstracted theological idea of God's grace, we do better to attend to the person of Jesus Christ to seek hints for our theological speech and our ethical and ecclesial behaviour. Grace is a mere descriptor of the person of Jesus, a person who must be attended to in His particularity.[19] In this particularity, we may well perceive something of the complexity of the tension pointed to above. Jesus' attitude to those who might be perceived to be religious outsiders to the Kingdom of God (sinners, tax collectors, Samaritans and gentiles) presents a situation which is far from easy to summarize in binary terms.[20] Rather, His relationships with those who seem to be outsiders arises from His person-to-person relationships.[21]

Furthermore, while there is no doubt that Jesus speaks at times in clearly separationist tones, it is not always so clear as one might automatically think as to which side of the binary separation we belong – a point which surely complexifies

---

Being, ed. Wayne Whitson Floyd and Hans-Richard Reuter, trans. Martin H. Rumscheidt, Dietrich Bonhoeffer Works (Minneapolis, MN: Fortress, 1996), 160–1.

19. These are themes I have discussed elsewhere in relation to Barth. See Tom Greggs, '"Jesus Is Victor": Passing the Impasse of Barth on Universalism', *SJT* 60 (2007): 196–212.

20. Although this book is expressed more in terms of a theology of the religions, for some of this complexity, see Gerald O'Collins, *Salvation for All: God's Other Peoples* (Oxford: Oxford University Press, 2008).

21. We should think, for example, of the likes of the Samaritan woman at the well, the Roman centurion whose faith Jesus commends and the Syrophoenician woman.

the matter. As one speaking to the religious people and institutions of his own age (different to our own), we do well to consider who it is that Jesus speaks against in our own times. If God's word continues to speak to us, surely we cannot simply associate the words of Jesus that are directed at the institutional insiders of his own day (the priests and the Pharisees, for example) as simply historical statements about one particular and singular instance of religiosity in His own cultural context.[22] If God continues to speak to us by the power of His Holy Spirit through His word, we must ask the question when faced with Jesus' assertions

---

22. Such singularly historical readings have not only avoided having to address the convicting nature of these passages in the New Testament, they have also led to dangerous anti-Semitic readings of New Testament texts. Biblical scholars have tended to blame anti-Semitic readings on what they regard as overly simplistic analogies drawn between, for example, Pharisees/Jews and legalists (in the popular sense of the term). Such analogies are, arguably, attempts to move beyond 'singularly historical readings'. The infamous, oft-cited example of this is Ernst Käsemann's discussion of 'the hidden Jew in all of us' ('Paul and Israel', in *New Testament Questions of Today* (London: SCM, 1969), 186). For criticism of this and comparable notions, see Daniel Boyarin, *A Radical Jew: Paul and the Politics of Identity* (Berkeley: University of California Press, 1994), 209–14. All of that said, criticism by biblical scholars of such analogies is not always done entirely in good faith. For example, Adolf von Harnack, *What Is Christianity?*, trans. T. B. Saunders (Philadelphia, PA: Fortress, 1957), 50–1 writes:

> [Jesus] came into immediate opposition with the official leaders of the people, and in them with ordinary human nature in general. They thought of God as of a despot guarding the ceremonial observances in His household; he breathed in the presence of God. They saw Him on in His law, which they had converted into a labyrinth of dark defiles, blind alleys and secret passages; he saw and felt Him everywhere.

Crucially, for Harnack, 'they' refers specifically to the *Jewish officials* whom Jesus confronted. This is important since Matthew Thiessen (an up-and-coming NT scholar who draws attention to and attempts to subvert ahistorical, anti-Semitic readings of the NT) quotes Harnack in an inaccurate way. In *Jesus and the Forces of Death: The Gospels Portrayal of Ritual Impurity Withing First-Century Judaism* (Grand Rapids, MI: Baker Academic, 2020), 3, Thiessen writes:

> Consider the words of the early twentieth-century German theologian Adolf von Harnack: '[Jews] thought of God as of a despot guarding the ceremonial observances in His household; [Jesus] breathed in the presence of God. [The Jews] saw Him only in His law, which they had converted into a labyrinth of dark defiles, blind alleys and secret passages; [Jesus] saw and felt Him everywhere.' Harnack's words describe Judaism as dead legalism focused on external ceremonies and then contrast this negative portrayal of Jewish religiosity to Jesus' free spirituality. One can see in Harnack's claims the belief that Judaism is a religion while Christian is a relationship with God.

about judgement – where are we in this text as God addresses His speech to us? What is perhaps most uncomfortable is that as the religious (even if many of us may be uncomfortable with that descriptor) of our own generation, we may be wise to see ourselves as those in scripture who presume we are the furthest inside, for whom the reality may well be that we are on the outside (read here the Pharisees). Are we correct to assume that we are the insiders always, or should we see ourselves as those who presume and perceive themselves to be the insiders while simultaneously excluding others and playing God in thinking we are able to make eschatological judgements about other humans?

Throughout the gospels, we are able to see this undermining of the insider– outsider binary, with those who perceive themselves as insiders finding their self-perceived confidence in their position before God. Jesus is the one who is not only treated as an outsider but who proclaims the Kingdom of God to be for those we might perceive as outsiders: it is the prostitutes and tax collectors (the perceived outsiders) who will enter the Kingdom of God before those who are perceived to be and perceive themselves to be the insiders (Mt. 21.31). And we must be wary of simply ignoring the judgements pronounced on the Scribes and Pharisees as if they were directed only by these historical groups. The living nature of scripture means that these judgements must be understood afresh and anew now for we who might also be judged under the harsh words of Jesus: 'Woe to you ... For you lock people out of the kingdom of heaven. For you do not go in yourselves, and when others are going in, you stop them ... For you cross sea and land to make a single convert, and you make the new convert twice as much a child of hell as yourselves.'[23] It seems that for the religious of Jesus' time and for ourselves, this saying is sure: judgement begins in the house of God.[24]

Lest we think that these charges apply only to historical figures in New Testament times and to see them as otherwise is to engage in flights of hermeneutical fancy, Jesus not only presents us with a discussion which points backwards in history but which points forwards to the apocalypse. In this, we can see at a future point (and not simply a past one) a level of surprise and shock by those who presume themselves to be insiders in some of Jesus' most disturbing binary language: as those who live before the *eschaton*, these warnings surely apply equally as strongly to us as to Jesus' contemporaries. In short, in Jesus' pointing to the future judgement, we are even historically here in the text. In some of the seemingly clearest indicators of Jesus' binary approaches to eschatology, we read about both

---

By supplying in square brackets 'Jews' rather than 'official leaders of the Jewish people', Thiessen has refracted Harnack's words so that they appear to be opposing Jesus to Judaism in general as a religion (an opposition Thiessen regards as anti-Semitic and then spends the rest of his book deconstructing). But Harnack, at least in this instance, is opposing Jesus with Jewish officials, not Judaism in general, while also drawing a line from the historically specific mindset of those leaders to something about human nature in general.

23. Mt. 23.15.
24. This language is picked up from 1 Pet. 4.17.

the sheep and the goats saying: 'Lord, when was it that we saw you hungry or thirsty or a stranger or naked or sick or in prison, and did not take care of you?'[25] Evidently, the eschatological determination of the individual is not simply based on any empirical visibility as to which section of humanity we belong to prior to the judgement, but on the way in which we treat the least of Jesus' brothers and sisters. This appears to lead to surprise and questioning of Jesus' judgement: those who expect to be sheep find themselves as goats, and those who expect to be goats find themselves as sheep. Clearly, there is no easy equating of those who in history are seen to be on the inside or outside with those who at the end find themselves on the inside or outside respectively. Matters are a little more complex than that.

The danger in pointing to such verses for our tradition is that all too easily we can slip into a movement away from grace back again towards a works-based approach to salvation.[26] However, evangelical 'activism' is an activism which flows from faith and is enabled by faith. Indeed, the context of Jesus' words here might seem to point in that direction: the sheep inherit the kingdom which was prepared for them from the foundation of the world (Mt. 25.34), and thus at a deeper level not one which simply becomes theirs by virtue of their actions. How best to understand these acts is thus not a straightforward issue to consider; this is no simple works-based soteriology. But it is equally not a soteriology which confuses the correct belief about justification by faith alone with the grace that justifies through faith.

---

25. Mt. 25.44, cf. 25.37-39. I must acknowledge here the insights of Christopher Rowland, 'The Lamb and the Beast, the Sheet and the Goats: "The Mystery of Salvation" in Revelation', in *A Vision for the Church: Studies in Early Christian Eschatology in Honour of J. P. M. Swete*, ed. Markus Bockmuehl and Michael B. Thompson (Edinburgh: T&T Clark, 1997), 181–92. Rowland advocates that Matthew's eschatological teaching must be read in the context of the whole narrative. When one does this, 'the Gospel leaves readers uncertain whether they can have the assurance that they are among the "sheep" rather than the "goats" ... Indeed, there is a surprise at the identity of the children of God when the Last Assize takes place' (188). Rowland asserts a similar hermeneutical key for Revelation.

26. Clearly, there would be dangers in building an eschatology from any one text singularly. The *sensus plenior* of scripture is what should be desired and sought. A focus on Mt. 25 alone might well lead one along dangerous lines away from justification by faith alone. However, this text is drawn on in order to recognize the warning voice of scripture to an all too self-assured sense of the Christian ability to judge and too great a willingness to systematize the mysteries of salvation into simple dogmatic statement. This essay does not want to undermine justification by faith alone, but to recognize its benefits and challenges in a different way from that often assumed – through the life of discipleship and the assurance of salvation. As Bonhoeffer puts it, 'Because we are justified by faith, faith and obedience have to be distinguished. But their division must never destroy their unity, which lies in the reality that faith exists only in obedience, is never without obedience.' Dietrich Bonhoeffer, *Discipleship*, ed. Geffrey B. Kelly and John D. Godsey, trans. Martin Kuske and Ilse Tödt, Dietrich Bonhoeffer Works 4 (Minneapolis, MN: Fortress, 2003), 64.

One might do well, however, to attend to the reality that as human beings we are determined by our acts: none of us is an absolute being, but we are all the results of the actions we undertake within the contingencies of our human histories. This is a problem for eschatology. Not only are we confronted with a situation of often seeking to describe the absolute judgements made over non-absolute beings, but we are also confronted with issues regarding justice, such as what we consider comprises a person, and whether the whole of a person is the person at the moment of death, and whether a person who dies at an earlier age should be judged in the same way as a person who lives to their dotage.[27] Do we consider potential or only actuality in terms of the way we seek to understand an individual's eschatology? If we understand a person to be made up of the acts in which that person engages (i.e. if what a person does is constitutive of who a person is), then we may begin to be able to move beyond such binary articulations of eschatology which give rise to these issues. If the act of a person is here determinative of the person's place among either the sheep or the goats, rather than who the person understands or perceives herself to be, we must consider what this means for eschatological reflection. It is the acts of a person which are judged here with regard to those for whom the kingdom was prepared before the foundation of the earth. In seeking to emphasize this, but not dangerously morphing it into a works-based salvation, we may say that these actions themselves arise from God's grace towards us: in His grace, He enables us to engage in following after Him with acts of grace which make our being correspond with that of His, which He self-determines through His own acts of grace.[28] Thus, as human beings we are human becomings, whose acts begin to transform our lives to correspond to the will and grace of God. It is these acts which are judged.

But still there remains the issue of how to deal with these acts in terms of non-absolute beings – indeed, beings who are always becomings by virtue of ongoing history and temporality. What constitutes a person who progresses towards her end? Is the end of a person's life the fullest or even the only point at which a person truly is who she is? Is a person the same person today as she was ten years ago and so on? As historical creatures from the perspective of history, none of us is singularly a saint, and none singularly a sinner: for all, there are acts which are sinful and acts which are gracious.[29] Once again (as in the previous section of this

---

27. Cf. John E. Sanders, 'Is Belief in Christ Necessary for Salvation?', *EvQ* 60 (1988): 249.

28. 'In so far as God not only is love, but loves, in the act of love which determines His whole being God elects.' *CD* II/2, 76. For more on the self-determining nature of God's act, see Eberhard Jüngel, *God's Being Is in Becoming. The Trinitarian Being of God in the Theology of Karl Barth* (Edinburgh: T&T Clark, 2001). See further, Paul T. Nimmo, 'Election and Evangelical Thinking: Challenges to Our Way of Conceiving the Doctrine of God', 29–43; and Paul Dafydd Jones, 'The Atonement: God's Love in Action', 44–62, both in *New Perspectives for Evangelical Theology: Engaging with God, Scripture and the World*, ed. Tom Greggs (London: Routledge, 2010).

29. The saint is clearly only ever *simul iustus, simul peccator*.

essay with regard to Christian sinfulness), the binary divide in terms of categories of peoples does not sit easily. Even the most heinous of sinners will have brought about joy and grace throughout their life (even if only as a child to their mothers); and even the most holy of saints is still a justified sinner. A strong belief in the absolute depravity of humanity, however, must surely determine that no good can be produced apart from God.[30] When faced with these issues and the difficulties of knowing to which side we ourselves belong at the great judgement, we may well be wise to say only that God judges those acts which arise from His grace to be in correspondence with His will, and those which do not to be contrary to Him. The surprise of those on the side of the sheep may well indicate that there are some (perhaps many) whose actions of grace arise from God's graciousness without an overt recognition of this: 'Lord, when was it that we saw you?' This may seem strange to our conversionist impulses, but it is surely a reminder that faith is never simply cognition: that is only ever the path to *gnosticism*. Faith is life lived in correspondence to God; in short, faith is innately actualistic. Such realizations help us to understand more deeply the meaning of judgement. Often wrongly confused with condemnation (*katakrinein*), the Greek word for judgement (*krinein*) bespeaks 'separation'. Judgement should not be considered as an act of destruction, but one in which there is separation. And while this may be absolute, it need not necessarily apply to categories of humans as if each were comprised of absolute beings. Paul writes, for example:

> The work of each builder has become visible, for the Day will disclose it, because it will be revealed with fire, and the fire will test what sort of work each has done ... If the work is burned, the builder will suffer loss; the builder will be saved but only as through fire.[31]

There is clearly, for Paul, a further reward for the builder whose foundation survives (v. 14): there are clear future eschatological (as well as present existential) benefits to a life converted to faithful activism. But there is not an absolute judgement made over the non-absolute human, whose acts are judged. Moltmann speaks of this as 'God's creative justice' and advocates:

> The image of the End-time 'fire' is an image of the consuming love of God. Everything which is, and has been, in contradiction to God will be burnt away, so that the person who is loved by God is saved, and everything which is, and has been, in accord with God in that person's life is saved.[32]

---

30. Indeed, a belief in the *creatio ex nihilo* must also determine that that which is good can only come from God.

31. 1 Cor. 3.13, 15.

32. Jürgen Moltmann, *In the End – the Beginning: The Life of Hope*, trans. Margaret Kohl (London: SCM, 2004), 143. Cf. Jürgen Moltmann, *The Coming of God: Christian Eschatology*, trans. Margaret Kohl (London: SCM, 1996). In this, Moltmann sees judgement not as an end but as a beginning (250–2).

Again, this is not to lead us from dogmatic separationism to dogmatic universalism, but to open our theology up to a generous particularism which recognizes the complexities of scripture and of human life. In this way, our emphasis on conversion does not fall into the trap of becoming tainted by post-enlightenment notions of knowledge as abstract bodies of information: no doctrinal statement (even one about the infallibility of scripture or substitutionary atonement) can ever save us. Our understanding of conversion must be to a life of following after Christ in faith – engaging not in acts that save us (as only God in His grace can do that) but in acts that correspond to God's grace. This does not lessen the urgency of mission or of conversion: to live a life without Christ is an unthinkable possibility for the person of faith, and it is to live a life within (existentially and eschatologically) the possibilities of death and hell. However, in this, it is necessary to realize that any acts that correspond to God's grace must flow from God's grace (even if at best met abductively by ourselves through conversion), and it is necessary to find something of the grace of God in the good acts of each builder since it is God who alone brings about goodness within the depravity of humanity.

If the previous section demonstrated the co-sinfulness of all, this section seeks to understand how to describe the goodness of those who appear to be on the outside while making us aware of the acts we engage in as those who perceive ourselves to be on the inside, a perception which may actually place us on the wrong side of our own binary divide. In both, it is necessary to move beyond simple binary language in eschatology.

Attending to the now and attending to God

What does this mean for our emphasis on conversion? Are we depreciated in our place before God? It may be no bad thing for us to be humbled for a while on this score: conversion is only ever a response to grace and never grounds for self-aggrandizement over and against the rest of humanity. However, there is no real reason for such a recognition of the complexities of these eschatological matters to undermine the importance of conversion or to dampen evangelistic zeal. Clearly, a life lived in correspondence to the will of God is the life desired by God and by His church. Lives which result in people determined by their acts of faith in response to God's grace are not only lives which will receive great eschatological reward (we do well here to remember language of Jesus about treasures stored in heaven), but they are also lives which will be filled with the Holy Spirit and the fruits that the Spirit brings. A peace in the present regarding eschatological issues in the future is no small matter, and one which has sizeable pastoral implications. It determines that our eschatological reflection does not merely fulfil the function of preaching 'the gospel at gun point'[33] but offers a possibility of finding peace in the present.

---

33. This is the charge Barth cited against Billy Graham. See Eberhard Busch, *Karl Barth: His Life from Letters and Autobiographical Texts* (London: SCM, 1976), 446.

Eschatology is not a reflection on the teaching of the church about ongoing and continued egoism for all eternity – an egoism grounded in a belief that *I* will go on. Eschatology is, instead, about both life (eternal life) and life more abundantly (full and deep life).[34] Eschatology is not simply about the future; it is about attitudes regarding the present.

Having advocated the need to move beyond simple binary articulations of eschatology given the complexity of the biblical witness, it may now seem odd to advocate the assurance that turning to Christ can bring for the convert. However, herein lies the difference between insurance and assurance. Faith is no contractual insurance policy but is about following after Jesus in a full hope that in the end is God.[35] When as converts we focus on the true and ultimate *eschaton* for all creation – God – then our other concerns, worries and preoccupations are relativized.[36] Here, one may see the clear and full reason for faithfulness: we are saved from the hell of unbelief, and made truly human in the life of faith as we are enabled by acts in correspondence to God's will to become the human beings we have been destined to be from and to all eternity. This is no limitation of justification by faith, but a recognition of its right and proper place – not as if the doctrine were a means of salvation, but instead seeing it as a second-order reflection on the means of the assurance of salvation brought by the realization that before us ultimately is God, the same God whose being we already know is self-determined by the acts of His grace. The life for those without this assurance is a life without its blessings and its peace. This is surely as strong a story and as positive an impulse for the spreading of the *Good* News as there can be. The urgency of conversion is an urgency for transformation of individuals in the present, and through them a transformation of the world.

This has radical political, social and economic implications.[37] However, these political implications are far from those normally associated with evangelical eschatologies – those of building up power in the world and engaging in a binary divisive clash of civilizations: such eschatologies pertain more to Babylon than to the New Jerusalem.[38] When faced with the reality that before us stretches an

---

34. See Jn 10.10.

35. For all that members of the evangelical community may be uncomfortable with J. A. T. Robinson, in the title of his book at least he was right. See J. A. T. Robinson, *In the End God* (London: Collins, 1968).

36. This point puts quibbling discussions about pre- or post-millennialism into sharp relief.

37. For a solid introduction to eschatology and politics, see Robert W. Jenson, 'Eschatology', in *The Blackwell Companion to Political Theology*, ed. William T. Cavanaugh and Peter Manley Scott (Oxford: Blackwell, 2007), 444–56.

38. We do well to remember the power dynamics of the early church which present situations in which they *as the weak and powerless* have true power not in this world but by virtue of eschatological justice. The New Testament Church is as far from a Christian superpower as is possible, and any direct deductions for present nation-state politics cannot be made on the basis of the small and oppressed early Christian Church's eschatology: present

eternity in which is God, the matters of this life begin to be seen for what they are. This is not in a way that should result in an other-worldly focus, but a clear focus on this world. Not divorced from the world as insiders to outsiders, we are judged by the acts which we do that will determine the beings we are in our becomings. Those beings we are becoming are not determined by the strength and power we gain in this world or by the perceptions of those who understand themselves to be insiders in worldly terms. Instead, present worries about ourselves are put into context by a God who will judge our acts based on the way in which we treat the least of Christ's brothers and sisters. The eschatological call to evangelicals is a call to activism in the present, but this must be an activism which arises out of self-sacrifice rather than self-righteousness. If we are to take scripture seriously on eschatological matters, it is time that we cease seeing the specks in our brothers' and sisters' eyes (placing them on the wrong side of the binary divide) and begin to address our own attitudes to money, status and power. When much of the world has little if anything to eat and no fresh water, lacks basic medical provision and finds itself suffering oppression, evangelicals must ask ourselves what our response will be to Jesus' saying:

> I was hungry and you gave me food, I was thirsty and you gave me something to drink, I was a stranger and you welcomed me, I was naked and you gave me clothing, I was sick and you took care of me, I was in prison and you visited me.[39]

Responding to God's grace through conversion determines a following after God's ways throughout life. This is the way of learning to separate (to judge) what is passing from what is eternal through the acts of our lives which determine our being in correspondence to the grace of God, and which display the fruits of the Spirit that arise from that correspondence.

To end where this chapter began, evangelical self-identity often seeks to maintain itself by being countercultural to the world. This is no innately bad thing. The questions to be asked concern more to whom and to what it is we seek to be countercultural. To be countercultural by seeing ourselves as the righteous insiders destined to be eternally on the Lord's side brings with it the folly of a self-perceived insider status that fails to recognize the grace of God to sinners (even sinners like ourselves) and the grace of God in acts of human graciousness. It fails to recognize that in the end is God, and not our own self or our categorization of people. Our challenge in our activism is to be properly and eschatologically countercultural. The call upon evangelical theology is to be countercultural to a culture dominated by the ego (even in eschatological discourse).[40] It is a call to

---

nations (even Christian ones) are not the historical concern but the place of the eschatological rewards of the faithful in a situation of oppression and injustice.

39. Mt. 25.35-36.
40. For more on this theme, see Elizabeth Kent, 'Embodied Evangelicalism: The Body of Christ and the Christian Body', in *New Perspectives for Evangelical Theology*, 108–22.

be counter to those very aspects of society to which we have assimilated – market forces and consumerism, in which worth and value is confused with monetary cost.[41] These so-called values (unlike our actions towards the weak, powerless and poor) will only ever pass away – things to be consumed by the purging fire of God.

Eschatology is about trusting the end to God, for He is the ultimate.[42] And for us now, it is about building up treasure in heaven, and attending to the places where we find Christ now rather than simply waiting to see Him face to face while realizing the connection between these two moments: it is about tending to the starving, helping the oppressed, visiting the prisoner, aiding the sick and welcoming the stranger. For in these acts are our eternal determinations. We must move beyond a simple binary, so often understood through vaguely *gnostic* or enlightenment understandings of knowledge; lives of faith governed by the cross, scripture, conversion and activism are far more than this. Lives lived in response to God's gracious salvation must begin to be lives transformed into grace. In Wesley's words, they shall be lives

> Changed from glory into glory
> 'Til in heaven we take our place,
> 'Til we cast our crowns before thee,
> Lost in wonder, love and praise.[43]

This transformation does not belong only to the future, but begins now as we become children of God, and as our gracious acts correspond to the grace of our Father in heaven.

---

41. One could point here to a range of ways in which evangelicalism could be called to be countercultural. However, the reason for choosing principally financial issues is because this is an aspect of society into which evangelicalism has integrated despite all of the difficult biblical passages about use of money. The focus on this one aspect is not meant to be exhaustive but indicative: issues to do with finance are pointed towards as they are so often ignored and as they themselves comprise issues at the hard of human sociality.

42. On ultimate and penultimate things, see Dietrich Bonhoeffer, *Ethics*, ed. Clifford J. Green, trans. Reinhard Krauss, Charles C. West and Douglas W. Stott, Dietrich Bonhoeffer Works 6 (Minneapolis, MN: Fortress, 2005), 146–70.

43. Hymns and Psalms (London: Methodist Publishing House), no. 267 ('Love Divine, All Loves Excelling').

Chapter 10

APOKATASTASIS: PARTICULARIST UNIVERSALISM IN ORIGEN (*c.* 185–*c.* 254)

Origen grew up in a Christian family, spending his formative years studying and then teaching in Alexandria, before moving to Caesaria where he continued to teach and also to preach. He lived through a period of persecution: his father was martyred and he himself is thought to have died as the result of injuries sustained through the Decian persecution. Origen is famed for many things: he is arguably the first ever systematic theologian, and his *De Principiis* is perhaps the first attempt at a thoroughgoing dogmatics; he was an avid biblical commentator and exegete; he revived the theological school in Alexandria; he created the Hexapla;[1] and he even offered corrections to the Septuagint. However, Origen is perhaps best known in theological circles for one thing above all – his advocacy of universal salvation.[2] When systematic theology mentions Origen's universalism in passing, however, it often does so without subtlety or recognition of the complexity that exists in Origen's corpus with regard to his infamous doctrine of *apokatastasis*, pointing automatically, instead, to its supposed condemnation. Indeed, one does well to remember that *apokatastasis* was not directly or singularly anathematized at the fifth ecumenical council in 553 CE, and it is also worth noting that the condemnations of 553 CE were no doubt more directed at Origenism than at Origen himself.[3] 'Origenism' quickly became a complaint not only against those whose thoughts were claimed (not always accurately) to have been derived from Origen, and, as Edwards puts it, 'once an embittered combatant had found reason for branding one of his opponents an Origenist, Origen might be tarred with every

---

1. This was six versions of the Old Testament (in its various editions and translations) laid side by side for comparison.

2. Much of the argument in this chapter is based on my more detailed engagement with Origen in Tom Greggs, *Barth, Origen, and Universal Salvation* (Oxford: Oxford University Press, 2009). Other aspects of the discussion have also been considered in Tom Greggs, 'Exclusivist or Universalist? Origen "the Wise Steward of the Word" (*Comm. Rom.* V.1.7) and the Issue of Genre', *International Journal of Systematic Theology* 9 (2007): 315–27.

3. See Gregory MacDonald, 'Introduction: Between Heresy and Dogma', in *'All Shall Be Well': Explorations in Universalism and Christian Theology, from Origen to Moltmann*, ed. Gregory MacDonald (Eugene, OR: Cascade Books, 2011), 1–25.

heresy that malice could lay at his opponent's door'.[4] To attend to Origen's account of universalism in detail is no doubt a useful enterprise in order to dispel certain assumptions about his work.

This essay seeks not only to outline Origen's particular version of the doctrine of universal salvation but also to comment on the way in which Origen's universalism does not stand in stark opposition to a particularist agenda. I will take as read in this chapter that Origen is a universalist, though this has variously been a point of dispute.[5] I will instead seek to explain how Origen's belief in *apokatastasis* is related to other of his dogmatic and systematic concerns, and seek to advocate that Origen's version of universalism does not undermine (but arises from) concerns with particularity. To do this, I will first consider the relationship between *apokatastasis* and pre-existence in Origen; second, address Origen's teaching on Christ's *epinoiai*; and third, discuss the relationship between his version of universalism and diversity, growth and sanctification.

Origen on Apokatastasis: *Pre-existence and restoration*

Origen is traditionally interpreted to be an arch-universalist, offering ultimate salvation even to the devil. However, his doctrine of universal salvation is neither universally dominant in his many and varied writings nor univocally affirmed throughout all of Origen's writings. There is, indeed, something of a tension in Origen's works, with strong affirmations at certain points of his corpus of God's sovereign grace, and clearly advocated separationism at other points in his writings. Certainly, *for pastoral reasons* Origen seems nervous about affirming a doctrine of universal salvation in, for example, his homiletic writings.[6] Yet the mapping of Christian theology offered in his systematic theology, along with certain comments offered in his commentaries, clearly suggests that Origen imagined an ultimate end in which all would be well, and God's final victory would be triumphant.

Because of the way in which Origen's articulation of universalism is connected to his systematic mapping of the Christian faith, it is necessary to consider the

---

4. Mark J. Edwards, *Origen against Plato* (Aldershot: Ashgate, 2002), 5. For further on the relationship between Origen and Origenism, and on the political nature of the Origenist controversy, see Elizabeth Clark, *The Origenist Controversy: The Cultural Construction of an Early Christian Debate* (Princeton, NJ: Princeton University Press, 2002).

5. For the perspective that maintains that Origen is a separationist, see Fredrick W. Norris, 'Universal Salvation in Origen and Maximus', in *Universalism and the Doctrine of Hell: Papers Presented at the Fourth Edinburgh Conference on Christian Dogmatics 1991*, ed. Nigel M. de S. Cameron (Carlisle: Paternoster, 1992), 35–58. I have, however, advocated elsewhere that this perspective is erroneous; see my *Barth, Origen, and Universal Salvation*, chs 3, 4, 6 and 7; and my 'Exclusivist or Universalist?'

6. For further details on this point, see my 'Exclusivist or Universalist?'

doctrines that are interdependent with his discussion of universal salvation. If one were to imagine systematic theology as an enterprise that might crudely be thought of as being a little like the interrelation of cogs and levers in a great mechanism, clearly how one manoeuvres certain cogs will determine what happens to the other ones. With universal salvation, this is no different than with any other doctrinal concern. Origen does not write his theology with the propositional concerns, relating to the logical outcomes of positions, that one sees within a hundred years of his death in the debates such as those between Arius and Athanasius, and the multivocity of his theological speech is no doubt left wanting by the standards of later ages. However, Origen's doctrine of *apokatastasis* does arise from his consideration of other doctrinal concerns (and vice versa), and it is necessary to attend to these.

First, one should note that the universalist strand in Origen's theology is strongly connected to his doctrine of the soul. For Origen, souls are substances which exist in all living things. He believes that the word for 'soul' (*psuche*) derives from the word for cooling (*psuchesthai*), the reason for this connection being that the soul cooled as it moved away or was moved away from its participation in the divine fire. It is this cooling in fervour from the divine fire (perhaps related in some way to boredom or over-satisfaction) which is the basis for the soul's fall from contemplation of God. Despite this fall, however, the soul retains its ability to be restored to its original position and nature in relation to God.[7] While it is appropriate to speak of souls as pre-existing from Origen's perspective, with their existence beginning in the eternal fire of God, souls are not eternal in the way that God is eternal: they are 'ingenerate' only in such a way as to be unable to be procreated like bodies.[8]

In Origen's anthropology, the soul is the seat of reason,[9] and Jesus' work of salvation is in relation to that which is rational: he is the one who 'shines on those who are rational and intellectual'.[10] Salvation is necessary, according to Origen, because while souls have the capacity for reason, they may or may not engage actively in the pursuit of it.[11] Christ's work of salvation is, therefore, to save humanity from the irrational.[12] The mechanism of salvation is the soul's

---

7. *Princ.* II.8.3.

8. G. L. Prestige, *God in Patristic Thought* (London: SPCK, 1952), 51; cf. Khaled Emmanuel Anatolios, 'Theology and Economy in Origen and Athanasius', in *Origeniana Septima. Origenes in der Auseinandersetzungen des 4. Jahrhunderts*, ed. W. A. Bienert and U. Kühneweg (Leuven: Peeters, 1999), 166.

9. *Princ.* II.1.2; III.1.13.

10. *Comm. Jo.* I.24.

11. *Comm. Jo.* I.29; Ronald E. Heine, ed., *Origen Commentary on the Gospel According to John*. The Fathers of the Church: A New Translation 80 and 89 (Washington, DC: Catholic University of America Press, 1989, 1993) (hereafter in this essay referred to as 'Heine'), I.190, 72.

12. *Comm. Jo.* I.42.

participation in reason, which is part of its participation in the Logos who is the fount of all reason. The relationship of the Logos to all rational creatures is the special salvific activity of the second member of the Trinity:[13] 'God the Father bestows on *all* the gift of existence; and a *participation* in Christ, *in virtue of his being the word or reason,* makes them rational.'[14] Humans share in rationality as a result of their participation in the work of the Christ in making humans rational.[15] This sharing in rationality is universal among humans: all humans share to some degree (even if just in terms of potentiality) in the rationality of the Logos, and 'all rational beings are partakers of the word of God, and so have implanted within them some seeds, as it were, of wisdom and righteousness, which is Christ'.[16] The Logos is present in all rational creatures,[17] and all human souls have some relation to reason even if this reason is not exercised.[18] Origen utilizes two terms that help to make this distinction: *logika* (all humans) who are distinct from the *logikoi*, a title which can only be applied to the saints. It may be useful to differentiate here in Origen's writing between some form of *passive* participation in the Logos, who supplies reason to all humans (*logika*), and *active* participation in the Logos, through exercise of the human will towards reason (in the *logikoi*).

Because of this differentiated relationship between the Logos and all rational beings, the basis for Origen's universal salvation is one of participation: all rational beings participate variously in the Logos. However, this participatory relationship is not simply passive, and Origen's universalism might usefully be thought of in more contemporary terms as some version of compatibilism in which human freedom and divine determinism are not in conflict. It is not simply, in Origen's account, that there is a triumph of God's will which crushes any sense of human particularity or freedom: Origen is still determined to retain the necessity of active human engagement in working out salvation. Although Origen is clear

---

13. *Princ.* I.3.7. The special remit of the first member of the Trinity is that of everything that possesses natural life, and the third's is the life of the saints.

14. *Princ.* I.3.8, emphasis added.

15. O'Leary suggests that the Son's work for Origen is primarily the perfecting of humanity's innate participation in the Logos (Joseph S. O'Leary, 'The Invisible Mission of the Son in Origen and Augustine', in *Origeniana Septima: Origenes in Den Auseinandersetzungen Des 4. Jahrhunderts*, ed. W. A. Bienert and U. Kuhneweg [Leuven: Leuven University Press, 1999], 610).

16. *Princ.* I.3.6. We should be careful to note that this position is not uniformly articulated in Origen's writing. For a contrasting perspective in Origen, see *Comm. Jo.*, II.4 (Heine, II.60, 109).

17. E.g., *Princ.* I.3.5.

18. Henri Crouzel, *Origen*, trans. A. S. Worrall (Edinburgh: T&T Clark, 1989), 95. Layton, on the other hand, argues that even negative and sinful actions can be seen as rational, as in the case of Judas (Richard A. Layton, 'Judas Yields a Place to the Devil', in *Origeniana Septima: Origenes in Den Auseinandersetzungen Des 4. Jahrhunderts*, ed. W. A. Bienert and U. Kuhneweg [Leuven: Leuven University Press, 1999], 534).

that the greater work of salvation is on the part of God, he is equally clear that humans also have some involvement in it, completing the work of salvation by their active participation in the process of becoming *logikoi*.[19] Nevertheless, this active engagement is not exclusive and only for the saints. Participation in Christ as Logos is not merely reserved for those who recognize God's work of salvation, but it is a participation in which *all* things take a part. For example, all things which have received power participate in Christ insofar as he is power,[20] and all things which have come into being as the result of Wisdom participate in Christ who is all Wisdom – even those who fail to recognize the Wisdom by which they were created.[21] This is connected to Origen's doctrine of the *epinoiai* (see below).

Origen's teaching on the universal participation of rationality in the fount of all reason (the Logos) is the condition for his teaching on *apokatastasis*.[22] Since pre-existent souls have moved from their participation in the divine fire, for Origen, salvation takes place through a *return* and *restoration* of God's perfect, creating will: 'when the Son is said to be subjected to the Father the perfect *restoration* of the entire creation is announced, so when his enemies are said to be subjected to the Son of God we are to understand this to involve the salvation of those subjected and the restoration of those that have been lost'.[23] The pre-fallen condition is what is restored for human beings, and in this way God's creating will and his redeeming will are innately connected. Salvation is seen ultimately as the 'perfect restoration of the whole of creation'.[24] Given Origen's discussion of the soul which was originally a participant in the divine fire but cooled, the restoration that takes place is a restoration to a life in full communion and participation with God – restoration to the full participation in God that the soul once enjoyed. This is the ultimate hope of salvation, in contrast to the present situation of limited, partial and distinct modes of participation in the Logos that the soul presently has. Crucially, this eschatological vision involves the whole of creation, and all human beings. All that is created will be restored. Origen grounds this in theological reflection on 1 Cor. 15.28: 'God will be all in all.' He writes: 'when "God shall be all in all," they [all creatures] also, since they are a part of all, may have God even in

---

19. *Princ.* III.1.18.
20. *Comm. Jo.* I.38.
21. *Comm. Jo.* I.39.
22. For a discussion of the use of this term in the fathers, see Morwenna Ludlow, *Universal Salvation: Eschatology in the Thought of Gregory of Nyssa and Karl Rahner* (Oxford: Oxford University Press, 2000), 38–44.
23. *Princ.* III.5.7, emphasis added.
24. Cf. Brian E. Daley, *The Hope of the Early Church: A Handbook of Patristic Eschatology* (Cambridge: Cambridge University Press, 1991), 58. We can note here a distinction between Origen's version of universal salvation and that of Gregory of Nyssa; see Ludlow, *Universal Salvation*, 258. This is not, however, to deny the transformative nature of restoration for Origen; see John Behr, *The Formation of Christian Theology I: The Way to Nicaea* (Crestwood, NY: St. Vladimir Seminary Press, 2001), 172.

themselves, as he is in all things'.²⁵ The restorative aspect of this eschatological end is the process of the soul becoming a second time what it was before.²⁶

The return of the soul to full participation in God takes place, according to Origen, over a long period of time that might involve purgation and punishment.²⁷ However, this punishment is not absolute,²⁸ but is instead intended to reform the soul:²⁹ punishment is a mechanism of salvation, rather than the determination of condemnation. There is, therefore, no *permanent* hell in Origen's thought, as Origen's sense of God's graciousness always allows for a further opportunity of reform in future ages. Origen asserts that even 'the worst sinner, who has blasphemed the Holy Spirit and been ruled by sin from beginning to end in the whole of this present age, will afterwards in the age to come be brought into order, I know not how'.³⁰ His theory of cycles of ages before and beyond this age allows that even those seemingly beyond any salvation in the present age will receive grace in the future. For Origen, the will of God must be fulfilled for the unjust as for the just:³¹ salvation, therefore, involves all creation and not simply a limited few.

The epinoiai *and varied participation in the Logos*

Origen's articulation of universalism is not one in which a dominant universal undermines all particularity, variety and difference. As Paul considers himself to be 'all things to all', so, Origen writes, 'the Saviour … in a way much more divine than Paul, has become "all things to all," that he might either "gain" or perfect "all things" '.³² Origen does not simply concern himself with binary categorizations when it comes to salvation (the elect compared to the rejected, or sinners compared to the righteous), but is fully aware of the breadth of human interactions with God:

> The Savior, therefore, is first and the last, not that he is not what lies between, but it is stated in the terms of extremities to show that he himself has become 'all things' But consider whether the 'last' is man, or those called the underworld

---

25. *Princ.* I.7.5.
26. *Princ.* II.8.3. This is not, however, the cyclical and endless determinism of Stoicism.
27. However, Origen does on another occasion suggest that purgation might take place 'in the twinking of an eye' (*Comm. Matt.*, XIV.9). There may be lines of continuity here in terms of Rahner's discussion of purgatory (Karl Rahner, 'Purgatory', *Theological XIX: Earth and Ministry* (London: Darton, Longman and Todd, 1984), 181–93).
28. *Princ.* II.10.7. See F. W. Farrar, *Mercy and Judgment: A Few Last Words on Christian Eschatology with Reference to Dr. Pusey's 'What Is of Faith?'* (London: Macmillan, 1881), 330; and P. Tzamalikos, *The Concept of Time in Origen* (Bern: Lang, 1991), 393.
29. *Princ.* I.6.3.
30. *Prayer* XXVII.15.
31. *Prayer* XXVI.6.
32. *Comm. Jo.* I.34 (Heine, I.217, 76).

beings, of which the demons also are a part, either in their entirety or some of them.[33]

Origen interprets Jesus' being the first and the last not in simple temporal terms, but in terms of personal understanding and relationship: the Saviour is first and last to everything in salvation – an angel to angels, a human to humans and so on. Salvation thus seems even to stretch (in speculation and logical outcome at least) to the demonic:[34] the work of the Logos cannot be limited.[35] Origen is insistent that Jesus came for the benefit of (at least) the whole human race.[36]

This logic forms part of Origen's doctrine of the *epinoiai*, or titles of Christ. The form of the Logos is varied depending on the ability of those to whom he directs his economy to receive him. Thus, for Origen, there is constancy in the divine *form* of the Logos, but variety in his *revelation*. Origen's teaching on the titles of Christ is found in its fullest form in the first book of his *Commentary on John*,[37] though it is also present elsewhere.[38] At a basic level, the teaching concerns the reality, for Origen, that 'we do not … all come to him [Christ] in the same way, but each one according to his own proper ability'.[39] Therefore, Christ is 'named in different ways for the capacity of those believing or the ability of those approving it'.[40] Attention is given to the plurality of Christ's names in order to allow for the plurality of means by which one might come to and know the Saviour.[41]

33. *Comm. Jo.* I.34 (Heine, I.219, 77).

34. The salvation of the devil and demons was a point of major concern to later critics and defenders of Origen. We must note that Origen never explicitly claims that Christ becomes a demon, albeit that may well be the logical implication to Origen's thought. Indeed, in his *Letter to Alexandrian Friends*, Origen is not prepared to extend salvation to the devil and demons.

35. Cf. Rowan D. Williams, 'Origen: Between Orthodoxy and Heresy', in *Origeniana Septima: Origenes in Den Auseinandersetzungen Des 4. Jahrhunderts*, ed. W. A. Bienert and U. Kuhneweg (Leuven: Leuven University Press, 1999), 13.

36. E.g., *Cels.* II.33, II.52; *Comm. Jo.* VI.37, I.24.

37. *Comm. Jo.* I.9–11, 22–42.

38. E.g., *Princ.* I.2.1, 4; *Hom. Gen.* I.7; 14.1; *Hom. Exod.* 7.8; *Cels.* 2.64-66. For a list of further passages in Origen's corpus concerning Christ's *epinoiai*, see Benjamin Drewery, *Origen and the Doctrine of Grace* (London: Epworth, 1960), 115–17.

39. *Hom. Gen.* 1.7.

40. *Hom. Exod.* 7.8.

41.

> I frequently marvel when I consider the things said about the Christ by some who wish to believe in him. Why in the world, when countless names are applied to our Savior, do they pass by most of them in silence? Even if they should perhaps remember them, they do not interpret them in their proper sense, but say that these name him figurally. (*Comm. Jo.*, Heine, 1.125)

In his *Commentary on John*, Origen lists and explains the titles of Christ as a precursor to understanding what it is to speak of the Son as *Logos*.[42] Origen laments the tendency of his own contemporaries to 'stop in the case of the title "Word" alone, as if they say that the Christ of God is "Word" alone'.[43] In order to understand Christ as *Logos*, Origen goes on to cite and seek to explain what it means to speak of the Christ under the following titles: 'light of the world', 'true light' and 'light of men',[44] the resurrection, the way, truth, lite, door, shepherd, king, 'teacher' and 'lord', 'son', 'true vine', 'bread of life', 'first and last', 'an angel of great counsel', 'wisdom', 'cornerstone', 'the last Adam', 'a sharp sword', 'a chosen arrow "hidden in the quiver" of the Father', 'servant', a lamb, a man, the advocate, propitiation, power, 'sanctification', 'redemption', 'justice', 'good teacher', 'great high priest', 'Judah', 'Jacob' and 'Israel', 'David', 'rod', 'flower', and 'stone'.[45] He asserts that each of these titles is found in the biblical corpus, and he looks to what he understands to be figural names of Christ in the Hebrew Bible alongside the titles found in the New Testament. It is the multiplicity and superabundance of the biblical titles of Christ that forces Origen to think beyond the traditional titles by which Christ is named. There is order at the highest level of the aspects of Christ (Wisdom and *Logos*), but no one title of Christ is to be so crushingly dominant as to destroy the power of any other.

Origen sees the plurality of the names as a function of the highest title of Christ – Wisdom. He writes:

> And if we should carefully consider all the concepts applied … [to Christ], he is the beginning only insofar as he is wisdom. He is not even the beginning insofar as he is the Word, since 'the Word' was 'in the beginning', so that someone might boldly say that wisdom is older than all the concepts in the names of the first-born of creation.[46]

The Wisdom of God exists hypostatically and eternally according to Origen;[47] and subsisting in Wisdom 'was implicit every capacity and form of creation that was to be'.[48] Wisdom contains, in Origen's thought, the potentiality of all creation in its diversity. By virtue of that, she also contains the many *epinoiai* of Christ, which exist for the sake of the variety of creation.

---

42. *Comm. Jo.*, Heine, I.153–57.
43. *Comm. Jo.*, Heine, I.125.
44. *Comm. Jo.*, Heine, I.168–80.
45. *Comm. Jo.*, Heine, I.181–265.
46. *Comm. Jo.*, Heine, I.118. However, elsewhere Origen sees Wisdom and Word as basically synonymous (*Princ.*, I.2.3). On the order of *epinoiai*, see Ronald E. Heine 'Epinoiai', in *The Westminster Handbook to Origen*, ed. John A. McGuckin (Louisville, KY: Westminster John Knox, 2004), 93–4.
47. *Princ.* I.2.2.
48. *Princ.* I.2.2.

This economic focus of the *epinoia* is important in Origen. Origen differs here from more heterodox presentations of the concept found in the likes of the *Acts of John* and the *Acts of Peter*.[49] While a few titles belong to Christ by essence, others were taken *on for the sake of creation*. Origen asserts: 'wisdom alone would remain, or word, or life, and by all means truth, but surely not also the other titles which *he took in addition because of us*'.[50] There is thus an economic focus to the vast majority of the *epinoiai*. While more heterodox versions of the teaching are focused on Christ's nature, leading to some version of docetic Christology focused on the incompatibility of the Logos and flesh,[51] Origen's version of the teaching is focused on Christ's *work* and is thereby primarily soteriological. Origen is able to differentiate in relation to the *epinoiai* between that which Christ is *in himself* and that which Christ is *for us*,[52] and between that which Christ is not 'for himself' but is 'for others'.[53] The vast majority of the titles of Christ that exist do so because, in his being Wisdom, there is in him the blueprint for *all* the world, which must be reached in its created diversity and variety by the economy of God. The *epinoiai* are, therefore, the way in which the One God reaches out to the plurality and diversity of *all* creation.[54] This doctrine is thus not one in which the focus is on Christ's ontology but upon soteriology, a soteriology that encompasses the whole of the created order in recognition of created plurality. For Origen, the *epinoiai* are primarily concerned with the capacity of creation to know Christ. Thus, without being docetic, Origen can speak of how Jesus' appearance was not simply the same for all who saw him, but varied 'according to their individual capacity'.[55] This doctrine extends, therefore, the hope of salvation far beyond the walls of the church: Christ is not simply known by one salvific title, but by many, and is, therefore, able to relate to more than simply those who name him 'Saviour' or 'Lord'.

Furthermore, one does well not to think of a rigid hierarchy in terms of the *epinoiai* in Origen's presentation (beyond the essential titles listed above). One cannot think of a simple superiority for those who utilize names associated more with the naming of Christ in churches. As noted above, Origen is saddened, for example, by the overly exclusive focus on the title *Logos,* and given that this belongs

---

49. On this topic, see John A. McGuckin, 'The Changing Forms of Jesus', in *Origeniana Quarta*, ed. Lothar Leis (Innsbruck, Austria: Tyrolia, 1987), 215–22.

50. *Comm. Jo.*, Heine, I.123, emphasis added.

51. See McGuckin, 'The Changing Forms of Jesus', 215–17.

52. E.g., *Comm. Jo.*, Heine, I.248 and 25.

53. *Comm. Jo.*, Heine, II.125–6.

54. See Jean Daniélou, *Origen*, trans. Walter Mitchell (London: Sheed & Ward, 1955), 257: 'the argument that between absolute unity and the multiplicity of creatures there must be a being who is one and yet shares in that multiplicity'. Cf. Rowan D. Williams, 'The Son's Knowledge of the Father in Origen', in *Origeniana Quarta*, ed. Lothar Leis (Innsbruck, Austria: Tyrolia, 1987), 147; and Williams 'Origen: Between Orthodoxy and Heresy', 12–13.

55. *Cels.* II.64, cf. *Hom. Gen.* 7.8.

to the titles Christ possesses by nature as well as for others, his disappointment surely points to the significance of each of the titles of Christ. Origen does compare the *epinoiai* to the steps of the temple, and he also points out that there are certain logical relations between certain of them: one must be on the 'way' to arrive at the 'door' and so on.[56] However, Origen does not offer a hierarchy of how each of these titles is related to the complete plurality of the titles of Christ, and it is difficult to know from Origen, therefore, which of the titles corresponds to which stage in the progression towards 'the Holy of Holies'. Origen's focus is not the relative heights of the *epinoiai* but on the full plurality of titles for a diverse world. His concern is to offer hope to the full breadth of creation, which has its full blueprint in God who will redeem it. Despite (or better, within) this diversity, God is able to work his ultimate salvific purposes, and bring all things to full and complete unity in God:[57]

> Finally, when the world was in need of variety and diversity, matter lent itself to the fashioning of the diverse aspects and classes of things in wholly obedient service to the Maker, as to its Lord and Creator, that from it he might produce the diverse forms of things heavenly and earthly. But when events have begun to hasten towards the ideal of all being one as the Father is one with the Son, we are bound to believe as a logical consequence that where all are one there will no longer be any diversity.[58]

This unity marks Gods ultimate salvific work, and comes with full recognition of the variety and plurality of creation.

Diversity, growth and sanctification

It is worthy of note that in Origen's system, there is no removal of the idea of diversity in relation to the exercise of human will, and while he accounts for the full plurality of creation and suggests a universal participation of the rational in the Logos, this does not come at the expense of precluding space for growth in faith and sanctification. Humans are sanctified by participating in Christ's sanctification,[59]

---

56. *Comm. Jo.* VI.26.

57. According to Clark, Jerome rejected the *apokatastasis* because it did not allow sufficient room for a differentiation of heavenly rewards based on ascetic renunciation. While he could allow the ultimate forgivability of sins, he was more strongly committed to a hierarchy in the afterlife. See Elizabeth A. Clark, 'The Place of Jerome's Commentary on Ephesians in the Origenist Controversy: The Apokatastasis and Ascetic Ideals', *Vigiliae Christianae* 41 (1987): 155.

58. *Princ.* III.6.4.

59. *Comm. Jo.* I.39. Indeed, it is through sanctification that humans become like Christ, who is the image of God (*Cels.* VIII.17). In a similar manner, all righteousness and justice flow to the individual from the one Righteousness and Justice who is Christ. See *Comm. Jo.* VI.3 (Heine, VI.40, 179).

and the nature of participation means that some may participate more fully and actively than others.⁶⁰ For Origen, the work of Christ is not only an objective work but also includes a pedagogical soteriology,⁶¹ involving the self-disclosure of God and human progression in the knowledge of God.⁶² This is focused upon those who believe in Christ, and progress is something for which the believer must strive with the help of the Trinity: 'In this way, through renewal of the ceaseless work on our behalf of the Father, Son, and Holy Spirit, renewed at every stage of our progress, we may perchance just succeed at last in beholding the holy and blessed life.'⁶³ It is to the journey towards holiness that the individual is chosen in Christ. For Origen, exercise of the will in terms of progress towards God is considered entirely continuous with predestination. Origen describes predestination thus: 'in the letter to the Ephesians it is written concerning all those to be saved that the Father "chose" them "in him," "in Christ," "before the foundation of the world" *that they should be "holy and blameless before him, having destined them in love to be his sons through Jesus Christ"* (Eph i:3–5)'.⁶⁴ To be chosen is to be chosen for sanctification.⁶⁵ This is the mechanism by which the flesh becomes obedient to the will of the soul and finally the soul reaches the stage at which it is perfect.⁶⁶

Spiritual growth is not confined to the present world for Origen⁶⁷ but also follows in the afterlife:

Alike in these ages that are 'seen' and 'temporal' and in those that are 'not seen' and 'eternal', all those beings are arranged in a definite order proportionate to the

---

60. The soul, which is made after-the-image of God, comes to be after-the-likeness of God (Crouzel, *Origen*, 95); there are clearly multiple points and tremendous variety between these two conditions.

61. E.g., *Comm. Matt.* X.9.

62. See Karen Jo Torjesen, 'Pedagogical Soteriology from Clement to Origen', in *Origeniana Quarta*, ed. Lothar Leis (Innsbruck, Austria: Tyrolia, 1987), 370–8. Young understands Origen's understanding of God's wrath and propitiation in this sense (Frances M. Young, *The Use of Sacrificial Ideas in Greek Christian Writers from the New Testament to John Chrysostom*, Patristic Monograph Series 5 (Cambridge, MA: Philadelphia Patristic Foundation, 1979), 168–70).

63. *Princ.* I.3.8.

64. *Prayer* V.5, emphasis added.

65. According to Daley, Origen 'demythologizes' eschatological thought in a pastoral direction. This is in order that Christians realize that there is a continuity between the present life and the future: humans thus grow towards union with God (Daley, *The Hope of the Early Church*, 48).

66. *Hom. Jos.* 22.2.

67. In this way, Origen may prepare the way for Gregory of Nyssa (Daniélou, *Origen*, 213). However, there is discontinuity here with Maximus the Confessor, who speaks of 'rest' in eternal life (Andrew Louth, *Maximus the Confessor*, Early Church Fathers [London: Routledge, 1999], 66–8).

degree and excellence of their merits. And so it happens that some in the first, others in the second, and others even in the last times, through their endurance of greater and more severe punishments of long duration, extending, if I may say so, over many ages, are by these very stern methods of correction renewed and restored, first by the instruction of angels and afterwards by that of powers yet higher in rank, so that they advance through each grade to a higher one, until at length they reach the things that are 'invisible' and 'eternal', having traversed in turn, by some form of instruction, every single office of the heavenly powers.[68]

Sanctification is, therefore, possible in future ages beyond the present and takes place through punishment and instruction from the angels. There is, therefore, in more modern terms, not only a version of post-mortem conversion taking place here but also a post-mortem sanctification. The early version of the doctrine of purgatory presented by Origen is offered not only negatively in terms of punishment[69] but also more positively in terms of a growth towards holiness.[70]

For believers, the work of salvation takes place in the present through the economy of the Holy Spirit.[71] The saints in the present partake of the 'sanctifying power' of the Holy Spirit,[72] and according to Origen the Spirit 'dwells with the saints alone'.[73] In this, the Spirit provides for the sanctification of the Christian, enabling the Christian to grow in the present towards God. This is a central aspect of Origen's teaching.[74] Although Origen clearly affirms

68. *Princ.* I.6.3.

69. On the doctrine of divine punishment, see Morwenna Ludlow, 'Universal Salvation and a Soteriology of Divine Punishment', *Scottish Journal of Theology* 53 (2000): 449–71; Joseph W. Trigg, 'Divine Deception and the Truthfulness of Scripture', in *Origen of Alexandria: His World and His Legacy*, ed. Charles Kannengiesser and William L. Petersen (Notre Dame: University of Notre Dame, 1988), 159–62; R. P. C. Hanson, *Allegory and Event: A Study of the Sources and Significance of Origen's Interpretation of Scripture* (London: SCM, 1959), 335–40; and Farrar, *Mercy and Judgment*, 330. To compare Origen's understanding to that of the so-called Gnostics and to Clement of Alexandria, see Daley, *The Hope of the Early Church*, 25–7, 44–6.

70. See also Daley, *The Hope of the Early Church*, 57–8.

71. This is also related to Origen's doctrine of baptism, and the particular work of the Holy Spirit in that. See Drewery, *Origen and the Doctrine of Grace*, 172–3; Crouzel, *Origen*, 223–4; Kilian McDonnell, 'Does Origen Have a Trinitarian Doctrine of the Holy Spirit?' *Gregorianum* 75 (1994): 20–1.

72. *Princ.* I.1.3.

73. *Princ.* I.3.5.

74. Daniélou, *Origen*, 103: 'In Origen's view, Christianity is not so much a set of doctrines as a divine force for changing men's hearts.' For Hadot, this is the purpose of all ancient philosophy: 'The philosophical notion of spiritual progress constitutes the very backbone of Christian education and teaching. As ancient philosophical discourse was for the philosophical way of life, so Christian philosophical discourse was a means of realizing the Christian way of life' (Pierre Hadot, *What Is Ancient Philosophy?*, trans. Michael Chase

apokatastasis,⁷⁵ through the Holy Spirit the Christian is able to move towards God in the present, and thus is made holy. Origen writes: 'There is also available the grace of the Holy Spirit, that those beings who are not holy in essence may be made holy by participating in this grace.'⁷⁶ In the present, the Spirit leads humans to their perfection⁷⁷ and brings a purification that awaits all things in the here and now.⁷⁸ According to Origen, the Spirit cleanses the Christian, and offers the remission of sins, and in so doing transforms the Christian into the sweet scent of Christ.⁷⁹ Human will continues to have a role here, and the path to perfection is such that the more one is purified, the more one receives the Spirit. Origen writes that 'the purer the soul is returned, the more generously the Spirit is poured into it'.⁸⁰ However, sanctification comes ultimately from without the Christian, as it is the Spirit who brings about all of the sanctifying work of God: 'All sanctification, both in our hearts and in our words and deeds ... come from the Holy Spirit in Christ Jesus.'⁸¹ Although this particular work of the Spirit is a work in the present with Christians specifically, it is nevertheless eschatologically ordered.⁸² The present work of the Spirit is to sanctify the church in order to bring it to future perfection in heaven.⁸³ In the *process* of this restoration, Christians receive Christ and the Spirit as the deposit of their future salvation.⁸⁴ Through the operation of the Holy Spirit, one is able to see how for Origen there is still space for Christian particularity and the quest for the holy life even within a universalist system. There is in Origen a version of universality that still allows for a greater relationship of the Logos to the saints than that which he has to all other rational creatures. For Origen, it is true that 'he [Christ] is the Savior of all men, especially of the faithful'.⁸⁵ Restoration is universal, but the process of restoring begins actively with those who by the power of the Holy Spirit have faith in Christ.⁸⁶

[Cambridge, MA: Harvard University Press, 2004], 240). According to Crouzel, it is the Spirit who transforms the human from being after the image to being after the likeness of God (Crouzel, *Origen*, 97–8; cf. *Fr. Eph.* III on Eph. 1.5).

75. *Princ.* I.7.5.
76. *Princ.* I.3.8.
77. *Comm. Matt.* XIII.18.
78. *Comm. Rom.* 2.13.32.
79. *Hom. Lev.* 2.2.5.
80. *Comm. Rom.* 6.13.7, emphasis added.
81. *Hom. Luc.* 26.6.
82. See Williams, 'The Son's Knowledge of the Father', 4–8.
83. *Comm, Rom.* 8.5.2.
84. *Hom. Lev.* 4.3.2.
85. *Comm. Jo.* VI.37 (Heine, VI.285, 245).
86. Edwards interprets this in terms of Origen's understanding of two resurrections, in which the saint partially anticipates in her mortal body what will be completed after death and will then be the portion of all humanity (Mark J. Edwards, 'Origen's Two Resurrections', *JTS* 46 (1995): 510). Edwards also rejects Crouzel's belief that one should sharply distinguish between Hades and Gehenna in Origen's system (511, 517); cf. Henri

It is around this point, indeed, that one might detect the reason for the seeming dichotomy in Origen between points in his corpus that appear to affirm universal salvation and points which seem to point towards some version of separationism. Origen is desirous that the future prospect of the universal salvation of Christ does not undermine a desire for the holy life in the present; indeed, it is through progress and holiness that the *apokatastasis* will take place. For pastoral reasons, therefore, he is prepared at times to point towards a limited salvation reserved only for believers. Salvation, in Origen's theology, comes through progression towards God, by the aid of the Son and the Holy Spirit, and universalism should not be preached if it might in any way be considered to impede the growth towards full rationality and holiness, which is the mechanism by which God will restore creation to something even more glorious than its pre-fallen original condition was. For Origen, universal redemption should never, therefore, remove particularity, plurality, history and growth in faith, but should be a hope that arises from seeking to understand the Christian life in the context of a pluralistic and diverse world: he seeks to give account both of the reasons for being Christian and following the life of faith, and of God's engagement with those outside of the church. This is surely one of the great strengths of Origen's account of universal salvation. No doubt arising from a pastoral situation in which persecution was a reality, Origen's universalism is not one of cheap and easy grace. Nor is his account one that renders all of history impotent by virtue of an ultimate love principle that renders all that happens in this world of no significance. Whether successfully or not, Origen seeks to allow for free grace and for a degree of continuity between this life and the next in his account of universal salvation. Faith is important to him – important enough to suffer persecution – and his universalism does not undermine that reality. But, even in a situation of persecution, Origen remains convinced of God's manifold and plural engagements with his creation, both within and outside of the church. Realizing the wonderful complexity of God and his engagement with the world, and the plurivocity of scripture on the issue of who will be saved, Origen offers a hope for all creation that does not undermine

---

Crouzel, 'Hadès Et La Géhenna Selon Origène', *Gregorianum* 49 (1978): 291–331; Crouzel, *Origen*, 240–2, 264–6; Lawrence Hennessey, 'The Place of Saints and Sinners after Death', in *Origen of Alexandria: His World and His Legacy*, ed. Charles Kannengiesser and William L. Peterson (Notre Dame: University of Notre Dame Press, 1988), 293–312. For further discussion of the relationship between universalism and the special place of the saint see Adele Monaci Castagno, 'Origen the Scholar and Pastor', in *Preacher and Audience: Studies in Early Christian and Byzantine Homiletics*, ed. Mary B. Cunningham and Pauline Allen (Leiden: Brill, 1998), 65–87, which advocates that this dual understanding results from Origen's pastoral concern. Although the case is overstated, Celia E. Rabinowitz, 'Personal and Cosmic Salvation in Origen', *Vigiliae Christianae* 38 (1984): 319–29, sees this tension as explicable in terms of the separation between soteriology and eschatology in Origen's thought. I have dealt in detail with this theme elsewhere; see my *Barth, Origen, and Universal Salvation*, chs 6 and 7.

the particular hope of the church. His account of the Christian faith is one that is at once responsible to the faithful life of the church and to the full diversity of the world. In that way, while we may not wish to endorse all of the speculative system that Origen offers, his theology surely still has something significant to offer the present theological age.

Chapter 11

THE MANY NAMES OF CHRIST IN WISDOM: READING SCRIPTURE WITH ORIGEN FOR A DIVERSE WORLD

Aged four when my sister was born, I was asked by my mother what I thought the baby should be called. 'Spiderman Goldilocks Greggs' was my rather bold answer. Sadly (albeit perhaps not for my sister), my mother did not take my youthful advice. No doubt it was because this was a rather silly name, and names say much about us. Indeed, names can be telling of our social class, our age, our schooling.[1] Most of us are known by more than one name. I am always called 'Thomas' by my family, although the majority of my friends call me 'Tom' and old school pals call me 'Greggsy'. Many of us have nicknames, and those of us who are or have children or grandchildren will be known by names which arise from relationships – such as 'Mum' or 'Nana'.[2] It should perhaps be of little surprise to us, therefore, that Christ is endowed with many names in scripture, and that we should attend to the plurality of these and their significance. However, so often theologians are selective of only a few of Christ's titles which become the norm for all of the others. This chapter seeks to consider the wisdom of the many titles of Christ in scripture, and to do so in formative and creative dialogue with the third-century theologian, Origen.

For Origen, the multiplicity of the names and titles of Christ marks a crucial element of his teaching on the economy of the Son, and marks especially a function of Christ's nature as wisdom. In this chapter I assert that, for Origen, the plurality of these names demonstrates that one should recognize that the full diversity of the world must be taken seriously within God's plan of salvation: the universality of the One who will be 'all in all' is not such that it destroys particularity; rather it is a universality which is brought about through a recognition of God's willingness to be involved in the various particularities of creation through the person and

---

1. This is a theme on which the playwright, Alan Bennett, muses a great deal. See, for example, his *Telling Tales* (London: BBC Books, 2001), in which he observes the differing social standings and generations that names indicate.

2. Here and at other points, I must acknowledge a debt to Dr Janet Martin Soskice, who has not only stimulated much thought on the process of naming through conversations with her and her lectures at the University of Cambridge but also read and commented on an early draft of this chapter.

work of his Son.³ This essay seeks first, therefore, to outline Origen's teaching on the many titles (or *epinoiai*) of Christ in scripture. In a second section of the essay, this teaching is applied to contemporary theological concerns.

Origen's teaching on epinoiai

Origen's teaching on the titles of Christ is found in its fullest form in the first book of his *Commentary on John*.⁴ Elements of the doctrine are also to be found in *De Principiis*,⁵ *Homilies on Genesis*,⁶ *Homilies on Exodus*⁷ and *Contra Celsum*;⁸ and vestiges of the teaching can be found scattered throughout Origen's corpus.⁹ At a basic level, the teaching concerns the reality that 'We do not ... all come to him [Christ] in the same way, but each one "according to his own proper ability"'.¹⁰ Therefore, Christ is 'named in different ways for the capacity of those believing or the ability of those approving it'.¹¹ Attention is given to the plurality of Christ's names in order to allow for the plurality of means by which one might come to and know the Saviour.¹²

---

3. One may see here a parallel to elements present in David F. Ford, *Self and Salvation: Being Transformed* (Cambridge: Cambridge University Press, 1999), esp. chs 7 and 8. If Ford's concerns are to present the face of Jesus Christ as the foundation for face-to-face, person-to-person relationships of which humans cannot have a total overview, Origen's concern is to present the names of Christ as the foundation for a superabundant number of interpersonal relations with the Son of which humans cannot have a total overview.

4. *Comm. Jo.* I.9–11, 22–42. Origen, like David Ford who is presently writing a commentary on John's Gospel, was deeply fascinated by the fourth gospel. Sadly, only sections of Origen's commentary remain; but even these sections mark some of his most exciting and creative work.

5. *Princ.* I.2.1, 4.

6. *Hom. Gen.* I.7; I.14.1.

7. *Hom. Exod.* 7.8.

8. *Cels.* 2.64–6.

9. For a list of further passages in Origen's corpus concerning Christ's *epinoiai*, see Benjamin Drewery, *Origen and the Doctrine of Grace* (London: Epworth Press, 1960), 115–17.

10. *Hom. Gen.* 1.7.

11. *Hom. Exod.* 7.8.

12. This is a feature of Christianity which is given little attention, a fact that troubles Origen: 'I frequently marvel when I consider the things said about the Christ by some who wish to believe in him. Why in the world, when countless names are applied to our Saviour, do they pass by most of them in silence? Even if they should perhaps remember them, they do not interpret them in their proper sense, but say that these name him figurally' (*Comm. Jo.* I.125). Christian theology must attend to the many names and titles of Christ, rather than simply attending to one or a certain few.

In his *Commentary on John*, Origen lists and explains the titles of Christ as a precursor to understanding what it is to speak of the Son as *Logos* in Jn. 1.1: a method for enquiring into the meaning and significance of titles which might more straightforwardly be understood is necessary if one is to understand the complex title of *Logos* often attended to by theologians at the exclusion of other of Christ's names.[13] Origen laments the tendency of his own contemporaries to 'stop in the case of the title "Word" alone, as if they say that the Christ of God is "Word" alone'.[14] In order to understand Christ more fully as *Logos*, Origen goes on to cite and seek to explain what it means to speak of the Christ as 'light of the world', 'true light' and 'light of men';[15] 'the resurrection';[16] 'the way';[17] 'truth';[18] 'life';[19] 'door';[20] 'shepherd';[21] 'king';[22] 'teacher' and 'lord';[23] 'son';[24] 'true vine';[25] 'bread of life';[26] 'first and last';[27] 'an angel of great counsel';[28] 'wisdom';[29] 'cornerstone';[30] 'the last Adam';[31] 'a sharp sword';[32] 'a chosen arrow "hidden in the quiver" of the Father';[33] 'servant';[34] 'a lamb';[35] 'a man';[36] 'the advocate';[37] 'propitiation';[38] 'power';[39] 'sanctification';[40]

13. *Comm. Jo.* I.153–157.
14. *Comm. Jo.* I.125.
15. *Comm. Jo.* I.168–180.
16. *Comm. Jo.* I.181.
17. *Comm. Jo.* I.183.
18. *Comm. Jo.* I.186–187.
19. *Comm. Jo.* I.188.
20. *Comm. Jo.* I.189.
21. *Comm. Jo.* I.190.
22. *Comm. Jo.* I.191–200.
23. *Comm. Jo.* I.201–3
24. *Comm. Jo.* I.204.
25. *Comm. Jo.* I.205–6.
26. *Comm. Jo.* I.207–8.
27. *Comm. Jo.* I.209–25.
28. *Comm. Jo.* I.218. On this title, see further, Joseph W. Trigg, 'The Angel of Great Counsel: Christ and the Angelic Hierarchy in Origen's Theology', *JTS* 42 (1991): 35–51.
29. *Comm. Jo.* I.221–223, 243–6.
30. *Comm. Jo.* I.225.
31. *Comm. Jo.* I.225.
32. *Comm. Jo.* I.228, 229.
33. *Comm. Jo.* I.228, 229.
34. *Comm. Jo.* I.228, 230–3.
35. *Comm. Jo.* I.233–234.
36. *Comm. Jo.* I.236–239.
37. *Comm. Jo.* I.240–241.
38. *Comm. Jo.* I.240–241.
39. *Comm. Jo.* I.242.
40. *Comm. Jo.* I.247–251.

'redemption';[41] 'justice';[42] 'good teacher';[43] 'great high priest';[44] 'Juda';[45] 'Jacob' and 'Israel';[46] 'David';[47] 'rod';[48] 'flower';[49] and 'stone'.[50] Each of these titles, Origen believes, is found in scripture, and he traces what he understands to be names of Christ in the Hebrew Bible as well as in the New Testament. It is attention to the superabundant complexity of scripture that will not allow Origen to condense Christ into a system, or to focus on merely one aspect of title of his person. While there is order at the highest level of the aspects of Christ (wisdom and *Logos*), no one title of Christ is to be so crushingly dominant as to destroy the power of any other.

Origen sees this plurality of names as an aspect of the highest title of Christ – wisdom.[51] The wisdom of God exists hypostatically and eternally in Origen's thought;[52] and subsisting in wisdom 'was implicit every capacity and form of creation that was to be'.[53] This is because, according to Origen's interpretation of Prov. 8.22-23, 'she was created as a "beginning of the ways" of God, which means that she contains within herself both the beginnings and causes and species of the whole creation'.[54] Wisdom contains, therefore, the potentiality of all creation in its diversity. By virtue of that, she also contains the many *epinoiai* of Christ which exist for the sake of the variety of creation.

---

41. *Comm. Jo.* I.247–251.
42. *Comm. Jo.* I.252–254.
43. *Comm. Jo.* I.254.
44. *Comm. Jo.* I.255–258.
45. *Comm. Jo.* I.259.
46. *Comm. Jo.* I.260.
47. *Comm. Jo.* I.261.
48. *Comm. Jo.* I.261–264.
49. *Comm. Jo.* I.263–264.
50. *Comm. Jo.* I.265.
51. He writes:

> And if we should carefully consider all the concepts applied … [to Christ], he is the beginning only insofar as he is wisdom. He is not even the beginning insofar as he is the Word, since 'the Word' was 'in the beginning', so that someone might boldly say that wisdom is older than all the concepts in the names of the first-born of creation. (*Comm. Jo.* I.118)

However, one should note that elsewhere Origen sees Wisdom and Word as basically synonymous (*Princ.* I.2.3). On the order of *epinoiai*, see Ronald E. Heine, 'Epinoiai', in *The Westminster Handbook to Origen*, ed. John A. McGuckin (Louisville, KY: Westminster John Knox, 2004), 93–4.

52. *Princ.* I.2.2.
53. *Princ.* I.2.2.
54. *Princ.* I.2.2.

It is here that one should begin to separate the presentation of this teaching by Origen from so-called Gnostic presentations of the concept in the likes of the *Acts of John* and the *Acts of Peter*.[55] Alongside the priority of wisdom, three other titles are given a higher status than the rest. These are the only titles which Christ possesses by essence. In considering which titles came first, Origen suggests: 'wisdom alone would remain, or word, or life, and by all means truth, but surely not also the other titles which *he took in addition because of us*'.[56]

Evident in this is a separation between the singularly Christological nature of certain of the titles and the economic aspect of the vast majority of the other *epinoiai*. While so-called Gnostic versions of the teaching are focused on Christ's nature, leading to some version of docetic Christology focused on the incompatibility of the *Logos* and flesh,[57] Origen's version of the teaching is primarily soteriological. This is demonstrated clearly in the likes of *Comm. Jo.* I.248, 251 in which Origen differentiates (in his discussion of 1 Cor. 1.30)[58] between that which Christ is and that which Christ is 'for us'. Similarly, Origen notes that there are certain *epinoiai* which Christ is not 'for himself' but 'for others'.[59] *The vast majority of the titles of Christ which exist in his being wisdom exist because, in his being wisdom, there is in him the blueprint for all the world which must be reached by the economy of God. The titles are, therefore, the way in which the One God reaches out to the plurality and diversity of all creation.*[60] Not in the first place purely Christological, they are an aspect of Origen's teaching on salvation and creation (two doctrines which for Origen can never be prized apart): rather than principally concerning the nature of Christ, Origen is concerned with the capacity of creation to know Christ. Thus, without being docetic, Origen can speak of how Jesus' appearance was not simply the same for all who saw him but varied 'according to their individual capacity'.[61]

While there are titles which are prioritized (wisdom, *Logos*, life and truth), one should not, however, think of a rigid hierarchy in terms of the rest of the titles in

---

55. On this topic, see John A. McGuckin, 'The Changing Forms of Jesus', in *Origeniana Quarta*, ed. Lothar Leis (Innsbruck: Tyrolia-Verlag, 1987), 215–22.

56. *Comm. Jo.* I.123 (emphasis added).

57. See McGuckin, 'The Changing Forms of Jesus', 215–17.

58. 'He is the source of your life in Christ Jesus, who became for us wisdom from God, and righteousness and sanctification and redemption.'

59. *Comm. Jo.* II.125–126.

60. Daniélou notes that 'the argument that between absolute unity and the multiplicity of creatures there must be a being who is one and yet shares in that multiplicity' is a crucial aspect of Origen's thought (Jean Daniélou, *Origen*, trans. Walter Mitchell [London: Sheed & Ward, 1955], 257). See also Rowan Williams, 'The Son's Knowledge of the Father in Origen', in *Origeniana Quarta*, ed. Lothar Leis (Innsbruck: Tyrolia-Verlag, 1987), 147; Rowan D. Williams, 'Origen: Between Orthodoxy and Heresy', in *Origeniana Septima: Origenes in den Auseinandersetzungen des 4. Jahrhunderts*, ed. W. A. Bienert and U. Kühneweg (Leuven: Leuven University Press, 1999), 12–13.

61. *Cels.* II.64; cf. *Hom. Gen.* 7.8.

Origen's presentation of the *epinoiai*. This is evidenced even with those which have priority: that Origen laments an overly exclusive focus on the title *Logos* is surely indicative of the significance of each of the titles, since even a higher title cannot stand alone. Origen does speak of the titles being comparable to the steps of the temple,[62] and he perceives that there are certain logical relations between certain of them: thus, for example, one must be on the 'way' to arrive at the 'door'.[63] However, Origen does not expound a clear hierarchy of how each of these related *epinoiai* relates to the *full* plurality of the titles of Christ: so, while a prioritized order exists between Christ as 'way' and 'door' and between Christ as 'shepherd' and 'king', there is no indication of how Christ as 'way' might relate to Christ as 'shepherd' and 'king' and so on. It is difficult to determine from Origen, therefore, which of the titles corresponds to which stage in the progression towards 'the Holy of Holies'. Origen's principal concern is not the relative heights of the *epinoiai* but the full plurality of titles for a diverse world, grounded in the belief that both the titles of Christ and creation find their diversity in his being wisdom.

What wisdom does this doctrine yield for today's world?

In considering what use may be made of this ancient reflection on scripture, I wish to focus on the fact that this doctrine is *not* simply an explanation of Christian progression. The emphasis in Origen on the spiritual growth of Christians and the pedagogical work of Christ is well documented.[64] However, it would be wrong to consider that Origen's teaching on *epinoiai* falls under this category of his thought. The teaching on *epinoiai* should, instead, be considered alongside his (in)famous belief in *apokatastasis*,[65] if indeed *apokatastasis* and spiritual growth can be separated for Origen.[66] The *epinoiai* of Christ allows Origen to speak of

62. *Comm. Jo.* 19.38.
63. *Comm. Jo.* 19.39.
64. Regarding growth, Daniélou, *Origen*, argues that, in this way, Origen prepares the way for Gregory of Nyssa (213). This is fundamentally different to the development of the thought of Maximus the Confessor who seeks to speak of 'rest' in eternal life, despite the parallels with Origen noted by A. Louth, *Maximus the Confessor* (London: Routledge, 1999), 67. On Christ's pedagogical work, see Karen Jo Torjesen, 'Pedagogical Soteriology from Clement to Origen', in *Origeniana Quarta*, ed. Lothar Leis (Innsbruck: Tyrolia-Verlag, 1987), 370-8); Frances M. Young, *The Use of Sacrificial Ideas in Greek Christian Writers from the New Testament to John Chrysostom*, Patristic Monograph Series 5 (Cambridge, MA: Philadelphia Patristic Foundation, 1979), sees Origen's understanding of God's wrath and propitiation as an aspect of this pedagogical work (168-70).
65. On *apokatastasis*, see Tom Greggs, 'Exclusivist or Universalist? Origen "the Wise Steward of the Word" (*Comm. Rom.* V.1.7) and the Issue of Genre', *International Journal of Systematic Theology* 9 (2007): 315-27.
66. See here Brian E. Daley, *The Hope of the Early Church. A Handbook of Patristic Eschatology* (Cambridge: Cambridge University Press, 1991), who advocates that Origen

the economy of the second person as it relates to the whole of humanity in all of humanity's variety.

If priority is given to the economy of salvation (rather than to Christology) in Origen's teaching on the *epinoiai*, as I have advocated above, it is not the case that one gains knowledge of Christ's nature as each one of these titles (door, truth, life, etc.) and is then able to participate in the economic function of the title; it is quite the reverse. Participating in Christ as these things enables one to know him under the titles. Hence, Origen writes:

> God made 'all things in wisdom'. Many creatures, on the one hand, have come into existence by participation in wisdom, while they do not apprehend her by whom they have been created. Very few, however, comprehend not only the wisdom concerning themselves, but also that concerning many beings, for Christ is all wisdom. But each of the wise participates in Christ to the extent that [s]he has capacity for wisdom, insofar as Christ is wisdom.[67]

Many things could be said about the logic and content of this short passage, but what one must recognize for these purposes is a variable participation in Christ dependent on the capacity one has for wisdom. This, however, is the important thing to note: it is not participation in Christ which leads to participation in wisdom, but the varied participation in wisdom (in creation) dependent upon capacity which enables varied participation in Christ who is 'all wisdom'. It is a participation in the economy which brings us to knowledge of the person (mediated through the title 'wisdom'), not knowledge of the name which brings us to the economy. To use an analogy, building on the starting point of this chapter, I call my mother 'mum' because I participate in a relationship with her of mother and son. If I called a stranger I had just met on the street 'mum', it would be to a large extent meaningless. Even if I called her 'mum' for the remaining days of my life, if I never participate in the mother–son relationship with her, she will never be my mother. What makes my mother my mother and allows me to call her by that

---

'demythologizes' eschatological thought in a pastoral direction to ensure that Christians realize that there is a continuity between the present life and the future, as all humans grow towards union with God (48). On the relationship between growth towards God and a doctrine of divine punishment, see Morwenna Ludlow, 'Universal Salvation and a Soteriology of Divine Punishment', *SJT* 53 (2000): 449-71; Charles Kannengiesser and William L Petersen, eds, *Origen of Alexandria: His World and His Legacy* (Notre Dame: University of Notre Dame, 1988), 157-64; R. P. C. Hanson, *Allegory and Event: A Study of the Sources and Significance of Origen's Interpretation of Scripture* (London: SCM, 1959), 336-40; and F. W. Farrar, *Mercy and Judgment: A Few Last Words on Christian Eschatology with Reference to Dr. Pusey's "What is of faith?"* (London: Macmillan, 1881), 330. To compare Origen's understanding to that of Gnostics and Clement of Alexandria, see Daley, *The Hope of the Early Church*, 25-7, 45-7.

67. *Comm. Jo.* I.245-246.

title is that she *is* my mother and we participate in a mother–son relationship. As a result of that relationship, I name her thus: the already extant relation determines the name, and not the name the relation. For Origen, Christ's titles are not simply epithets I give to him; they are names that I may call him by *because I already participate in that relation to him.*

The previous example given was a positive one from the perspective of Christian faith – Christ's title of wisdom. However, one can also see the same logic employed with those titles which must surely be understood to be further down the scale. Origen writes:

> We must also consider whether he [Christ] would not have become a shepherd if man had not been compared to 'senseless beasts nor become like them.' For if 'God saves men and beasts,' he saves what beasts he saves by granting a shepherd to those who have not the capacity for a king.[68]

Here the language is of 'beasts' (*ktēnē*) who need a shepherd because their limited capacities make them unable to participate in Christ's title of 'king'. The word *ktēnos* was even used of swine.[69] Given the exacting nature of the catechumenal process, one might find this a rather odd description for a fully fledged baptized 'Christian'. Thus, Christ's title of 'shepherd' enables those who only have the capacity of 'beasts' still to be reached by the economy of God contained in God's wisdom. They do not have to progress to the level of those with the capacity for a 'king' to find a way to participate in God's salvation in Christ. They are reached, instead, in their particularity. It might even be the case that Origen takes this a step further. In his *Commentary on Romans*, Origen discusses what he conceives to be the rather 'astonishing' title of 'a stone of stumbling and a rock of scandal'.[70] However, Origen believes this title is an important aspect of Christ's economy: Christ is the one who is able in this capacity and under this title in scripture, to allow those who are 'running down the road of destruction with swift feet' to participate in his salvation.[71] Thus, Christ is even able to encounter people running away from him as the stone that trips them up in front of hell. Similarly, he is a 'rod' to those in need of his punishment.[72] Christ has many names in scripture because there are many and diverse ways in which humans relate to him, and many and diverse ways in which he relates to the rest of humanity.

When faced as a Christian with a world which is complexly secular and religious,[73] such a teaching has much to commend it. Rather than throwing the truth of Christ like rocks at people's heads regardless of the capacity for someone to catch it or

68. *Comm. Jo.* I.122.
69. LSJ, s.v. ktēnos.
70. *Comm. Rom.* 7.19.8.
71. *Comm. Rom.* 7.19.8.
72. *Comm. Jo.* I.262–263.
73. On this, see David F. Ford, 'Gospel in Context: Among Many Faiths' (paper presented at the Fulcrum Conference, Islington, 28 April 2006); David F. Ford, 'Abrahamic

not,[74] Origen's teaching on the *epinoiai* presents us with a view of the economy of God which takes on board the variety of human capacity, differing situations and complexity of human life. He allows for a picture of God's salvation which is not starkly black or white, and which avoids binary language about salvation in order to escape simple categorization of people as either inside or outside the plan of God. Instead, he recognizes that the plan of God is a plan for all. But this universal does not come at the expense of obliterating all particulars. For Origen, there is a sense of the varied participation that humans have in the economy of God's salvation. Some people can only experience Christ as a 'stumbling block' while others may know him as 'flower'; others may know him as a 'teacher'; and still others will know him as 'Lord'. But in it all, each learns something of Christ in his many titles from participating in the economy and function of those titles, which are prefigured in his eternal and hypostatic existence as wisdom.

In an age apparently of so much religious conflict between elements of each of the Abrahamic faiths, to look to the *many* titles of Christ may be wise. We may be united with the other in certain of the titles of Christ. Furthermore, this need not only be in terms of our participation in his economy, without naming the title. In naming Christ (among all of his other titles) at least as 'Prophet' or as 'Rabbi', we may participate in and name an aspect of Christ's economy, recognized in these titles, alongside Muslims and Jews respectively. As Christians, we may be frustrated that this is not all that there is to Christ whom Origen rightly realizes is first and last. But, with Origen, perhaps we ought also to remember that this does not mean that Christ is not all that lies between, but has instead 'become "all things"'.[75] To focus on but one aspect or *epinoia* of Christ is to fail to attend to 'the fullness of him who fills all in all' (Eph. 1.23).

Dialogue: Towards Respect and Understanding in Our Life Together' (paper presented at the Inauguration of the Society for Dialogue and Action, Cambridge, 2006).

74. This was Tillich's criticism of Barth. See J. Heywood Thomas, *Tillich* (London: Continuum, 2000), 56. Such criticism also perhaps reflects Ford's concern that Christ fulfils the role of a *Bildungsroman* in Barth's *Church Dogmatics*. See David F. Ford, *Barth and God's Story: Biblical Narrative and the Theological Method of Karl Barth in the Church Dogmatics* (Frankfurt am Main: Verlag Peter Lang, 1985), 91–2. For a sample of Barth's reflections on the name 'Jesus Christ', see *CD* I/2, 10–25; IV/1, 16–21; IV/V, 91–100.

75. *Comm. Jo.* I.219.

Chapter 12

READING SCRIPTURE IN A PLURALIST WORLD: A PATH TO DISCOVERING THE HERMENEUTICS OF *AGAPĒ*

Introduction: Why might hermeneutics and agapē *belong together?*

The task of systematic theology might be considered to be the rational explication of the Christian gospel. However, the very purpose of this rational explication of the Christian gospel is to aid the reading of scripture: systematic theology might understand its goal to be the bringing together of biblical expression, to offer in turn flexible and lightweight guides for reading scripture. Systematics and hermeneutics are, therefore, deeply connected in any form of systematic theology which seeks to take the revelation of God's word in the flesh and history of Jesus Christ, and in the testimonies paid to Him in scripture, seriously. In this engagement in rationally explicating the Christian gospel, there inevitably needs to be some use made of philosophy. As Barth reminds us,

> In attempting to reflect on what is said to us in the biblical text, we must first make use of the system of thought we bring with us, that is, of some philosophy or other. Fundamentally to question the legitimacy of this necessity would be to question whether sinful man as such, and therefore with such possibilities of thought as are given to him, is called to understand and interpret the Word of God which encounters us in Scripture. If we cannot and must not dispute this, if we are not to dispute the grace and finally the incarnation of the Word of God, we cannot basically contest the use of philosophy in scriptural exegesis.[1]

This involves not only bringing philosophical categories to the engagement with the biblical text but also thinking philosophically about the manner in which one engages with the text. However, questions immediately rise regarding how this enterprise is engaged in legitimately, or appropriately theologically. Barth establishes five points in his discussion of the legitimate use of philosophy and philosophical categories in theology: we must be aware and clear about every scheme of thought we bring to the text and how this is different from the scriptural word; philosophy can have only the fundamental character of an hypothesis; use

---

1. *CD* I/2, 729–30.

of philosophy can claim no independent interest in itself; there are no essential reasons for preferring one particular scheme to another; and a scheme of thought is useful when it is determined and controlled by the text of scripture and the object within it.[2] While Barth rejects the idea of 'replacing philosophy by a dictatorial, absolute and exclusive theology',[3] he nevertheless cautions:

> As interpreters of Scripture, perhaps not in practice but in principle, we will be able to adopt a more friendly and understanding attitude to the various possibilities which have manifested themselves or are still manifesting themselves in the history of philosophy, and to make a more appropriate use of them, *if the object on which we reflect has put us on our guard against their particular genius*.[4]

If we are to think about the effect of the nature of the object on which biblical hermeneutics reflects, a question arises of what the best way is to think *theologically* about the use of the philosophical categories in the approach of texts. Are there ways in which the schemes of thought utilized might be determined and controlled by the text of scripture and the object within it? Put otherwise: Can we speak biblically about the task of biblical or theological hermeneutics?

One way, perhaps, of expressing *theologically* the enterprise of biblical or theological hermeneutics might be to say that it is the science of reading texts faithfully and hopefully simultaneously. The concern of hermeneutics is not only to attend to the text as authoritative source, seeking to read it *faithfully* in order to attend to what it is saying in its own terms but also to read the text *in the hope* that it might speak to communities today or may have spoken to communities of readers who have understood the text across its transmission through the years.[5] Hermeneutics, therefore, generally attends to the necessity of both explanation (*Erklärung*), an activity which involves the faithful reading of a text, and to understanding (*Verstehen*), which I identify as a hopeful enterprise that involves the belief that the reading of a text might offer, to use the words of Anthony Thiselton, 'a more personal, intuitive, or suprarational dimension'.[6] This engagement in seeking to understand these two horizons of a text requires in its own terms, furthermore, that it is not simply a speculative theoretical engagement in *Wissenschaft*, but a genuinely formative, communal way of approaching the text, in contrast to any individualistic and (ironically) universalized approach that

---

2. *CD* I/2, 730-4.
3. *CD* I/2, 734.
4. *CD* I/2, 735 (emphasis added).
5. Cf. Anthony C. Thiselton, *Hermeneutics: An Introduction* (Grand Rapids, MI: Eerdmans, 2009), 1-16.
6. Thiselton, *Hermeneutics: An Introduction*, 9. Clearly, not all hermeneutical theorists place emphasis on both aspects; Gadamer focuses only on the *Verstehen* aspect (see Anthony C. Thiselton, *The Hermeneutics of Doctrine* (Grand Rapids, MI: Eerdmans, 2007), xix; cf. Thiselton, *Hermeneutics: An Introduction*, ch. 11).

one might identify with the Enlightenment. For people of faith who read their texts ritualistically, ecclesially (in the broadest sense of this term) and devotionally, such a recognition of the formative and communal nature of texts needs little justification: as a Christian, I read the Bible not only to hear what Jesus said there and then but also in the hope that I will hear what Jesus says to my community by His Spirit here and now; and clearly I do not think that there is a necessary disjuncture between those two modes of reading but believe that the one helps to inform the other. As a preacher, the commentary work which helps me to prepare the sermon, while necessary, is nevertheless only a *preparation* and not the sermon in itself. The purpose of the sermon is to help the church to understand the meaning of the text in the contingent contemporaneity of the church's situation, but notably that contingent contemporaneity is not allowed simply to dominate the text: instead, the preacher and congregation should seek to listen carefully to the text, which is the basis of the explication of the word to the congregation.

There is much to commend the increased attentiveness to hermeneutics in the current theological and ecclesial climate. However, for the Christian theologian, I wish to suggest (perhaps boldly, if you will forgive me) that an attentiveness to reading the text faithfully and hopefully is surely a way of reading the text which falls short of a fully Christian approach. After all, faith and hope belong to a triad in which they are surpassed by love. In the words of St Paul in 1 Cor. 13.13: 'Faith, hope, and love abide, these three; and the greatest of these is love.' If hermeneutics has a formative and communal nature, then for Christian biblical or theological hermeneutics, it would surely be advantageous to consider what it means not only to read a text faithfully and hopefully but also to read a text lovingly.

The concern to read scripture in order to bring about love is one expressed by Augustine.[7] He considers that the building up of the love of God and of neighbour is essential to understanding and interpreting scripture appropriately. He writes: 'Whoever, then, thinks that he understands the Holy Scriptures, or any part of them, but puts such an interpretation upon them as does not tend to build up this twofold love of God and our neighbour, does not yet understand them as he ought.'[8] Indeed, Augustine considers a hermeneutic of love alongside the 'precise meaning which the author whom he reads intended to express' (what I have termed the *faithful* aspect of hermeneutics), and 'another meaning ... of Scripture than the writer intended' (which might be considered close to what I have termed the *hopeful* aspect of reading).[9] For Augustine, reading a text faithfully and lovingly (and perhaps hopefully) is central to the correct interpretation of scripture.

My purpose in this chapter is to seek to outline (and nothing more; and in this the chapter is a bit of an experiment) what characteristics a hermeneutics of love (*agapē*) might have, and to suggest that the practice of reading the Bible with members of other faith communities might, for the Christian, be just one example

---

7. I am grateful to Bill Danaher for reminding me of these passages in Augustine.
8. Augustine, *De Doctrina Christiana*, 1.36(40).
9. Augustine, *De Doctrina Christiana*, 1.36(41).

of such a process of reading a text lovingly. I wish to conclude by suggesting that this process might allow one, furthermore, to understand and explain texts better in relation to the theme of an insider/outsider binary, and where we locate the self and the other in the ecclesial reading of a text.

What does it mean to read lovingly? What might the hermeneutics of agapē mean?

An obvious danger in seeking to express the need to read a text lovingly, as a key Christian identifier in hermeneutics, is the capacity for love to become a universalized and liberal principle binding on all of the particularities and difficulties of a text. We can elide all difficulty by removing any confrontational, judgemental or difficult texts, or we might fail to engage with them on the basis of their being 'unloving'. Any notion of self,[10] particularity or difference could be seen as a failure for love, and a retreat could all too easily be made to a form of lowest common denominator approaches to texts in the fear of their potential offensiveness. However, it is precisely here that the importance of the particularity of Christian love must be emphasized.[11] Not only is love a principle for reading which may only be meaningful for Christian readers (it is not my place to judge on its worth as a means of reading texts for non-Christians), but the love of which Paul speaks is also itself carefully defined and articulated. As soon as one suggests, therefore, that love might be a basis for reading texts, it is necessary to consider what is meant by this specifically Christian love and to recognize its potential difference from other forms that love might take. The love which Paul speaks of, and which Christ reveals, is a particular form of love, made meaningful in the narrative of the New Testament. As Barth puts it,

> Christian love cannot in fact be equated with any other, or with any of the forms (even the highest and purest) of this other, just as this other love has obviously no desire to be confused with Christian. Nor can Christian love be fused with this other to form a higher synthesis. We cannot say of any other love that it is a kind of preparatory stage for Christian love. Nor can we commend Christian love by representing and portraying it as the purified form, the supreme climax, of this other love.[12]

---

10. In *De Doctrina Christiana*, 1.26, Augustine points to the fact that love of other does not exclude love of self. For Augustine, it is important that we love our neighbours *as ourselves*.

11. Cf. Anthony C. Thiselton, *The First Epistle to the Corinthians*, The New International Greek Commentary (Grand Rapids, MI: Eerdmans, 2000), 1033–4.

12. *CD* IV/2, 735.

To attend faithfully to the text of the New Testament requires that one attends (faithfully) to the particular and specific meaning of love in the text. This love is *agapē*, and (as will be indicated) the word is used in such a way that the self is not consumed by the other, a type of love which marks – perhaps – the theologically liberal and universalized understanding of the word, and which subjects all else to its love-principle (a version of love perhaps more akin to *eros* than to *agapē*).[13] We cannot, therefore, presume that we know what it means for a Christian to read texts lovingly; instead, we need to attend to the particular form that Christian love is described as taking. In that way, our understanding must be *faithfully* loving, as well as hopefully loving: the triadic reading of faith, hope and love must be held together, rather than any one (even love) coming to dominate at the expense of the others. While love is deemed in Christian theology to be 'the greatest of these three', it is such in relation to the other two, rather than at the expense of the other two.

The relation between a faithfully appropriate reading of the text and a loving reading of the text is an issue to which Augustine directs his attention in his discussion of the interpretation of scripture and the engendering of love. He differentiates between a way of reading the text to bring about love, which might not be the most appropriate way of rendering the author's original meaning, and a way of reading the text which is a deliberate form of deception. While he thinks that the former is not culpable of deception, he is directly concerned with those who wilfully deceive regarding the nature of the text:

> there is involved in deception the intention to say what is false; and we find plenty of people who intend to deceive, but nobody who wishes to be deceived. Since, then, the man who knows practices deceit, and the ignorant man is practiced upon, it is quite clear that in any particular case the man who is deceived is a better man than he who deceives, seeing that it is better to suffer than to commit injustice. Now every man who lies commits an injustice; and if any man thinks that a lie is ever useful, he must think that injustice is sometimes useful. For no liar keeps faith in the matter about which he lies. He wishes, of course, that the man to whom he lies should place confidence in him; and yet he betrays his confidence by lying to him. Now every man who breaks faith is unjust. Either, then, injustice is sometimes useful (which is impossible), or a lie is never useful.[14]

For Augustine, there cannot be a direct desire to deceive in the interpretation of a text offered: this would be an act against faith. It is not possible, therefore, to elide difference and particularity to a form of love principle which operates by rejecting the faithful claims of scripture, as this is an exercise in deceit. Even though

---

13. *CD* IV/2, 745. One must, however, be careful of demarcating too straightforwardly *eros* and *agapē* (see below).

14. Augustine, *De Doctrina Christiana*, 1.36(40).

Augustine's work has at times been interpreted in a more liberal way regarding his love hermeneutic, for him the bringing about of love cannot come at the expense of a faithful reading of the text. He is clear: 'Whoever takes another meaning out of Scripture than the writer intended, goes astray.'[15] Furthermore, even those who accidently misinterpret texts out of a desire to build up love, in doing this, go astray and must be corrected (albeit this correction is to be gentle and loving, since it corrects an activity motivated by good reasons). He writes:

> Whoever takes another meaning out of Scripture than the writer intended, goes astray, but ... if his mistaken interpretation tends to build up love, which is the end of the commandment, he goes astray in much the same way as a man who by mistake quits the high road, but yet reaches through the fields the same place to which the road leads. He is to be corrected, however, and to be shown how much better it is not to quit the straight road, lest, if he get into a habit of going astray, he may sometimes take cross roads, or even go in the wrong direction altogether.[16]

In the end, Augustine believes that such a well-motivated and loving approach may lead to loss of faith, and that both faith and love are required.[17] Love can never come at the expense of faith; the two are always bound together.

In direct relation to helping us to engage in a faithfully loving reading, St Paul offers tremendous help in his description of what comprises love:

> Love is patient; love is kind; love is not envious or boastful or arrogant or rude. It does not insist on its own way; it is not irritable or resentful; it does not rejoice in wrongdoing, but rejoices in the truth. It bears all things, believes all things, hopes all things, endures all things. Love never ends. (1 Cor. 13.4-8)

The point of this is not simply that Paul says Christians should follow a form of love defined by *agapē* (in contrast to, say, *eros*); whether one can engage in such definitional approaches to words is always questionable.[18] The point is, rather,

---

15. Augustine, *De Doctrina Christiana*, 1.36(40).
16. Augustine, *De Doctrina Christiana*, 1.36(41).
17. Augustine, *De Doctrina Christiana*, 1.37.
18. To that degree, the sort of the definition given by C. S. Lewis in *The Four Loves*, while perhaps theologically helpful, is hardly historically or linguistically accurate (C. S. Lewis, *The Four Loves* [Glasgow: Collins, 1960]). But equally, one might see the narrow definitional work of Margaret Mitchell in relation to the Corinthian letter as overly limiting in terms of the context of the letter: certainly, in terms of understanding the importance of the text now, the idea that love is simply a positive counterpoint to Corinthian factionalism is unhelpful (see Margaret M. Mitchell, *Paul and the Rhetoric of Reconciliation: An Exegetical Investigation of the Language and Composition of 1 Corinthians* [Louisville, KY: Westminster John Knox, 1991], 167).

that Paul defines what is meant by love for the Christian through his description of what *agapē* involves. In his majestic commentary on 1 Corinthians, Anthony Thiselton defines this love as follows:

> Love (*agapē*) denotes above all a *stance* or *attitude* which shows itself *in acts of will* as *regard, respect, and concern for the welfare of the other*. It is therefore profoundly *christological*, for *the cross* is the paradigm case of the act of *will* and *stance* which *places welfare of others above the interests of the self.* ... **love does not seek its personal good** (13:5) but the welfare of *the other*.[19]

Such a process of removing the prioritization of the interests of the self (but without wholly consuming the self) marks the central element of Christian love in its concern, respect and care for the other. This is not a form of love which does away, therefore, with otherness, but one which is based upon the otherness of the other to the self. Thus, if we are to apply the category of Christian love to the way in which Christians should read texts, such a love does not involve the removal of any difference or otherness (it is not about simply engaging with 'warm and fuzzy' texts only), but seeks, grounded in the recognition of the other's otherness, to place the interests of the other above the interests of the self, regardless of who the other might be.[20]

It is the issue of who those others might be that leads us to consider what it means to read texts lovingly in the current age of religious pluralism. We now live in a globalized culture in which, if we do not have neighbours of other faiths or none, we are more than aware of their presence through the instantaneous nature of the mass media. For all that such a situation may be referred to (with all due provisos) as postmodern, it is perhaps not so dissimilar to the *Sitz-im-Leben* of the First Epistle to the Corinthians from which the New Testament's teaching about love is taken: the commercial and pluralistic setting of Corinth has much that is common to the context of the twenty-first century,[21] and – after all – the issue of pluralism was a real one for the Corinthians who had to consider whether to eat meat sacrificed to 'false gods' (1 Cor. 8.1–11.1).[22] It is in consideration of this context that it is possible to turn directly to the issue of Scriptural Reasoning and its potential for hermeneutics.

---

19. Thiselton, *The First Epistle to the Corinthians*, 1035 (emphases original).

20. Cf. Thiselton: 'Christians are to respect and care for those who may not seem attractive or like us in their culture, gender, race, or concerns, but are fellow believers or human beings on whom God has set his love' (Anthony C. Thiselton, *I Corinthians: A Shorter Exegetical and Pastoral Commentary* [Grand Rapids, MI: Eerdmans, 2006], 219–20).

21. Thiselton, *The First Epistle to the Corinthians*, 10.

22. On Paul's response to the situation in Corinth and its potential ethical implications, see Bruce W. Winter, 'Theological and Ethical Responses to Religious Pluralism – 1 Corinthians 8–10', *TynBul* 41 (1990): 209–26.

How does Scriptural Reasoning help us read this way?

Scriptural Reasoning 'is a practice before it is a theory. It properly can only be known in its performance.'[23] Scriptural Reasoning involves Muslim, Jewish and Christian people reading each other's texts together in small group study. It began with David Ford, Daniel Hardy, Peter Ochs and Basit Koshul, and there are now various instances of the practice around the world. Scriptural Reasoning is difficult to describe for those who have not practised it, but might (crudely) be thought of as some form of inter-faith bible study.[24] It seems appropriate in suggesting that Scriptural Reasoning is a mode of engaging in a hermeneutics of *agapē* to attempt to describe and narrate a discussion, which while singular is in some ways exemplary of the sorts of interpretation of texts that sometimes happen in Scriptural Reasoning meetings. The context in which this discussion took place was a small group at the University of Cambridge who were undertaking an engagement with Surah 26.69-89, 102; 9.114 on Abraham. This had followed on from an early engagement with the difficult text in which Jesus commands us to hate our father and mother, wife and children, brothers and sisters (Lk. 14.26), a text with which we had rightly struggled. Confronted with the difficulty of Jesus' words, as a Christian I had sought to say something along the lines of: 'Well, of course, Jesus didn't really mean that; it's about priorities.' However, reading the Quran's teaching about Abraham and his disassociation from his father led one of our Jewish participants to talk about Abraham in the Torah – a man who thinks God's promise will be fulfilled through his wife's slave with whom he sleeps; who then sends his son and Hagar away; and who almost sacrifices his child. 'Abraham hates his father and wife and sons; Jesus is telling us to be like Abraham!' was the excited cry from our Jewish friend. In the context of this setting, we read the Quran to receive a Midrash through Torah on Luke.

This occasion led me to reflect (uncomfortably) on what sorts of hermeneutics were being engaged in this. We were led from a problem with the Christian text (most especially for the Christians sat in the room, all of whom loved their families) to a Quranic text discussion. The two seemed unlinked. But from this discussion of the Quran we were taken to the Torah by a Jewish participant who wished to help us to understand the Christian text by a thought that the Qur'an raised for her. Her intertextual interpretation was such that it did not de-problematize the Christian text, but that it did at least allow for a clearer sense of its not being a text that is so strange in the context of the narration of the strangeness and challenges of a scriptural life of faith. This was not a process which was self-beneficial for the Jewish and Muslim participants, but instead a process which arose out of what

---

23. Steven Kepnes, 'A Handbook for Scriptural Reasoning', *Modern Theology* 22 (2006): 370.

24. For further description of and reflection on Scriptural Reasoning, see David F. Ford, *Christian Wisdom: Desiring God and Learning in Love* (Cambridge: Cambridge University Press, 2007), ch. 8.

I might want to call, as a Christian, a hermeneutics of *agapē* – and which I might describe (in a way the others would not) as a love for the other for the other's sake, arising from the love of God, as it is revealed to me in the self-sacrifice of Jesus Christ. During the reading of this text, there was a reading which was loving extended by a Jewish colleague, allowed by Muslim colleagues and accepted by Christian colleagues.

Pointing towards the activities of non-Christians may well seem to suggest a return to the kind of liberal love principle about which I have already expressed nervousness. My desire here, however, is not to say that the non-Christian participants engaged in readings which were motivated by a wish to exemplify Christ's love, but simply to say that these kinds of moments in Scriptural Reasoning display, from a Christian perspective, a potential exemplification of what a hermeneutics of *agapē* might be. When we look at the detailed unpacking by Paul of what love (*agapē*) is like, several of the characteristics of that love are evident in such a reading. The activity was *patient*. Not only did it take time to come to such a reading, but the non-Christian participants were patient with a text which is difficult enough for Christians; and the Christians were patient in allowing members of other faith communities to read and interpret their texts. There was no blundering exclusivist impatience, but a willingness to wait patiently for God's timing.[25] The reading was also kind, seeking to offer a generous (another interpretation of the Greek word) reading of a text which was difficult for Christians; and it was received in generosity by Christians who did not forthrightly proclaim that it was a crucicentric text, or the likes. There was no bragging or envy involved, but also, notably, no inflated sense of self-importance. Not only was the reading offered as just one potential, but the text itself (difficult and jarring as it is for those for whom the family is central) was not dismissed, just as the reading was received without any sense that a member of another community could never read the text properly. The attempt to read the text without being rude is also a feature of the practice of Scriptural Reasoning: older readers should not interrupt younger ones; men should not interrupt women; no single voice should be allowed to dominate; and so on.[26] The very reading of scripture together with members of other Abrahamic communities is an enactment of a form of reading which does not insist on its own way: it is a form of hospitality to the other, who is allowed to join in the reading of the scripture which is sacred and holy to oneself. Furthermore, this invitation is waited for, and the reading 'does not elbow its way into conversations'.[27] This reading is not engaged in for the sake of proving the other wrong or the self right: in this way it is neither irritable nor resentful. As such, Scriptural Reasoning does not focus on the origins of Christianity in Judaism; or the origins of Islam in Christian and Jewish traditions.[28] It is not about a preoccupation with the self,

---

25. Thiselton, *The First Epistle to the Corinthians*, 1046–7 (cf. Heb. 6.15).
26. This is checked by a chair who should be sensitive to these issues.
27. Thiselton, *The First Epistle to the Corinthians*, 1050.
28. See Kepnes, 'A Handbook for Scriptural Reasoning'.

and the interests of the self in relation to the other (in terms of supersession or antecedence of claim), but is rather about reading with the other for the sake of God and of the other. Provocative and irritating behaviour is checked in the setting of Scriptural Reasoning,[29] and patience and graciousness is required. Yet, there is no desire for the creation of unifying principles or the identification of conceptual unities in the Scriptural Reasoning. In this much, it embodies a love which rejoices in that which is true. This quest for the truth (in all its particularity and with all of its potential pain)[30] in no ways undermines a reading which seeks to adopt the hermeneutics of *agapē*. After all, 'Would genuine love for the other seek premature closure of what troubles or challenges the other?'[31]

That love has an eschatological element, as that which never ends, and which exceeds faith and hope (things Calvin believed were no longer necessary after the *eschaton*), is also fitting as a descriptor of Scriptural Reasoning. In his 'Handbook for Scriptural Reasoning', Steven Kepnes identifies the eschatological element to Scriptural Reasoning as follows:

> The eschatological dimension of SR [Scriptural Reasoning] practice recognizes that … in the SR 'tent of meeting' people whose communities are otherwise at war with each other are sitting down in peaceful conversation. … [T]he liturgical aspect of SR can be seen in the belief that many SR members have that an ideal future time, a time of inter-religious peace, is anticipated, 'glimpsed' and even 'participated in' through SR practice.
>
> Imagining SR practice as a glimpse of the end time is extremely powerful because, as with all eschatological thinking, it necessarily has implications for the present. The new eschatology of SR calls into question some of the exclusivist and triumphantalist aspects of the traditional eschatologies of Judaism, Christianity,

---

29. Cf. Thiselton, *The First Epistle to the Corinthians*, 1052.
30. As I have put it elsewhere, we should not forget

> how uncomfortable those seats at the inter-faith table not only are but – if we are to be internally coherent and to be present as members of our own faiths – have to be. This is not to engage in something unloving; quite the opposite, it is to bear that discomfort out of love for the other. Surely such sacrificial love is an even greater virtue than that of tolerance: while tolerance pertains principally to ideas, love pertains to persons, and in sitting with those who believe different things than we do, we do not simply play with ideas but engage in love for the other. (Tom Greggs, 'Bringing Barth's Critique of Religion to the Inter-faith Table', *JR* 88 (2008): 83)

For further discussion of this theme, see Tom Greggs, 'Legitimizing and Necessitating Inter-faith Dialogue: The Dynamics of Inter-faith for Individual Faith Communities', *International Journal of Public Theology* 4 (2010): 194–211.

31. Thiselton, *The First Epistle to the Corinthians*, 227. Cf. here the discussion of Augustine and faithful readings of texts discussed above.

and Islam in which one religion triumphs over the other two. One practical result of face-to-face SR readings of eschatological texts of the three monotheistic traditions is that it becomes harder to maintain eschatologies that expect to overcome the religious particularities of each tradition. This allows for the re-imagining of a new type of end-time in which universal peace is won through preserving the particularity of the other instead of obliterating it. Here, the end-time can function as the ideal that pulls the traditions along with it to a future time of human fulfillment, a reign of justice and peace and communion with God. Reading scriptures together as a form of eschatological thinking also recalls past times of rich interaction between Jews, Christians, and Muslims and a beginning time of creation in which the world and the human was created as very good.[32]

The very activity of reading scriptures with members of other faith communities directs us towards the future time when many shall come from east and west to feast with Abraham, Isaac and Jacob (Mt. 8.11), and reminds the Christian reader that the Kingdom of God is always more than the limiting walls of the empirical *ecclesia*. Reading lovingly is an exercise in reading eschatologically, and we are helped to glimpse something of the vision of God's loving and peaceful kingdom through the simultaneous reading of scriptures together. This is not in a way which undermines the other's otherness, but in a way which traverses that otherness in the very otherness of God's love for us. Scriptural Reasoning may be just one of many ways of reading which aids the hermeneutics of *agapē*.

However, it may not simply be the case that Scriptural Reasoning may be just an exemplification of a hermeneutics of *agapē*, it may also help us to engage in deeper and more loving readings, even in non-Scriptural Reasoning settings. The hermeneutical process of reading with Abrahamic others is humbling, as it is offered and received in tremendous generosity, but also because in it is found not just the pleasantness of being with those other children of Abraham for its own sake, but what I have come to think of as the necessity (for me as a Christian) of being with these other children of Abraham for my own sake – for the sake of my reading of my scripture, for the sake of my Christian faith, for the sake of my life before God.

What about the self and the other?

It is here that I wish to consider the effects of reading with members of other religious communities on the majority of my readings of scripture, which find their home in daily devotional and weekly liturgical acts. If Scriptural Reasoning is a practice that might be described as embodying a loving hermeneutics, how does the process of reading with others form a hermeneutics of *agapē* which exist beyond the necessarily occasional readings of scripture with members of

---

32. Kepnes, 'A Handbook for Scriptural Reasoning', 381.

different faith communities?[33] My concern here relates to the issue of reading with an awareness of one's propensity towards self-deception: as Ricoeur reminds us, we should examine the manner in which we read with a good degree of critical suspicion. In reading with members of other faith communities, we are confronted with the reality that in approaching scripture, in the words of Thiselton, 'It is all too easy to opt for convenient or self-affirming interpretations.'[34] The very process of reading with others begins to undermine the capacity that one has, and occasional sleight of hand in which one engages, in terms of locating oneself in the text. Reading with members of other religious traditions raises issues for the all too easy self-identification with the insider. It also questions the identification of the other as the outsider, and it helps us to examine the all too simplified binaries which we tend to create in terms of our reading of our tradition in relation to the text.[35]

Christian readings of insiders and outsiders in the text of the New Testament are as slippery as they are confusing. It is perhaps wrong of me to point to a pastoral example to make this point, but the reduction of this argument to the absurd may nevertheless highlight tendencies many of us have.[36] The church to which I belong has a group of retired ladies who meet weekly (many of whom are in their eighties and all of whom are more pietistic Methodists than I am). I am deeply struck by their fellowship meetings by their capacity to read themselves as the insider at all points in the text. Thus, they are the moral insiders who obey the law (quite rightly, for they have lived good and Godly lives), but they are also able to see themselves in contrast to the Pharisees as – in a way that always draws a smile from me – the prostitutes who will enter the Kingdom of God first; just as they also see themselves as the prodigal son, Zaccheus and so on. The point that I am making is this: in the reading of texts, there is an almost irresistible desire to self-identify (typologically perhaps in the case of Christian theology) with the 'insider' or the hero, without once thinking about whether the other that one reads of in the text is someone who would be a repetition of one's self in the present, or whether that other in the text would be classed as the outsider in the contexts in which we find ourselves now.

33. I use the term 'necessarily occasional' here both to indicate the paucity of the practice in comparison to 'normal' forms of scriptural reading with intra-religious communities, and also because in order to remain genuinely particularist and genuinely inter-faith, there should be no suggestion that co-reading scripture with members of other communities should in some ways replace the faithful devotional and liturgical reading of scripture in which people of faith engage.

34. Thiselton, *Hermeneutics: An Introduction*, 5.

35. On binaries and how to overcome them, see the concluding chapter of Peter Ochs, *Peirce, Pragmatism and the Logic of Scripture* (Cambridge: Cambridge University Press, 2004).

36. I hope the reader will forgive my turning to a pastoral example. I do this in part not only to illustrate the point I am trying to make but also in part in recognition of Anthony Thiselton's deep and continuous engagement with the church throughout his career.

The Gospel confronts this issue directly, and not simply in Jesus' engagement with the Pharisees.[37] A repeated theme of the New Testament is that those who consider themselves most on the inside are the ones who are likely to receive a rude awakening. The eschatological parable of the sheep and the goats makes this point. Not only do those who think that they are goats discover that they are sheep, but those who presume they are sheep also discover that they are goats (Mt. 25.31-46). Furthermore, hero or insider status is often not related to being an insider to one's religious affiliation.[38] In the parable of the Good Samaritan, for example, the hero with whom as contemporary insiders most Christians identify is precisely the anti-hero outsider to the religious community to which this tale was narrated.[39]

Reading face to face with another, indeed with a member of another faith community, reading lovingly, confronts us with the need to engage with sensitivity with texts when we read by ourselves. It challenges us to contemplate where we locate ourselves in texts, and crucially has the effect of de-assuring us theologically of our insider status, our hubris and our self-created binary exclusivisms. The process of reading with religious others is not just a process which *displays* a loving reading, but it is one which *engenders* in a far more reaching way a reading which critically challenges the preoccupation with the self and the text, and points us towards the other, aiding us perhaps to understand something more of the ultimate otherness of God. As a Christian insider at the current juncture in the world's history, this should bring with it an awareness of Jesus' challenge not just (to employ earlier terms) *faithfully* to the insider status of the second temple Judaism (and notably not rabbinic Judaism) of which he was a part, but *hopefully* back to the insider status of contemporary Christianity, in its institutionalized religious form. And since faith and hope are always exceeded by love, it will perhaps bring us to read our texts (even the painful and exclusivist ones) lovingly in relation to the contemporary Jewish and Muslim other in the world today.

---

37. For a theological discussion of the Pharisees in the New Testament, see Dietrich Bonhoeffer, *Ethics*, ed. Clifford J. Green, trans. Reinhard Krauss, Charles C. West and Douglas W. Stott, Dietrich Bonhoeffer Works 6 (Minneapolis, MN: Fortress, 2005), 309–15.

38. For a more detailed discussion of this passage, see the essay in this volume, 'Beyond the binary: Forming evangelical eschatology'.

39. This is a theme I discuss in the essay in this volume, 'Preaching inter-faith: Finding hints about the religious other from the Good Samaritan'.

Chapter 13

PEOPLES OF THE COVENANTS: EVANGELICAL THEOLOGY AND THE PLURALITY OF THE COVENANTS IN SCRIPTURE

I

Engagement in inter-faith dialogue is never an easy task. It is born of difference, particularity and otherness to another who inevitably faces the same or similar concerns and questions as oneself. For evangelical Christians, engaging in inter-faith dialogue is more difficult than it is for many Christians. Following Bebbington's classical fourfold definition of evangelicalism,[1] as well as being crucicentric (focusing theology on the atoning death of Jesus Christ) and activist (responding to that death in works of faith), evangelicalism is marked from other forms of Christian spirituality by its biblicism (seeing scripture as the final authority in all matters of faith and practice) and its conversionism (emphasizing the decision of faith and seeking the conversion of others to Christianity).[2] There is, therefore, for evangelicalism, a double exclusivity which can serve to undermine the potential for inter-faith engagement: the first of these revolves around revelation, with the Christian scriptures being seen as God's final and absolute authoritative word to humanity; the second revolves around issues concerning salvation and the need for response to God's grace in the act of conversion.[3] For evangelicalism, there is

---

1. See David Bebbington, *Evangelicalism in Modern Britain: A History from the 1730s to the 1980s* (London: Unwin Hyman, 1989).

2. Larsen also offers a helpful characterization of evangelicalism, effectively adding to Bebbington's definition the condition that these are held in conjunction with orthodox protestant theology. See Timothy Larsen, 'Defining and Locating Evangelicalism', in *The Cambridge Companion to Evangelical Theology*, ed. Larsen and Treier (Cambridge: Cambridge University Press, 2007), 1–14. For further discussion of issues surrounding evangelical identity, see S. J. Grenz, *Revisioning Evangelical Theology: A Fresh Agenda for the 21st Century* (Downers Grove: IVP, 1993), esp. ch. 2.

3. These concerns clearly place evangelical theology in a different position than liberal theologies, such as that of John Hick. See, for example, his *God and the Universe of Faiths: Essays in the Philosophy of Religion* (London: Macmillan, 1973); *God Has Many Names: Britain's New Religious Pluralism* (London: Macmillan, 1980); *Problems of Religious Pluralism* (London: Macmillan, 1985); and *An Interpretation of Religion: Human Responses to the Transcendent* (London: Macmillan, 1989). However, it also puts evangelical theology

an emphatic insistence on the plain sense of Jesus' claim 'I am the way, the truth and the life', and this is expressed in terms of attending to the high authority of the Christian scriptures and to a life which seeks to be in personal relationship with Christ. It is this characterization which provides evangelicalism's identity as a trans-denominational movement, a movement focused on the uniqueness of Jesus Christ's atoning death, as learned about in scripture and as responded to by conversion.

However, if evangelicalism is to take its claim to biblicism seriously, there is a need to attend to *all* of the Bible, including those places in which one can identify some of the complexities found in the body of scripture.[4] A number of such texts revolve around the place of the religious other within scripture. While there are places in which there are clear binary separations of people (prophets of Baal do not seem to be prophets of the Lord!), there are other places in which it seems clear that God works outside of the twofold classification of insiders and outsiders to His promise which often underpins evangelical approaches to the text.[5] These narratives involve the various Samaritans and pagans with whom Jesus engages, but also figures such as Rahab, Melchizedek, Jethro and Ruth.[6] Taking biblicism seriously in these texts seems to demand questions of the traditionally articulated evangelical attitude to the way in which God works with His people – usually expressed as only being a relationship with Christians and (in most evangelical articulations) with Jews. The text demands a more complex reading, and to be genuinely biblicist involves attending to these. Crucially, while these themes are very much contemporary for a post-9/11 world, these complexifying elements do not arise external to the tradition, but are rather to be found through the plain sense of the texts of the Bible, whose unique status as the revelation of God must be affirmed by evangelical Christians. Recognizing the deep wealth of scriptural wisdom means that to be truly biblical (even in the plain sense) can never involve the hermeneutical naïveté of stating, 'the Bible said it, I believe it, that settles it'.[7] There is a glorious complexity to the God of all the universe – so infinite that He

in a different position than tradition-based theologies, which emphasize the role of tradition in theology; for these, there is more opportunity to 'change' or (better) 'develop' the theological stance of their churches, as is perhaps the case with Vatican II's *Lux Mundi*.

4. The evangelical propensity towards selective reading of texts is marked: while it is outwith the confines of this chapter, it is notable how little attention is paid, for example, to texts regarding money, despite the prolific number of them within the body of scripture.

5. On such an approach, see, for example, Nigel M. de S. Cameron, 'Universalism and the Logic of Revelation', in *The Best in Theology*, vol. 3, ed. J. I. Packer (Carol Stream, IL: Christianity Today, 1989), esp. 153 and 166; and David Fergusson, 'Eschatology', in *The Cambridge Companion to Christian Doctrine*, ed. Colin E. Gunton (Cambridge: Cambridge University Press, 1997), 241.

6. On this theme, see Gerald O'Collins, *Salvation for All: God's Other Peoples* (Oxford: Oxford University Press, 2008).

7. Richard Hays cites this as a worrying bumper sticker he has seen around America. See Richard B. Hays, 'Postscript: Seeking a Centred, Generous Orthodoxy', in *New Perspectives*

is best honoured by silence – and it should not be a surprise to evangelicals that there is a glorious complexity to the Word of that God.[8] Sure, the Bible contains the simple message of God's love and covenant with His people, but it also contains a depth of wisdom which grows ever deeper the further it is furrowed. As Richard Hays puts it, evangelical theologians must have the

> willingness to grapple with actual close readings of the biblical texts and to acknowledge the presence of tensions and perplexities that stimulate careful scholarly study and interpretation. To treat the Bible's complexity with this sort of alert respect is to grant it more, not less, authority than those interpreters who superimpose a priori propositional grids upon it … To acknowledge such complexities in both world and Scripture is not to be less evangelical, but to insist that the good news with which we are entrusted must truthfully acknowledge our created and fallen human condition and the historically contingent manner in which God has chosen to reveal himself to us.[9]

Furthermore, evangelical reading of scripture is not engagement with a static, dusty textbook, but a recognition of the living and active Word of God. This determines that for evangelicals, the Bible should not be read simply as a means of confirming predecided norms, but should be read as a means of facilitating God's personal encounters with His people to whom He still speaks by His Word and His Spirit. As Richard Briggs puts it,

> What is the *telos* (goal, purpose, end) of evangelical reading of Scripture? It is attentiveness to the God mysteriously present in Scripture. It is discipleship illumined by this inspired text in incomparable ways, though of course in the midst of multiple other illuminations. It is transformation before the whole canon received as God's providential ordering of many and various witnesses to his Word, the same 'many and various' voices which we saw brought together (mysteriously) in Christ in Hebrews 1:1–2.[10]

In the age of post-Christendom in which our neighbours (whom Christ in scripture calls us to love as ourselves) are people of other faiths and none, the true evangelical is to seek from the Bible God's purpose for lives of discipleship

---

for Evangelical Theology: Engaging God, Scripture and the World, ed. Tom Greggs (London: Routledge, 2009), 217.

8. Evangelicals recognize this complexity which arises from the plain sense in such disputes over dispensationalism and the like: the multivocity of scripture determines that the stronger the plain sense reading, the greater the level of hermeneutical or theological sophistication needed to allow that plain sense to stand.

9. Hays, 'Postscript', 217. See further, Richard Briggs, 'The Bible before Us: Evangelical Possibilities for Taking Scripture Seriously', in *New Perspectives for Evangelical Theology*.

10. Briggs, 'The Bible before Us', 26.

in this generation. Again, to quote Hays, 'If we believe that the word of God is living and active, sharper than any two-edged sword (Heb. 4.12), we should expect our encounter with that living word to challenge and change us.'[11] Faced with the contemporary, political need for peace within our world between people of different creeds, it is the task of the evangelical theologian to seek for the 'deep readings' of the scriptures which are so important and central to the life of evangelical faith:[12] while the conversionist impetus will undoubtedly remain within the evangelical psyche, the theologian must also attend to how properly to relate the conversionist impetus with an activist desire for the peace of the city. Central to this task is the engagement with these contemporary issues in a manner which is genuinely *evangelical*, speaking from within the tradition in order to shape and reform its engagement with the Bible, God and the world. Put sharply, the question is this: how can we be evangelical and open to God's presence with and promises for other people? This chapter seeks to offer just one potential example of such a theology.

As an evangelical who has wrestled with these themes, the practice of Scriptural Reasoning has facilitated a greater depth in the reading of my own scriptures in light of reading with others. Such readings have made me have to question the presumptions I have brought to the text in light of more genuinely plain sense readings of those for whom the Christian Bible is not their scripture. As an evangelical theologian, this has determined the need to ask questions both of the legitimacy of meeting with members of other faith communities to dialogue with them, and of the hermeneutics involved in learning more of oneself and one's scriptures in light of conversations with the other.[13] One such place in which this learning has taken place has been with regard to God's covenants (plural) of grace found in the Bible.[14]

In this essay, I wish to address these themes by examining the nature of covenant and covenants in scripture, and to do this by entering into dialogue with the Swiss

---

11. Hays, 'Postscript', 217.

12. The term 'deep reading' is borrowed from Ben Quash. 'Deep Calls to Deep: Reading Scripture in a Multi-Faith Society', in *Remembering Our Future: Explorations in Deep Church*, ed. Bretherton and Walker (Milton Keynes: Paternoster, 2007, 108–30.

13. These are themes I have developed in a little more detail elsewhere. See my essay in this volume, 'Legitimizing and necessitating inter-faith dialogue: The dynamics of inter-faith for individual faith communities'.

14. By covenants in the plural is meant such covenants as the Noahide, Davidic and Abrahamic covenants (to name but three), which each have different foci and 'reaches'. For a good overview of covenant and covenants in scriptural texts, see W. J. Dumbrell, *Covenant and Creation: A Theology of the Old Testament Covenants* (Carlisle: Paternoster, 1997); and Steven L. McKenzie, *Covenant* (St. Louis: Chalice, 2000), esp. 4–7. In this chapter, the scope of discussion is only covenants between God and humanity. For covenants between humans and nations, and so on, see D. J. McCarthy, *Old Testament Covenants: A Survey of Current Options* (Oxford: Blackwell, 1973), ch. 4.

theologian, Karl Barth. The chapter will, then, offer a Scriptural Reasoning-style theological reading of the Ishmael and Abraham narratives around the theme of covenant and promise, finally drawing some tentative conclusions for evangelical attitudes to Islam.

II

There is much discussion in theology about God's covenant (singular) with humanity. When spoken of in the singular, covenant involves God's relational dealings with humanity, seen supremely in the person of Jesus Christ – for Christians, God's full and complete covenant with humanity in whom all other covenants have their origin, meaning and end. Indeed, were one to insist on a central motif for the twentieth century's greatest theologian, Karl Barth, it would no doubt have to be God's covenant of grace with humanity in Jesus Christ – a theme which occurs at every point in his *Church Dogmatics*. This is hardly surprising when one considers that the word covenant ($b^e r \hat{\imath} t$ in Hebrew or *diathēkē* in Greek)[15] occurs in 260 verses in the Hebrew Bible, and a further 60 verses in the New Testament. Not all of these uses of the word describe the relationship between humanity and God, as in some uses the covenant is between human beings. However, there are a range of covenants in the Bible between God and humans. Within the Hebrew Bible, it is possible to identify a number of such discrete covenants with humanity, many involving differing 'reaches' of God (and levels of exclusivity). Among a notable number of others, these are sometimes identified as the Noahide, Abrahamic, Sinaitic, Davidic and the new Ezekelic covenants.[16]

Systematic theology has recognized (if only in passing) this range of covenants. Indeed, Karl Barth, for whom the theme of covenant is so important, on eight different occasions points to the plurality of covenants in scriptures, beyond the simple Christian recognition of the old and the new covenant.[17] Barth writes clearly and emphatically: 'The one covenant achieves historical form in the making of *a series of covenants*.'[18] For Barth, these covenants are not separate or distinct from the perspective of God, but are rather historical expressions of the one covenant – Jesus Christ. In this, Barth continues: 'This covenant is fulfilled, however, in the existence of the one Jesus Christ.'[19] Although Jesus Christ is the one

---

15. For an examination of the philology of *berit*, see D. J. McCarthy, *Old Testament Covenants: A Survey of Current Options* (Oxford: Blackwell, 1973).

16. For a presentation of the range of covenants within the Bible, see Steven L. McKenzie, *Covenant* (St. Louis: Chalice, 2000); and Dumbrell, *Covenant and Creation*.

17. The purpose of this essay is not to examine supersessionist implications of this, nor to examine the relationship between these two covenants; these issues require sensitive engagement beyond the scope of the present piece.

18. Karl Barth, *Learning Jesus Christ through the Heidelberg Catechism* (Grand Rapids, MI: Eerdmans, 1964), 52, emphasis added.

19. Barth, *Learning Jesus Christ*.

covenant God for humanity, this does not determine that there is not historical particularity and variance in the different historical instantiations of covenant before Jesus' historical becoming flesh. This particularity and distinctiveness is not, furthermore, suspended by Christ's incarnation for Barth:

> Jesus Christ is already the content and theme of this prehistory, of the Old Testament covenant. As prehistory, as revelation in expectation, the Old Testament covenant is characterised by its division into several covenants side by side, equipped with the same marks, even with the marks of the same uniqueness. Before the Sinaitic covenant we admittedly find the covenant with Abraham underlying the election of Israel, and again, before the Abrahamic covenant, the covenant with Noah, in which the particular covenant with Israel, even before it became an event, is already carried beyond its particularity and raised to universality. So, although it is already a reality from that early beginning, Israel's election is a present reality. In Deuteronomy we find that the covenant is to some extent a lasting ordinance, under which the Israel of the present stands, although it is still based upon the free love and lordship of God.[20]

According to Barth, and surely the tradition of God's immutability, the promises of God last forever, and thus must include the present post-resurrection world.

Given theology's propensity to speak in terms of 'the' covenant, or 'the old' and 'the new' covenant, it is appropriate for Barth to ask: 'Which of these covenants is *the* covenant intended by the Old Testament, and meant to be understood and attested as the original, central and true covenant?'[21] However, Barth's answer is apposite for the biblical texts: 'An answer in terms of the Old Testament texts themselves can only be to the effect that each one is in its own place and in its own way. For it is always the one covenant with the same direction and order.'[22] The attestation of scripture to the concrete plurality of covenants requires recognition. One could put this otherwise: if Jesus Christ is the primary objectivity of God's revelation, then in the various concrete covenants of God with creation, one can detect the secondary objectivity of God's revelation in concrete historical settings in which the covenant takes historical and contextual form.[23] Crucially, however, these contextual instantiations of God's covenant are not passing in nature, but are preserved owing to the nature of God, and their being *God's* promises. Barth helpfully states, discussing the nature of God as patient:

---

20. *CD* I/2, 81–2, emphasis added. Barth goes on in this section to recognize the covenant discussed in Jeremiah, Ezekiel and Deutero-Isaiah, as well as the covenant with David and Levi.
21. *CD* I/2, 82.
22. *CD* I/2, 82.
23. On primary and secondary objectivity, see Charles Marsh, *Reclaiming Dietrich Bonhoeffer: The Promise of His Theology* (Oxford: Oxford University Press, 1994), 31–3.

Does not the whole story of God's covenant with man, the covenant with Abraham, and the covenant at Sinai, and everything that happens in connexion with them – above all does not the fulfilment of all the promises of all these covenants in Jesus Christ, depend upon the fact that this covenant with Noah was concluded and kept and will always be faithfully kept? Does not the grace and mercy of God depend upon the fact that there is also a patience of God, that He grants space to the sinful creature, thus giving Himself space further to speak and act with it?[24]

Although these covenants are promised in Jesus Christ, the integrity and veracity of them for those to whom they are promised remains. Because they are covenants in Jesus Christ, the faithful mercy and patience of God determines that they are preserved for all of those to whom they are promised. Those standing under the covenants to Abraham, Moses and (even) Noah remain under such promises of *God*, since they are the very promises of God, and (for the perspective of Christian theology) grounded in the very nature and person of God as Jesus Christ.[25]

Barth clearly affirms and addresses the plurality of covenants in scripture, and their continued significance. However, this theme hardly makes a real impact in his theology. For Barth, there are twenty-seven mentions of covenants (in the

---

24. CD II/1, 413.
25. Indeed, Barth discusses the third use of the law under the covenants made to Israel:

> The Church lives by the covenants made between God and Israel. Again and again new agreements and mutual obligations are made between God and the men of this people. The number of them shows how unilaterally they have been kept. And if there is a remarkable preponderance of divine warnings at the very making of them, even more so does their fulfilment seem to consist almost regularly and entirely in the occurrence of the corresponding penal judgments. The Church recognises the pure and full comfort of the one covenant of grace kept by man as by God. But what does it recognize in it but the meaning and the determined purpose of the many covenants made with Israel? The Church lives by the 'lawgiving' which took place in Israel, regulating the life of the people with a view to the holiness required by the holiness of its Lord. The law of the Church is the faith which it has been given in the Lord by whose holiness the holiness of His people is created. Yet when it is obedient in this faith, it is doing no more than what is really required by Israel's Law. The Church lives by the 'worship' that is permitted and commanded Israel. The permission and the commandment consist in the priestly and sacrificial order which is given to the people and embraces its whole life. The Church exercises worship in spirit and in truth in view of the eternal High Priest and His sacrifice offered once for all. But it is the worship permitted and commanded Israel which is fulfilled in this way. The Church lives by the 'promises' given to Israel according to which the people is to be blessed and numerous, to possess the land, to be rich and powerful and happy under its king, and finally to see all peoples united in Zion. (*CD* II/2, 203)

plural) in his corpus, including mentions when he addresses simply 'old and new covenants', compared to 3,278 uses of the word 'covenant' (in the singular). While he affirms – rightly for evangelical theology – that all instantiations of covenant are instantiations of the one covenant of God with humanity in Jesus Christ, it must surely be admitted that (given the various ways in which covenants appear in scripture) he does not give due attention to the significance, even if only at the level of secondary objectivity, of there being a plurality of historical covenants, despite what he says about the plurality of covenants. The particularity and variance of God's dealings with his peoples does not receive discussion, and the particularity of each of the covenants (while affirmed by Barth) comes simply to be subsumed in each covenant being part of God's one full and complete covenant in Jesus.

While certainly Christian (and most especially evangelical) theologians must make the centrality of Jesus Christ key to all discussion of the univocity of scripture, to attend to scripture and to take scripture seriously involves recognizing the particular way in which God's covenant with humanity in Christ is established in concrete history. These instantiations of covenant need not, moreover, undermine God's single word to humanity – Jesus – but may be understood as enhypostatic subsistences of God's one eternal covenant with humanity in history.[26] To measure Barth by his own yardstick through judging him by scripture, it is surely necessary to say that the more evangelical approach to these themes involves attesting the multiplicity of covenants that confront the faithful reader of the Christian texts.

Theologians (and to their credit often evangelical ones) have often addressed these themes with regard to Israel. In the next section of this chapter, however, I wish to attend to the covenanting promise of God with Ishmael; for God's promises to Abraham are not simply worked out through Isaac, but also through his other son. For Ishmael and his descendants, the promise of God is sure, and God's patience endures: for the promises are made by the one and same God, the God of Jesus Christ. Evangelical theologians cannot simply be selective with regard to the promises made in scripture, but must surely give scripture the true power and authority to address the reader and speak to her. As well as the Judaeo-Christian tradition of Ishmael being the father of a powerful nation, in *The Tales of the Prophet*, which is the first part of Mohammad's biography, Ishmael is understood not only to be the father of the Arab nations but also the father of the greater *Ummah* of Muslim people. Attending to the texts around the promises made to him may enable evangelical Christians to see God's purposes worked outwith the bounds of the Christian (or even evangelical) community.

---

26. Webster discusses the ethical implications of Barth's an-/en-hypostasis distinction. I am wishing here to say something akin to what Webster says about Christ's humanity with regard to the covenant: because God's covenant with humanity is real, reality is given to all other covenants of God with humanity. Cf. J. Webster, *Barth's Moral Theology: Human Action in Barth's Thought* (Edinburgh: T &T Clark, 1998), 88–90. On an-/en-hypostasis, see *CD* I/2, 162–4, 216 *anhypostasis* only); and *CD* IV/2, 44–50. See also, Eberhard Jüngel, *God's Being Is in Becoming* (Edinburgh: T&T Clark, 2001), 96–7.

III

The figure of Ishmael and the stories surrounding him in the Hebrew Bible are ambiguous. Clearly, he is a son of Abraham, who is circumcised (Gen. 17.23-25) and thereby a member of God's covenant people: 'So shall my covenant be *in your flesh* an everlasting covenant' (emphasis added). As flesh from Abraham's flesh and as a circumcised male, Ishmael is also a fulfilment of God's promise to Abraham. Promises are also made, on various occasions, to Hagar and Ishmael:[27]

> The angel of the LORD also said to her, 'I will so greatly multiply your offspring that they cannot be counted for multitude.' And the angel of the LORD said to her, 'Now you have conceived and shall bear a son; you shall call him Ishmael, for the LORD has given heed to your affliction.' (Gen. 16.10-11)

And: 'As for Ishmael, I have heard you; I will bless him and make him fruitful and exceedingly numerous; he shall be the father of twelve princes, and I will make him a great nation' (Gen. 17.20). These promises are repeated even when it seems that Ishmael may die of thirst, having been turned out of his father's home:

> And God heard the voice of the boy; and the angel of God called to Hagar from heaven, and said to her, 'What troubles you, Hagar? Do not be afraid; for God has heard the voice of the boy where he is. Come, lift up the boy and hold him fast with your hand, for I will make a great nation of him.' Then God opened her eyes and she saw a well of water. She went, and filled the skin with water, and gave the boy a drink. God was with the boy, and he grew up. (Gen. 21.17-20)

Promises are not simply made to Hagar but also to Abraham regarding his first born son: 'As for the son of the slave woman, I will make a nation of him also, because he is your offspring' (Gen. 21.13). However, it is also clear that Ishmael is not (from the perspective of the biblical narrative) the primary choice for God's covenant. The narrative with Sarah makes this clear, and it is put emphatically by God thus: after the promise of Ishmael's blessing (Gen. 17.20), God states, 'But my covenant I will establish with Isaac, whom Sarah shall bear to you at this season next year' (v. 21).[28]

---

27. For an excellent and subtle discussion of texts surrounding Ishmael, and particularly surrounding Hagar, see Steven Kepnes, 'Hagar and Esau: From Others to Sisters and Brothers', in *Crisis, Call, and Leadership in the Abrahamic Traditions*, ed. Peter Ochs and William Stacy Johnson (New York: Palgrave Macmillan, 2009), 31–46. For further discussion from a Jewish perspective, see Jon D. Levenson, *Inheriting Abraham: The Legacy of the Patriarch in Judaism, Christianity and Islam* (Princeton, NJ: Princeton University Press, 2012), ch. 2, esp. 49–54.

28. It is equally possible to translate the 'but' in this sentence as 'and', and certain translations do this. While this may seem to make the statement less exclusivist, the force

It may seem strange, therefore, given the verse on *bᵉrît* (covenant) being established with Isaac (and by implication not Ishmael) to claim that these promises to Ishmael and Hagar are covenants as well. Gen. 17.21 is, indeed, a troubling verse,[29] because God has also just covenanted with Abraham that Ishmael shall be blessed. Furthermore, God has offered his everlasting covenant with all of Abraham's descendants. Thus, it seems that God says something (in vv. 20 and 21) like 'I make a covenant with Ishmael, but my covenant shall be established with Isaac.' Although the word *berit* is not used for Ishmael, it is difficult to see what else the repeated promises can be. Covenant is not simply that which takes place only when the word is cited (nor indeed, since the word is also used of human treaties): to say that would mean that theology would be required to say that Jesus is God's covenant only with regard to the places in which he is spoken of as *diathēkē*. We do well here to note Van Seters's argument that covenant in the Abrahamic material follows 'a divine oath of promise rather than the so-called treaty pattern of Deuteronomy'.[30] Issues (perhaps important to the concerns of evangelicals outside the Reformed tradition) such as the contingency of promise on the basis of response do not appear in the text. The promises made to Ishmael are certainly divine oaths. It is the very nature of God's inability to break such oaths (because of his patient faithfulness) that is the essence of God's covenant to humanity.[31] Even if the text does not use *berit* of the promises to Ishmael, there can be little doubt that they are indeed divine covenants with him and his offspring. What, then, is the significance of these promises to Ishmael?

First, these divine covenants arise out of the great and everlasting covenant made with Abraham. That this covenant is made with Abraham and his descendants, rather than simply Isaac and his, is of significance for the plain sense of the texts. There is a clear level of continuity even for the son who is not chosen by his father. If evangelicals are to take scripture seriously, we must ask why it is that the covenant is not simply made with Isaac's offspring, but with Abraham's, and what the significance of *all* of Abraham's flesh entering into God's covenant is. The promise is for *Abraham's* and not simply Isaac's descendants. It is hardly as if God is unaware of the added child of Abraham, and Ishmael is after all circumcised as Abraham enters into his covenant. Indeed, this is a point which is repeated on

---

of the exclusion is the statement about Isaac and Sarah, rather than which connective is inserted in the English.

29. This may explain why there is remarkably little on this verse in either the tradition or in contemporary biblical scholarship.

30. John Van Seters, *Abraham in History and Tradition* (New Haven, CT: Yale University Press, 1975).

31. Barth certainly sees God's promise to Hagar about Ishmael as arising out of His election: 'Even its [the covenant's] rejected members (just because of the separation which excludes them) are not forsaken, but after, as before, share in the special care and guidance of the electing God' (*CD* II/2, 217). Barth is stating here that there is a covenant for those outside the covenant.

three occasions, at ch. 17, vv. 23, 25 and 26. Ishmael is clearly a member of God's covenant with Abraham.[32]

Second, that there is continuity with Abraham and Abraham's covenant does not mean that there is not differentiation and particularity. A separate promise is given to Ishmael to that of Isaac. That there are many covenants in scripture should surely remind the Christian theologian that God does not operate in the world in a monotonous or monochrome manner. There is a feast of variety and particularity in God's dealing with all of His peoples in history. Even if there is a hierarchy in terms of the promises that God makes, as seems to be here with the preference of Isaac over Ishmael (and as is certainly the case for evangelical theologians with regard to God's covenant in Jesus Christ), this does not mean that God does not make promises and involve Himself with others. As the providential Lord over all of creation, this is hardly anything that might be unexpected. In the case of Ishmael, there are glorious and specific promises which are made that are different to those made to Isaac. Reading the stories of these two brothers, evangelicals must be challenged to recognize the manner in which God works with others who seem to be outside the 'chosen' (or a particular chosen) people, and we must break down fences with those different to ourselves in order to realize God is on the other side already ahead of us. This involves no removal of commitment to the heritage of evangelical faith (just as a promise is still made directly to Isaac which is distinct to that made to Ishmael), but it should surely warn us against the pernicious evangelical tendency to confine God's ways with the world simply to ways with evangelical communities. Certainly, the latter (evangelical communities) are true ways in which God relates to His people, but God – as the one Lord and the only God of all of the world – has other people with whom He operates differently as well.[33] The promise to Ishmael does not undermine the specificity and specialness of the promise to Isaac, but neither does the covenant with Isaac undo the distinctive promise to Ishmael. They stand in a non-competitive relationship, which is hardly surprising for a God who – as love – has an infinite amount of love from which to bestow His grace on people. Both covenants are separate and different, but both are the promises of God and mark His ways with His specific and distinctive peoples. When we move past, which we must, notions of seeing God as the 'biggest thing in the world' (which may be the definition of an idol, but never the Lord), the capacity to see God as an object of knowledge to know is denied, and we are able to recognize (as evangelical

---

32. Thus one might note that, if evangelicals are to affirm something like a (to my mind entirely false, erroneous and unbiblical) differentiation between covenants fulfilled in Jesus Christ and those not fulfilled in Jesus Christ (but are still promises of God), it is worth their remembering that Ishmael's promises are an outworking of the covenant with Abraham, a covenant which cannot but be seen to be a part of the one covenant of God in Jesus Christ.

33. Evangelicals must be careful of the dangerous narrowing of God's salvific work, which can sometimes display itself as 'Only me and thee are saved, and I am not so sure about thee.'

personalism and emphasis on individual relationship with God traditionally has done) that God is the Holy One to whom we relate. Just as human beings do not simply know each other in exactly the same way, but relate differently to different people, so too God's relations with His people do not need to be the same, but are differentiated, as is the case with Isaac and Ishmael.[34] The story of Ishmael demonstrates, moreover, that this differentiation is not binary, in terms of saved-damned or elected-rejected: it is a differentiated *positive* relationship of God to these different children of Abraham.[35]

That Ishmael relates to God is, third and furthermore, made exceptionally clear in the text: God, the Lord, is clearly the God of Ishmael as much as He is the God of Isaac. Genesis makes this abundantly evident (21.20): 'God was with the boy, and he grew up.' Certainly, he fights with his brother (though not so much that he is not involved in Abraham's burial in Gen. 25.9): God says, 'He shall be a wild ass of a man, with his hand against everyone, and everyone's hand against him; and he shall live at odds with all his kin' (Gen. 16.12). However, we cannot and should not confuse enmity with his kin (which, given the manner in which he is cast out for the 'favoured' child Isaac, is perhaps entirely understandable) with enmity with God. That he does not get on with his kin does not mean that God is not his God, with whom he is in relationship. To seek to relate this point to the present situation, similarly, evangelicals today should not confuse the tensions that exist between Islam and Christianity as in any way indicative of a lack of relationship with God for Muslims. The children of Abraham not getting along together means neither that they are not children of Abraham, nor that they are not in a relationship of promise with God. The Isaac and Ishmael stories make that overtly clear.

IV

If evangelicals are to take the whole of scripture seriously, then Ishmael is a figure that they have to consider. The living and active Word of God with its authority in all matters of faith cannot simply be cast aside with the excuse of historical contextualization which is not relevant to present: this is surely the very thing evangelicals fear in liberal approaches to the scriptures. The history that follows these scriptures recounts how the God of all history has fulfilled his promise to Ishmael in the people of Islam. This is not the place in which to discuss issues of supersession, nor the place to discuss the veracity of truth claims or the adequacy of response for Muslim people. On these issues, there will always be family tensions, as there were between the patriarchs, Isaac and Ishmael. But these tensions do not

---

34. This is not only the case with Isaac and Ishmael; the extent of the covenant with Noah (all of creation) and with Moses (those gathered at Sinai) also demonstrates God's varied relations with different people.

35. On non-binary approaches to salvation, see Tom Greggs *Barth, Origen, and Universal Salvation: Restoring Particularity* (Oxford: Oxford University Press, 2009).

mean that Ishmael and his descendants have not received the promise of God, who in His patience, mercy and faithfulness endures. Jesus' reminder regarding Zacchaeus should be a reminder for evangelicals regarding Ishmael: 'he too is a son of Abraham' (Lk. 19.9).

The current chapter has done little more than point to the existence in scripture of a plurality of covenants, which evangelicals especially need to take seriously; and has focused particularly on God's promises regarding Ishmael. The purpose has not been to unpack what the implications of these promises might be for contemporary evangelicalism's engagement with and understanding of Islam. On that we are at best only at the very beginning of the beginning, and there remains a huge amount of work to be done. The attempt has been made only to point to one place in the scriptural account which potentially asks evangelicals for some degree of *patient and humble complexifying* of their account of the covenanting activity of God with his people in relation to interpretation of the Holy Bible. Space does not allow a thorough examination of what the precise nature of the covenant might be, nor what the outworkings of this interpretation of the Ishmael narratives might mean for evangelicals in relation to the way in which they understand salvation, prophecy, providence or revelation: for issues of this kind, much further enquiry and engagement would be required. For now, the following provisional conclusions will have to suffice in the hope that they might engender humility, carefulness and future engagement with the theological and practical implications that arise from theological exegesis of the Ishmael narratives.

Evangelicals would do well to remember that Christians, too, are not the honoured chosen heirs, born of Sarah, but are adopted children in the family, spiritual heirs to Abraham without being physical ones.[36] Furthermore, there is the need to realize that we are adopted into a family that does not have an only son, but another heir to whom an enduring promise is given.[37] Such a reminder may help to change attitudes to Islam's perceived supersession of Christianity: Islam is not simply a newer religion than Christianity but has its basis on a much older promise – a promise made to Abraham and traced, not through Isaac, but through

---

36. James Dunn's words seem wise here:

> The old and new covenants should be seen not so much as two quite different covenants, but as two interpretations of the first covenant: the promise to Abraham. … Christianity is not so much an antithesis to Judaism as the means by which Gentiles were drawn into Israel (together with Jews) in fulfilment of Israel's historic mission to the nations. (James D. G. Dunn, 'Judaism and Christianity: One Covenant or Two?', in *Covenant Theology: Contemporary Approaches*, ed. Mark. J. Cartledge and David Mills [Carlisle: Paternoster, 2001], 54)

37. Nicholas Lash puts it thus: 'Moses, Jesus, Muhammad: three individuals who stand, in very different ways, at the particular beginnings of the stories of Judaism, Christianity and Islam. Behind all three of them stands Abraham' (Nicholas Lash, *The Beginning and the End of 'Religion'* [Cambridge, Cambridge University Press, 1996], 216).

Ishmael. Evangelicals do, after all, tend to make a similar move with regard to Judaism: as evangelicals, we tend not to question the promise God made in relation to Israel for rabbinical Judaism as opposed to templic Judaism, despite significant differences in religious practice. It may well be time to attend to God's three families who have arisen from one great promise to Abraham – a great promise which for Christians is a prefigurement of Jesus Christ, and which has its truth in Him; a promise which continues in God's faithfulness; and a promise made in scripture, which – as evangelicals especially – we cannot ignore. In attending theologically to the full breadth and depth of such a promise in scripture, we have the possibility of becoming more (and not less) evangelical.

Chapter 14

LEGITIMIZING AND NECESSITATING
INTER-FAITH DIALOGUE ON EXCLUSIVIST
GROUNDS: THE DYNAMICS OF INTER-FAITH FOR
INDIVIDUAL FAITH COMMUNITIES

Introduction

Inter-faith dialogue involves all of the complexities of human interaction.[1] Dialogue is not the same as papers written which state a position with the final full-stop in place, but instead involves person-to-person, face-to-face engagement with the other.[2] Dialogue involves speaking and listening, leading and being led, shaping and being shaped. It is not a series of monologues, nor is it a sermon or lecture. Dialogue is not simply bidirectional (I speak-you listen), but is, instead, complexly multidirectional (I speak-you listen-You speak-I listen-I rethink-I speak again and so on). It is not simply cognitive and theoretical, but fully personal and human. Dialogue is not only about the other with whom we dialogue, it is also about ourselves. In dialogue, we should not simply expect the other to be changed (if at all) but ourselves to be transformed: what one brings to dialogue is secondary to that which one takes from dialogue with the other.

Thus, this essay concerns the dynamics of inter-faith dialogue and considers the purpose of such dialogue. Put in its sharpest form, the chapter asks why religious people should engage in inter-faith dialogue and what inter-faith dialogue seeks to achieve. The focus of this chapter is, therefore, concerned with the step prior to engagement in inter-faith dialogue (in whatever form) and the mechanics of practices; it is concerned with the thinking prior to articulations of theologies of religions. Its concerns surround the reasons why religious people of any one faith tradition should be at all concerned to engage with members of any other religious community. Underlying the argument in this chapter are many of the concerns addressed by Paul Ricoeur,[3] whose thought has been particularly

---

1. I wish to thank Canon Professor Anthony C. Thiselton and the anonymous referees of the previously published version of this essay for their helpful comments.

2. See David F. Ford, *Self and Salvation: Being Transformed* (Cambridge: Cambridge University Press, 1999), 17–44.

3. See Paul Ricoeur, *Oneself as Another*, trans. Kathleen Blamey (Chicago: University of Chicago Press, 1992).

utilized in the field of theologies of inter-faith engagement (especially by David Ford). However, the focus of this chapter is more specifically not only the legitimacy of people of any one religious tradition engaging with any other but also whether one can speak of the necessity of such engagement in order to be genuinely and more fully persons of an individual faith community. In an age in which religion is a burning issue in the geopolitical sphere, the need for peoples of different religions to engage may seem clear; what is less clear is whether there is legitimacy for and an imperative to members of individual faith communities to engage with the religious other on the exclusive grounds of their individual faith. This chapter thus seeks to advocate that theology done in the service of individual faiths needs, as a priority, to engage in legitimizing and necessitating dialogue with the religious other primarily as the religious other (rather than singularly as the political other), in recognition that full expressions of any one faith may well involve a sensitivity to and a positive attitude towards members of other faith commitments.

Hence, this chapter asserts that the effects of inter-faith dialogue on oneself need to be brought back to the individual religious community. However, it argues that this cannot be done in such a way as to undermine the particularity and integrity of an individual community, but needs to be done in a manner which allows that community to become more genuinely the community of faith it already is. Practitioners of inter-faith engagement should bring what they learn through dialogue back to the faith community of which they are a part, but do so in a way that engages on terms internal to that community. By this I mean that the internal reasoning of an individual tradition should be employed to legitimize and necessitate engagement with another tradition. Members of faith communities need to know not just how to engage with the other but why engaging with the other is a priority and how an individual tradition can and does provide the resources for it to be a priority. Clearly this priority will be different for different faith communities, and for some it will not even be an issue. However, this fact does not undermine the need for faiths to engage on the basis of their own particularities. That inter-faith dialogue may not be an issue that needs legitimizing for some communities may actually underscore the need for particularity; a particularity that recognizes that some traditions will not see the need for this engagement on the basis of particularity as essential to their individual particularity. The central point of this chapter is simply this: it is incumbent on individual faith communities and traditions to engage in dialogue with others on the basis of their individual particularity. Put concretely, a Christian should engage with a Muslim on the basis of Christianity; a Muslim should engage with a Christian on the basis of Islam; and so on. Engagement on the basis of a religion is not only because in this there is genuine inter-*faith* dialogue but also because legitimacy for engaging with the other (which can at times be difficult and seem counter-intuitive to a tradition) must be grounded on the basis of a tradition.

Diagnosing some possible problems

The concerns of this essay arise from an awareness of three possible problems with the present situation. The first problem is that faith communities do not need the religious other, and inter-faith dialogue is not seen as a high priority for many communities. Faced with running buildings and finances, practising individual religious rites, clarifying a sense of individual and collective identity within a complexly religious and secular society,[4] dealing (in the instance of diaspora communities) with issues concerning being a religious minority and (at least in western Europe) contending with the onslaught of secularism,[5] individual religious communities in the present generation have enough to contend with without engaging with members of other faith communities, who similarly have plenty of other priorities that seem higher than inter-faith dialogue. One can see how a vicious cycle can ensue. Moreover, many religious communities (especially monotheistic faiths) understand themselves to be exclusive, and to engage and dialogue with the religious other would be a denial or betrayal of that exclusivity whereby inter-faith dialogue might be seen to undermine particularity or to relativize a uniquely considered or revealed perspective on the divine.[6] Individual communities and faith members can fear the pollution of the outsider that may reduce the integrity of their community and, instead of bringing dialogue between two others, may create a *tertium quid*. These concerns often lead to an alienation between religious communities, and at worst can lead to various forms of violence. This violence is not only in terms of terrorist acts carried out in the

---

4. The phrase 'complexly religious and secular' is borrowed from Prof. David Ford.

5. Although the growth of secularism is debated by those who see a contemporary resurgence of religion, advocates of the secularization thesis still attest to its continuing validity (especially in Europe); cf. Scott M. Thomas, 'Taking Religious and Cultural Pluralism Seriously: The Global Resurgence of Religion and the Transformation of International Society', *Millennium: Journal of International Studies* 29 (2000): 815–41; Grace Davie, *Europe: The Exceptional Case: Parameters of Faith and the Modern World* (London: Darton, Longmann & Todd, 2000); David Martin, *The Religions and the Secular: Studies in Secularization* (London: Routledge & Kegan Paul, 1969); David Martin, *Reflections on Sociology and Theology* (Oxford: Clarendon Press, 1997); and Peter L. Berger, ed., *The Desecularization of the West* (Grand Rapids, MI: Eerdmans, 1999).

6. Although this chapter speaks in rather general terms (at this point), it is written by a Christian living in the West and, therefore, betrays the concerns of one living as a Western Christian. These concerns will no doubt be put differently by others. While it may seek to consider shared problems, along with MacIntyre it is aware that shared problems do not provide traditions with 'a neutral standard in terms of which their respective achievements can be measured. Some problems are indeed shared. But what importance each particular problem has varies from tradition to tradition, and so do the effects of failing to arrive at a solution.' Alasdair MacIntyre, *Whose Justice? Which Rationality?* (London: Duckworth, 1988), 348.

name of individual religious communities but also in terms of the antagonism that can exist at localized levels between, for example, mosques and churches that are located on different sides of the street. What compounds these problems is that many of those involved in inter-faith dialogue are often so concerned with the good and proper work that they are doing that they are distanced from those in their religious communities who see the religious other as insurmountably different from themselves. For many of those engaging in inter-faith dialogue, the complexities of doing so alongside the religious other (perhaps inevitably) leads them to focus on the religious other rather than reforming members of their own faith community; thus, they run the danger of being primarily identified as members of an inter-faith community rather than (or at least only secondarily) members of an individual faith community.

The second possible problem lies in the fact that exclusivist members of faith communities often perceive that which unites those engaged in inter-faith dialogue as being some form of liberalism that exists outside of the claims and traditions of individual faith communities.[7] For this reason, the liberal practitioner of an individual religion is seen by conservative and exclusivist members of the faith community to be an outsider to the very community of which they claim to be a part. Hence, liberals come to be seen as not fully genuine or authentic parts of the community but are instead identified primarily as 'liberals' and only secondarily as members of a faith community, who read and interpret their faith through their external liberal framework. The dialogue between such liberals is seen as no dialogue at all by exclusivists, and it risks seeking agreement and commonality between religions around a lowest common denominator.[8] Such dialogue is seen as symptomatic of a pluralistic approach to religion in modernity that fails to recognize distinction, particularity and exclusivity by imposing the universal category of 'religion' onto all individual faiths, and seeing each individual religion as merely one instantiation of the generalized universal. Consequently, those who meet to engage in inter-faith dialogue are often not the ones who need to do so: since liberals are not going to engage in physical violence against the religious other (albeit they may engage in 'violence' to the otherness of the other), it is exclusivists who most need to meet the religious other in face-to-face dialogue. Clearly, this does not mean that all exclusivists will engage in violence towards the other, but it is from the extremities of exclusivist forms of communities that fundamentalisms arise. Proponents of inter-faith dialogue need to engage these problems, and direct an imperative towards exclusivist practitioners of faiths to engage in inter-faith dialogue that is legitimized and necessitated on the practitioner's terms.

Third and relatedly, the recognition of the importance of inter-faith dialogue for the present situation of discord globally and in localized communities seemingly

---

7. See MacIntyre, *Whose Justice? Which Rationality?*, 326–48.

8. See, for example, Hick who speaks of 'the Real' as opposed to 'God', John Hick, *An Interpretation of Religion: Human Responses to the Transcendent* (London: Macmillan, 1989), 10; and John Hick, *Problems of Religious Pluralism* (London: Macmillan, 1985), 39–44.

stemming from religion determines that there are public and political dimensions to inter-faith dialogue. This leads to the need for those engaged in inter-faith work to transcend the normal categories and manner of theological engagement (be it the seminar, academic article or technically framed monograph) and to recognize the implications of theology for political decisions: the audience for theologians of the religions is not only the academy or the individual community of faith but also the *polis*. That is, the outworking of inter-faith dialogue may hope to involve, as a by-product, community cohesion and peace between the nations. If, however, inter-faith dialogue is to be pursued for the public good, the very people who would most benefit from engagement in it are those for whom it is most difficult – those who do not understand themselves as existing within or being a part of liberal pluralism. Moreover, while inter-faith dialogue has political implications, it cannot be engineered or directed by the state, but, in order that it engage those who need to be engaged most strongly, should arise from within the community of faith. To engage those whose primary identity is their individual religion (before their sense of nation/statehood or liberal democracy), it is necessary to engage on the basis of the exclusivist and conservative elements of each faith in order to legitimize dialogue with the religious other, and to direct the faith community to the religious other. Directives from external secular powers will only undermine an individual faith's sense of its internal authority, and will lead conservative factions again to fear that the inter-faith project results in the reduction of any one particular faith to a bland common religion understood only from an outsider, secular perspective, whereby religion becomes the religion of the enlightenment, tolerated by the state only inasmuch as it is not too fervent. In this there is a difficult balance to strike: the state clearly sees the importance of inter-faith dialogue; however, the impetus for this work (for the reasons outlined) cannot come from politicians, but must come from within faiths.

In light of this diagnosis, this chapter advocates that one major priority for inter-faith dialogue is the reformation of individual faith communities to make them more fully the community their faith calls them to be. Dialoguing with the religious other leads one back to one's own individual faith community and identity, and the need to engage in a reconciling reformation and transformation of the self, in light of the other, in order to make the faith community more genuinely itself. By this I mean that meeting with the religious other should lead members of a faith community back to their own community; it should lead to a rethinking of identity in light of the religious other in order truly and more intensively to become oneself. For example, a Christian engaging in dialogue with a Muslim should seek to understand how to frame that dialogue for her or himself in light of the Christian faith, and how to engage in that dialogue in a manner that does not undermine Christian identity but reinforces and allows for deep and intense Christian identity, a depth of identity that would not be possible without that dialogue with the Muslim.[9] Furthermore, this identity may become

9. See Ben Quash, '"Deep Calls to Deep": Reading Scripture in a Multi-Faith Society', in *Remembering Our Future: Explorations in Deep Church*, ed. L. Bretherton and A. Walker (Milton Keynes: Paternoster, 2007), 108–30.

so deep that it necessitates communication with other Christians in order that they, too, can become even more overtly, deeply, intensely and particularly Christian. In this way, inter-faith dialogue becomes central to being exclusively and intensely Christian, leading even conservative Christians to engage in dialogue in order to be genuinely Christian and to fulfil their Christian calling. This virtuous cycle needs to undermine the potential vicious cycles above. While clearly one cannot presume that all members of all faith communities will have this virtuous cycle as a primary concern (there will be other non-competing reasons for engaging in inter-faith dialogue), the concern to be genuinely and fully a member of a faith community is innate to all who understand their identity as related to their faith commitment. The basic argument of this chapter is, therefore, that faiths should begin to understand what is internal to their tradition that makes inter-faith dialogue a necessity for intense and particular religious self-identity: what is there in Christianity, Islam, Judaism and all other faiths that determines that engaging in inter-faith dialogue makes a practitioner respectively more Christian, Muslim, Jewish and so on? In seeking to discover this, we can begin to undermine the potential problems of inter-faith dialogue diagnosed above and recognize the need for inter-faith dialogue on conservative or exclusivist terms for the good of the world, but motivated entirely from within individual faiths.[10]

The purpose of inter-faith dialogue: Changing ourselves and not the other

To solve some of the problems with dangerous theo-politics, it is necessary in the first instance to engage in the 'theo' aspect of the theo-political. Problematic elements of individual traditions' self-expressions need to be dealt with in terms internal to the tradition itself, and faced with this the practitioner of inter-faith dialogue has a dual agenda. By engaging with the religious other, the practitioner of inter-faith engagement is in dialogue with other religious traditions, but, by engaging in the activity of dialogue with the religious other, practitioners of any individual faith are also in dialogue with the particular tradition of their own faith. In this way the transformative nature of inter-faith dialogue can become reformative for the individual communities of those who engage in it. For practitioners of inter-faith dialogue to make a difference in the public realm, there may be a need to engage in reparative reasoning in relation to one's own tradition, looking deeply within one's own tradition to resource a repair of it, in this instance in terms of the relationship

---

10. This may also refer to those who are not exclusivist; see, for example, J. A. DiNoia, 'Christian Universalism: The Nonexclusive Particularity of Salvation in Christ', in *Either/Or: The Gospel or Neopaganism*, ed. C. E. Braaten and R. W. Jenson (London: Eerdmans, 1995), 37–48.

between one's own tradition and other religious traditions.[11] This repair is not an engagement in changing a particular community into something new or different; it is, instead, an engagement in making that community more genuinely and truly the community it claims to be by seeking to repair its reasoning from within. Practitioners in inter-faith dialogue should make reformation of their tradition a priority in order to legitimize the practice for other members of their community on the basis of their particular tradition; better still, they should seek to use their tradition in order to understand engagement with the other as a priority.

There is certainly a level of 'chicken and egg' about this: one needs to engage with the religious other in order to recognize the transformative nature of that engagement to lead one back to one's own tradition in order to legitimize that engagement with the religious other, so that others too feel they can engage in it. However, this cyclical model of inter-faith engagement has the potential to become a further virtuous cycle, with the possibility of bringing healing in the public realm. Engagement in inter-faith, with attentiveness to intra-religious dialogue, brings about the possibility of engaging those who are not comfortable with it, including those who are fearful of meeting around a shared common principle like liberalism. In short, such attentiveness determines an engagement with those internal to a tradition, who need to engage with the other, and it determines that this is done on their terms in a manner which recognizes the exclusive claims of religious traditions.

Consequently, there is a clear need for practitioners of inter-faith dialogue to think in terms of the prior step to do these activities, and the term 'reformation' is appropriate to this activity. In order to engage those who think that inter-faith dialogue is alien to a tradition, it is necessary to look back into the tradition to search for an imperative to engage with religious others in light of the politics of today. By reaching deeply into each individual tradition, it may be possible to reach more clearly out to others in reconciliation and to see the reasons for doing so; not to change others or completely change ourselves, but rather to reform ourselves in order to be truly who we should be in light of the religious other.

Meeting around Scripture

Clearly, the manner in which different traditions approach inter-faith dialogue varies depending on the tradition.[12] Indeed, even within Christianity, different

---

11. See Nick Adams, 'Making Deep Reasoning Public', *Modern Theology* 22 (2006): 385–401, esp. at 400–1. For further performances of this practice, see Peter Ochs, 'Abrahamic Theo-politics: A Jewish View', in *The Blackwell Companion to Political Theology*, ed. Peter Scott and William T. Cavanaugh (Oxford: Blackwell, 2007), 519–34; and Ben Quash, 'Deep Calls to Deep', in *Remembering Our Future: Explorations in Deep Church*, ed. L. Bretherton and A. Walker (Milton Keynes: Paternoster, 2007), 108–30.

12. Cf. MacIntyre, *Whose Justice? Which Rationality?*, 348.

traditions will engage variously dependent on the way in which authority operates within their tradition: while exclusivist Protestant traditions might look to the Reformation principle of *sola scriptura*, for the Roman Catholic Church the magisterium will need to be considered. This does not mark a denial of the argument that follows, however: it is recognition of the complexity involved in the enterprise of legitimizing and necessitating inter-faith dialogue. Nevertheless, from a Western perspective, living in a world in which there seems (at least as it is portrayed by the media) to be considerable discord between members of the Abrahamic faiths determines that there is a need for engagement between people who understand their exclusivities (variously) from the perspective of their scriptures.[13] The key to legitimizing and even necessitating inter-faith dialogue on exclusivist grounds for 'people of the Book' surely lies within the teaching of their sacred books. In the contemporary geopolitical situation, it would be beneficial for Muslims, Jews and Christians to engage with members of other faith communities on the grounds of biblical or Qur'anic imperative. In this way, engagement is neither at the behest of an external secular power nor out of conformity to an external intellectual movement; it is instead on the exclusive basis of a particular religious tradition.

For me, this realization has arisen from my involvement in Scriptural Reasoning,[14] through which I have been led to consider the issues that are at the centre of this essay. Meeting with others has led me to look at my own scriptures with new perspectives. However, what fascinates me most in this enterprise is my reading of the Christian scriptures in light of engaging in the practice of reading those scriptures alongside another; this has enabled me to see the legitimacy and necessity of engagement with the other (ironically) on the exclusive grounds of my own revelational exclusivity. In engaging in dialogue, as a result of the pressing political situation in the West and a belief in the Christian imperative to peace, I have found it necessary simultaneously to seek the legitimacy of such a practice on the basis of my theology. As a theologian who takes the uniqueness of Christ, scripture and the creeds as the foundations for my speech about God, I am not someone who finds inter-faith dialogue natural or easy. I engage in dialogue because of the importance of this activity for a theology that recognizes its role in the public sphere. Yet, to retain my integrity as a theologian, that public theology should correspond to my private thinking. Meeting around scripture has allowed this two-way engagement to take place: by reading with members of another faith

---

13. The status of the scriptures of each of these traditions clearly varies both internal to the traditions and between them: for Christianity the Word is supremely seen not in the Bible but in the incarnate Jesus.

14. On the practice of Scriptural Reasoning, see David F. Ford, *Christian Wisdom: Desiring God and Learning in Love* (Cambridge: Cambridge University Press, 2007), 273–303; David F. Ford and C. C. Pecknold, eds, *The Promise of Scriptural Reasoning* (Oxford: Blackwell, 2006); and David F. Ford, 'God and Our Public Space: A Scriptural Wisdom', *International Journal of Public Theology* 1 (2007): 63–81, at 71–3.

community, I have been led by their otherness back to my own faith community. However, this has not made my community any less particularly or intensely Christian, but rather more fully particular and intense in its identity as Christian. Meeting with the other has simultaneously determined the need to reflect on the theological legitimacy of engaging with the religious other. Moreover, in seeking legitimacy for this dialogue, I have found the necessity of it, a necessity grounded in the very basis of being a Christian.

I have faced this issue of reformation both as a lecturer in the academy and as a preacher in the pulpit. Since meeting with the other has led me back to reforming myself and my community in order to be more truly the community we are called to be, this involves as a preacher not only legitimizing the practice of meeting with members of other faith communities but also urgently calling from the pulpit for the necessity of doing so, not on political or secular grounds but on exclusively biblical and theological grounds. Furthermore, engagement with the Abrahamic other around the practice of Scriptural Reasoning has led to a heightened awareness in my reading of the Christian Bible of the place of the religious other within its narrative.

In describing experiences of Scriptural Reasoning to 'secular' people (including some politicians), I have witnessed fascination with the idea that Scriptural Reasoning provides the possibility of religious people engaging with each other 'on their own terms', and that solutions to the local and global problems between members of faith communities might actually be found within the very particularities of the communities themselves. The ability to explain and interpret one's religious text to and with members of other faith communities has the potential to include even the most conservative, orthodox or 'fundamentalist' of believers, and it does so on the basis of their particularity and on their agenda. Given this, Toynbee Hall in London has engaged in a pilot scheme for young people called 'Justext'. The feasibility of curriculum development within schools is presently being considered, as a way of recognizing the religious particularity and commitments of students within Religious Studies, which often presents individual religious traditions as relativized individual instantiations of a universal human phenomenon, or it treats religions thematically seeking consensus and agreement around a common core or lowest common denominator. An interesting feature of these early discussions has been the recognition of the need to legitimize students' (and their parents') engagement in the practice. Indeed, the awareness of issues of legitimacy is reflected in the adult practice of this kind of inter-faith dialogue on the London-based Scriptural Reasoning website, which states that the material has been developed and run under the Jewish *halachic* and Islamic *shari'a* supervision of the London Beth Din and the Fatwa Committee of the Islamic Cultural Centre and London Central Mosque respectively.[15] The need to engage in intra-faith legitimization as the prior step to inter-faith dialogue is clear.

---

15. The Scriptural Reasoning Society, http://www.scripturalreasoning.org.uk (accessed 24 November 2020).

Some hints for one particular community: Looking to Christ to understand Christianity and the other

In line with the programmatic purpose of this chapter, the above questions can only be answered from the particular perspective of any one religious tradition for that particular tradition. Writing as a protestant Christian, I seek to consider these issues by attending to the protestant Christian tradition. Moreover, in keeping with the purpose of this chapter, the legitimizing and necessitating of inter-faith dialogue will be done on the basis of the exclusive claims of the Christian tradition: that is, by attending to its scriptures, creeds, Christology and the Trinity. In other words, the very particular things that divide Christianity from other religious communities will be utilized to resource legitimizing dialogue. This is hardly a new practice, and many academics have found resources for legitimizing engagement with the other within the Trinitarian nature of the Christian tradition, the Christian doctrine of God, the Christological focus of Christian theology, pneumatology, Christian wisdom or Christian scripture.[16] This chapter in no way seeks to displace such work; it seeks rather to supplement it and to accentuate the place for necessitating and legitimizing inter-faith dialogue for those who find it difficult to engage in it (given their exclusivist commitments to their respective traditions). As a Methodist preacher, I offer hints which seek to have a homiletic note to them as they endeavour to engage the Christian public and not only the academy.[17] Given this homiletic note, it is the Christian scriptures and Jesus as portrayed in it that form the principal foci of my endeavour. Throughout what follows, it should be remembered that the public and religious lives of people and nations in the ancient world were in many ways inseparable. It is also necessary to remember that thinking of Jesus' dealings with non-Jewish peoples as dealings with proto-institutionalized Christians is anachronistic. While the passages discussed may reflect concerns of early communities rather than reflections on the historical Jesus, Jesus' dealings with non-Jewish people cannot be seen as making these people into some form of Christian: we are never told, for example, that Samaritans or pagans who feature in the Gospel accounts ceased to be Samaritans or pagans. Indeed, given that the New Testament makes much of the inclusion of

---

16. See, for example, Rowan Williams, *On Christian Theology* (Oxford: Blackwell, 2000), 167–80; Gavin D'Costa, *The Meeting of Religions and the Trinity* (Edinburgh: T&T Clark, 2000); David B. Burrell, *Knowing the Unknowable God: Ibn-Sina, Maimonides, Aquinas* (Notre Dame: University of Notre Dame Press, 1987); *CD* IV/3, 691–2; Eugene F. Rogers Jr, 'Supplementing Barth on Jews and Gender: Identifying God by Analogy and Spirit', *Modern Theology* 14 (1998): 43–82; Ford, *Christian Wisdom*; and Charles H. Pinnock, *A Wideness in God's Mercy: The Finality of Jesus Christ in a World of Religions* (Grand Rapids, MI: Zondervan, 1992), 25–9.

17. See the essay in this volume, 'Preaching inter-faith: Finding hints about the religious other from the Good Samaritan'.

the first gentiles in the community,[18] one can hardly suppose that the gentiles and Samaritans Jesus came across became integral members of the first community or proto-Christians during his lifetime.

Jesus as religious outsider

It is a noticeable theme in John's gospel that Jesus is at times seen not only as an outsider but more specifically as a religious outsider.[19] This is most curiously evident in a discussion about the true heirs of Abraham, where Jesus is called a Samaritan (Jn 8.48). It is a noteworthy feature of this story that Jesus, who speaks of God as his father, is immediately contrasted with those who call Abraham their father. 'Abraham is our father' (NRSV, Jn 8.39) and 'We are descendants of Abraham and have never been slaves to anyone' (NRSV, Jn 8.33) is the cry from those opposing Jesus. This is heightened all the more in questioning Jesus' authenticity as a heir of Abraham by referring to him as a Samaritan – even if some form of heir of Abraham, a wrong and wayward heir. Jesus is religiously wrong. These aspects of John's gospel could be interpreted in dangerously anti-Semitic ways; the church must repent of its past tendency to do this. However, the challenge for the Christian in an age of institutionalized Christianity, who sees her or himself as the religious insider, is to remember Jesus as an outsider to the religious legitimacy of his age, whose claim to Abraham was disputed and who was seen as a Samaritan. Interestingly, Jesus never challenges the discussion of him as a Samaritan; he only challenges the accusation that he is demon possessed (Jn 8.49). Jesus is one who cannot be captured simply within the bounds of institutional religion of any kind; or as Barth puts it, Christ is 'the Abolition [*Aufhebung*] of Religion'.[20] In an age in which there is perceived to be much discord between the rival Abrahamic faiths, the Christian tradition is wise in its relations with the other Abrahamic traditions to remember its Lord was once considered an illegitimate Abrahamic heir, and it should, therefore, not be quick to question the legitimacy of claims on Abraham by others.

Jesus is not only a religious outsider in Judea, the Samaritans see Jesus as a religious outsider too: 'The Samaritan woman said to him, "How is it that you, a Jew, ask a drink of me, a woman of Samaria?"' (NRSV, Jn 4.9). In Samaria, Jesus is seen as a Jew; in Judea, on one occasion, he is seen as a Samaritan. Institutional religions of his age on different sides see Jesus as a religious outsider. Moreover, it also seems that, according to John's gospel, religious outsiders identify with Jesus, and in Jerusalem it is Greeks who wish to see Jesus (Jn 12.20-21). That Jesus was once perceived as a religious outsider and approached by religious outsiders surely

---

18. See Henry Wansborough, *The Lion and the Bull: The Gospels of Mark and Luke* (London: Darton, Longman & Todd, 1996), 141–2.

19. I am indebted here to discussions with Mark Edwards, University of Oxford, UK.

20. *CD* I/2, §17. See further, Tom Greggs, 'Bringing Barth's Critique of Religion to the Inter-faith Table', *JR* 88 (2008): 75–94.

challenges the Christians' response to those they themselves perceive as religious outsiders from their own insider perspective today.

Jesus and the Samaritans

A related theme to this is Jesus' dealings with the Samaritans more generally. The Samaritans were the descendants of the Jews who did not go into exile and were hostile to the rebuilding of the Jerusalem temple. Their purity as a people was called into question, and, although they recognized only the first five books of the Jewish scriptures, they did not follow Jewish ritual. These issues were focused on the establishment of a rival temple at Mt Gerezim, and the recognition of a different line of priestly descent.[21] Their proximity to and alienation from the Jewish people led to fierce rivalry between the peoples. I wish to contend that Jesus' dealings with the Samaritans are significant to the present age of local and international theo-politics. There are several notable features in this.

The first is how Jesus both attends to and teaches about practical, physical human needs in his dealings with Samaritans. In the story of Jesus cleansing the ten lepers in Luke's Gospel, one of the lepers Jesus heals is a Samaritan, and it is he who returns to thank Jesus (Lk. 17.16-19). Jesus attends to the Samaritan's physical needs by curing him of his leprosy. This in itself attends to the Samaritan leper's need for physical human contact with others, which would have been prevented by his disease. A similar issue of attending to the physical needs of the other is seen from the alternative perspective in terms of Jesus asking the Samaritan woman at the well for a drink (Jn 4.7). Here, the Samaritan woman is invited to respond to Jesus' thirst, his physical needs, despite his religious otherness. While a spiritual point is made from this, the woman is nevertheless concerned that she cannot attend to Jesus' needs, as she has no bucket and the well is deep. Physical needs are also pointed to in the famous story of the Good Samaritan (Lk. 10.25-37). Feeling pity for the injured man, the Samaritan tends to his physical needs: 'He went to him and bandaged his wounds, having poured oil and wine on them. Then he put him on his own animal, brought him to an inn, and took care of him' (NRSV, Lk. 10.34). Christians are charged in their relation with the religious other to respond with mercy to the physical needs of the religious other, and to recognize the mercy with which others may attend to them.

The second notable feature of Jesus' dealings with Samaritans is in terms of the issue of God. Jesus' attitude as a Jewish man towards the Samaritans, as a disputed Abrahamic people, may say something to Christians about contemporary issues between Abrahamic peoples. This is not to deny all of the complexity surrounding

---

21. For more on the Samaritans, see Everett Ferguson, *Backgrounds of Early Christianity*, 2nd edn (Grand Rapids, MI: Eerdmans, 1993), 378, 499–501 and Richard Bauckham, 'The Scrupulous Priest and the Good Samaritan: Jesus' Parabolic Interpretation of the Law of Moses', *NTS* 44 (1998): 475–89 at 487.

these types of questions, but to seek hints from the Gospels on these themes. In the aforementioned story of the ten lepers, Luke recounts:

> Then one of them, when he saw that he was healed, turned back, praising God with a loud voice. He prostrated himself at Jesus' feet and thanked him. And he was a Samaritan. Then Jesus asked, 'Were not ten made clean? But the other nine, where are they? Was none of them found to return and give praise to God except this foreigner?' (NRSV, Lk. 17.15-18)

Despite fears of religious pollution and the rejection of Samaritan cultic practice, there is no question here of the God whom the Samaritan praises, and he is not made into a 'proper' Jew before his praise is deemed appropriate. The fact that the Samaritan is religiously other to the remaining nine healed lepers is emphasized in Jesus speaking of him as a 'foreigner'; yet, it is this religious other who praises God appropriately. Similarly, in the Johannine account of the woman at the well, Jesus replies to the woman's question about the legitimacy of worship on Mt Gerezim or the Jerusalem temple saying:

> Woman, believe me, the hour is coming when you will worship the Father neither on this mountain nor in Jerusalem … the hour is coming, and is now here, when the true worshipers will worship the Father in spirit and truth, for the Father seeks such as these to worship him. God is spirit, and those who worship him must worship in spirit and truth. (NRSV, Jn 4.21-24)

While Jesus recognizes the woman's religious otherness, this is in the context of the woman still worshiping. Worship of God is redefined by God's nature: since God is spirit, God cannot be contained within the bounds of any one temple. The importance of institutionalized religion, therefore, is relativized by the very ultimacy of God.

Third, the Samaritan other is seen as an example to follow. This is clear in the story of the ten lepers, and it is most overt in the story of the Good Samaritan. Jesus could have told this story in a way that allowed the hero to be a Jewish person who was prepared to place the humanity of another above religious affiliation.[22] He could have made the Samaritan the injured party, but he does not do this. Jesus makes the Samaritan the hero, and, shockingly, Jesus tells his audience to behave like the Samaritan instructing them to 'Go and do likewise' (Lk. 10.37). Hence, Jesus' audience are commanded to be like the religious other in their ethical behaviour, at the cost of ritual and religious purity – the religious contamination of the dead body (Lk. 10.31-32).[23]

---

22. Christopher Rowland, *Christian Origins* (London: SPCK, 1985), 142.
23. On ritual purity, see Bauckham, 'The Scrupulous Priest and the Good Samaritan'.

Jesus and the gentiles

A further theme that may be explored is Jesus' interaction with the gentiles. This is clearly not a major part of Jesus' ministry, and such interactions are relatively scarce;[24] however, their scarcity is not necessarily indicative of a lack of importance. For the contemporary setting, the scarcity may be a reminder that there is no substantialized 'thing' called 'inter-faith'. Interactions with other religious traditions do not displace particularity, nor should they become the normative expression of religious identity: Christians are and remain Christians; Muslims are and remain Muslims; Sikhs are and remain Sikhs; and so on. From a Christian perspective, the question is not about a reorientation entirely and exclusively onto the religious other; the question is about how to understand that religious other in times such as the present with its perceived public tensions and difficulties. This does not replace the mission of the church, but leads to the question of how the church is truly to be the church in the world in light of these themes, as one element of the church's identity. Thus, the Christian should attend to and seek hints from Jesus' interaction with gentiles as religious others.

The first feature to note is that Jesus does not make the gentiles into Jews, nor even call them out of their present religious particularity: Jesus does not make the religious other into the correct *homo religiosus*, neither does he create gentile Christians; that is clearly not part of his mission. Even in his reticent dealing with the Syrophoenician woman (Mk 7.24-30), Jesus responds to her needs without denying the religious distinction between them. The problematic nature of Jesus calling her a 'dog' cannot easily be brushed aside,[25] and is in itself indicative of the difficulties of inter-faith relations. However, she is not required to become Jewish: there is a place for her in the plan of God, albeit a different one to the place for the preferred Jewish people, and her faith makes her child well.

More positively, in Jesus' dealing with the Roman centurion (Mt. 8.5-13 and Lk. 7.1-10), Jesus responds to the faith that the centurion (no doubt a pagan) places in Jesus' ability to cure his servant, stating: 'Truly I tell you, in no one in Israel have I found such faith. I tell you, many will come from east and west and will eat with Abraham and Isaac and Jacob in the kingdom of heaven' (NRSV, Mt. 8.10-11). In comparison to the people of his own religion, then, Jesus praises the faith of these religious others. In an age of pluralism, it does the Christian well to remember this praise, especially when confronted with the piety of religious others today. Jesus' prophetic proclamation concerning those who will eat in the kingdom of heaven is indicative of a prophetic expectation that there will be feasting alongside the religious other at the *eschaton*: the centurion is no heir of Abraham, Isaac and Jacob, but he will feast with them.

---

24. E. P. Sanders, *Jesus and Judaism* (London: SCM, 1985), 219–21.

25. See Morna D. Hooker, *The Gospel According to St Mark* (London: A&C Black, 1991), 183. See also, Adele Yarbro Collins, *Mark*, Hermeneia (Minneapolis, MN: Fortress, 2007), 366–8 (and the literature cited in n. 49 regarding ethnicity and gender).

What we may see in Jesus is an opening up to the otherness of others. Barth put it thus:

> If we see Him, we see with and around Him in ever widening circles His disciples, His people, His enemies and the countless millions who have not yet heard His name. We see Him as theirs, determined by them and for them, belonging to each and every one of them.[26]

For Christians, who, in their particularity, seek to follow Christ, there exists the necessity of facing the reality of the religious other in the societies in which we live. This is not about ignoring differences or particularity, but it is rather about tending to their needs (and allowing them to tend to ours), recognizing their faith and hoping for a future feast alongside them. Inter-faith dialogue is not about ignoring Christian particularity but instead following the example of Christ.

Conclusion

There is much more that could and needs to be said about these themes as they confront religious people in our world today. From the Hebrew Bible, there is scope for reflection on the holy pagans (such as Jethro, Rahab and Melchizedek), the lack of hospitality shown to Israel from foreign nations, the exile and the commands regarding the strangers in the land. However, to illustrate the need for particularity and exclusivity in approaching the reasons for inter-faith dialogue, this chapter has looked only to the New Testament, which is exclusively and uniquely Christian. It is not the place for the Christian to give the reasons why a Jewish person might wish to engage in dialogue with them, neither for that matter why any member of any other tradition should do likewise. It is, instead, the place of the Jewish, Muslim, Hindu, Sikh and Buddhist to reflect on these questions by looking deep within their own traditions.

Inter-faith issues are deeply complex; they belong to the individual traditions and, in an age of reputed conflict, to the public arena. These issues need to be faced in recognition of their dual aspects; that is, from inside the church, temple, mosque and synagogue, as well as from the perspective of community cohesion, education policy, human rights and international relations. Such issues need to be preached and considered in the internal life of religious communities, as they seek to discover their place in the public sphere.

What I have attempted in this chapter is to forward a programmatic agenda for faith communities to consider why, for their self-identity, it might be both legitimate and necessary to engage positively with the religious other. I have done this with an illustration of how the issues might be faced by one individual community in the hope that members of different communities might also

---

26. *CD* III/2, 216.

continue to consider these themes. Attempts at dealing with the issues will need to be done with attentiveness to the full complexity of human living. However complex, it is incumbent on faiths to address these issues, if they are to be seen neither as things to be 'smuggled into some last secret place',[27] nor as forces for division or clashes of absolutes, but as forces for the good, coexisting alongside one another, in the healing of communities and the world.

---

27. Dietrich Bonhoeffer, *Letters and Papers from Prison*, ed. John W. de Gruchy, trans. Isabel Best et al., Dietrich Bonhoeffer Works 8 (Minneapolis, MN: Fortress, 2010), 457.

Chapter 15

PREACHING INTER-FAITH: FINDING HINTS ABOUT THE RELIGIOUS OTHER FROM THE GOOD SAMARITAN

It is never an easy time to be a preacher, but today's generation brings with the task of preaching a level complexity that has rarely been the case. This complexity revolves around preaching in a society which is complexly religious and secular.[1] In an age in which the dominance of Christendom has considerably declined in Western Europe,[2] preachers are confronted with the question of how best to proclaim the good news of Jesus Christ in a multicultural and multifaith society, with all of the shifting claims on identity and competing loyalties that being a member of such a heterogeneous society brings with it. This does not only involve issues about how to preach to and about the unchurched non-believer, and the struggles to maintain numbers in our congregations; but it also brings with it the complexity of knowing how to preach about members of other faith communities, and how, as Christians, we are supposed to understand and relate to these other religionists. Put sharply, the Christian preacher must face not only how to preach in an age of declining congregations and a perceived increased level of secularism;[3] the preacher must also face how to preach in a setting of religious pluralism.[4] It is this latter issue that the present essay concerns.

---

1. I owe this turn of phrase (as I owe so many things) to Prof. David Ford.

2. See Grace Davie, *Europe: The Exceptional Case. Parameters of Faith in the Modern World* (London: Darton, Longman & Todd), esp. ch. 1. We should be careful, however, not to overestimate the idea that secularization even in Europe is taking place in a united and unified direction. See, for example, David Martin, *Reflections on Sociology and Theology* (Oxford: Clarendon Press, 1997); and David Martin, *The Religious and the Secular: Studies in Secularization* (London: Routledge and Kegan Paul, 1969).

3. It may be that even if there is not a unidirectional process of secularization taking place, many Christians *perceive* this as happening; this perception may well be as important as the actual factual evidence.

4. For statistics on the religious composition of societies, see David B. Barrett, George T. Kurian and Todd M. Johnson, *World Christian Encyclopaedia*, 2nd edn (Oxford: Oxford University Press, 2001).

The problems of preaching in a pluralistic setting are compounded by the method of our preaching. Methodists, of whom I am one, as members of a Protestant denomination, are bound at least to consider the principal of *sola scriptura* in their approach to homiletics. Engaging with the Bible is central to the task, and the text is the basis for the way that we preach. The calling of the preacher is to 'preach the Gospel' and 'the message of salvation to all, in season and out of season'; and we affirm that this is 'a responsibility rooted in the word of God'.[5] The task is intimately related to scripture. However, preaching is not simple exegesis: exegesis forms the basis of preaching and is the prior step to the preached word, but it is not in and of itself preaching. Preaching needs to 'go' somewhere: although it stems from the individual, in this sense of needing to 'go' somewhere at least it is a congregational activity. Preaching is, therefore, not simply about the words of scripture, but the words of scripture *as they meet communities of the church in the world in the present*. Preaching is about speaking the words of scripture into the situations those communities face in the world in the present age, because in every age and generation preachers are called to preach the word of God to their particular age and generation. It would be inappropriate, therefore, for a preacher in the twenty-first century to preach exactly the same sermon in the same way as a preacher in the eighteenth century: while called to the same task and responsibility rooted in the word of God, we are called to serve different ages and different contexts. And in order to serve the present age, we must face the issues of the present age. For us, this is an age which faces a significant need for religious people to face questions about the relations between the religions. But to do this, the preacher cannot deny her calling to preach the word of God and the message of salvation to all: even in this age, and herein lies the rub, our calling is to be preachers of the word.

Facing these issues as preachers can lead one to something of a quandary. The preacher is called to preach Christ and him crucified, and our task, in the words of Charles Wesley, is that we must '[our] every sacred moment spend / In publishing the sinners' friend'.[6] The earliest members of the tradition to which I belong preached the good news in fields to seek to gain converts for Christ. As Methodists, we are born of revivalism. But if, as preachers, we seek to preach to our congregations, and if that in turn means that we need to take contemporary issues seriously, facing the contemporary need for peace between peoples of different religions is paramount in importance. A member of another Protestant tradition, Karl Barth, once said the preacher should read both the Bible and the newspaper together.[7] Preaching involves confronting and considering contemporary issues in light of the word of God, and the word of God in light of contemporary issues. It is a task of wrestling with scripture, until we receive a blessing in today's age and

---

5. *The Methodist Worship Book* (Peterborough: Methodist Publishing House, 1999), 332.

6. *Hymns and Psalms* (London: Methodist Publishing House, 1983), no. 767 ('Give Me the Faith which Can Remove').

7. 'Barth in Retirement', *Time Magazine* 82.22 (31 May 1963): 35–6.

generation. In an age of community fragmentation and conflict and of geopolitical turmoil surrounding the war against terror, there could be few greater blessings than peace between peoples of different faiths – and from a Western perspective, particularly peace between the children of Abraham. In light of these themes, the preacher must ask how it is that we stay true to scripture with all of its exclusivist claims[8] *and* assist our congregations to understand their place within a pluralistic and multifaith nation and world.

My own engagement with these issues has been sharpened in recent years through my involvement in Scriptural Reasoning (the reading of the sacred scriptures of Judaism, Christianity and Islam beside each other).[9] This activity has led me to reconsider the relations between peoples of different faiths, but crucially it has done this around the shared reading of scripture together. What has most interested me about this engagement in Scriptural Reasoning has been the way in which it has affected my own private, or singularly Christian, reading of the Bible, and the fresh insights this has brought about with regard to the religious other in my own sacred text. One might call this pre-Scriptural Reasoning scriptural reasoning. This chapter marks an engagement in such a mode of reasoning. My suggestion here is that we must seek hints from scripture and be attentive particularly to positive assessments of the religious other within the text, in order to repair a tradition which can seem confrontational and divisive in terms of the possibilities of its exclusivist preaching.[10] There are many places in scripture to which one could look for direction – Rahab, Melchizedek, Jethro, the centurion whose slave is dying, to name but a few of these 'holy pagans' found within the text of scripture.[11] However, in this chapter, I would like to model just one way of approaching this issue by considering the famous story of Jesus – the Good Samaritan (Lk. 10.25-37).

---

8. By this I mean such passages as: 'Those who believe in him are not condemned; but those who do not believe are condemned already, because they have not believed in the name of the only Son of God' (Jn 3.18).

9. On this practice, see David F. Ford, *Christian Wisdom: Desiring God and Learning in Love* (Cambridge: Cambridge University Press, 2007), 273–303; David F. Ford and C. C. Pecknold, eds, *The Promise of Scriptural Reasoning* (Oxford: Blackwell, 2006); and David F. Ford, 'God and Our Public Space: A Scriptural Wisdom', *International Journal of Public Theology* 1 (2007): 71–3.

10. This method is sometimes referred to as 'reparative reasoning'. See Nick Adams, 'Making Deep Reasoning Public', *Modern Theology* 22 (2006): 400–1. This practice is well modelled in Peter Ochs, 'Abrahamic Theo-politics: A Jewish View', in *The Blackwell Companion to Political Theology*, ed. Peter Scott and William T. Cavanaugh (Oxford: Blackwell, 2007), 519–34.

11. See Charles H. Pinnock, *A Wideness in God's Mercy: The Finality of Jesus Christ in a World of Religions* (Grand Rapids, MI: Zondervan, 1992), esp. 25–9.

Relations between Jews and Samaritans

In order to gain the full impact of this parable, it is necessary to recognize the level of hostility, stretching back many centuries, that existed between Jews and Samaritans.[12] Relations between the northern and southern kingdoms of Israel following the period of the united monarchy of Saul, David and Solomon were never particularly good. When the northern kingdom fell in 722–721 BCE, the Assyrians deported the Israelites and brought in pagans from neighbouring nations who worshipped Yahweh alongside other gods. This was a practice that 2 Kgs 17.41 suggests was carried out by the descendants of these new inhabitants, thus polluting the purity of the theology and ritual of the northern nation.[13] Moreover, in the years 589 and 587 BCE the ancient Jewish people were disrupted by the most cataclysmic disaster of their history to that point. Having been brought to the promised land, having built the temple and centralized the cult upon it, the people were sent into exile by Nebuchadnezzar. The effects of this were enormous, and most significant among them was the loss of the temple in 587 BCE.[14] The people who retuned following the exile began to understand themselves as superior to the people who had remained in the land, and to their neighbours to the north who lived around the city of Samaria. The root of this antagonism seems to be the opposition of the authorities in Samaria to the rebuilding of the temple and the city walls of Jerusalem. The Samaritans had their own rival priesthood and temple at Mount Gerezim and opposed the Jerusalem cult, even enacting violence towards pilgrims travelling through Samaria.[15] From the Judean side, against the experience of the exile, the Gerezim temple was seen as a rival place of worship to the centralized Jewish worship in Jerusalem.[16] Furthermore, not only was this rivalry seen as an affront to the returned exiles and their second temple, but it was also associated with ritual and theological impurity through the pollution of foreign gods.

This is the background to the story of the Good Samaritan. As a result of this history and hostility, Jews refused to engage with Samaritans in their everyday lives. One can also see this reflected in John's Gospel: 'The Samaritan woman

---

12. Christopher Rowland, *Christian Origins* (London, SPCK, 1985), 142.

13. See Lawrence Boadt, *Reading the Old Testament* (New York: Paulist Press, 1984), 459.

14. This is a very brief account of a very complex matter. For more on this history of this crucial period of the history of Judea and Israel, see Bernhard W. Anderson, *The Living World of the Old Testament*, 4th edn (Harlow: Longman, 1993), ch. 14; Martin Noth, *The History of Israel*, 2nd edn (London: A&C Black, 1965), 253–356; John Bright, *A History of Israel*, 3rd edn (London: SCM, 1998), 343–60; Roland De Vaux, *Ancient Israel: Its Life and Institutions* (London: Darton, Longman & Todd, 1973), 312–43.

15. Richard Bauckham, 'The Scrupulous Priest and the Good Samaritan: Jesus' Parabolic Interpretation of the Law of Moses', *NTS* 44 (1998): 487.

16. Everett Fergusson, *Backgrounds of Early Christianity*, 2nd edn (Grand Rapids, MI: Eerdmans, 1993), 378.

said to him, "How is it that you, a Jew, ask a drink of me, a woman of Samaria?" (Jews do not share things in common with Samaritans).'[17] Here, the animosity and otherness of the other is such that the other is seen as insurmountably alien – so much so that one cannot even engage in sharing such a basic human need as a glass of water.

Issues of religious identity: 'Go and do likewise'

It is clear, therefore, that discussion of Samaritans in the New Testament involves the issue of religious identity.[18] For all of the levels of continuity between Jewish and Samaritan peoples, there was also a clear level of discontinuity and otherness. This issue is picked up very clearly in the story of the Good Samaritan. In reply to the question 'Who is my neighbour? (Lk. 10.29), Jesus tells a shocking story which indicates that one's neighbour is not necessarily a member of one's own religious community but can be a member of another religious community, and which indicates that members of one's own community are not necessarily the best neighbours one has.

In this story, a Jewish man is attacked by robbers and is left half-dead (Lk. 10.29). A priest walks by and passes on the other side of the road; a Levite does the same thing (Lk. 10.31-32). Almost certainly, this was to avoid contact with a potential dead body, which would lead to ritual uncleanness.[19] Even if that is not the case, the highest-ranking member of the religious community (the priest), on whom the command to avoid corpse defilement rested most clearly, and the next highest-ranking member of the community (the Levite) fail to help a person in need. Then enters a figure who would instinctively be understood by the community to be the villain figure, and we are left wondering what the Samaritan will do if even the priest and Levite have passed this victim by. But the Samaritan is moved with pity; bandages the wounds of the man; pours oil and wine on them; puts him on his animal; takes him to an inn; takes care of him; gives the innkeeper two denarii; tells the innkeeper to care for this man; and says he will repay all that is spent by the innkeeper (Lk. 10.33-35). Jesus asks rhetorically who the neighbour is in this situation. This is a very challenging story about being neighbourly towards others. In the words of Rowland, this indicates that 'responsibility to one's neighbour does

---

17. Jn 4.9.

18. This is disputed in Bauckham, 'The Scrupulous Priest and the Good Samaritan.' However, this piece underplays the hostility between Jewish and Samaritan peoples. Clearly, the Samaritan is not a gentile. However, this does not undermine the religious difference and antagonism it may well increase it: the Samaritans did not worship from a position of ignorance; they should have known better.

19. Rowland, *Christian Origins*, 142–3; E. V. Barrell and K. G. Barrell, *St Luke's Gospel: An Introductory Study* (London: John Murray, 1982), 93; Bauckham, 'The Scrupulous Priest and the Good Samaritan', 475–85.

not depend on racial or religious ties, for there can be no limit made on the extent of the demand made by those in need'.[20]

However, what I am struck by is this: if this is only a story about being neighbourly towards others, why not make the hero the Jewish man and the victim the Samaritan? It would have worked powerfully enough. A priest and a Levite fail to be compassionate to this Samaritan, but an ordinary Jewish person, moved with compassion, helps the Samaritan in his need. This, too, would indicate that responsibility to one's neighbour does not depend on religious or racial ties: to be a good Jewish person (a good religious insider), one should be like this ordinary Jewish man rather than the members of the community who are the religiously professional or elite. The point might have worked equally as well: which of the Jewish people was more neighbourly? Jesus does not tell the story that way, however. He makes the Samaritan, the religious other, the hero. In reading this story in today's generation, one must be attentive to the way in which it speaks homiletically into issues surrounding peace between the religions: it is a story about religious identity and relations between different faith communities. If we understand the Jewish victim, priest and Levite typologically to be members of our own Christian community and the Samaritan to be a religious outsider to our community,[21] Jesus radically disrupts our expectations by making the religious other the one who is neighbourly towards us as religious 'insiders'. He does not tell a story in which we are neighbourly towards the religious other. Instead, we are the ones in need of the neighbourliness of the other; the other is the hero, the type that we are to emulate.[22]

The power of the final words of Jesus in this pericope should not fail to address the church. Following a story about the religious other, we are told: 'Go and do likewise' (Lk. 10.37). Jesus commands us to behave not like the religious professionals and elite of our own community but like the one who is neighbourly *from another religious community*. We are told to behave like the religious other. Moreover, the issue is more complex than this. We are not always in the driving seat in terms of our dealings with the religious other, according to Jesus. It is not simply a case of our assisting and aiding the religious other who needs us, but a realization of our need to be assisted and aided by the religious other (as in the case of the victim here). We are not simply the paragons of these virtues to display

---

20. Rowland, *Christian Origins*, 142.

21. Clearly, it is not acceptable to read this story within the Christian community to be about the contemporary Jewish community. Its setting is *within* the Jewish religious community of the first century CE and should, therefore, in our setting in the twenty-first century in which Christianity exists as a world religion not be understood as a story about Jewish people, but a story which is a critique of the Christian church – the religious insiders who use this as an authoritative text.

22. On the notions of ironic need and indebtedness here, see Mark A. Proctor, '"Who Is My Neighbor?" Recontextualizing Luke's Good Samaritan (Luke 10:25–37)', *JBL* 138 (2019): 203–19.

them for others to follow; we ourselves may need at times to be helped by the religious other, and we should emulate that gracious service directed towards us. Christians are not in charge in an inter-faith setting; there is genuine reciprocity. The Good Samaritan demonstrates this. He is the hero who tends to the Jewish person when his own community do not come to his aid. The religious insider requires the religious outsider here: the outsider is quite literally vital to him. As Christians, therefore, we should not only at times be prepared to emulate the neighbourliness of religious others, but we need to be prepared to receive it. Our place is not simply to patronize others but to be prepared to be cared for by them.

Not about tolerance: Who tolerates the victim?

Inter-faith issues are not simply about tolerance. While tolerance is no innately bad thing, it nevertheless is a very weak virtue.[23] Tolerance involves inactivity and allows for distance. It allows people to co-exist side by side without having to interact, or without engaging. Tolerance involves no sociality and no deep engagement with the humanity of the other.[24] It is a worst-case scenario of 'positive' community relations. Whenever we are tempted to think of the virtues of tolerance, it is helpful to personalize the concept. Tolerance pertains better to ideas than to people, and when we speak of tolerance as being an acceptable mode of interaction (or more accurately non-interaction) with other human beings, we should be mindful of what that sounds like to the one we tolerate: 'I tolerate you' is hardly an affirming or positive relation with the other when put in these interpersonal terms. What is more, tolerance can involve a level of superiority on the part of the one tolerating: it is akin to saying, 'I am prepared to put up with you; it would be better for me if you were not here; but you are so let's just get on with it and not bother one another.'

In the light of the parable of the Good Samaritan, tolerance is simply not good enough for the Christian. There are two people in this story who engage in the activity of tolerating. They are the priest and the Levite. They do not make the victim's situation directly any worse, but they do nothing to help. They do not order that he is got rid of or kick him out of sight; they simply cross over the road and progress on the other side as if they had not come across the man. Their inactivity is the inactivity of tolerance. They make no attempt to engage with the victim, and there is no attempt at allowing the man's life to intersect with their own. They pass along parallel paths, and never cross over to the other. This is all the more powerful if the priest and Levite did not presume the man was Jewish (i.e. if they thought he was a religious other); after all, how were they (or indeed the

---

23. See further Tom Greggs, 'Bringing Barth's Critique of Religion to the Inter-faith Table', *JR* 88 (2008): 83, 87–8.

24. I am grateful to the late Prof. Daniel W. Hardy for discussions around these ideas.

reader) necessarily to know? The actions of the Samaritan, on the other hand, that we are told to emulate by Jesus, are radically alien to the notion of tolerance. These are actions of love, or *agapē*. The Samaritan engages in a level of self-sacrifice in order to assist this poor victim that he comes across. Moved by pity, he sacrifices his own wine and oil, his own transport, his time and care, and his money to aid this half-dead man.

The engagement with the religious other is not, if we seek to think of this passage in light of the contemporary context, simply one in which the other should be tolerated. If we are to learn from this passage about the Good Samaritan, our engagement with the religious other should involve action. Jesus tells us to 'Go and *do* likewise' (Lk. 10.37). Neighbourliness is seen not in being prepared to live on the other side of the street and pass each other by on the other side of the road but by being prepared to cross over the road and interact with the needs of the other. Neighbourliness involves sacrificial love, the ethical hermeneutic of *agapē* which relativizes tolerance and exposes it for the unloving inactivity that it is. To be a genuine neighbour and to understand who our genuine neighbours are involves being active in each other's world, helping with and sharing in pain and need, along with being prepared to receive help and aid when we need it. This is how our interaction with the religious other is to be – not the tolerance of a variety of communities that exist side by side, but the loving interaction of persons and communities of difference. This is not to deny our traditions or our exclusivity. It is, rather, as Christians, to recognize that part of our exclusive revelation (the New Testament) involves the imperative to be like the religious other who is neighbourly, and to do likewise with the others we come across. There is a gospel imperative not to walk on the other side, but to cross over and discover what other people's needs are, even if they are members of other faith communities.

Attending to present needs not future judgements

Linked to the above point, there is the need in moving from tolerance to *agapē* to prioritize present needs rather than future theological judgements. Here, the Samaritan does not pause to ask theological questions about his relationship with the victim on the wayside. He does not seek first to understand this other's place in the kingdom of God. He does not ask whether interacting with this man will involve a level of ritual impurity (which may well have been a concern for the priest and Levite). The Samaritan does not question the eschatological destination, revelational authentication or soteriological implication of this man whom he comes across. The Samaritan simply tends to the needs of the person as he finds him. He simply seeks to be a good neighbour.

Inter-faith activity should, on the basis of this text, seek to attend fully to present needs rather than worrying constantly about future destinations. For a teleological religion such as Christianity, future destinations obviously have implications to the way in which we understand the other in the present, and these are themes I have addressed elsewhere.[25] However, these themes are secondary to the commandment to love one's neighbour as oneself. It is an interesting feature of the story of the Good Samaritan that it comes within the context of a lawyer who asks Jesus about how to inherit eternal life (Lk. 10.25). Jesus states that this involves loving God with all one's heart, soul, strength and mind, and loving one's neighbour as oneself (Lk. 10.27).[26] Yet Jesus goes on to discuss neighbourliness in terms of a religious other that one is to emulate. The concerns of eternal life involve at some level being only secondarily (at best) concerned with the future destination of the other: in order to gain eternal life for ourselves, we must see the other as a neighbour even if we cannot be certain of their eventual destination. It would be better to say that we should not worry about the eternal destination of the other: that is a concern of God. To attend to the other's needs in the here and now is true neighbourliness and the primary concern for humanity.

Certainly, it is imperative that we cannot divide people into categories of religious insiders and religious outsiders, and allow this to determine how we interact with them in terms of our neighbourliness towards other people. Like the Samaritan we, too, must not even pause to read presupposed eschatological judgements about insiders and outsiders back onto present communities, and allow that to dictate how we interact and are neighbourly with the other. Christian neighbourliness and love has no notion of creed or religious distinction. The Christian is to be as loving to members of other faith communities as to the person she sits next to in the pew. This is by no means easy, but it is the ethics of the Good Samaritan.

Stories such as these radically interrupt our notions of insiders and outsiders. One might have thought the priest and Levite here would have been insiders, who would tend to the victim, a fellow seeming insider of their own community. But as Jesus tells the story, it is these religious officials who appear to be outsiders, and the presumed outsider (the religious other in the Samaritan) who appears to be on the inside.[27] Insiders and outsiders are determined by whether we love God and our

---

25. See, for example, Tom Greggs, '"Jesus is Victor": Passing the Impasse of Barth on Universalism', *Scottish Journal of Theology* 60 (May 2007): 196–212; Tom Greggs, 'Exclusivist or Universalist? Origen "The Wise Steward of the Word" (CommRom. V.1.7) and the Issue of Genre', *International Journal of Systematic Theology* 9 (July 2007): 325–7; and Tom Greggs, *Barth, Origen, and Universal Salvation: Restoring Particularity* (Oxford: Oxford University Press, 2009).

26. On the parable as Jesus' instruction on how to interpret the Law, see Joshua Marshall Strahan, 'Jesus Teaches Theological Interpretation of the Law: Reading the Good Samaritan in Its Literary Context', *Journal of Theological Interpretation* 10 (2016): 71–86.

27. This is a theme which is picked up throughout the New Testament. See Christopher Rowland, 'The Lamb and the Beast, the Sheep and the Goats: "The Mystery of Salvation" in Revelation', in *A Vision for the Church: Studies in Early Christian Ecclesiology in Honour of J. P. M. Swete*, ed. Marcus Bockmuehl and Michael B. Thompson (Edinburgh: T&T Clark, 1997), 181–91.

neighbour as ourselves. It is not our place to ask this question of any other faith; that should never be the Christian's concern. The Christian's concern is to ask this of herself. Put sharply it is this: are we prepared to love the other (the one who is distinct, even the religious other) as we love ourselves? Put concretely for us in the world today facing our contemporary issues, are we as concerned about issues that face Muslim and Jewish and Sikh and Hindu communities and individuals as we are about issues that face Christian communities and individual Christians? Or, does the injured Muslim matter as much to us as the injured Christian? If we are to do as Jesus says and to behave as the Good Samaritan did, the answer needs to be a resounding 'yes'. This is difficult, but the message of Jesus is never easy.

Conclusion

To conclude, it is important for the preacher to unite the need to preach the word of God and the need to preach to the contemporary world with all of its questions about conflict ostensibly between religions and religious communities. In the Methodist Church, to be true to our heritage, we must do this by looking deeply into scripture to resource positively our dealings with the religious other. We must seek what messages there are in the Bible for the healing and reconciliation of communities and the world, a healing and reconciliation which must begin locally – with the interaction of members of individual congregations with those of other faiths. This must be a priority in the preaching of the word. This priority is not on the basis of some external liberal agenda, but – as I have hoped my interpretation of the Good Samaritan might indicate – on the basis of the message of the good news of Jesus Christ. Engagement with the needs of members of other faith communities is an imperative from scripture: it is part of loving our neighbour as ourselves. There is, therefore, no discontinuity between preaching inter-faith and preaching Christ and him crucified. Engagement with the other, tending to her needs and allowing her to tend to ours in no way lessens our individual identity; it does not involve capitulating on central doctrines of the church. On the contrary, engaging with the religious other involves demonstrating practically in the here and now the self-sacrificial love of Jesus Christ in his directedness towards the other; it heightens our Christian identity. It is not our place to worry about eschatological endpoints of members of other faith communities; that is a concern of God's. Nor is it our place to worry about how others will understand us from the position of their own creed; that is a concern of those other communities. It is only our place to do as the Samaritan does – to move beyond simple tolerance and to tend to the needs of the other as they arise. In doing that we live responsibly before God who creates and guides the world, and we love our neighbour as we love ourselves.

CONCLUSION

The essays in this book are occasional pieces. They were written over the course of more than a decade. They engage with a variety of interlocutors from a variety of traditions and spanning almost 1,800 years of history. They draw on a range of biblical texts. And they address a range of individual topics. However, there is a core series of concerns that these different essays engage. This core revolves around how to understand the life of the church within the economy of God in the givenness of the church's contemporary situation. This understanding of the church rests, therefore, within an account of the gracious activity of God in the world; and this account itself rests on an account of who God (the God of salvation) is in God's revelation. In all these discussions, the very uniqueness and particularity of the God who is known to us in Jesus Christ by the Holy Spirit is the centre from which and end to which all the reflections take place. It is the God of the gospel and the gospel of that God who is the subject of all the essays discussed, as they seek to expound upon how God relates to the world in all its complexities and contingencies, and to the church which exists within and for that world in all its complexities and contingencies.

The reflections on the church and the world are based upon a prior reflection on salvation and the God of grace who saves. It is this primary divine self-determining of God's relationship to the world that further determines all of God's ways with the world. The world is created from, through and towards the divine self-willing of salvation: salvation is not merely something God does, but, in this singular act in Jesus Christ by the Spirit, it is who the constant and eternal God is. The saving God is the God of salvation; the God who brings good news is the God of the gospel; the God who creates, sustains, reconciles and redeems is the God of grace. Creation is the external context for salvation, but salvation is the internal purpose for creation. *This* God is the subject and object of theological enquiry: God is sovereign and free even over conceptualizations of God, and even the most confident theology must be checked by the overwhelming and blinding, mysterious light of revealed grace. This theological insight is that which creates a climate of both theological confidence and theological humility: confidence grounded in the revelation of God in Jesus Christ by the Holy Spirit; humility that this God is the one with whom theology is concerned and the one who – as such – cannot be grasped or contained in the limits of religious and theological speech.

The implications of these insights are that the church must speak of itself with both a sense of its existence as a work of the act of God, trusting that the church's constancy and telos is held in God's constant living. But this is also grounds for the church not to confuse itself with the God who brings it into being, preserves it in faithfulness and will bring it to its end. It is for this reason that the church must always be the *ecclesia semper reformanda*. The church is not the condition of salvation but is itself the result of God's saving grace. The church is not the foundation of salvation but is itself conditioned by salvation. There is an important asymmetry here. This asymmetry means, furthermore, that the church's confident dependence on the economy of God should inculcate a sense of generosity (in all the church's particularity) towards the world and those outwith the church's walls. The church is the terminus for revelation – the context in which revelation is known. But as such, the church is not the singular locus of God's saving work: the church knows of and witnesses to the reality of God's grace in the world; the church knows the economy of God's grace and, in that, knows that the whole world exists because of and with the purpose of the divine economy. The church cannot confuse its religious form or its self-conceptualization with the God of all creation (or, indeed, with the totality of God's relationship to all creation). Instead, remembering that the object and subject of theology is God should lead the church to point beyond itself to the God who is its origin and end, and whose glorification is its purpose as it moves ever towards the eschaton when God shall be all in all.

It is for these reasons that treating the church and a theology of those of different faiths or none might wisely be undertaken together. The same humility which the God of the Gospel should engender in the church which reflects upon its origins and relationship to that God should also be engendered in the church as it relates to those outside of it. Ecclesial humility and hope for the world outside the church belong hand in hand. Furthermore, since the church is a provisional, proleptic and anticipatory community of redeeming grace, a focus on the saving of activity of God within the world is appropriate to the church's self-understanding of its role and purpose as a community which exists for the sake of the world in which it is brought into being by God. The provisional nature of the church reminds it that the church is wedded to the world this side of the eschaton as it anticipates redemption. Furthermore, the givenness of the context in which the church exists for the world is in and of itself important to the church's form in the particular, contingent contemporaneities within which the church is brought into being by God. To reflect on the context the church finds itself in with the issues this raises is not a matter of contextual theological reflection but an outworking of the dogmatic recognition of the contingency of the church's own life in the quotidian, givenness of space–time. Witnessing to the hope of the gospel in the world rests on the constancy and sufficiency of that gospel and (as several essays attempt to demonstrate) the supreme relevance of the gospel in its capacity to speak into every age and even into the current complexly secular and religious one; but it also rests on the purpose for which the church is created in the divine economy – to speak into its given context in its contingent quotidian form in which the church lives.

In this sense, the occasionalism of these essays is entirely appropriate to the subjects written about. In speaking, even confidently and dogmatically, about these themes, there can never be a final word: there is a need for the church ever to reform. These essays, like all of theology, cannot ever be considered a final word and should never contain an over-determined systematicity. That they are working papers in dogmatics is not only true to the form in which the papers were originally written but is also dogmatically appropriate to the topics herein. There must always be a provisional form to such reflections. The hope of this book, ultimately, therefore, is not that others (who will come from different traditions and certainly hold different perspectives) will repeat their insights or exercise that woeful form of cautious theology which can always express 'anxieties' without anything constructive or hopeful; but, rather, that these essays will give rise to other (necessarily occasional) works on the church in a complexly secular and pluralist world. And, more importantly, the hope is that these essays are seen as good news – a good news others would wish in their own occasional forms to proclaim and reflect upon.

BIBLIOGRAPHY

Adams, Nick. 'Making Deep Reasoning Public'. *Modern Theology* 22 (2006): 385–401.
Anatolios, Khaled Emmanuel. 'Theology and Economy in Origen and Athanasius'. In *Origeniana Septima: Origenes in der Auseinandersetzungen des 4. Jahrhunderts*, edited by W. A. Bienert and U. Kühneweg, 155–72. Leuven: Peeters, 1999.
Anderson, Bernhard W. *The Living World of the Old Testament*. 4th edn. Harlow: Longman, 1993.
Anselm. 'Cur Deus Homo'. In Anselm, *Anselm: Basic Writings*, translated by Thomas Williams, 237–326. Indianapolis, IN: Hackett, 2007.
Augustine. *On Christian Teaching*. Translated by R. P. H. Green. Oxford: Oxford University Press, 1997.
Aulén, Gustav. *Christus Victor: An Historical Study of the Three Main Types of the Idea of the Atonement*. New York: Macmillan, 1969.
Avis, Paul. *Becoming a Bishop: A Theological Handbook of Episcopal Ministry*. London: Bloomsbury, 2015.
Avis, Paul. *Reshaping Ecumenical Theology: The Church Made Whole?* London: T&T Clark, 2010.
Ayres, Lewis. *Nicea and Its Legacy: An Approach to Fourth-Century Trinitarian Theology*. Oxford: Oxford University Press, 2004.
Barclay, John M. G. 'Universalism and Particularism: Twin Components of Both Judaism and Early Christianity'. In *A Vision for the Church: Studies in Early Christian Eschatology in Honour of J. P. M. Sweet*, edited by Markus Bockmuehl and Michael B. Thompson, 207–24. Edinburgh: T&T Clark, 1997.
Barrell, E. V., and K. G. Barrell. *St Luke's Gospel: An Introductory Study*. London: John Murray, 1982.
Barrett, David B., George T. Kurian and Todd M. Johnson. *World Christian Encyclopaedia*. 2nd edn. Oxford: Oxford University Press, 2001.
'Barth in Retirement'. *Time Magazine* 82.22 (31 May 1963): 35–6.
Barth, Karl. *Fragments Grave and Gay*. London: Collins Fortress, 1971.
Barth, Karl. *God, Grace and Gospel*. Scottish Journal of Theology Occasional Papers 8. Edinburgh: Oliver & Boyd, 1959.
Barth, Karl. *Learning Jesus Christ through the Heidelberg Catechism*. Grand Rapids, MI: Eerdmans, 1964.
Bauckham, Richard. 'The Scrupulous Priest and the Good Samaritan: Jesus' Parabolic Interpretation of the Law of Moses'. *New Testament Studies* 44 (1998): 475–89
Bauer, Walter. *Orthodoxy and Heresy in Earliest Christianity*. Philadelphia, PA: Fortress, 1971.
Bebbington, David. *Evangelicalism in Modern Britain: A History from the 1730s to the 1980s*. London: Unwin Hyman, 1989.
Behr, John. *The Formation of Christian Theology I: The Way to Nicaea*. Crestwood, NY: St. Vladimir's Seminary Press, 2001.

Belcher, Jim. *Deep Church: A Third Way Beyond Emerging and Traditional*. Downers Grove: IVP, 2009.
Bennett, Alan. *Telling Tales*. London: BBC Books, 2001.
Binney, Thomas. *Dissent Not Schism*. London: Robinson, 1885.
Boadt. Lawrence. *Reading the Old Testament*. New York: Paulist Press, 1984.
Bonhoeffer, Dietrich. *Act and Being*. Edited by Wayne Whitson Floyd and Hans-Richard Reuter. Translated by Martin H. Rumscheidt. Dietrich Bonhoeffer Works 2. Minneapolis, MN: Fortress, 1996.
Bonhoeffer, Dietrich. *Discipleship*. Edited by Geffrey B. Kelly and John D. Godsey. Translated by Martin Kuske and Ilse Tödt. Dietrich Bonhoeffer Works 4. Fortress, 2003.
Bonhoeffer, Dietrich. *Ethics*. Edited by Clifford J. Green. Translated by Reinhard Krauss, Charles C. West and Douglas W. Stott. Dietrich Bonhoeffer Works 6. Minneapolis, MN: Fortress, 2005.
Bonhoeffer, Dietrich. *Letters and Papers from Prison*. Edited by John W. de Gruchy. Translated by Isabel Best et al. Dietrich Bonhoeffer Works 8. Minneapolis, MN: Fortress, 2010.
Bonhoeffer, Dietrich. *Life Together and Prayerbook of the Bible*. Edited by Geffrey B. Kelly. Translated by Daniel W. Bloesch and James H. Burtness. Dietrich Bonhoeffer Works 5. Minneapolis, MN: Fortress, 2004.
Bonhoeffer, Dietrich. *Sanctorum Communio: A Theological Study of the Sociology of the Church*. Edited by Clifford J. Green. Translated by Reinhard Krauss and Nancy Lukens. Dietrich Bonhoeffer Works 1. Minneapolis, MN: Fortress, 1998.
Boring, M. Eugene. 'The Language of Universal Salvation in Paul'. *Journal of Biblical Literature* 105 (1986): 269–92.
Boulton, Matthew Myer. *God against Religion: Rethinking Christian Theology through Worship*. Grand Rapids, MI: Eerdmans, 2008.
Briggs, Richard. 'The Bible before Us: Evangelical Possibilities for Taking Scripture Seriously'. In *New Perspectives for Evangelical Theology: Engaging with God, Scripture, and the World*, edited by Tom Greggs, 14–28. Oxford: Routledge, 2010.
Bright, John. *A History of Israel*. 3rd edn. London: SCM, 1998.
Brittain, Christopher. 'Why Ecclesiology Cannot Live by Doctrine Alone: A Reply to John Webster's "In the Society of God"'. *Ecclesial Practices* 1 (2014): 5–30.
Brunner, Emil. *The Misunderstanding of the Church*. Philadelphia, PA: Westminster, 1951.
Burrell, David B. *Knowing the Unknowable God: Ibn-Sina, Maimonides, Aquinas*. Notre Dame: University of Notre Dame Press, 1987.
Busch, Eberhard. *Karl Barth: His Life from Letters and Autobiographical Texts*. London: SCM, 1976.
Calvin, Jean. *Commentary on Ephesians*. Calvini Opera.
Calvin, Jean. *Institutes of the Christian Religion*. Edited by John T. McNeill. Louisville, KY: John Knox Press, 1960.
Cameron, Nigel M. de S. 'Universalism and the Logic of Revelation'. In *The Best in Theology, Vol. 3*, edited by J. I. Packer, 153–68. Carol Stream, IL: Christianity Today, 1989.
Carter, David. 'Catholicity and Unity'. *One in Christ* 40 (2005): 67–84.
Castagno, Adele Monaci. 'Origen the Scholar and Pastor'. In *Preacher and Audience: Studies in Early Christian and Byzantine Homiletics*, edited by Mary B. Cunningham and Pauline Allen, 65–87. Leiden: Brill, 1998.

Chase, Michael. 'Time and Eternity from Plotinus and Boethius to Einstein'. ΣΧΟΛΗ 8 (2014): 68–110.
Clark, Elizabeth A. 'The Place of Jerome's Commentary on Ephesians in the Origenist Controversy: The Apokatastasis and Ascetic Ideals'. *Vigiliae Christianae* 41 (1987) 154–71.
Clark, Elizabeth A. *The Origenist Controversy: The Cultural Construction of an Early Christian Debate*. Princeton, NJ: Princeton University Press, 2002.
Clough, David L. *On Animals: Volume 1: Systematic Theology*. London: T&T Clark, 2012.
Coffey, David. *Deus Trinitas: The Doctrine of the Triune God*. Oxford: Oxford University Press, 1999.
Colle, Ralph Del. 'John Wesley's Doctrine of Grace in Light of the Christian Tradition'. *International Journal of Systematic Theology* 4 (2002): 172–89.
Colle, Ralph Del. *Christ and the Spirit: Spirit-Christology in Trinitarian Perspective*. Oxford: Oxford University Press, 1997.
Congar, Yves. *I Believe in the Holy Spirit*. Volume 2. New York: Crossroad, 2013.
Cranfield, C. E. B. *The Gospel According to St Mark*. Cambridge: Cambridge University Press, 1963.
Cray, Graham, ed. *Mission-Shaped Church: Church Planting and Fresh Expressions of Church in a Changing Context*. London: Church House, 2004.
Crouzel, Henri. 'Hades et la Gehenna selon Origene'. *Gregorianum* 49 (1978): 291–331.
Crouzel, Henri. *Origen*. Translated by A. S. Worrall. Edinburgh: T&T Clark, 1989.
Cyprian. *De Lapsis: The Unity of the Catholic Church*. Translated by Maurice Bévenot. Oxford: Clarendon, 1971.
D'Costa, Gavin. *The Meeting of Religions and the Trinity*. Edinburgh: T&T Clark, 2000.
Daley, Brian E. *The Hope of the Early Church: A Handbook of Patristic Eschatology*. Cambridge: Cambridge University Press, 1991.
Daly, Mary. *Beyond God the Father: Toward a Philosophy of Women's Liberation*. Boston, MA: Beacon Press, 1973.
Daniélou, Jean. *Origen*. Translated by Walter Mitchell. London: Sheed & Ward, 1955.
Davie, Grace. *Europe: The Exceptional Case: Parameters of Faith and the Modern World*. London: Darton, Longman & Todd, 2000.
Davie, Gracie. *Religion in Britain since 1945: Believing without Belonging*. London: Blackwell, 1994.
DeHart, Paul J. *The Trial of the Witnesses: The Rise and Decline of Postliberal Theology*. Oxford: Blackwell, 2006.
Dietrich Bonhoeffer, *Creation and Fall: A Theological Exposition of Genesis 1–3*. Edited by John W. de Gruchy. Translated by Douglas Stephen Bax, Dietrich Bonhoeffer Works 3. Minneapolis, MN: Fortress, 2004.
DiNoia, J. A. 'Christian Universalism: The Nonexclusive Particularity of Salvation in Christ'. In *Either/Or: The Gospel or Neopaganism*, edited by C. E. Braaten and R. W. Jenson, 37–48. London: Eerdmans, 1995.
Drane, John. *After McDonaldization: Mission, Ministry and Christian Discipleship in an Age of Uncertainty*. London: Darton, Longman & Todd, 2008.
Drane, John. *The McDonaldization of the Church: Spirituality, Creativity, and the Future of the Church*. London: Darton, Longman & Todd, 2000.
Drewery, Benjamin. *Origen and the Doctrine of Grace*. London: Epworth Press, 1960.
Dullaart, Leo. *Kirche und Ekklesiologie*. Munich: Chr. Kaiser, 1975.
Dulles, Avery. *Models of the Church: A Critical Assessment of the Church in All Aspects*. New York: Doubleday, 1987.

Dulles, Avery. *The Catholicity of the Church*. Oxford: Oxford University Press, 1985.
Dumbrell, W. J. *Covenant and Creation: A Theology of the Old Testament Covenants*. Carlisle: Paternoster, 1997.
Dunn, James D. G. 'Judaism and Christianity: One Covenant or Two?'. In *Covenant Theology: Contemporary Approaches*, edited by Mark. J. Cartledge and David Mills, 33–55. Carlisle: Paternoster, 2001.
Ebling, Gerhard. *Luther: An Introduction to His Thought*. London: Collins, 1970.
Edwards, Mark J. 'Origen's Two Resurrections'. *Journal of Theological Studies* 46 (1995): 502–18.
Edwards, Mark J. *Catholicity and Heresy in the Early Church*. Aldershot: Ashgate, 2009.
Edwards, Mark J. *Origen against Plato*. Aldershot: Ashgate, 2002.
Farrar, F. W. *Mercy and Judgment: A Few Last Words on Christian Eschatology with Reference to Dr. Pusey's 'What Is of Faith?'*. London: Macmillan, 1881.
Fee, Gordon. *God's Empowering Presence: The Holy Spirit in the Letters of Paul*. Peabody, MA: Hendrickson, 1994.
Fergusson, David. 'Eschatology'. In *The Cambridge Companion to Christian Doctrine*, edited by Colin E. Gunton, 226–44. Cambridge: Cambridge University Press, 1997.
Fergusson, David. *State, Church and Civil Society*. Cambridge: Cambridge University Press, 2004.
Fergusson, Everett. *Backgrounds of Early Christianity*. 2nd edn. Grand Rapids, MI: Eerdmans, 1993.
Ford, David F. 'Abrahamic Dialogue: Towards Respect and Understanding in Our Life Together'. Paper presented at the Inauguration of the Society for Dialogue and Action. Cambridge, 2006.
Ford, David F. *Barth and God's Story: Biblical Narrative and the Theological Method of Karl Barth in the Church Dogmatics*. Frankfurt am Main: Peter Lang, 1985.
Ford, David F. *Christian Wisdom: Desiring God and Learning in Love*. Cambridge: Cambridge University Press, 2007.
Ford, David F. 'God and Our Public Space: A Scriptural Wisdom'. *International Journal of Public Theology* 1 (2007): 63–81.
Ford, David F. 'Gospel in Context: Among Many Faiths'. Paper presented at the Fulcrum Conference. Islington, 28 April 2006.
Ford, David F. *Self and Salvation: Being Transformed*. Cambridge: Cambridge University Press, 1999.
Ford, David F. *The Future of Christian Theology*. Oxford: Wiley-Blackwell, 2011.
Ford, David F., and C. C. Pecknold, eds. *The Promise of Scriptural Reasoning*. Oxford: Blackwell, 2006.
Ford, David F., and Daniel W. Hardy. *Living in Praise: Worshipping and Knowing God*. 2nd edn. Grand Rapid, MI: Baker Academic, 2005.
Frei, Hans. *Types of Christian Theology*. New Haven, CT: Yale University Press, 1994.
Gibbs, Eddie, and Ryan K. Bolger. *Emerging Churches: Creating Christian Community in Postmodern Cultures*. Grand Rapids, MI: Baker Academic, 2005.
Giles, Kevin. *Jesus and the Father: Modern Evangelicals Reinvent the Doctrine of the Trinity*. Grand Rapids, MI: Zondervan, 2006.
Giles, Kevin. *The Eternal Generation of the Son: Maintaining Orthodoxy in Trinitarian Theology*. Downers Grove: IVP, 2012.
Giles, Kevin. *The Trinity and Subordinationism*. Downers Grove: IVP, 2002.
Graham, Jeannine Michele. *Representation and Substitution in the Atonement Theologies of Dorothee Sölle, John Macquarrie and Karl Barth*. New York: Peter Lang, 2005.

Green, Clifford. *Bonhoeffer: A Theology of Sociality*. Rev. edn. Grand Rapids, MI: Eerdmans, 1999.
Gregg, Robert C., and Dennis E. Groh. *Early Arianism: A View of Salvation*. London: SCM Press, 1981.
Greggs, Tom. *Barth, Origen, and Universal Salvation: Restoring Particularity*. Oxford: Oxford University Press, 2009.
Greggs, Tom. 'Being a Wise Apprentice to the Communion of Modern Saints: On the Need for Conversation with a Plurality of Theological Interlocutors'. In *The Vocation of Theology Today: A Festschrift for David Ford*, edited by Rachel Muers and Simeon Zahl, 21–4. Eugene: Cascade, 2013.
Greggs, Tom. 'Beyond the Binary: Forming Evangelical Eschatology'. In *New Perspectives for Evangelical Theology: Engaging with God, Scripture and the World*, edited by Tom Greggs, 153–6. Abingdon: Routledge, 20107.
Greggs, Tom. 'Bringing Barth's Critique of Religion to the Inter-faith Table'. *Journal of Religion* 88 (2008): 75–94.
Greggs, Tom. *Dogmatic Ecclesiology volume 1: The Priestly Catholicity of the Church*. Grand Rapids, MI: Baker Academic, 2019.
Greggs, Tom. 'Exclusivist or Universalist? Origen "The Wise Steward of the Word" (*Comm. Rom.* V.1.7) and the Issue of Genre'. *International Journal of Systematic Theology* 9 (2007): 315–27.
Greggs, Tom. '"Jesus Is Victor": Passing the Impasse of Barth on Universalism'. *Scottish Journal of Theology* 60 (2007): 196–212.
Greggs, Tom. 'Legitimizing and Necessitating Inter-faith Dialogue: The Dynamics of Inter-faith for Individual Faith Communities'. *International Journal of Public Theology* 4 (2010): 194–211.
Greggs, Tom. 'Pessimistic Universalism: Rethinking the Wider Hope with Bonhoeffer and Barth'. *Modern Theology* 26 (2010): 495–510.
Greggs, Tom. 'The Order and Movement of Eternity: Karl Barth on the Eternity of God and Creaturely Time', in *Eternal God, Eternal Life: Theological Investigations into the Concept of Immortality*, edited by Philip G. Ziegler, 1–24. London: T&T Clark, 2016.
Greggs, Tom. *Theology against Religion: Constructive Dialogues with Bonhoeffer and Barth*. London: T&T Clark, 2011.
Greggs, Tom. 'Tolerance Isn't Enough!'. *Emerging Culture* (Spring 2007): 12–13.
Gregory of Nyssa. *Life of Moses*. Translated by Abraham J. Malherbe and Everett Ferguson. Mahwah: Paulist Press, 1978.
Grenz, Stanley J. *Revisioning Evangelical Theology: A Fresh Agenda for the 21st Century*. Downers Grove: IVP, 1993.
Grudem, Wayne. *Evangelical Feminism and Biblical Truth*. Sisters: Multnomah, 2004.
Grudem, Wayne. *Systematic Theology: An Introduction to Biblical Doctrine*. Downers Grove: IVP, 1994.
Gunton, Colin E. 'The Church on Earth: The Roots of Community'. In *On Being the Church*, edited by Colin E. Gunton and Daniel W. Hardy, 48–80. Edinburgh: T&T Clark, 1989.
Gunton, Colin. *Theology through the Theologians: Selected Essays 1972–1995*. London: T&T Clark, 1996.
Hadot, Pierre. *What Is Ancient Philosophy?* Translated by Michael Chase. Cambridge, MA: Harvard University Press, 2004.
Hanson, R. P. C. *Allegory and Event: A Study of the Sources and Significance of Origen's Interpretation of Scripture*. London: SCM, 1959.

Hardy, Daniel W. 'Created and Redeemed Sociality'. In *On Being the Church: Essays on the Christian Community*, edited by Colin E. Gunton and Daniel W. Hardy, 21–47. Edinburgh: T&T Clark, 1989.
Hardy, Daniel W. *Finding the Church: The Dynamic Truth of Anglicanism*. London: SCM, 2001.
Hardy, Daniel W. *God's Ways with the World: Thinking and Practising Christian Faith*. Edinburgh: T&T Clark, 1996.
Hardy, Daniel W. 'Receptive Ecumenism – Learning by Engagement'. On *Receptive Ecumenism and the Call to Catholic Learning*, edited by Paul D. Murray, 428–41. Oxford: Oxford University Press, 2008.
Hauerwas, Stanley. *Christian Existence Today: Essays on Church, World, and Living In Between*. Grand Rapids, MI: Brazos, 2001.
Hauerwas, Stanley. *Hannah's Child: A Theologian's Memoir*. London: SCM, 2010.
Hays, Richard B. 'Postscript: Seeking a Centred, Generous Orthodoxy'. In *New Perspectives for Evangelical Theology: Engaging God, Scripture and the World*, edited by Tom Greggs, 216–18. London: Routledge, 2009.
Healy, Nicholas M. 'What Is Systematic Theology?'. *International Journal of Systematic Theology* 11 (2009): 24–39.
Healy, Nicholas M. *Church, World and the Christian Life: Practical-Prophetic Ecclesiology*. Cambridge: Cambridge University Press, 2000.
Heine, Ronald E. 'Epinoiai'. In *The Westminster Handbook to Origen*, edited by John A. McGuckin, 93–5. Louisville, KY: Westminster John Knox, 2004.
Heitzenrater, Richard P. *Wesley and the People Called Methodist*. Nashville, TN: Abingdon, 1995.
Hennessey, Lawrence. 'The Place of Saints and Sinners after Death'. In *Origen of Alexandria: His World and His Legacy*, edited by Charles Kannengiesser and William L. Peterson, 293–312. Notre Dame: University of Notre Dame Press, 1988.
Hick, John. *An Interpretation of Religion: Human Responses to the Transcendent*. London: Macmillan, 1989.
Hick, John. *God and the Universe of Faiths: Essays in the Philosophy of Religion*. London: Macmillan, 1973.
Hick, John. *God Has Many Names: Britain's New Religious Pluralism*. London: Macmillan, 1980.
Hick, John. *Problems of Religious Pluralism*. London: Macmillan, 1985.
Hooker, Morna D. *The Gospel According to St Mark*. London: A&C Black, 1991.
Hunsinger, George. *How to Read Karl Barth: The Shape of His Theology*. New York: Oxford University Press, 1991.
Hymns and Psalms. London: Methodist Publishing House, 1983.
Jackson, W. Daniel. 'The Logic of Divine Presence in Romans 3:23'. *Catholic Biblical Quarterly* 80 (2018): 293–305.
Jenson, Robert W. 'Eschatology'. In *The Blackwell Companion to Political Theology*, edited by William T. Cavanaugh and Peter Manley Scott, 444–56. Oxford: Blackwell, 2007.
Jenson, Robert W. *Systematic Theology, Volume 2*. Oxford: Oxford University Press, 1999.
Jillions, John A. 'Three Orthodox Models of Christian Unity: Traditionalist, Mainstream, Prophetic'. *International Journal for the Study of the Christian Church* 9 (2009): 295–311.
Jinkins, Michael. *The Church Faces Death: Ecclesiology in a Post-Modern Context*. Oxford: Oxford University Press, 1999.

Johnson, Luke Timothy. *Contested Issues in Christian Origins and the New Testament*. Novum Testamentum Supplements 146. Leiden: Brill, 2013.
Jones, Paul Dafydd. 'The Atonement: God's Love in Action'. In *New Perspectives for Evangelical Theology: Engaging with God, Scripture and the World*, edited by Tom Greggs, 44–62. London: Routledge, 2010.
Jüngel, Eberhard. *God as the Mystery of the World: On the Foundation of the Theology of the Crucified One in the Dispute between Theism and Atheism*. London: Bloomsbury, 2014.
Jüngel, Eberhard. *God's Being Is in Becoming. The Trinitarian Being of God in the Theology of Karl Barth*. Edinburgh: T&T Clark, 2001.
Jüngel, Eberhard. *Theological Essays II*. London: Bloomsbury, 2014.
Kalaitzidis, Pantelis. 'Theological, Historical, and Cultural Reasons for Anti-Ecumenical Movements in Eastern Orthodoxy'. In *Orthodox Handbook on Ecumenism: Resources for Theological Education*, edited by Pantelis Kalaitzidis, Dietrich Werner and Thomas E. FitzGerald, 134–52. Oxford: Regnum Books International, 2014.
Kannengiesser, Charles, and William L Petersen, eds. *Origen of Alexandria: His World and His Legacy*. Notre Dame: University of Notre Dame, 1988.
Kasper, Walter. *Jesus the Christ*. 2nd edn. London: T&T Clark, 2011.
Kent, Elizabeth. 'Embodied Evangelicalism: The Body of Christ and the Christian Body'. In *New Perspectives for Evangelical Theology: Engaging with God, Scripture and the World*, edited by Tom Greggs, 108–22. London: Routledge, 2010.
Kepnes, Steven. 'A Handbook for Scriptural Reasoning'. *Modern Theology* 22 (2006): 367–83.
Kepnes, Steven. 'Hagar and Esau: From Others to Sisters and Brothers'. In *Crisis, Call, and Leadership in the Abrahamic Traditions*, edited by Peter Ochs and William Stacy Johnson, 31–46. New York: Palgrave Macmillan, 2009.
Kovach, Stephen D., and Peter R. Schemm, Jr. 'A Defense of the Doctrine of the Eternal Subordination of the Son'. *Journal for the Evangelical Theological Society* 42 (1999): 461–76.
Küng, Hans. *The Church*. London: Burns & Oates, 1968.
Larsen, Timothy. 'Defining and Locating Evangelicalism'. In *The Cambridge Companion to Evangelical Theology*, edited by Timothy Larsen and Daniel J. Treler, 1–14. Cambridge: Cambridge University Press, 2007.
Lash, Nicholas. *The Beginning and the End of 'Religion'*. Cambridge, Cambridge University Press, 1996.
Layton, Richard A. 'Judas Yields a Place to the Devil'. In *Origeniana Septima: Origenes in Den Auseinandersetzungen Des 4. Jahrhunderts*, edited by W. A. Bienert and U. Kuhneweg, 531–41. Leuven: Leuven University Press, 1999.
Lefèbvre, Joseph Cardinal. 'Obedience to the Pope'. In *Obedience and the Church*, edited by Karl Rahner et al., 43–56. London: Geoffrey Chapman, 1968.
Levenson, Jon D. *Inheriting Abraham: The Legacy of the Patriarch in Judaism, Christianity and Islam*. Princeton, NJ: Princeton University Press, 2012.
Levison, John R. *Filled with the Spirit*. Cambrdige: Eerdmans, 2009.
Lewis, C. S. *The Four Loves*. Glasgow: Collins, 1960.
Lewis, C. S. *The Screwtape Letters: Letter from a Senior to a Junior Devil*. London: Collins, 1942.
Liddell, Henry George, Robert Scott and Henry Stuart Jones. *A Greek-English Lexicon*. 9th edn. Oxford: Clarendon, 1996.
Lindbeck, George A. *The Nature of Doctrine: Religion and Theology in a Postliberal Age*. London: SPCK, 1982.

Louth, Andrew. *Maximus the Confessor*. Early Church Fathers. London: Routledge, 1999.
Ludlow, Morwenna. 'Universal Salvation and a Soteriology of Divine Punishment'. *Scottish Journal of Theology* 53 (2000): 449–71.
Ludlow, Morwenna. *Universal Salvation: Eschatology in the Thought of Gregory of Nyssa and Karl Rahner*. Oxford: Oxford University Press, 2000.
Lumen Gentium. Vatican Council II.
Luther, Martin. *Concerning the Ministry*. In *Church and Ministry II*, edited by H. Lehmann and C. Bergendoff. Luther's Works 40. Minneapolis, MN: Fortress, 1958.
Luther, Martin. *Katechismuspredigten (1528)*. Weimarer Ausgabe 30.1.
Luther, Martin. *Lectures on Genesis Chapters 1–5*. Edited by Jaroslav Pelikan. Luther's Works 1. St Louis: Concordia, 1958.
Luther, Martin. *On the Councils and the Church*. In *Church and Ministry III*, edited by Eric W. Gitsch, Luther's Works 41. Philadelphia, PA: Fortress, 1966.
Luther, Martin. *Predigten und Schriften (1523)*. Weimarer Ausgabe 11.
Luther, Martin. *Selected Psalms III*. Edited by Jaroslav Pelikan and Daniel E. Poellot. Luther's Works 14. St. Louis: Concordia, 1958.
Luther, Martin. *That a Christian Assembly or Congregation Has the Right and Power to Judge All Teaching and to Call, Appoint, and Dismiss Teachers, Established and Proven by Scripture*. In *Church and Ministry I*, edited by Eric W. Gritsch, Luther Works 93. Philadelphia, PA: Fortress, 1970.
Luther, Martin. *The Freedom of the Christian*. In *Career of the Reformer I*, edited by H. J. Grimm and H. Lehmann. Luther's Works 31. Philadelphia, PA: Fortress, 1957.
Macaskill, Grant. 'Apocalypse and the Gospel of Mark'. In *The Jewish Apocalyptic Tradition and the Shaping of New Testament Thought*, edited by Benjamin E. Reynolds and Loren T. Stuckenbruck, 53–77. Minneapolis, MN: Fortress, 2017.
MacIntyre, Alasdair. *Whose Justice? Which Rationality?* London: Duckworth, 1988.
Maican, Petre. 'The Form of Christ: Sketching an Ecumenical Ecclesiology for Eastern Orthodoxy'. PhD dissertation, University of Aberdeen, Aberdeen, 2016.
Marsh, Charles. *Reclaiming Dietrich Bonhoeffer: The Promise of His Theology*. Oxford: Oxford University Press, 1994.
Martin, David. *Reflections on Sociology and Theology*. Oxford: Clarendon Press, 1997.
Martin, David. *The Religious and the Secular: Studies in Secularization*. London: Routledge and Kegan Paul, 1969.
McCall, Thomas H. *Which Trinity? Whose Monotheism?* Grand Rapids, MI: Eerdmans, 2010.
McCarthy, D. J. *Old Testament Covenants: A Survey of Current Options*. Oxford: Blackwell, 1973.
McCormack, Bruce L. 'Grace and Being: The Role of God's Gracious Election in Karl Barth's Theological Ontology'. In *The Cambridge Companion to Karl Barth*, edited by John Webster, 92–110. Cambridge: Cambridge University Press, 2000.
McDonnell, Kilian. 'Does Origen Have a Trinitarian Doctrine of the Holy Spirit?' *Gregorianum* 75 (1994) 5–35.
McGuckin, John A. 'The Changing Forms of Jesus'. In *Origeniana Quarta: Die Referate des 4. internationalen Origeneskongresses (Innsbruck, 2.-6. September 1985)*, edited by Lothar Leis, 215–22. Innsbruck: Tyrolia-Verlag, 1987.
McIntyre, John. *The Shape of Pneumatology: Studies in the Doctrine of the Holy Spirit*. Edinburgh: T&T Clark, 1997.
McKenzie, Steven L. *Covenant*. St. Louis: Chalice, 2000.

Meyers, Carol L. 'Gender Roles and Genesis 3:16 Revisited'. In *The Word of the Lord Shall Go Forth*, edited by Carol L. Myers and M. O'Connor, 337–54. Philadelphia, PA: Eisenbrauns, 1983.
Mitchell, Margaret M. *Paul and the Rhetoric of Reconciliation: An Exegetical Investigation of the Language and Composition of 1 Corinthians*. Louisville, KY: Westminster John Knox, 1991.
Moffitt, David M. *Atonement and the Logic of Resurrection in the Epistle to the Hebrews*, Novum Testamentum Supplements 141. Leiden: Brill, 2011.
Moltmann, Jürgen. *In the End – the Beginning: The Life of Hope*. Translated by Margaret Kohl. London: SCM, 2004.
Moltmann, Jürgen. *The Coming of God: Christian Eschatology*. Translated by Margaret Kohl London: SCM, 1996.
Neder, Adam. *Participation in Christ: An Entry into Karl Barth's Church Dogmatics*. Louisville, KY: Westminster John Knox, 2009.
Newman, John Henry. *An Essay on the Development of Christian Doctrine*. London: Penguin, 1974.
Nimmo, Paul T. 'Election and Evangelical Thinking: Challenges to Our Way of Conceiving the Doctrine of God'. In *New Perspectives for Evangelical Theology: Engaging with God, Scripture and the World*, edited by Tom Greggs, 29–43. London: Routledge, 2010.
Nimmo, Paul T. *Being in Action: The Theological Shape of Barth's Ethical Vision*. London: T&T Clark, 2007.
Norris, Fredrick W. 'Universal Salvation in Origen and Maximus'. In *Universalism and the Doctrine of Hell. Papers Presented at the Fourth Edinburgh Conference on Christian Dogmatics 1991*, edited by Nigel M. de S. Cameron, 35–72. Carlisle: Paternoster, 1992.
Noth, Martin. *The History of Israel*. 2nd edn. London: A&C Black, 1965.
O'Collins, Gerald. *Salvation for All: God's Other Peoples*. Oxford: Oxford University Press, 2008.
O'Grady, Colm. *The Church in the Theology of Karl Barth*. Washington, DC: Corpus Books, 1969.
O'Leary, Joseph S. 'The Invisible Mission of the Son in Origen and Augustine'. In *Origeniana Septima: Origenes in Den Auseinandersetzungen Des 4. Jahrhunderts*, edited by W. A. Bienert and U. Kuhneweg, 605–22. Leuven: Leuven University Press, 1999.
Ochs, Peter. 'Abrahamic Theo-politics: A Jewish View'. In *The Blackwell Companion to Political Theology*, edited by Peter Scott and William T. Cavanaugh, 519–34. Oxford: Blackwell, 2007.
Ochs, Peter. *Another Reformation: Postliberal Christianity and the Jews*. Grand Rapids, MI: Brazos Press, 2009.
Ochs, Peter. *Peirce, Pragmatism and the Logic of Scripture*. Cambridge: Cambridge University Press, 2004.
Oliver, Simon. *Philosophy, God and Motion*. London: Routledge, 2005.
Origen. 'On Prayer'. In *Origen*, edited and translated by Rowan A. Greer, 81–170. New York: Paulist, 1979.
Origen. *Commentary on John*. Edited and translated by A. Menzies. Ante-Nicene Fathers 10. Grand Rapids, MI: Eerdmans, 1979.
Origen. *Commentary on Matthew*. Edited and translated by J. Patrick. Ante-Nicene Fathers 10. Grand Rapids, MI: Eerdmans, 1979.
Origen. *Commentary on the Epistle to the Romans*. Edited and translated by Thomas P. Scheck. The Fathers of the Church 103. Washington, DC: Catholic University of America Press, 2001.

Origen. *Commentary on the Gospel According to John*. Edited and translated by Ronard E. Heine. The Fathers of the Church 80, 89. Washington, DC: Catholic University of America Press, 1989, 1993.

Origen. *Contra Celsum*. Edited by Henry Chadwick. Cambridge: Cambridge University Press, 1965.

Origen. *Homilies on Genesis and Exodus*. Edited and translated by Ronard E. Heine. The Fathers of the Church 71. Washington, DC: Catholic University of America Press, 1982.

Origen. *Homilies on Joshua*. Edited by Cynthia White. Translated by Barbara J. Bruce The Fathers of the Church 105. Washington, DC: Catholic University of America Press, 2002.

Origen. *Homilies on Leviticus*. Edited and translated by Gary Wayne Barkley. The Fathers of the Church 83. Washington, DC: Catholic University of America Press, 1990.

Origen. *Homilies on Luke*. Edited and translated by Joseph T. Lienhard. The Fathers of the Church 94. Washington, DC: Catholic University of America Press, 1996.

Origen. *On First Principles: Being Koetschau's Text of the De Principiis into English, Together with an Introduction and Notes*. Edited and translated by G. W. Butterworth. Gloucester, MA: Smith, 1973.

Owen, John. *The Works of John Owen*. Vols. 15, 16. Edinburgh: Banner of Truth, 1968.

Pannenberg, Wolfhart. *Basic Questions in Theology, Volume 1*. Minneapolis, MN: Fortress, 2008.

Pannenberg, Wolfhart. *Jesus – God and Man*. 2nd edn. Translated by Lewis L. Wilkins and Duane A Priebe. Louisville, KY: Westminster John Knox Press, 1982.

Pannenberg, Wolfhart. *Metaphysics and the Idea of God*. Grand Rapids, MI: Eerdmans, 1990.

Pannenberg, Wolfhart. *Systematic Theology, Volume 3*. Translated by Geoffrey W. Bromiley. London: T&T Clark, 2004.

Pardes, Ilana. *Countertraditions in the Bible: A Feminist Approach*. Cambridge, MA: Harvard University Press, 1992.

Pinnock, Charles H. *A Wideness in God's Mercy: The Finality of Jesus Christ in a World of Religions*. Grand Rapids, MI: Zondervan, 1992.

Prestige, G. L. *God in Patristic Thought*. London: SPCK, 1952.

Proctor, Mark A. '"Who Is My Neighbor?" Recontextualizing Luke's Good Samaritan (Luke 10:25–37)'. *Journal of Biblical Literature* 138 (2019): 203–19.

Quash, Ben. 'Deep Calls to Deep: The Practice of Scriptural Reasoning'. http://www.interfaith.cam.ac.uk/resources/scripturalreasoningresources/deepcallstodeep. Accessed 3 June 2016.

Quash, Ben. '"Deep Calls to Deep": Reading Scripture in a Multi-Faith Society'. In *Remembering Our Future: Explorations in Deep Church*, edited by L. Bretherton and A. Walker, 108–30. Milton Keynes: Paternoster, 2007.

Rabinowitz, Celia E. 'Personal and Cosmic Salvation in Origen'. *Vigiliae Christianae* 38 (1984): 319–29.

Rahner, Karl. 'Purgatory'. In *Theological Investigations, Volume 19: Faith and Ministry*, 181–93. London: Darton, Longman & Todd, 1984.

Rahner, Karl. *Bishops: Their Status and Function*. London: Burns and Oates, 1964.

Rainey, David. 'The Established Church and Evangelical Theology'. *International Journal of Systematic Theology* 12 (2010): 420–34.

Ramsay, Michael. *The Gospel and the Catholic Church*. London: Longman, 1936.

Richardson, Paul. 'Britain Is No Longer a Christian Nation'. *Sunday Telegraph* (27 June 2009).
Ricoeur, Paul. *Oneself as Another*. Translated by Kathleen Blamey. Chicago: University of Chicago Press, 1992.
Ritschl, Albrecht. *The Christian Doctrine of Justification and Reconciliation*. New York: Scribner, 1902.
Robinson, J. A. T. *In the End, God: The Christian Doctrine of the Last Things*. London: Collins, 1968.
Rogers, Eugene F., Jr. 'Supplementing Barth on Jews and Gender: Identifying God by Analogy and Spirit'. *Modern Theology* 14 (1998): 43–82.
Rowland, Christopher. *Christian Origins*. London, SPCK, 1985.
Rowland, Christopher. 'The Lamb and the Beast, the Sheep and the Goats: "The Mystery of Salvation" in Revelation'. In *A Vision for the Church: Studies in Early Christian Ecclesiology in Honour of J. P. M. Sweet*, edited by Marcus Bockmeuhl and Michael B. Thompson, 181–91. Edinburgh: T&T Clark, 1997.
Rupp, E. Gordon. *Protestant Catholicity*. London: Epworth, 1960.
Sanders, E. P. *Jesus and Judaism*. London: SCM, 1985.
Sanders, John E. 'Is Belief in Christ Necessary for Salvation?'. *Evangelical Quarterly* 60 (1988): 241–59.
Schillebeeckx, Edward. *Church: The Human Story of God*. New York: Crossroads, 1990.
Schleiermacher, Friedrich. *The Christian Faith*. 2nd edn. Translated by H. R. Mackintosh and J. S. Stewart. Edinburgh: T&T Clark, 1928.
Schmemann, Alexander. 'Ecclesiological Notes'. *St Vladimir's Seminary Quarterly* 11 (1967): 35–9.
Schwöbel, Christoph. 'The Creature of the Word: Recovering the Ecclesiology of the Refomers'. In *On Being the Church: Essays on the Christian Community*, edited by Colin E. Gunton and Daniel W. Hardy, 110–55. Edinburgh: T&T Clark, 1989.
Scriptural Reasoning Society. http://www.scripturalreasoning.org.uk (accessed 24 November 2020).
Seeters, John van. *Abraham in History and Tradition*. New Haven, CT: Yale University Press, 1975.
Sell, Alan. 'The Holy Spirit and the Church: Some Historical Soundings and Ecumenical Implications'. Paper presented at the Society for the Study of Theology Conference. York University, 26–28 March 2012.
Sonderegger, Katherine. *Systematic Theology: Volume 1: The Doctrine of God*. Minneapolis, MN: Fortress, 2015.
Soskice, Janet. *The Kindness of God: Metaphor, Gender, and Religious Language*. Oxford: Oxford University Press, 2007.
Stamforth, Maxwell, and Andrew Louth, eds. *Early Christian Writings: The Apostolic Fathers*. London: Penguin, 1987.
Strahan, Joshua Marshall. 'Jesus Teaches Theological Interpretation of the Law: Reading the Good Samaritan in Its Literary Context'. *Journal of Theological Interpretation* 10 (2016): 71–86.
The Methodist Worship Book. Peterborough: Methodist Publishing House, 1999.
Thiselton, Anthony C. *Hermeneutics: An Introduction*. Grand Rapids, MI: Eerdmans, 2009.
Thiselton, Anthony C. *The First Epistle to the Corinthians*. New International Greek Testament Commentary. Grand Rapids, MI: Eerdmans, 2000.
Thiselton, Anthony C. *I Corinthians: A Shorter Exegetical and Pastoral Commentary*. Grand Rapids, MI: Eerdmans, 2006.

Thiselton, Anthony C. *New Horizons in Hermeneutics: The Theory and Practice of Transforming Biblical Reading*. Grand Rapids, MI: Zondervan, 1992.
Thiselton, Anthony C. *The Hermeneutics of Doctrine*. Grand Rapids, MI: Eerdmans, 2007.
Thomas, J. Heywood. *Tillich*. London: Continuum, 2000.
Thomas, Scott M. 'Taking Religious and Cultural Pluralism Seriously: The Global Resurgence of Religion and the Transformation of International Society'. *Millennium: Journal of International Studies* 29 (2000): 815–41.
Tillich, Paul. *Systematic Theology: Volume 2: Existence and the Christ*. Chicago: University of Chicago Press, 1975.
Tillich, Paul. *Systematic Theology*. Combined Volume. Digswell Place: James Nisbet, 1968.
Torjesen, Karen Jo. 'Pedagogical Soteriology from Clement to Origen'. In *Origeniana Quarta: Die Referate des 4. internationalen Origeneskongresses (Innsbruck, 2.-6. September 1985)*, edited by Lothar Leis, 370–9. Innsbruck: Tyrolia-Verlag, 1987.
Trible, Phyllis. *God and the Rhetoric of Sexuality*. Philadelphia, PA: Fortress, 1986.
Trigg, Joseph W. 'The Angel of Great Counsel: Christ and the Angelic Hierarchy in Origen's Theology'. *Journal of Theological Sudies* 42 (1991): 35–51.
Trigg, Joseph W. 'Divine Deception and the Truthfulness of Scripture'. In *Origen of Alexandria: His World and His Legacy*, edited by Charles Kannengiesser and William L. Petersen, 147–64. Notre Dame: University of Notre Dame, 1988.
Tzamalikos, P. *The Concept of Time in Origen*. Bern: Lang, 1991.
Vaux, Roland De. *Ancient Israel: Its Life and Institutions*. London: Darton, Longman & Todd, 1973.
Wagner, J. Ross. '"Baptism into Christ Jesus" and the Question of Universalism in Paul'. *Horizons in Biblical Theology* 33 (2011): 45–61.
Wansborough, Henry. *The Lion and the Bull: The Gospels of Mark and Luke*. London: Darton, Longman & Todd, 1996.
Ware, Bruce. 'How Shall We Think About the Trinity?' In *God under Fire: Modern Scholarship Reinvents God*, edited by Douglas S. Huffman and Eric L. Johnson, 253–78. Grand Rapids, MI: Zondervan, 2002.
Ware, Bruce. *Father, Son, and Holy Spirit: Relations, Roles, and Relevance*. Wheaton: Crossway, 2006.
Webster, John. *Barth's Moral Theology: Human Action in Barth's Thought*. Edinburgh: T&T Clark, 1998.
Webster, John. *God without Measure: Working Papers in Christian Theology: Volume 1: God and the Works of God*. London: T&T Clark, 2016.
Webster, John. '"In the Society of God": Some Principles of Ecclesiology'. In *Perspectives on Ecclesiology and Ethnography*, edited by Pete Ward, 200–22. Grand Rapids, MI: Eerdmans, 2012.
Webster, John. 'The Identity of the Holy Spirit: A Problem in Trinitarian Theology'. *Themelios* 9 (1983): 4–7.
Webster, John. *Word and Church: Essays in Christian Dogmatics*. Edinburgh: T&T Clark, 2001.
Wesley, John. *The Works of John Wesley, Volume 1: Sermons I*. Edited by Albert C. Oulter. Nashville, TN: Abingdon, 1984.
Wesley, John. *The Works of John Wesley Volume 2: Sermons II*. Edited by Albert C. Outler. Nashville, TN: Abingdon Press, 1985.
Wesley, John. *The Works of John Wesley Volume 3: Sermons III*. Edited by Albert C. Outler. Nashville, TN: Abingdon Press, 1986.
Williams, Colin W. *John Wesley's Theology Today*. London: Epworth, 1960.

Williams, Rowan D. *Arius: Heresy and Tradition*. London: SCM, 2001.
Williams. Rowan D. *On Christian Theology*. Oxford: Blackwell, 2000.
Williams, Rowan D. 'Origen: Between Orthodoxy and Heresy'. In *Origeniana Septima: Origenes in den Auseinandersetzungen des 4. Jahrhunderts*, edited by W. A. Bienert and U. Kühneweg, 3–14. Leuven: Leuven University Press, 1999.
Williams, Rowan D. 'The Son's Knowledge of the Father in Origen'. In *Origeniana Quarta: Die Referate des 4. internationalen Origeneskongresses (Innsbruck, 2.-6. September 1985)*, edited by Lothar Leis, 146–53. Innsbruck: Tyrolia-Verlag, 1987.
Winter, Bruce W. 'Theological and Ethical Responses to Religious Pluralism – 1 Corinthians 8–10'. *Tyndale Bulletin* 41 (1990): 209–26.
World Council of Churches. *Baptism, Eucharist and Ministry*. Faith and Order Paper 111. Geneva: World Council of Churches, 1982.
Yarbro Collins, Adela. *Mark: A Commentary*. Hermeneia. Minneapolis, MN: Fortress, 2007.
Yeago, David. 'The New Testament and Nicene Dogma'. *Pro Ecclesia* 3 (1994): 152–64.
Yoder, John Howard. *The Politics of Jesus*. Grand Rapids, MI: Eerdmans, 1996.
Young, Frances M. *The Making of the Creeds*. London: SCM, 2002.
Young, Frances M. *The Use of Sacrificial Ideas in Greek Christian Writers from the New Testament to John Chrysostom*. Patristic Monograph Series 5. Cambridge, MA: Philadelphia Patristic Foundation, 1979.
Zahl, Simeon. 'The Spirit and the Cross: Engaging a Key Critique of Charismatic Pneumatology'. In *The Holy Spirit and the World Today*, edited by Jane Williams, 111–29. London: Alpha, 2011.

INDEX

activism 133–8, 160, 165
agapē (*see* Christian love)
Anselm 30 n.8
Aquinas, Thomas 27 n.1, 44 n.4
Augustine 14, 49 n.13, 90, 112 n.29, 128, 195–8
Ayres, Lewis 92–3

baptism 33–6, 80–1
Barclay, John 152
Barth, Karl 15, 23, 40, 49–50, 53–4, 56, 65, 73, 84, 91, 96, 100, 101, 103, 128–30, 135–6, 139, 141, 145–7, 156, 193–4, 196, 211–14, 216 n.31, 231, 235, 238
Bauckham, Richard 232 n.21, 233 n.23, 240 n.15, 241 n.18
Bennett, Alan 183 n.1
Binney, Thomas 117 n.45
Bonhoeffer, Dietrich 36, 37, 41 n.33, 70, 73, 76, 82, 84–5, 125–6, 129 n.21, 131, 133–4, 136, 142–4, 146–7, 155, 160 n.26, 166 n.42, 236 n.27
Briggs, Richard 209
Brunner, Emil 88 n.1

Calvin, John 16 n.37–8, 17, 19, 57, 76–7, 79, 80, 90, 91–2, 93, 94, 102 n.42, 115, 120, 121, 127–8
Carter, David 121 n.60
Christian love 107, 111–12, 195–9, 201, 244, 245 (*see also* love)
church
  invisibility 75, 127–9
  as representative 140, 141, 143–4
  as witness 41, 57, 83–5, 145–7
Clark, Elizabeth 168 n.4, 176 n.57
Clough, David 30 n.7
communion of saints, 79, 89, 97–102, 103–4
Congar, Yves 19, 23 n.65, 26
conscience 109, 117

conversion 154, 156, 163, 210
critique of religion 137
Cyprian 25, 27, 113–14

Daniélou, Jean 175 n.54, 178 n.74, 187 n.60, 188 n.64
Davie, Grace 59 n.1, 62 n.10, 125 n.1, 126 n.7, 223 n.5, 237 n.2
DeHart, Paul 146 n.94
Del Colle, Ralph 34 n.20, 67 n.35, 122 n.61
Didymus the Blind 22
difference 38, 111–12, 123, 199, 217–18
divine
  agency 11, 14, 18, 20–1, 79
  aseity 12–14, 44 n.4, 52
  eternity 45–8
  freedom 46 n.5, 50, 138
  grace 29, 30, 32, 52, 153–7, 161–2, 163, 165, 247–8
  judgement 162
Drane, John 9 n.1, 133 n.34
Dunn, James 219 n.36

Edwards, Mark 94 n.24, 113 n.33, 167–8, 179 n.86
epinoiai (*see* titles of Christ)
eucharist (*see* holy communion)

faith 52, 90, 110, 160, 162, 164, 180, 198
Ford, David 53, 99 n.36, 100 n.37, 184 n.3, 190 n.73, 191 n.74, 200, 221 n.2, 223 n.4, 228 n.14, 237 n.1, 239 n.9

gentiles 234–5
Giles, Kevin 88 n.3
gnosticism 162, 166, 187
good works 111, 112
Green, Clifford 139 n.59
Gregory of Nyssa 56 n.39
Gunton, Colin 10 n.11, 31 n.14, 79, 118, 120, 134 n.39, 141 n.67

Hardy, Daniel 37 n.27, 38 n.29, 53, 74 n.4, 81, 119 n.53, 120, 127, 154 n.9
Harnack, Adolf von 31 n.9, 158 n.22
Hauerwas, Stanley 84 n.21, 135 n.43
Hays, Richard 208 n.7, 209, 210
Healy, Nicholas 9 n.1, 74 n.4, 100 n.39, 224 n.8
hell 111, 163, 172
Hick, John 207 n.3
holiness 77, 79, 180 (*see also* sanctification)
holy communion 113–14, 81, 139
Holy Spirit
    and anthropos 33–5, 55–6
    and assurance 63–4
    and church 18–19, 25, 35–42, 68–9, 74–9, 84–5, 117–22, 128–9, 132, 137
    fruit 24, 66–7, 69, 116–17, 132 n.31, 137, 163, 165
    perfecting work 22, 24, 179
    presence 22, 23, 25, 55, 68–9, 78, 83–4, 118–19, 132
humility 70–1, 248

Ignatius 113, 139 n.57
illumination 45, 52, 122–3
image of God 29–30, 55, 176 n.59, 177 n.60
Islam 218–20

Jenson, Robert 75–6, 119, 164 n.37
Jinkins, Michael 60, 76, 125 n.3, 144 n.87, 145
Judaism 158 n.22, 219 n.36, 232–3
Jüngel, Eberhard 35 n.21, 49 n.16, 161 n.28, 214 n.26
justification 141, 160

Kepnes, Steven 200 n.23, 201 n.28, 202–3, 215 n.27
Kingdom of God 24, 78, 159, 203

Larsen, Timothy 153 n.7, 207 n.2
Lash, Nicholas 104, 219 n.37
Lewis, C. S. 137 n.52, 198 n.18
Lindbeck, George 93
love
    divine 48, 50, 52, 66, 155–6, 161 n.28
    human 14, 57, 63, 66
Luther, Martin 16 n.37, 22, 28 n.4, 65 n.23, 66, 93, 94, 95, 102, 120

MacIntyre, Alasdair 223 n.6, 224 n.7, 227 n.12
Martin, David 223 n.5, 237 n.2
mission 25, 61, 163
Moltmann, Jürgen 162

Neutel, Karin 82 n.16
Nimmo, Paul 127 n.8, 161 n.28
non-absolute beings 157–63

O'Grady, Colm 129 n.20
O'Leary, Joseph 170 n.15
Origen 51 n.24, 167–81, 183–91
Owen, John 15–16, 121 n.58

Pannenberg, Wolfhart 16 n.39, 17, 25, 38 n.28, 46 n.6, 48 n.11, 53, 54, 78, 87 n.1, 92 n.15, 103 n.45
participation
    in Christ 28, 32, 33, 35, 38, 39, 41, 189–91
    in divine glory 52–7
    in grace 29, 30, 32, 33, 41
    in the Logos 170–1
    in the work of God 133–4
Pentecost 25, 36, 38–9, 68, 75–6, 119
philosophy 178 n.74, 193–4
pluralism 1, 199
prayer 24, 82, 112
preaching (*see* proclamation)
predestination 177
pre-existence, 168–72
priesthood of all believers 16 n.37, 82, 144, 147
proclamation 73, 80, 96, 102, 120, 136–7, 195, 237–9, 246
promise 70, 212–17, 219–20
punishment 172, 178

Quash, Ben 108 n.10, 210 n.12, 225 n.9, 227 n.11

radical reformation 138 n.53
Ramsay, Michael 116 n.43
rationality 170
redemption 24–5
religious identity 225–6, 234, 241–3
repentance 64–6, 70
revelation 23, 91, 212

Ricoeur, Paul 204, 221
Rowland, Christopher 160 n.25, 233 n.22, 240 n.12, 241–2, 245 n.27
Rupp, Gordon 119 n.50

salvation
  as co-humanity 28, 33, 36–7, 82–3
  economy of 19–20, 30–1, 189
  objective 23, 35, 154
  subjective 30 n.9, 154, 177
Samaritans 232–3, 240–1
sanctification 81–3, 112, 117, 119–20, 121–2, 135–6, 176–9
Schillebeeckx, Edward 12
Schleiermacher, Friedrich 17, 30 n.9, 63 n.14, 64 n.21
Schwöbel, Christoph 20, 116 n.43
Scriptural Reasoning 108 n.10, 200–3, 228–9, 239
scripture principle (see *sola scriptura*)
secularism 223, 237
Sell, Alan 118 n.46
separationism 151–2, 156, 157–8, 163, 168 n.5
sin 154–5
  cor incurvatus in se 24, 28–30, 40

depravity 154–6
the fall 28–30
sola scriptura 87, 89–90, 95, 99–100, 102–4, 238
spiritual growth (*see* sanctification)

Thiessen, Matthew 158 n.22
Thiselton, Anthony 96 n.28, 194, 199, 201, 202 n.31, 204
Tillich, Paul 102, 191 n.74
titles of Christ 173–6, 184–8
tolerance 202 n.30, 243–4
Trinity 11, 18, 19–20, 50–1, 88, 146

Van Seters, John 216

Webster, John 9–12, 18 n.45, 20, 21, 22, 23, 43 n.2, 44 n.4, 50, 214 n.26
Wesley, Charles, 53, 166, 238
Wesley, John 61–7, 69, 70, 71, 73, 106–12, 115, 116, 122–3
Williams, Rowan 88 n.2, 101, 173 n.35, 175 n.54, 179 n.82, 187 n.60, 230 n.16
wisdom 171, 174–5, 186–90
worship 24–5, 57, 77, 108, 213 n.25, 233

www.ingramcontent.com/pod-product-compliance
Lightning Source LLC
Chambersburg PA
CBHW062122300426
44115CB00012BA/1774